A TOWERING FLAME

A unique and historical work on the Revolution of 1905 and Latvian anarchists... If I were president, then I'd make this book compulsory reading.

Andris Vitoliņš, Arterritory.com

Ruff's historical research is written in the best traditions of academic writing ... the fast-moving and compact way of story-telling, which is more characteristic of the detective genre, seems to be effortlessly natural... One of us [a Latvian] should take care that this wonderful story gets a sequel.

Viktors Dāboliņš, *Latvju Teksti*

Like a master of popular "puzzles", in the course of many years the author found and identified the scattered and before now partly hidden fragments, and put them together in an easily comprehensible, unified picture, in which countless people and events are interconnected, and where everything acquires meaning... a quiet, convincing story, richly supported by historical facts.

Maira Asare, *Kultūres Diena*

Just finished your Towering Flame. Thank you for the compassionate, sobering account. Enjoyed it very much... well researched, well written, candid... I have shared this book and suggested reading it to many — excellent work!!

Lolita Čigāne, Member of Parliament of the Latvian Republic

British historian Philip Ruff's decades-long researches have cast new light on a fascinating period in both Latvian and British history.

Mike Collier, Chief Editor, Latvian Public Media English Service

In telling the story of Jānis Žāklis, the 1905 revolution in Latvia, and the anarchist movement it spawned, Ruff avoids the traps of simplistic celebration or condemnation — a marvellous work of historical rediscovery.

John Patten, Kate Sharpley Library

About the author

Anarchist historian Philip Ruff was born in Birmingham in 1952. During the 1970s and '80s Philip was an active proponent of revolutionary anarchism as a member of the Anarchist Black Cross; as well as being a prolific contributor to a wide range of anarchist publications (including *Black Flag*, the Cienfuegos Press *Anarchist Review* and *Anarchy* magazine) as author, editor, cartoonist and publisher. Describing himself today as a "retired anarchist", Philip has since 1986 specialised in researching into Latvian social history, with a special emphasis on the 1905 revolution and Latvian anarchism. He first visited Latvia in 1988 and lives in London.

Philip Ruff

A Towering Flame

*The Life and Times of the Elusive Latvian
Anarchist Peter the Painter*

BREVIARY STUFF PUBLICATIONS
2019

Published in 2019 by Breviary Stuff Publications,
BCM Breviary Stuff, London WC1N 3XX
breviarystuff.org.uk
Copyright © Philip Ruff, 2012, 2018, 2019

The centipede device copyright © Breviary Stuff Publications

The right of Philip Ruff to be identified as the Author of this Work has been asserted by him
in accordance with the Copyright, Designs and Patents Act 1988.

Copyright for photographs: David Campbell, 53, 54, 56, 57; Ira Gruntmane, 2, 3, 4, 5, 6, 23,
24, 66, 70; Latvian War Museum (Latvijas Kara muzeja - LKM), 7, 9, 12, 13, 14, 15, 17, 19, 29,
32, 62, 63, 64; Līvija Rēfelde, 10, 21; George Rosen, 28, 45, 46, 47; Donald Rumbelow, 30, 31,
33, 34, 35, 48, 61; Sakharov Centre (Moscow), 65; Melindria Tavoularis, 22, 26, 42, 43, 44.
Unless otherwise acknowledged, the remainder of the photos are
from the collection of the author.

First published in Latvian translation as *Pa stāvu liesmu debesīs: Nenotveramā
latviešu anarchista Pētera Māldera laiks un dzīve* by Dienas Grāmata, Riga 2012

A CIP record for this book is available from
The British Library

ISBN (hardback): 978-0-9929466-8-5
ISBN (paperback): 978-0-9929466-5-4

Contents

Images

Introduction to the English language edition
by Mike Collier

I had heard about Philip Ruff and his book *A Towering Flame* long before I read it or had the good fortune to meet its author. As someone earning a living writing in English while living in Latvia, I would often be asked: "Have you read the book about Jānis Žāklis? You should!"

To make life easy for myself I tried to find an English language edition of the book, which I saw all the time in Latvian bookshops and libraries (often on the shelves reserved for the most popular titles). I was out of luck because this book written in English by an Englishman was only available in Latvian. This is just the first of many endearing idiosyncrasies with which I associate Philip. He is a historian without a historian's training, but displays a far more dedicated approach to tracking down and engaging with sources than many academics would dare attempt. Stories of him marching into KGB facilities and simply demanding to be shown classified documents are legendary (in fact, his visit to the KGB in Riga was by appointment). Amazingly this fearless strategy, dangerous to the point of foolhardiness when he pursued it in the 1980s, yielded remarkable results.

A Towering Flame is a book that probably no Latvian historian would have thought of writing, and no other English historian would have attempted. By bringing together the original London police files on the 'Houndsditch Murders' with previously unknown archival material from Latvia, Philip has been able to bring a new perspective to the activities of the Latvian anarchists. Philip is someone who understands the anarchist movement from the inside. It is clear that while not condoning all the acts of violence perpetrated by the Latvian anarchist movement, he has a respect and even admiration for their commitment to their cause and what might be termed their "rules of engagement" that communicates itself in the text.

Who were Peter the Painter and his associates, and what precisely happened to them, still grabs headlines today. But it is the account of why the anarchist cells formed, how they operated and what they saw as their ultimate aims that is, in my opinion, the most fascinating aspect of this story. Indeed, while the names of 'Peter the Painter' and the 'Siege of Sidney Street' are still part of folk memory in the United Kingdom (though most people would be hard-pressed to explain what exactly they signify), it is almost exclusively through Philip's tireless research that any awareness of the Latvian anarchists exists in Latvia itself. Yet for a few years, Peter the Painter was the most famous Latvian on the planet, with the police force of the world's largest and most powerful empire dedicated to catching him at any price and by any means.

Until now, the actual fate of Peter the Painter was a matter of legend and lazy assumption. In this book Philip Ruff blasts through that wall of obscurity with all the force of a well-primed anarchist bomb, revealing a far more fascinating and convincing account of Jānis Žāklis' ultimate destiny and the no less interesting but frequently more gruesome fates of his comrades. In doing so, Philip performs a singular task: writing a missing chapter in the histories of both Latvia and the United Kingdom that, in my opinion, deserves to be thought of as the definitive work on its subject matter.

While I had to learn Latvian in order to read *A Towering Flame*, thanks to this new English-language edition you don't have to. So now the British public can discover a missing chapter of its history just as the Latvian public did.

Mike Collier
Riga, December 2017

Mike Collier is a British-born author and journalist who has lived in Latvia since 2007.

Introduction to the Latvian edition

It may seem odd that a book about a lost epoch of Latvian history should be written by an Englishman, but this it is not an exclusively Latvian story. Some of it has been told before — in England, as a true crime story; in Latvia, as Soviet propaganda. But until I first travelled to Latvia in 1988 no one had attempted to put all the pieces together as a work of social history. The result, I hope, illuminates a series of events that impacted upon both nations.

The principal characters all made their presence felt in England as suspects in a murder mystery that spiralled into folk legend. Outside Latvia none of the authors who have written about these events have had much understanding of the "bigger story" which lay behind them — the 1905 revolution in the Baltic and the armed resistance to Russian state terrorism which followed it. In Latvia, the "bigger story" of 1905 was made smaller by the distortions of Soviet historiography, and the Latvian anarchists were edited out of history altogether.

So here, for the first time in any language, is the real story of what happened. Inevitably there are gaps and omissions. I don't claim this to be a definitive account. My hope is that it may inspire others to carry on from here, and take the story of Peter the Painter further.

Though written in English, I am happy that this book is being published first in the Latvian language — for this I am entirely indebted to Lauris Gundars, both for his excellent translation and for his first suggesting the project to Dienas Grāmata.

Sources

This book is based on original primary research conducted in England from 1986, and in Latvia since 1988. Additional material has been gathered from archives and individuals in Australia, Germany, Spain, Russia, and the USA. It brings together, for the first time, information from the City of London Police files on the Houndsditch Murders (currently held by the London Metropolitan Archives (LMA)) with extensive archival research in Latvia; most notably in the archives of the Central Committee of the Latvian Communist Party (including unpublished memoirs and letters) and the files of the tsarist police and Okhranka, held in the Latvian State History Archives (Latvijas Valsts vēstures arhivā (LVVA)) in Riga. It is supplemented by personal interviews and correspondence, including with relatives of Peter the Painter and other direct participants in this story; and with a wide body of published primary sources held by the Latvian National Library — most notably the encyclopedic four volume work *Latvijas revolucionāro cīnītāju pieminas grāmata* (The memorial book of Latvian revolutionary fighters of the 1905 revolution, Riga 1976-1987); and the earlier two volume work on which it was based, edited by R. Endrups & U. Feldmanis. *Revolucionārās cīņās kritušo piemiņas grāmata* (The memorial book of those fallen in the revolutionary struggle. Prometejs, Moscow, 1933 and 1936).

Acknowledgements
My thanks to the staff of the Brotherton Library, Leeds University; Eliass
Museum of History & Art, Jelgava; Kate Sharpley Library; Kuldiga Museum;
Latvian State History Archives (Latvijas Valsts vēstures arhivā (LVVA)) and
Latvian State Archives (Latvijas Valsts arhivā (LVA)), Riga; Latvian National
Library (Latvijas Nacionālās bibliotēkas (LNB)), Riga; Latvian War Museum
(Latvijas Kara muzeja (LKM)), Riga; Marx Memorial Library, London; London
Metropolitan Archive (LMA); Misina Library, Riga; National Archives of
Australia (NAA); National Archives (PRO), Kew, London; Library of the
London School of Economics (LSE); Library of the School of Slavonic & East
European Studies, London.

Sadly, many of the people who have helped me over the years have not lived
to see the publication of this book..

My grateful thanks go to the relatives of some of the principal characters in
this story, who have helped to humanize my understanding of ordinary people
caught up in extraordinary events; most notably to those of the extended Žāklis
family in Latvia, Russia, Australia and the USA: Fēliks Bauze; Līvija Didrihsone;
Ira Gruntmane; Ugis Gruntmanis; Aivars Kalējs (who deserves special mention
for his additional research in the Latvian archives); Aldis, Krisjanis & Tālis
Putniņš; Vēsma Putniņš (nee Upeniece); Līvija Rēfelde; Malvīne Sakne; Ruta
Zaksa; Aina Žakle; Ausma Žakle-Kalēja; Juris Žāklis. And to Alfred Driscoll
(son of Luba Milstein and Fricis Svars); Maija Eliase (daughter of Kristaps
Eliass); Catherine Golden (daughter of Luba Milstein and Alfred Dzirkalis);
Melita "Letty" Norwood (daughter of Aleksandr Zirnis); George Rosen (son of
Jānis Celinš); Melindria Tavoularis (granddaughter of Luba Milstein and Fricis
Svars).

Thanks also to Ilga Apine; Bruno Ašcuks; Pauls Bankovskis; Alberts Bels;
Boris Borisov; Jānis Borgs; David Campbell; Hans-Ulrich Dillmann; Aivars
Dombrovskis; Stanislavs Garkājs; Richard Handyside; Ros Kane; Vladimir
Kārklinš; Pēteris Krupnikov; Columba Longmore; Viktor Lorencs; Andris
Mellakauls; Dzidra Paeglite; John Patten; Eric Pleasants; Dainis Pozins; Andris
Puļķis; Anita Rumbina; Donald Rumbelow; Mark Saunders; Maruta Sproge;
Valentīns Šteinbergs; Andris Straumanis; Boris Volodarsky; Richard
Whittington-Egan; Horace "Harry" Young, Vita Zelče; Artis Zvirgzdiņš.

My special thanks, for her invaluable assistance, must go to Lilita Garkāja.

Last but not least, huge thanks to Dienas Grāmata, and to my editors: literary
editor, Gundega Blumberga and scientific consultants, Inta Rozenvalde and
Vents Zvaigzne.

I dedicate this book to my daughter, Olive Kane, for inspiring me to begin;
and to my wife and friend Irene Ruff, without whom it would never have been
finished.

Philip Ruff
London, April 2012

Postscript
My search for Peter the Painter has not stopped since this book was published in
Latvia in 2012. The text has been significantly updated and corrected twice since
then to take account of new information. The acknowledgements, above, have
similarly been updated to add my thanks to those people who have come forth
with new detail or clarification. My sincere thanks go to Breviary Stuff
Publications for their persistence and dedication to bringing this story to an
English-speaking audience, and to Mike Collier for his introduction.

Philip Ruff
London, May 2019

Principal characters

Jānis Celiņš (1884-1956): anarchist; former Latvian Social Democrat from Sigulda; a defendant in the Houndsditch trial; a.k.a. Bārddzinis — The Barber, John Rosen.

Alfrēds Dzirkalis (1887-1961): anarchist from Liepāja; a defendant in the Houndsditch trial; a.k.a. Mazais (Shorty), Chochol, Karl Hoffman.

(?) Hartmanis (1884-1910): anarchist from Liepāja; principal shooter at Houndsditch; died at 59 Grove Street; a.k.a. Puika (Kid), George Gardstein, Karl Muromets, Muromtsev, P. Morin, Jānis Stencels.

Juris Laivinš (1886-?): anarchist; former Latvian Social Democrat from Alsviki (Aluksne); a defendant in the Houndsditch trial; a.k.a. Jurķis, Yourka, George Dubov, Charles Lambert.

Jēkabs Peterss (1886-1938): Latvian Social Democrat from Nīkrāce (Aizpute); chief defendant in the Houndsditch trial; a.k.a. Svanelis, Jacob Colnin.

Kristaps Salniņš (1885-1939): Latvian Social Democrat from Riga; a.k.a. Grishka, Jan Sproge, G. Sander, Jacob (and Christopher) Fogel, Alfrēds (and Christopher) Laubergs, Rudzewice, Schpoyas, Zavadsky, Osip, Onkulit, Viktor Hugo.

Fricis Svars (1885-1911): anarchist; former Latvian Social Democrat from Liepāja; killed in the Siege of Sidney Street; a.k.a. Friczals, Fričelis, Buldogs, Kārlis Dūmnieks, Bobrikov, Karpovics, Pēteris Svare, Peter Trohimschik, Adolf Brown.

Jānis Žāklis / Žākle (1883-?): anarchist; former Latvian Social Democrat from Jaunlutrini (Saldus); a.k.a. Mērnieks (The Land Surveyor), Tālbergs, K. R. Schtern, Straume, J. Churin or Chirens, Peter Piatkov, Pēteris Mālderis (Peter the Painter).

Preface
My Search for Peter the Painter

'Where shall I begin, please your Majesty?'
'Begin at the beginning,' the King said gravely, 'and go on till you come to the end: then stop.'

Lewis Caroll, *Alice's Adventures in Wonderland*

The Houndsditch murders of 1910 are still regarded today as the single worst case of police murder in British history. The Latvian anarchists held responsible entered into East London folklore when, trapped inside a house in Stepney, they took on Winston Churchill and the British Army in "The Siege of Sidney Street". Two died, but no one ever accounted for the mysterious Peter the Painter, popularly supposed to be the leader of the gang and to have escaped the burning house during the battle.

The story inspired two major feature films — *The Man Who Knew Too Much* (Alfred Hitchcock, 1934), and *The Siege of Sidney Street* (Monty Berman & Jimmy Sangster, 1960) — as well as a slew of books, all with different theories on the background to the shootings and the identity of those involved: Peter the Painter was a tsarist police agent; he was Stalin; he was the brother of a Metropolitan Police interpreter; he never existed; he did exist and became an agent of Lenin's Cheka in Russia. At the start of the 1970s, when the bombing campaign of the Angry Brigade[1] pushed the word "anarchist" back into the headlines, one of the groups under investigation by Special Branch called itself "The Siege of Sidney Street Appreciation Society". As recently as 2003 one of the contributors to a London Weekend Television documentary about the Houndsditch murders called Peter the Painter "the Osama Bin Laden of his time".

It was in that LWT documentary in 2003 that I first put forward evidence to support my identification of Peter the Painter as Jānis Žāklis.[2] I had looked for an answer to the mystery of "Peter the Painter" where no one else, amazingly, had ever thought to look — inside Latvia.

My detective work in Latvia since 1988 has resulted in proof positive of the real identity of Peter the Painter and unearthed the real story of his life and revolutionary career. But more than that, it has opened a window on the hitherto unknown history of Latvian anarchism and of the 1905 revolution in the Baltic which gave rise to it. This wider story reveals the violent events in London — shocking as they may appear — to be part of a much bigger story of class war, revolution and survival.

* * *

Looking back, now I realise that I have spent almost a lifetime searching for a solution to this mystery.

"He looks like Peter the Painter", my Grandmother used to whisper knowingly of any suspicious character lurking in the street when I was a boy. Were painters not to be trusted, I wondered?

My Granny had been in service in London before the First World War, but not for long. Her rebellious streak, inherited by me, would not permit her to accept meekly the life of drudgery and class brutality imposed on those "below stairs". She told the Lady in the big house what to do with her rotten job and brought herself and her tales of Peter the Painter back home to Birmingham, where I was born. I watched the films and read all the books. Every popular theory about Peter the Painter seemed to me utter nonsense. But one book, first published in 1973, by Donald Rumbelow had the tantalising aura of being based on something solid. His account, based on the original case papers — discovered by Donald in cardboard boxes, put out for burning, in Snow Hill police station, where he was then a serving City of London policeman — had a ring of authority to it. It was Rumbelow, with a policeman's dedication to uncovering the killer of three of his predecessors, who first made a convincing case for Jēkabs Peterss having fired the fatal shots at Houndsditch. My own investigation has convinced me that Rumbelow is wrong; but I have his book, whose theory of Jēkabs Peterss' guilt I shared at first, to thank for inspiring my own quest. The information rescued by Rumbelow suggested a more significant story yet to be told. But it was only part of the picture. To find out more I would have to go to Latvia.

In 1988 I arrived in Latvia, then still part of the Soviet Union, as a tourist; not knowing any Latvian or Russian, and armed only with a few addresses of people who might be of help. Against all odds and by virtue of sheer bloody cheek alone, I made enough headway by knocking on doors to return to Riga in the summer of 1989 under a business visa to do proper research, with the co-operation of the Latvian Committee for Cultural Relations with Countrymen Abroad, known more simply as the "Culture Committee"; in reality part of the public relations arm of the KGB.

One of the people I met in Riga was a member of the Latvian Academy of Sciences, Professor Valentīns Šteinbergs, who had just published a short biography of Jēkabs Peterss; the man I believed to be the Houndsditch shooter. It seemed at first possible to collaborate in writing the real story behind the London events, but it wasn't to be. My ideas and those of Professor Šteinbergs proved to be incompatible; something brought home to me when I interviewed a "Public Relations Officer" of the KGB, who finished our conversation by wishing me luck in my endeavours and tossing a copy of Šteinbergs's book to me as a token of my visit to KGB Headquarters. Serious history would be welcomed, but this book (Šteinbergs's biography of Peterss) was more like *The Three Musketeers*, the KGB man remarked disparagingly.

This second trip to Latvia was not wasted though. As well as interviewing the KGB (wasn't it usually the other way around?) and visiting Riga Central Prison (the site in 1905 of a famous rescue mission led by Jānis Žāklis to free two revolutionary leaders), I toured the normally "closed" (to foreigners) areas of Liepāja, Kuldīga, Jelgava and Tukums in search of information; and I did collect some important material. But my search in Soviet archives was sometimes frustrated by the limits of Glasnost. When I asked for information about Fricis Svars (one of the two men killed at Sidney Street), during a visit to the Archive of the Central Committee of the Latvian Communist Party, my request was brushed away with the words, "We are only interested in the *revolutionaries*". Svars had been expelled from the Party, and that was that. The quest seemed hopeless until my last visit to the Museum of the Revolution, on the last morning of my visit, when I opened the last file I had requested to see. What I found inside changed everything. Here at last was the first proof that Peter Piatkov, Peter the Painter, was Jānis Žāklis.

But what proof can I offer that all the previous theories about Peter the Painter are flawed, and that he was really Jānis Žāklis?

The myth of Peter the Painter began on 30th January 1911, after the Siege of Sidney Street, when the police issued a 'wanted' poster bearing two photographs of Peter Piatkov: 'alias Schtern, alias "Peter the Painter", age 28 to 30 years, height 5 feet 9 or 10 inches, complexion sallow, clear skin, hair and medium moustache black, otherwise clean shaven, eyes dark, medium build, reserved manner. Dress, brown tweed suit (broad dark stripes), black overcoat (velvet collar rather old), black hard felt hat, black lace boots, rather shabby. A native of Russia, an anarchist.'

The City Police and Special Branch made strenuous efforts to identify and trace him, contacting police forces all over the world for assistance. The fact that George Gardstein was found dead in Piatkov's room initially made him a prime suspect. When it became obvious that Piatkov was not at Houndsditch when the shootings occurred the police quietly switched their attention to other suspects. But the famous photographs of Peter the Painter had already been widely circulated and the legend of a mysterious "Mr. Big" had started to have a life of its own.

The police never issued a public notice to say that Piatkov was no longer wanted, so the myth remained. But when it came to the test, on every occasion that the London Police were offered possible sightings of Peter the Painter abroad, or were asked by foreign police forces if further action was required to arrest him, the answer was always the same: that there was no evidence on which to base either an arrest or extradition. Justice Grantham, in his surprising intervention in the Old Bailey trial, admitted: 'There is no evidence to show that the man Peter the Painter was one of the murderers'.[3]

A good-looking man with regular features, particularly striking dark eyes and brown hair, Piatkov was described in London as rather shabby, and of reserved manner, but the famous studio portrait used on the wanted poster shows him to have been decidedly elegant. Several people who knew him in London remarked on his refined appearance and commented that it put them in mind of a doctor or an artist. Sara Trassjonsky was somewhat in awe of him and is generally regarded as his "sweetheart" (a term first used of her in 1946 by J. P. Eddy[4]), but there is no evidence that her feelings were reciprocated. Piatkov corresponded at the same time with a girlfriend (apparently his wife) in Kiev, Lidija Schwarz (Anna). Although he painted the scenery for an amateur dramatic production that several friends were involved with, he was not integrated into the social scene of which Fricis Svars was something of a "star". He was known specifically as Svars' friend, and no-one that hadn't known him in Latvia seems to have known his real name. He was an amateur watercolorist (as was Svars — they both played musical instruments too), and it is assumed that he was called "The Painter" because he habitually worked as a house painter, or because of his contribution to the theatre production. Svars, though, offered an alternative explanation on one occasion by telling Luba Milstein that "Peter" was studying art. In London he was also called "the Frenchman", possibly because he arrived from France and had lived there, or because he was a Francophile and affected French manners. The fluent and cultured French of his long formal statement after witnessing a fatal road accident in June 1909 impressed the French police and astonished the examining magistrate. He also spoke Latvian, Russian, English, German and Yiddish.

Piatkov came to London to see Fricis Svars. For someone with Svars' considerable reputation as a fighter to have been such a close friend, to have been so guarded about his real identity and to have been so notably deferential towards him, Piatkov must have been someone of even greater importance in Latvia's revolutionary movement. The similarities between Piatkov and Ģederts Eliass, who had helped free Svars from the clutches of the Riga secret police in 1906, seem at first too many to be merely coincidental. Photographs of Eliass and Piatkov reveal a strong likeness; both were Francophiles and painters; Maija Eliase, Ģederts' niece, confirms that he was in London at the appropriate period; 'somewhere around 1911'.[5] Their close links, Svars' conversion to Anarchism notwithstanding, would make it logical for Eliass to stay with Svars when in London.

Juris Laiviņš (George Dubov), who stood trial alongside Jēkabs Peterss for the murders, had taken Peter a small water-colour on the day of the Houndsditch shootings, to get his opinion of it — implying that Piatkov was regarded (as Eliass was) as something of an authority on painting. Ģederts Eliass spent the years 1909-1913 in Brussels, where he wrote for the Latvian Social Democracy's newspaper *Cīņa*, under the pen name Blaumanis and studied at Brussels Academy of Art. After he graduated from there in 1913 he moved to Paris and studied painting until 1914, when he returned to Latvia and withdrew from active politics.

Even Eliass' niece and the sceptical experts at Jelgavā's Eliass Museum of History and Art were eventually convinced by this theory when they examined the evidence in 1989. It turned out to be wrong. The material uncovered in Riga proves conclusively that Peter Piatkov was the leader of the attack on Riga Central Prison, and many more armed actions, during the 1905 Revolution, and subsequently the recognised leader of the Latvian anarchist movement: Jānis Žāklis. This discovery renders the mistaken acceptance of the Eliass theory more understandable: Eliass was not Peter the Painter, but he worked with him as a fighter in Latvia, Russia and Finland. If Eliass was in London in 1911 it was probably as an observer, for the Foreign Committee of the Latvian Social Democracy in Brussels, at Jēkabs Peterss' trial.

The Riga material also gives new substance to information obtained by the City of London Police, the true significance of which, lacking independent corroboration, has hitherto gone unheeded. Amongst the papers found in Grove Street was a letter from New York, penned by a Latvian anarchist who had previously belonged to the *Melnais Karogs* (Black Flag) group in Paris. The letter concerned a sectarian quarrel among the Latvian émigrés in America, prompted by an article in the Latvian Social Democracy (LSD) press. The article roundly attacked the Latvian anarchists in Paris, directing particular condemnation at a certain *Metrneek*.[6] The original is not on file, but *Metrneek* (a non-existent word) seems likely to be a mistranscription of the Latvian word *Mērnieks* (Land Surveyor), Jānis Žāklis' nickname; placing Žāklis in Paris at the same time as Piatkov.

Žāklis (Schahklis in old script) can also be written as Jaklis, Jakle, Zhakle or Schaakle. In August 1912, the City Police received a letter from Kiev which claimed that Peter the Painter returned to a relative in Kuldīga called Johan Shakle, that he left Russia as J. Pjetov and that in London he used the name Peter Schivopisez (*zhivopisets* is Russian for painter). On 12th September, Superintendent Ottaway added the note: 'The man referred to is no doubt "Peter the Painter" against whom the evidence is insufficient to extradite.'[7]

On 16th December 1912, the Russian Consul General in London wrote to Ottaway: 'I received today from the Russian Foreign Office a letter informing me that the man who was implicated in the attempted burglary of Harris's Jewellery Shop at Houndsditch called Peter the Painter has now been identified as being possibly the peasant of the Province of Courland, district of Goldingen (Kuldīgā) Evan Evanovitch (Janis Janisoff) Jakle alias Jaklis. He was born on 19th July 1883, his father is called Evan Evanovitch, his mother Margaritha. He has a brother called Karl, and sisters Anna, married to a man called Sakee (Sakne), Mary, Catherine and Milda, all the above named live on a farm called Kounen, in the district of Talsen. Janis Jakle or Jaklis is wanted by the police at Goldingen for having absconded and evaded Military Service. He is known to be at present in Germany, but his whereabouts are not established. I beg to inform you of the above so that you may take advantage of the information at your discretion.'[8]

Confirmation that Žāklis was Piatkov is provided by the thin file I found in Riga's Museum of the Revolution. In it are several photographs, starting with the tsarist police mugshots of a dishevelled prisoner — 1904 arrest photographs of Žāklis in Bobruisk — and ending with an original studio portrait; instantly recognisable as the picture that appeared in London on the wanted poster of Peter Piatkov, (see images 1, 7, 14, 20). On the back is written: "Žāklis in America as Tālbergs". Tālbergs was the maiden name of his mother, Margarieta Žākle.

Jānis Žāklis disappears from Soviet histories after 1906. His career after leaving the LSD is of no interest to Party historians. All that is known is that he became an anarchist, emigrated to the USA and was in London. The interlude in America, where the famous studio portrait was taken, would explain how Žāklis spoke English before arriving in London. As the Latvian anarchist movement's principal organiser of this period, it is interesting to note that Žāklis' departure from the USA corresponds with the appearance there of the journal *Brīvība* (Freedom), which Svars helped to edit in London, and that Piatkov's escape from London corresponds with the appearance in Paris of the journal *Melnais Karogs*. Both journals were financed from the proceeds of expropriations. The November 1910 issue of *Brīvība* included a short report signed by Mērnieks (Žāklis), as the treasurer of the London Group, Liesma (The Flame).[9]

Problems with publishers and the collapse of the Soviet Union in 1991 forced me to shelve my investigation; but I returned to the project in 2000. And in 2003 I returned to Latvia (now an independent country) with my secret weapon: my wife Irene Ruff, whom I first met in Riga in 1989 when she worked as a translator for Valentīns Šteinbergs. It is Irene, a native Latvian educated at Moscow University, whom I have to thank for making the completion of this work possible. Together we have been able to unearth a wealth of new material in the Latvian National Archives in Riga (Latvijas Valsts arhīvā — formerly the archives of the Latvian Communist Party) which prove beyond doubt that Peter Piatkov was Jānis Žāklis; most notably the tsarist police files on Žāklis, and unpublished memoirs by two Latvian revolutionaries who knew Žāklis in Latvia and Europe, who both identity him as the man wanted in London as Peter the Painter. Those accounts, by Voldemārs Skare and Juris Daberts, are perhaps the most telling for their rendering of "Peter the Painter" in Latvian. There are three Latvian words for painter: *krāsotājs*, painter and decorator; *gleznotājs*, portrait artist; or *mālderis*, a crude dauber. Skare and Daberts both say Žāklis was Peter the Painter, but refer to him in Latvian irreverently as Pēteris Mālderis (Peter the Dauber); implying that he wasn't a very good artist, or may have believed himself to be better than he was.

The London TV documentary, "London's Scariest Mysteries — the Houndsditch Murders" (LWT 2003), attracted a great deal of interest in Latvia, where the violent events in London were previously unknown, and resulted in a string of articles in the Latvian press about my researches. Among the journalists who covered the story, and who accompanied Irene and myself on a road trip around Courland, was the author, Pauls Bankovskis, whose 2002 novel *Mister Latvija* was inspired by the characters associated with the Houndsditch robbery. His feature article about my search for Peter the Painter (with photographs of Žāklis, Piatkov, Peterss and Svars) appeared in the colour supplement of *Sest-Diena*, the Saturday edition of Latvia's most important daily, *Diena*. Bankovskis wrote that my search for Peter the Painter had become an obsession.

'The Englishman, who looks like a bespectacled school teacher, has studied the history of Latvian anarchists and the revolutionary movement for years... Gradually this research turned into an obsession in a way. Listening to his stories, versions and hypotheses, watching the enthusiasm with which he is trying to find some more crumbs of information to add to his study, an involuntary recollection dawns upon my mind of a film called "Possession" — about a romantic obsession caused by a letter found by chance in a library... Soon enough, looking through the dusty files of a local museum and examining topographic maps, I also start getting visions of what I would so much like to find and discover...'[10] The obsession it seemed was becoming contagious, but it also produced results.

After another article, this time by Raivis Buris in the daily *Lauku Avīze*,[11] an elderly lady came forth who remembered being at school with someone with the Žāklis surname. As a result of her information I was able to get in touch with a distant relative of Peter the Painter, and eventually to trace the surviving members of the Žāklis family in Latvia, Russia, Australia and America. On successive trips to Latvia, Irene and I were able to find and visit all of the important locations associated with Jānis Žāklis and the Žāklis family, and to meet in particular two women directly related to Peter the Painter; granddaughters of his brother Karlis and of his sister Anna. They offered compelling evidence that their relative really was Peter the Painter: family photographs of the same faces and places depicted in photographs belonging to Peter Piatkov in London. Years of secrecy surround the fate of Jānis Žāklis; the Žāklis family today have little more than half-remembered rumour to dispel the mystery. It was a retired historian, Andris Puļķis, who had been threatened with dire consequences by the Soviet authorities because of his interest in the Latvian anarchists, and who was in the grip of a terminal illness when I interviewed him in 2003, who offered the first convincing theory of what happened to Peter the Painter, and put me on the track of the last piece in the jigsaw.

The story pieced together in this book is much more than the solution to a simple murder mystery. It places the revolutionary activities of Peter the Painter and the Latvian anarchists in the context of the centuries old struggle of the Latvian people for freedom, against foreign occupation and social injustice. In a world traumatised today by a global "war on terror", in which Peter the Painter has been likened to Osama Bin Laden, it demonstrates that the actions of the Latvian anarchists in London were not the "terrorism" they have been compared to; but rather part of a resistance movement against the *state* terrorism of an autocratic Russian government. The tragic course of modern Latvian history — from the 1905 Revolution against German exploitation and a monolithic Russian empire, which denied the existence of a separate Latvian identity; through the first Latvian Republic of 1918-1940; to the triple trial of Soviet-Nazi-Soviet-again occupation, accompanied by state sponsored terror, wartime holocaust, mass deportations to Siberia and an involuntary incorporation into the Soviet Union which only ended in 1991 — are proof enough, if proof is needed, that the struggle of the Latvian anarchists was not without moral foundation; that the will to resist oppression is always present. And for Latvians today, coming to terms with their turbulent past and seeking to find a secure identity for themselves in an uncertain future, perhaps the story of Peter the Painter and the remarkable group of young Latvian anarchists who emerged from the 1905 Revolution may offer an antidote to the national shame voiced by the poet Vizma Belševica, when she imagined witnessing the unopposed slaughter of the pagan Latvians by German crusaders in the middle ages:

> "I want to burn [...]
> To climb towards heaven on a towering flame
> And scream out the injustice by which my nation
> With fiery iron was beset and slaughtered"[12]

In 1912 Superintendent John Ottaway of the City of London Police believed that Peter the Painter was Jānis Žāklis. The material discovered in Latvia during the writing of this book over a hundred years later show that he was right. London's most enduring mystery since Jack the Ripper is solved. And a lost epoch of Latvian history has been restored.

Notes

1   Often cited as "Britain's first urban guerrilla group", the Angry Brigade (1970-1972) used guns and bombs in a series of symbolic attacks against property.

2   "London's Scariest Mysteries — the Houndsditch Murders" (London Weekend Television, 2003)

3   James Edward Holroyd, *The Gaslight Murders: The Saga of Sidney Street and the Scarlet 'S'* (London, 1960), p. 105

4   J. P. Eddy, *The Mystery of Peter the Painter* (London, 1946), pp. 27, 31-32.

5   Interview with Maija Eliase, Jelgava, 16th June, 1989.

6   Files of the City of London Police, "Houndsditch Murders", Box 534G/1.4: Letter from 'Werner Upits', London Metropolitan Archives.

7   Ibid. 534C/1.8: Letter from Kiev, 17th August 1912.

8   Ibid. 534C/1: Letter No.9457: Russian Consul General to Superintendent Ottaway, 16th December 1912.

9   *Brīvība* No. 6, November 1910.

10   Pauls Bankovkis, 'Melnais Pēteris' (Black Peter), *SestDiena* (Rīga), 11-17th October, 2003.

11   Raivis Buris, 'Latviešu bin Ladens' (The Latvian Bin Laden), *Lauku Avīze* (Riga), 21st October, 2003.

12   Vizma Belševica, 'Indriķa Latvieša piezīmes uz Livonijas hronikas malām' (The Notations of Henricus De Lettis in the Margins of the Livonian Chronicle). Belševica, Vizma: *Gadu gredzeni*. Riga, 1969, p. 93.

Prologue
The Houndsditch Murders
Dramatic reconstruction

Friday, 16th December 1910

Police Constable Walter Piper listened. The sounds were like drilling, sawing and breaking away of brickwork. He followed Max Weil out of the back room and went upstairs. In the second floor back bedroom he leaned out of the window and looked across at Exchange Buildings, but the yards below were hidden from view. When they came downstairs the noises were still there. Piper decided to investigate.

It was a windy night outside in Houndsditch. The snow covered street was deserted. Piper looked again at the shop next door to Max Weil's. The window read 'No. 119. H. S. Harris. Goldsmith-Silversmith. Established 1865.' This particular shop had only been open since May. He was still only a probationary constable, but he prided himself on knowing his beat. Everything seemed normal. The bostwick gate over Harris' was locked. He peered through the window. The observation light was on and the inner office door was open, so that he could see the jeweller's heavy iron safe in the corner.

Piper turned, and with Max Weil in tow, headed up Houndsditch and swung right into Cutler Street. On the corner with Exchange Buildings the lights were still on in the Cutler's Arms. He turned right again, and knocked on the door opposite the pub. Number 12 Exchange Buildings. This little cul-de-sac ran parallel to Houndsditch. One of these places must back on to Harris' shop.

The Abrahams family, occupants of number 12, were tenants of long standing. Nobody was working in the yard at the back, they assured Piper.

He moved on to number 11. It had an old fashioned folding shop-front. Three windows covered by green shutters. Through the gap at the top Piper could see the gleam of gaslight. He knocked on the door. It opened almost immediately and a foreign, furtive-seeming man looked out at him.

Piper asked, "Is the missus in?"

The man shook his head. "She has gone out".

"Right. I will come back."

He was unsure of what to do next. The suspicious foreigner had closed the door to number 11. He tapped again, lightly, at number 12. "How far is Harris' from here?" he asked. Going through to the narrow back yard he tried to puzzle out the distance for himself. Then he left and walked back towards Cutler Street. A man stood watching him from the shadows at the mouth of the cul-de-sac. As Piper got nearer, the man walked off.

Piper supposed he had better go for help. In Houndsditch he bumped into two constables from neighbouring beats, Ernest Woodhams and Joseph Choate, and started to tell them the story. He missed out the bit about going to Exchange Buildings.

Choate took up position in Houndsditch where he could keep watch on the front of the jeweller's shop. Woodhams went round to cover the back from the entrance to Exchange Buildings. Piper set off again for Bishopsgate Police Station to get reinforcements. Before he had gone much further he met Sergeant Robert Bentley and two Detective Constables, James Martin and Arthur Strongman. Bentley sent Strongman back to the station, then followed Piper to see Max Weil.

Weil took Bentley through to the back of his shop, as he had done with young Piper. The noises could still be heard. As they were talking the hammering stopped. Bentley went out onto Houndsditch and found that Strongman had returned with sergeants Tucker and Bryant and a constable called Smoothey. Piper didn't see what happened next; Bentley ordered him to take Choate's place in front of Harris' shop.

Stationing Smoothey on the corner with Cutler Street, and leaving Woodhams where he was, Sergeant Bentley led the other five policemen to the door of number 11 Exchange Buildings. It was 11.30pm. No one had any idea that Piper had already been to the house fifteen minutes before.

Bentley knocked on the door. It opened.

"Have you been working or knocking about inside?" Bentley asked.

The face that looked back at him gave no answer.

"Don't you understand English?"

Still no answer.

"Have you got anybody in the house that can? Fetch them down."

The mute foreigner pushed the door to but didn't close it, and went upstairs.

Behind Bentley one of the other policemen called, "Open the door or we're going to smash it in."

At that moment the lights went out in the Cutlers' Arms.

Bentley pushed the door open and stepped into a small lobby facing the stairs. To his right was a small room in which a large fire blazed in the grate. In the middle of the room a table was spread with food. There was no one there. As Sergeant Bryant pushed in behind him, Bentley looked up and saw the legs of a man standing in front of him on the stairs, his face hidden in shadow.

Bentley asked, "Is anybody working here?"

"No."

"Can I have a look in the back?"

"Yes."

"Show us the way."

The darkened figure on the stairs pointed towards the room. "In there".

Bentley stepped into the room. As he did so a man came in through the back door, moved between the policeman and the table and opened fire with a squat looking pistol.

In the same moment the figure on the stairs opened fire. Bullets struck Bentley in the shoulder and neck. Staggering backwards he collapsed with his head over the doorstep. Behind him, Bryant was hit in the arm and chest. Stumbling over Bentley's body into the cul-de-sac, he collapsed.

Woodhams, running towards the shooting, was felled by a bullet to the thigh. As he sank into unconsciousness, one of the men in the house stepped out of the door and shot Sergeant Tucker twice, in the hip and the heart. Strongman caught him by the arm as he fell, dragging him the length of Exchange Buildings. Tucker collapsed, dead.

One man was shooting now from the doorway as the figure who shot Tucker fired two more shots and retreated inside to reload.

At that moment a third man burst from number 9 and advanced up the cul-de-sac, firing methodically to clear an escape route. Stricken with terror, Detective Constable Martin turned tail and ran into the house opposite.

The gunman had almost reached the end of the cul-de-sac when Constable Choate caught hold of his wrist and tried to wrestle the long barrelled pistol from his grip. The man pulled the trigger again and again as Choate desperately pushed the gun away from his body. Four bullets went into the policeman's thigh, calf, and foot. The centre of the exploding whirlwind seemed to shift to Choate. From the doorway of number 11, the man who had shot Bentley and Tucker (having reloaded) ran out to help his comrade and fired two deliberately aimed shots into Choate's back. In that instant a fourth gunman appeared from number 9 and ran forward, firing wildly at Choate. But it was the policeman's attacker whom the shot hit in the back.

After the shooting came dazed silence. Bentley lay dying on the doorstep of number 11. Bryant, propped against the outside wall next to the door, sat badly wounded. Woodhams and Choate lay sprawled in the middle of the cul-de-sac. Choate was dying. Tucker was dead already. Strongman and Martin were both in shock but unharmed. The gunmen picked up their wounded comrade and carried him away into the night.

They turned right into Cutler Street away from the police and headed east. As they reached the corner with Borers Passage, a man came round the corner and almost collided with them. It was Isaac Levy, manager of a Walthamstow tobacconists shop, returning home. He saw three men coming towards him, walking in the middle of the street. The middle one was being supported by the other two as though drunk. Behind them, a woman wearing a fur hat and carrying a large muff. He was two yards from them and could see their faces clearly in the gas light on the corner. He didn't notice a fourth man, ahead of the others in the darkness.

Drawing level with him, the two men supporting their wounded comrade turned with pistols pointing at Levy's face and both spoke in broken English.

"Don't follow us".

"Don't follow!"

Saturday, 17th December 1910

Detective Superintendent John Ottaway of the City of London Police took charge of the investigation just before midnight. From an inspection of the scene, it was obvious that the people who had occupied numbers 9 and 11 Exchange Buildings had been interrupted as they tunnelled through the wall into Harris' to rob the safe of its contents (valued later at £7,000).

In number 11 the fire was still burning in the grate. Tea, bread, jam, and sardines were laid out on the table. There was also a pressure gauge, a double blowpipe fitted with seven feet of flexible metal tubing, rubber tubing, and two stop-cocks. Besides the table, a gas stove, an armchair, three upholstered chairs, and a chest of drawers completed the room's furniture. Pieces of oil cloth were spread on the floor. Two of the windows by the door had been broken by bullets. There were bullet holes in the ceiling. The bullets had passed through and lodged in the ceiling of the first floor bedroom above. The bedroom was bare except for a bed and another upholstered chair matching the three below. Downstairs, the back door through which the man with the gun had come, opened onto a small yard measuring fourteen feet by three. In the yard were a sink at one end and a toilet at the other. Near the sink were signs that someone had climbed over into the yard of the unoccupied number 10 next door. Similar signs showed that somebody had also climbed over into number 9, from where the entry into Harris' jewellers had been under way.

In the yard of number 9 were broken bricks and a cylinder of oxygen-compressed gas. The toilet seat was covered with brown paper upon which lay diamond-pointed drills, a carpenters' brace, chisel, crowbars, and a specially constructed wrench with jagged jaws for tearing metal. In the wall backing onto Harris' a hole nine inches deep, and measuring 24 inches by 20 inches, had been made. Inside the house were 63 feet of rubber tubing fixed to a gas pipe, freshly mixed mortar, sand, wax candles, and asbestos boards. Whoever these people were they knew their business. Ottaway set about doing his.

Saturday morning passed in intense activity. Ottaway's detectives were desperate for anything that might lead them to the gang who had shot five policemen. The break came just after mid-day. Detective Inspector Frederick Wensley telephoned the City Police with the news that a Doctor Scanlon had just reported attending a man at 59 Grove Street, Whitechapel. The man had been shot in the back sometime during the night and was in a serious condition. The bad news was the press had also got hold of the information.

Minutes before the reporters descended, Detective Inspector Thompson of the City Police, accompanied by Wensley and several other armed detectives from H Division (covering the East End), arrived at 59 Grove Street, three quarters of a mile east of Houndsitch. The upstairs flat was rented to a young Latvian, Fricis Svars, and his girlfriend Luba Milstein.

In the front room they found a man lying fully dressed on a narrow bed facing the door, a blood stained overcoat at his feet. He was dead. In the back room was a woman, interrupted as she bent over the fireplace, burning photographs and papers.

The dead man's pockets contained thirty 7.65mm pistol cartridges, a drill, a key to number 9 Exchange Buildings, and welder's goggles. In his overcoat pockets were a fully loaded magazine clip, seven more loose cartridges of the same calibre, a key to 59 Grove Street, and a wallet holding various letters written in what turned out to be Latvian. Under the mattress at the head of the bed was a fully loaded 7.65mm Dreyse pistol, and two spare magazine clips of 7.65mm ammunition. A man's cloth cap containing six Mauser pistol rounds and twenty three assorted rifle cartridges lay on the table in the centre of the room.

Elsewhere in the flat were found: more letters and papers in Latvian, a box of fifty cartridges, a cartridge belt, a dagger, a mandolin, a tambourine, a violin, two oil paintings, and a water colour signed "Yourka, 15.12.1910". A slip of paper bore the inscription, "G. Dubov, 20 Galloway Road, Shepherd's Bush".

As well as the letters, the dead man's wallet revealed a passport in the name of Schafishi Kahn Hirsh (Riga), and a membership card for the Latvian anarchist-communist group (London) – The Flame (*Latviešu anarhistu-komunistu grupas "Liesma" - Londona*) bearing the signature of Grīnbergs. According to Doctor Scanlon, the dying man had given his name as George Gardstein. The evidence showed he also used the names Morountzev, Mourrometz, P. Morin, and Janis Karlovitch Stenzel... It was going to be an uphill struggle sorting out who he really was.

The arrested woman was less of a mystery: Sara Rosa Trassjonsky, a Polish Jew who worked with Luba Milstein as a seamstress.

The only other piece of intelligence the police possessed was that the flat was shared by a third occupant, a Latvian artist who lived (where now the dead man lay) in the front room — Peter Piatkov, Peter the Painter.

I

1883 to January 1905
A Painter and Artist, or Dauber

> I first met him in Riga in 1904. By profession he was a painter and
> artist. He was a brown-haired man with dark brown eyes and a rosy
> face, of average height but strong build, wore a moustache.
>
> Voldemārs Skare[1]

The Baltic provinces of Russia — today's Latvia and Estonia — were still a
feudal world in 1883, when Peter the Painter was born near the small town of
Saldus (Frauenberg) in the Latvian countryside. A possession of Germany since
the 13th century, and variously of Sweden, and Poland, Latvia was only
incorporated into the Russian empire at the end of the 18th century. In return
for their support for the Russian tsar, the German barons were permitted to
retain their power over the lives of the peasants, as the landowning elite in
Latvia. Such was the zeal of the Baltic barons in defending the autocracy of the
Romanovs that the last of the tsars (himself more German than Russian)
considered them more loyal than even his own nobles, and many of them
occupied influential positions in the service of the Russian state.

Descended from the Teutonic Knights who "civilised" pagan Latvia during
the great Northern Crusade, the Baltic barons looked down arrogantly on the
Latvian peasants as an inferior race, demanding total servility. When the Latvian
peasants were emancipated (1817 in Courland, 1819 in Livonia; predating the
abolition of serfdom in Russia proper which was not abolished until 1861), the
owning of land was forbidden to them. Freed of serfdom, the peasants were
forced to exist as farmhands or, at best, able only to lease land owned by the
barons. Like the black plantation workers in America after the abolition of
slavery, the lives of the rural population in Latvia were controlled totally; living
in tied cottages and often only receiving wages-in-kind at inflated prices from
the equivalent of the "company store".

Ironically, this process of "civilising" imperialism was conducted in a country
which of all the lands ruled by the tsar most resembled Western Europe. While
the urban proportion of European Russia was no more than 13 per cent of the
population, almost a third of the two and a half million Latvians lived in the
towns. And unlike the Russian *muzhik*, most Latvian peasants could read and
write. By the end of the 19th century the literacy rate in Latvia was more than
three times greater than the Russian average. The early emancipation of serfdom
in Latvia was brought about by the pressing needs of industrial capitalism. Huge
Russian markets and increases in trade heralded a rapid expansion of industry in
the Baltic. An ambitious programme of railway construction was launched and
the Baltic Sea ports expanded. By the end of the 19th century Latvia had an
industrial labour force of nearly a million. Riga ranked third, next to Moscow
and St. Petersburg, in the volume of industrial output and number of workers.

But while life changed in the cities, the growth of industrialisation had little impact on rural Latvia. Amid the idyllic beauty of the Courland countryside the harsh life endured by peasants in small towns like Saldus, Sabile (Zabeln), Talsi (Talsen) and Kuldiga (Goldingen) remained almost untouched. After agrarian reforms in the 1860s Latvian peasant farmers were grudgingly permitted to own land, but few of them could afford the prohibitive payment instalments demanded. The oppressive power of the German barons was felt in everything.

Like former slave-owners everywhere the barons, whose families had ruled over the big estates since the Baltic lands were first subdued by fire and sword in the 12th century, regarded any Latvian female within reach as fair game. It was common for the German nobility to father illegitimate children with Latvian farm girls. The usual way of avoiding scandal was to marry off the unfortunate woman to a young Latvian boy, and install the newly weds on a farm of their own. Given the near impossibility of otherwise owning land neither family of the happy couple would see reason to complain about the generous settlement. Something like this happened in the Žāklis family.

According to family folklore Kristaps Žāklis (20th October 1826–16th August 1889) was the illegitimate son of Baron Heinrich von Mirbach (1805-1875) and a Latvian servant girl on his estate at Jaunmuiža (Neuhof), called Marija. In time-honoured tradition, the pregnant Marija was hastily married off to a Latvian youth called Adam (the brother of Peter the Painter's great-grandfather), from Aknukalni farm in Šķēde. The birth of the child came during the period when Latvians (now free of serfdom) first acquired family names; usually taken from nature or the geographical area in which they lived. Perhaps it was Baron von Mirbach who bestowed a Latvian surname *Žākle* on his bastard son (in old script *Schahkle*: meaning a forked tree, or pitchfork), to give the impression of Latvian parentage. When Kristaps Žāklis came into manhood and married a local girl called Steppe, von Mirbach gave the couple a small plot of land at Rijnieki (Rednieki farm), in the parish of Lutriņi (Luttringen; today Jaunlutriņi) just north of Saldus, where they raised five children. One of them was called Jānis Žāklis. But this Jānis (1863-1940) was not the man who grew up to become Peter the Painter – he came from a different branch of the family.

Both branches of the Žākle family come from Ermanis Žāklis (1770-1849), father of Adam and Juris. Juris Žāklis married Ilze Zveja (1790-1880) and they had a son called Jānis (born *c.* 1822). He in turn had two sons: another Jānis (born 23rd June 1851, died 24th June 1908) and Juris (born 1856). This second Jānis (in the Russian style, Ivan Ivanovich; John son of John) became in turn the father of Peter the Painter. The distant and unspoken connection to an illustrious member of the German nobility explains a number of otherwise inexplicable events in the subsequent life of the Žākle family; and perhaps the hatred displayed in adulthood by Peter the Painter to the Baltic barons.

The birth of Peter the Painter is documented in the Church Books for the parish of Lutriņi, which tell us that 'Jahn son of Jahn Schahkle' was born at 6am on 19th July 1883, at the family farm called Svītes (Svitte), in the parish of Lutriņi.[2]

Baby Jānis was the third child of six: elder brother Kārlis (born 25th March, 1879) and sister Anna (born 2nd July, 1880), followed afterwards by younger sisters Charlotte Marija (born 3rd August, 1885), Katrīna (born 13th March, 1890), and Milda (born 7th January, 1895).

Both of the Žāklis parents were enigmatic figures. The father, Jānis (Jahn), was the cousin of an unacknowledged son of one of the most powerful German families in the Baltic. His farm at Svitēs was the ancestral home of his branch of the Žākle family, but only as tenant farmers. His luck changed when he married Margarieta Tālberga. It was she who had bought the farm at Svitēs from the local Baron sometime in the 1870s in the time when the land was being redistributed, and it remained registered in her name until she sold it, after her husband's death, to one of her son-in-laws in 1913. For a Latvian woman like Margarieta Tālberga, to be able to buy land was extremely unusual, so she must have come from a wealthy family. In any event, she was a singular woman, and for some reason not well liked by her husband's relatives, who avoided her in later life.

An explanation for both of these things may lie in the fact that, although listed as 'Lutheran' in official documents, Margarieta Tālberga was born into a Jewish family in Kuldiga. Her father, Krishs Talbergs, seems to have died before her marriage and her widowed mother, Lote (Charlotte) Tālberga, lived with the Žākles at Svitēs. Lote converted to Lutheranism late in life and is noted in the Church Books as being 'Baptised' in 1885. Perhaps Margarieta Žākle, who as a 'Lutheran' could buy land denied to Jews by law, was never quite accepted into the extended Žākle clan because of her Jewish background.

A modern psychological profiler looking at a "terrorist" suspect today would no doubt make much of Peter the Painter's family background: distant cousin to a bastard descendant of a German noble; with a Jewish grandmother and a mother shunned by the family; carrying a big chip on his shoulder about rich landlords and despising the petty parochialism of country people; a sensitive child, driven to overthrow all authority and ignorance and pursue a utopian vision plucked from his large collection of books.

The young Jānis Žāklis was a bright boy and in 1891, at the age of eight, he started school at Neuhof, close to Lake Laidzes, just outside Talsi. His parents by then had taken on a second, rented, farm nearby called Kūle (Kuhlen). The young Žāklis remained at school in Neuhof until he was eleven, and it could be that one of his teachers, Gustavs Lācis, who was later to figure in police reports about the local revolutionary movement in 1905, may have had an influence on the schoolboy.

After leaving Neuhof, Žāklis was sent away to Kuldiga, to spend the next four years pursuing his secondary education in a private fee-paying school. He left the school in 1898 at the age of sixteen and entered the fifth form at Kuldiga's classical German Gymnasium,[3] a prestigious fee-paying high school built in 1868 that was usually reserved for the Baltic nobility, whose alumni (some 20 years prior to Žāklis arriving there) included Eduard Graf von Keyserling, tenth child in one of the most powerful aristocratic families in Courland, who later found fame in Germany as a novelist.

For a Latvian to attend a German Gymnasium the family would normally have had to have been wealthy, or to have some strong German connection. Sometimes a Lutheran church Pastor might promote a clever boy to

"Germanise" him; but it would serve equally well if it were commonly known that a particular family was related, albeit illegitimately, to a local Baron. In the case of Jānis Žāklis his education was paid for only in part by his father. The remainder of the cost was borne by his uncle, Juris Žāklis, a successful engineer in the army, holding the rank of Colonel in a Sapper Battalion stationed in the important garrison city of Bobruisk, Belarus (Byelorussia), who acted as his guardian and seems to have been a key figure in times of family crisis.

The atmosphere in Kuldiga on the shore of the river Venta, with its famous waterfall and a large park in the heart of the town, was entirely German and provincial, though most of the teaching at the Gymnasium would have been conducted in Russian. As well as Russian, Žāklis received tuition in French and German, both of which he spoke fluently in addition to Latvian, English and Yiddish, learned from his Mother. He also learned to play the violin, painted portraits and had a passion for reading. Early in 1901, at the age of eighteen, Žāklis dropped out of this cultured environment before the end of the course, on the grounds of weak health and because he did not have enough money to stay.[4] The Head of the Vidzeme guberna Gendarmerie, gathering information to send to London in 1912, noted, 'Žāklis studied in the Kuldiga gymnasium, but he did not finish the course, leaving the sixth form on 24 March 1901, as a result of a letter by his uncle and guardian, because he did not succeed very well.'[5]

It could be that Žāklis did not succeed very well in Kuldiga because his mind was on other things. Žāklis was highly intelligent and noted for his fine collection of books.[6] He had also embraced the dangerous new ideas of revolutionary socialism that were gaining popularity in Latvia at the time. The national and social humiliation felt by Latvians towards the German landowners in the second half of the 19th century produced a "National Awakening" that coincided with a movement known as the *Jaunā Strāva* (New Current); Marxist intellectuals and writers like the poet Jānis Rainis who brought revolutionary literature into the country from abroad. Forbidden books also came into Latvia with the teachers and specialists employed from Germany, where the ideas of Social Democracy were legal; and it could be that Žāklis was encouraged to read socialist literature by one of his German teachers at the Gymnasium.

When Žāklis dropped out of college he went home to his parents' farm at Kūle outside Talsi. His father, Jānis senior, though still classed as a "peasant" in the strict social hierarchy of the times, was by now a successful farmer, who the police noted, 'has his own farm with land at Svitēs ... and rents another farm... A well-to-do man'.[7]

The Svitēs farm was now occupied by Žāklis' older sister Anna, who had married a local man, Herman Sakne. Big brother Kārlis had also married and was living with his wife at a third farm in the district called Kļaviņe. Back with his parents and three younger sisters at Kūle, Žāklis would doubtless have come under pressure from his family to stop daydreaming, and buckle down to either finishing his studies or earning his keep by working on the farm. But the bookish teenager was too preoccupied with ideas of revolution to take much notice.

In Talsi, Žāklis became friends with Jānis Linde (Lindulis, 1870-1942), a man some thirteen years older than himself, who worked as a bookseller. Sometime in

1901 the two men founded the first illegal socialist group in Talsi, but Žāklis was the main organiser. Soon afterwards they were joined by a twenty-seven year-old socialist called Jūlijs Kažemirs, who had come from Riga to work in Talsi as a teacher at the Russian Orthodox School. Thanks to Kažemirs, by February or March 1902 they had established contact with the illegal Baltic Latvian Social Democratic Workers Organisation (BLSDSO) in Riga, and had organised four small groups among the local farm workers. In April 1902 the four cells came together as an affiliated section of the BLSDSO, under the direction of the Talsi Committee of the BLSDSO — Žāklis, Linde and Kažemirs — and it wasn't long before their presence was felt.

Looking back in 1925, Jānis Linde wrote that: 'Like all our Latvian towns and villages, Talsi is a very sleepy and peaceful corner of the Earth. Everybody lives withdrawn into their shells, like snails, and doesn't like to be disturbed. Narrow-mindedness and rigidity are their characteristic traits. Twenty-five years ago it was even more so. And suddenly ripples started to appear in this quiet back-water. As if some naughty boys started to throw pebbles into it…' The first pebble was thrown on Christmas night, 1902. The Lutheran church in Talsi celebrated with a Christmas tree and a choir singing 'From Heaven will be brought to me…' accompanied by the church organ. But the next morning leaflets appeared on the church doors, on the stairs, on walls of houses and in the streets proclaiming: 'Too long you have been fooled and sedated; too long you have waited for a Saviour and Messiah from Heaven'.

The second pebble came in the form of hectographed leaflets with a cartoon (probably drawn by Žāklis) depicting 'How Father Gruuns hanged his coachman', which had a big effect on the country people. The Lutheran Pastor from Arlava, Father Gruuns, on the way home from a child's christening, had quarrelled with his coachman and pushed him off his seat. The poor humiliated coachman took 'his Lord's punishment' so close to heart that he hanged himself. Linde notes with some satisfaction that 'Father Gruuns was later shot in 1906, when he travelled down some road'.[8]

Leaflets produced by the Talsi Committee were distributed among farm workers on all the large estates in the district, and began to appear more frequently, spreading over a wide area; as far away as the Baltic coast, Lake Engure, Kandava and Sabile. To the authorities it was clear that an organisation was at work.

'Who were those mischief makers, those dare-devils, who dared to stand up against the Lords and the Church, against the sanctioned by God Tsar and the state order? Of course, they were not from Talsi itself; they were not the self-satisfied philistines or their kin. They were country youths, some were educated people who worked in Talsi in various institutions and young school teachers from the surrounding country schools, teenagers who had read a book or two and knew how people lived in other countries, who thirsted for more freedom.'[9]

The agitation demanded an improvement to the harsh conditions endured by the farm workers. On one Talsi estate the workers announced a strike against being paid in rotten potatoes. The Talsi Committee used the strike as a means of getting their revolutionary message across. In the summer of 1903 Žāklis wrote a hectographed appeal signed by the Committee, 'To the Land Workers', calling on them to unite in small groups to defend their class interests against the barons. It was later published in the monthly journal *Sociāldemokrāts* (The Social Democrat).[10]

Over the spring of 1903 Žāklis became acquainted through friends in Talsi with 20-year-old Fricis Ratkalns. The pair discovered that they shared common interests and views and became friends. According to a statement extracted from Ratkalns under torture by the Talsi police: 'Žāklis had a lot of good books and Ratkalns was very interested in his library, and borrowed books off him (philosophy, etc). From reading Žāklis' books Ratkalns first learned of the social problems of mankind. He discussed these books with Žāklis. They also discussed the situation in Russia, and Žāklis told him about his beliefs and actions in opposition to the government in Russia. Žāklis started giving him illegal literature. He went for walks in the forest with Žāklis, who taught him how to hectograph texts. They distributed the proclamations together among the people at the forest celebration [the pagan Midsummer's Eve *Ligo* festival, celebrated in Latvia on the evening of 21st/22nd June]. Žāklis gave him 100 copies. He distributed 70 in Talsi and 30 among the people at Mūrnieki. Ratkalns told the police that there were two hectographs in the district – one was from Riga, one from Talsi, but he didn't know where they were kept. He thought the hectograph might be with Žāklis at the farm Kūle [just outside Talsi], or in the forest where all the illegal literature of the Talsi organisation was kept'.[11]

On 16th July 1903 police in the area of Valdemārpils (Sasmaken) near Talsi found six copies of the proclamations 'Beware of Spies!' and 'To the Land Workers' nailed to a post. During the investigation into the origins of this seditious propaganda Fricis Ratkalns was betrayed to the police by a former schoolmate called Kārlis Celms. Celms told the police that late in the evening of 13th July, during a celebration in the forest near to the Mūrnieki estate in Nurmuižas (Nurmhousen), Ratkalns had given him a proclamation in Latvian titled 'Beware of Spies!' which he burned immediately. On 24th July the police descended on Ratkalns at his uncle's house at Valdemārpils, searched his room in the attic and took him into custody. During the search the police found handwriting evidence that Ratkalns had copied the hectographed proclamations. During his third interrogation on 14th August 1903, Ratkalns admitted he was guilty, and that on 13th July he had given out two copies, and copied out part of the proclamation himself. He also confessed, under torture by the policeman Grigorovich, that the text he copied was given to him by Jānis Žāklis.[12]

The information extracted from Ratkalns confirmed the suspicions of the Talsi police about Žāklis and other agitators in the district whom they had under observation. Ratkalns was charged with spreading seditious proclamations signed by the Talsi Committee of the BLSDSO and transferred to prison in Jelgava.

A formal case against Žāklis was opened on 31st July 1903, but when police searched the Žāklis farm at Kūle he had already disappeared, together with his friend Andreas Briģis (Brigge) and two other suspects – Jansons, a former student from Jelgava, and Pekmanis.[13]

Though the police were not aware of it at the time, Žāklis sought sanctuary with his sister, Anna, and her husband, Herman Sakne, at Svitēs.[14] But the family obviously deemed it safer that the fugitive leave Courland altogether, so Žāklis was packed off to live with his benevolent uncle Juris in Bobruisk, where his parents probably hoped he would forget about fomenting revolution among the farm workers and get down to studying for his certificate of education.

On 10th September 1903 the Head of the Courland Gendarmerie finally concluded, on the evidence of Ratkalns and the search of Žāklis' home, that there was sufficient cause to order the arrest of Žāklis and the other suspects in the case, and instructed his assistant to work out the details with the Office of the Prosecutor.[15] Fricis Ratkalns was released on 1st October 1903 because of ill-health and placed under 'special observation' in his home parish of Stende, north of Talsi.

While the Courland police searched fruitlessly for Jānis Žāklis around Talsi, he was safely under the wing of his uncle Juris in Bobruisk, 700km away in Byelorussia, studying (his family hoped) for his exams. But if his parents imagined sending their son to Bobruisk would keep Žāklis out of trouble they had picked the wrong place. Just like Latvia, the border province of Byelorussia was seething with discontent. In 1898 the capital, Minsk, was the venue for the founding congress of the Russian Social Democratic Labour Party (RSDLP). The provincial garrison city of Bobruisk was a major centre of socialist and trade union activity, and a stronghold of the Jewish workers Bund (which had 700 members in the city). Clashes with the police were frequent. By September 1903 the situation had grown so volatile that the Bund feared that a pogrom was imminent in Bobruisk and formed its own Fighting Organisation to defend Jewish workers from attack. The funerals of workers and Bund members killed in clashes with the police invariably turned into street demonstrations, with revolutionary speeches.

On 1st May 1904, the workers in Bobruisk celebrated with a general strike. The railway station closed. Mass meetings of up to 800 people in one place were held in the forests outside the city, and socialist proclamations were distributed by the thousand. A parade of a thousand workers marched down Bobruisk's central street with a carnival air. Among the crowds many were demanding more resolute action against the government — one of them was Jānis Žāklis. Unfortunately for Žāklis, his subversive activities in Bobruisk had not escaped the attention of the local police. On 28th May 1904 Žāklis was arrested at the house of his uncle and interrogated, as part of an investigation opened on 10th April, about the distribution of illegal socialist literature in the region. He was charged specifically under Articles 252, 252a and 318 of the Criminal Code with crimes against the state, for the possession of illegal literature.[16]

Because of a lack of cells in Bobruisk prison, Žāklis was held temporarily at the Municipal Police Directorate, and then transferred to the 'investigatory isolator' prison in Minsk. If the book-loving young Žāklis had ever read Bram Stoker he must have wondered if he was being delivered to Dracula's castle when he arrived in Minsk. A mock Gothic pile known as Pishchala's Castle (after the architect Rudolf Pishchala) built in 1825, Minsk prison sits astride a hill-top in the middle of the city dominating the view beneath it. The grim looking structure is a three-floored rectangular building with a round tower at each corner, ringed by a high stone wall. Still in use as a prison today, it is now only possible to admire the architecture in autumn and winter; in the spring and summer the white turrets are hidden among the trees which have grown around the prison walls.

In Minsk prison Žāklis was photographed and the pictures were added to his file on 4th June 1904.[17] It was the discovery of these prison mug shots in 1989 (see image 7), in what was then the Museum of the Revolution (now the Latvian War Museum) in Riga, which provided the first piece of conclusive evidence for the identification of Jānis Žāklis as Peter the Painter. The mug shots show in full face a tousle-haired unshaven prisoner; dressed in a collarless shirt beneath a light-coloured jacket; the jaw set and deep piercing eyes glaring defiantly at the camera; in profile instantly recognisable as the face in the posed studio portrait of Peter Piatkov.

On 5th June 1904, the day after his photograph was added to the growing file on him, Žāklis reached the age when he was eligible for military service.[18] Understandably he was unable to answer the call when it came. Incredibly, in view of the long list of violent crimes with which Jānis Žāklis was subsequently associated, this single offence of evading conscription in 1904 is the only thing for which he ever remained wanted under his real name.

On 13th July 1904 Žāklis sent a letter of appeal from Minsk prison to the Gendarmes Directorate of Courland Province, asking that he be released on bail because there was no evidence against him: 'Considering that at present I am in detention only because of the investigation started by the Gendarmes Directorate of the Courland Province, and also taking into account that there is no evidence which can prove my complicity in this case, I am asking the Gendarmes Directorate of the Courland Province to release me from custody on bail, placing me under police observation until the case comes to court.'[19]

Two days after his arrest the Minsk police completed a four-page questionnaire, detailing what was known about Žāklis, and on 31st July 1904 sent a copy of it to the Head of the Courland Gendarmerie.[20] The police in Courland took the charges levelled against Žāklis in Minsk as confirmation that he was guilty of doing the same thing in Talsi. On 30th August 1904 he and Ratkalns were both formally charged under Article 252 of the Criminal Code, in connection with the Talsi proclamations. Bail was set at 300 roubles, with the stipulation that the defendants reside at officially sanctioned addresses under strict police supervision. Fricis Ratkalns, though, had no intention of standing trial. On hearing the charges he immediately ducked the police surveillance and disappeared abroad, to England.[21] Jānis Žāklis was ordered to be released from Minsk Prison on bail and be sent under special police observation to Valmiera, in Livonia, because the case in Minsk required no further investigation.[22] There was only one problem – he didn't have 300 roubles bail.

On 23rd September 1904 the Head of Minsk Police wrote to the prison, asking to hurry up the release of Žāklis because he should have been freed on 30th August.[23] A week later he was informed that the reason for the delay in releasing Žāklis was because they were still waiting for the bail money. The 300 roubles bail was finally paid on 27th September and Žāklis was released from prison after four months in custody. The Head of the Minsk police issued Žāklis with a travel document and put him on a train to Valmiera, where he was expected to reside under police observation.[24] But Žāklis had no intention of staying in Valmiera.

On 2nd October 1904 Žāklis arrived at Ābeļ (Apple Tree farm), a new farm his father was renting in Briņķi-Pedvāle, situated in the beautiful Abava river valley, near the small country town of Sabile, 120km from Riga. From there Žāklis wrote to the Directorate of the Courland Gendarmerie saying he was suffering with a complication of a cold and lodged an appeal against the order to reside in Valmiera, asking for retrospective permission to stay in Sabile: 'Taking into account that I caught a cold on the way from Minsk to Valmiera, and my illness developed a complication, making me physically unable to go there, and considering that I don't have any means of sustenance to live there, and also considering that in the case started against me by the Gendarmes Directorate of the Minsk Province I was released on bail and chose as my place of residence estate Ābeļ, rented by my father in Courland Province, Talsi District, Briņķi-Pedvāle parish, to which effect I handed in signed papers to the above-mentioned Gendarmes Directorate, I am asking the Gendarmes Directorate of the Courland Province to put me under police observation in Sabile, a place which is six versts (6.4km) away from estate Ābeļ.'[25]

The Police agreed and allowed Žāklis to live in Sabile, but fearing he might escape abroad like Ratkalns, placed him under special observation.[26] On 12th October the head of Courland Gendarmerie noted that permission had been granted for Žāklis to live in Sabile, 'where he is at present'.[27] Žāklis also stayed for part of the time with his parents at Ābeļ.[28]

Žāklis seems to have been earning some sort of income in Sabile as a sign-writer and painter (the profession which gave him his nickname), but was clearly milking his ill-health for all it was worth. On 21st October 1904 the police reported that Žāklis was suffering from a chest infection and was unable to work.[29] But Žāklis didn't let this supposed illness stop him from getting back in touch with political developments.

A lot had been happening while he had been away. Jansons and Pekmanis, two co-conspirators wanted in the Talsi case, had fled to America; the teacher Jūlijs Kažemirs had accepted a job at the prestigious Riga Polytechnic Institute (now the University of Latvia) and moved to the capital. The Talsi BLSDSO had grown to 150 members. At its First Congress held in June 1904, while Žāklis was in prison in Minsk, it united with the Social Democrats of neighbouring Tukums to form the Talsi-Tukums branch of a new Marxist party, the Latvian Social Democratic Workers Party (*Latvijas sociāldemokrātiskās strādnieku partijas* (LSDSP)); the first Latvian political party. Jānis Linde, though, says that the link with Tukums was 'a bad decision', and existed in name only: 'It was even more difficult to keep in contact with Tukums, than with Riga. It was an artificial fusion of two organizations, enforced from above, which was quite useless... Tukums carried on with their own activities and did not even try to establish any contacts with Talsi. And Talsi as well went about their business independently.'[30]

But Jānis Žāklis wouldn't have been concerned too much about matters in rural Talsi while he sat in Sabile under police observation. New vistas were opening up in Riga.

In September 1904, a Federative Committee of the Riga Social Democratic

Organisations was created to coordinate the activities of the LSDSP and the Bund; the smaller group of Russian Marxists (RSDLP) in the city refused to take part, on the basis that they were ideologically opposed to federalism. The Federative Committee was nonetheless a major force, representing the organised workers' movement in the Latvian capital, and was increasingly engaged in labour disputes and strikes across the city. And those strikes were increasingly growing violent.

Despite being under police surveillance and with two sedition cases hanging over his head, Jānis Žāklis contrived to get back to where the action was. Linde says that 'Žāklis left for Riga in the autumn of 1904',[31] but this is impossible. The police case notes on Žāklis show that, officially at least, he remained resident in Sabile until early in January 1905. But he did manage to dodge the police and spend time in Riga without permission, as attested by Voldemārs Skare, who recalls his first meeting Žāklis: 'I first met him in Riga in 1904. By profession he was a painter and artist. He was a brown-haired man with dark brown eyes and a rosy face, of average height but strong build, wore a moustache.'[32]

The clandestine presence of Žāklis in Riga was risky, but went unnoticed by the police. What he was doing there would soon become apparent.

By 28th October 1904 the police case against Žāklis in Talsi was complete, but the hearing was delayed because his personal documents (passport, birth certificate, army call-up papers, school diploma showing that he completed five classes from the classical gymnasium) had not been forwarded.[33] Žāklis was questioned about this lack of documents on 31st October 1904. He told the Talsi police that all his documents had been kept by the police in Minsk.[34] The officer in charge of the Minsk case wrote to Courland, forwarding the missing documents to the head of the Talsi District police on 6th November and they were recorded as received on 10th November 1904.[35] The Talsi investigation, Case No. 2201 (which had begun on 31st July 1903), was formally closed on 6th November 1904 and the case papers were sent to the District Court in Liepaja on 10th November.[36] The evidence against Žāklis and Ratkalns consisted of the two proclamations, pencil notes on the struggle of the workers, and a letter from Ratkalns to his sister, Julia.[37] When the case came to court, the Liepaja Prosecutor noted: 'Experts concluded that the handwriting on the hectographed proclamations # 1 & 4 was that of Ratkalns. During his third interrogation on 14 August 1903, Ratkalns admitted he was guilty, and that on 13 July he had given out two copies, and copied out part of the proclamation himself. He also told the police (under torture by Grigorovich) that the text he copied was given to him by Žāklis. His evidence supported evidence the police had already gathered about people under observation. Ratkalns only told the police of rumours about people, not facts. For that reason they were not arrested. Žāklis was charged in 1904 in connection with this case because of another investigation that was going on in Minsk (Byelorussia) in which he was under investigation. Žāklis made no admission of guilt. Both defendants were first imprisoned but then released under special observation by the police.'[38] With Ratkalns having flown the coop to England, the prosecutor concluded there was not enough evidence to proceed against Žāklis and the investigation should be closed.[39]

On 23rd December 1904 the remaining case against Žāklis, in Minsk, was also closed and all charges dropped for lack of evidence.[40] On 29th December Žāklis signed a statement that he had been informed of the outcome of his case.[41] The police noted that Žāklis was still living under secret observation at Ābeļ.[42] Two days later, on 31st December 1904, the police lifted their observation on Žāklis.[43]

On 11th January 1905 Žāklis' personal documents were returned to him by the police. It was only two days before an event which would shake Latvia to the core and mark the outbreak of the 1905 Revolution; Latvia's second *Awakening*.

In this brief moment of calm before the storm Jānis Žāklis vanished. The name Žāklis does not appear in the files of the Russian police, or *Okhranka*[44] again until seven years later, when he is identified as being the suspect known as Peter the Painter wanted by the police in London. In the interim, the police admitted: 'Žāklis was never registered in the city of Riga as a resident, where he lived after 1904. About his present whereabouts, we don't know. We don't know if he took part in the revolutionary movement. Neither do we know what name he might have used in the revolutionary movement. We know of no reward for his capture...'[45]

Notes

1   Latvijas Nacionālā bibliotēka (LNB) — PA17/4/3/24.524/77-24.526. Voldemārs Skare, *Materiāli par 1905. gada revolūciju un tas darbiniekiem.* (Material on the 1905 revolution and its participants), p. 149. (Riga, 1950. Unpublished manuscript of 170 pages).
2   Latvijas Valsts vēstures arhivā (LVVA): 9393/235/2/1471, #68, Abschrift der Luttringenscen Kirchenbuches pro 1883. Lutrinu (Luttringen Church Book for 1883), notes the birth on 19th July 1883, and the baby's christening on 21st August 1883.
3   LVVA 4569/1/32, #273, Kurzemes guberna Gendarmerie: Personal file on Jan Janisov Žāklis, 31st July 1903, Case No. 2201. The former German Gymnasium in Kuldiga is at 19 Kalna iela.
4   Ibid.
5   LVVA 4568/15/225,Vidzeme guberna Gendarmerie: Letters from agents #66, 4th October 1912.
6   LVVA 4569/1/32, #196-199, Statement of Ratkalns (aged 21), 1903.
7   Ibid. #273.
8   Lindulis (Jānis Linde), 'Revolūcijas fakti un dokumenti: Talsu revolūcija' (Facts and documents of the Revolution: The Talsi Revolution), *Domas* No. 7, Riga 1925.
9   Ibid.
10 *Latvijas revolucionāro cīnītāju pieminas grāmata* I. Sēj: 1. daļa. (The memorial book of Latvian revolutionary fighters of the 1905 revolution. Vol. 1- Part 1. Riga, 1976), p. 56.
11 LVVA 4569/1/32, #196-199.
12 Ibid. #132: The conclusions of the Liepaja Prosecutor in the case of Ratkalns & Žāklis, 1904.
13 Ibid. #203, 13th September, 1903, and # 262, 11th March 1904.
14 Ibid. #277, Police report, 5th June 1904.
15 Ibid. #214, Report by the Head of the Courland Gendarmerie, 10th September 1903.
16 Ibid. #141.
17 Ibid. #278, Letter from Bobruisk to Minsk.
18 Ibid. #276.
19 Ibid. #282, Letter (in Russian) from Jānis Žāklis, 13th July 1904.
20 Ibid. #273 & 274, Information sheet No. 456 of the Gendarme Directorate of Minsk Province, 30th May 1904.
21 Ibid. #107, September 1904; & #112, 2nd October 1904.
22 Ibid. #102.
23 Ibid. #292, Report from the Head of Minsk Police, 23rd September 1904.
24 Ibid. #296, Report 30th September 1904. The original travel document issued to Jānis Žāklis survives on file: LVA 4569/1/32. #309.
25 Ibid. #116, Letter (in Russian) from Jānis Žāklis to the Directorate of Gendarmerie for Courland Province, 7th October 1904 (stamped "received", 9th October, 1904, # 4898).
26 Ibid. #120.
27 Ibid. #300, 13th October 1904, Report from the head of Courland Gendarmerie.
28 LVVA 4568/15/225, 'Letters from agents', #64: Letter from Courland to the authorities in Vidzeme, 28th September 1912, when the *Okhranka* was gathering evidence to transmit to London.
29 LVVA 4569/1/32. #122.
30 Lindulis (Jānis Linde), *Revolūcijas fakti un dokumenti: Talsu revolūcija,* op. cit.
31 Voldemārs Skare, *Materiāli par 1905. gada revolūciju un tas darbiniekiem,* op. cit., p. 149.
32 Ibid.
33 LVVA 4569/1/32. #125.
34 Ibid. #310, Police report 3rd November 1904.
35 Ibid. #311-#318.
36 Ibid. #112 and #13.
37 Ibid. #129.
38 Ibid. #132.
39 Ibid. #133.

40 Ibid. #150.
41 Ibid. #156.
42 Ibid. #140.
43 Ibid. #157.
44 'Okhranka', more usually called *Okhrana* by English-speakers; the colloquial name for the Russian political police. The name derives from the Security Division (*Okhrannoe Otdelennie*) of the Department of State Police, created by the Ministry of Internal Affairs (MVD) in 1880. A central Special Department (*Osobyi Otdel*) of eight sub-divisions directed security operations against revolutionaries within the Russian Empire's borders. The Special Department also controlled a Foreign Security Agency (*Zagranichnaia Okhranka*), based at the Russian Embassy in Paris, which conducted operations against émigré revolutionaries in Western Europe, the Balkans, the Near East and North America.
45 LVVA 4568/15/225, 'Letters from agents', #66: Vidzeme guberna Gendarmerie, 4th October 1912.

2

January to September 1905
The Times of the Land Surveyor

> Our leader was comrade J. Žākle (Mērnieks) — a brave comrade with
> a lot of fighting experience.
>
> Eduards Medne[1]

Jānis Žāklis never used his real name again. From the beginning of 1905, when
he disappeared from Sabile and moved to Riga, Žāklis hid behind a succession
of false identities, but to his comrades in the revolutionary movement he was
known simply as Comrade Mērnieks — the Land Surveyor.

The name is an allusion to a book published in 1879 — *Mērnieku laiki* (The
Times of the Land Surveyors) by the brothers Reinis and Matiss Kaudzites. The
first novel written in Latvian, *Mērnieku laiki* appeared during the period that
Latvians consider their first *National Awakening*,[2] which challenged the notion
fostered by the Baltic Germans that the Latvian language was nothing more than
an uncouth peasant dialect, incapable of conveying ideas or culture. The book
was an important event in the social history of Latvia. It was the first piece of
Latvian literature which didn't look back to an ancient past, but took its subject
matter from the everyday life of the Latvian peasants. The authors used people
they themselves knew as prototypes for the characters and situations familiar to
the reader. The novel depicts life in Piebalga around 1870, when the land was re-
measured during a period of land reform and the borders between different
farms were re-drawn by the Land Surveyors; *Mernieku*.

The character of Mērnieks Feldhauzens, the mysterious surveyor, is
surrounded by rogues and conmen, mysterious thefts, murders and deceit but he
remains righteous. His secret adventures become more and more complicated.
When the local swindler Grabovskis impersonates him to organise a campaign
of fraud and robbery, Feldhauzens pays his assistant Rankis to shoot the
impostor. But in the dark Rankis shoots the wrong man and kills the innocent
Kaspars Gaitins. Later in the story a gang of villains rob and blackmail
Feldhauzens, who manages to extricate himself only by paying a large ransom.
These adventures, in which seemingly respectable citizens are relieved of
dishonestly acquired wealth, may have influenced the choice of Žāklis'
nickname. In symbolic terms Mērnieks, as the person who redistributes the land
to the peasants, is an agent of social change. In 1911 the anonymous author of
an article in the Latvian anarchist press (quite possibly Žāklis himself) likened
the antics at a congress of revolutionary teachers during November 1905 to the
comical situations described by the Kaudzites brothers in *Mērnieku laiki*.[3]

For the police and *Okhranka*, Mērnieks became a spectre they sought
desperately to identify as the man deemed their most intelligent and dangerous
enemy. As one of the principal leaders of the 1905 Revolution, Jānis Žāklis
took on the stature of a Latvian *Scarlet Pimpernel*.[4] But the connection between

the seditious draft dodger from Lutrini and the notorious Comrade Mērnieks was never made.

Even in 1912 the Russian authorities had to admit they knew nothing about Žāklis after the start of 1905: 'We don't know if he took part in the revolutionary movement. Neither do we know what name he might have used in the revolutionary movement.'[5] The most the *Okhranka* ever established was, 'In 1905 the peasant from Courland, near the town of Frauenberg, Ivan Ivanovich Žāklis, stayed in Riga, where he provided the Latvian revolutionaries with arms.'[6]

The acquisition of arms was one among many new responsibilities thrust on the twenty-one-year-old Žāklis at the start of 1905, after a massacre of epic proportion ignited the Latvian revolution.

Trouble had been brewing in Latvia for some time. By the end of 1904 a strong workers' strike movement had emerged in Riga, Liepāja and other cities. Clashes with armed police at meetings and demonstrations were frequent. The workers invariably defended themselves with improvised coshes, knuckle-dusters and even revolvers. In December 1904, 1,100 workers of the Lange Shipyard went on strike for five days. The Jute factory was on strike for ten days, and the workers at Eikert's textile factory were also on strike. The strikes were accompanied by demonstrations with political slogans and red banners.

On 11th January 1905, the day Žāklis received his personal documents back from the Courland police, the Riga Federative Committee brought the city to a halt with a general strike called in sympathy with the victims of Bloody Sunday in St. Petersburg, where three days before peaceful demonstrators had been massacred by the Imperial Guard.

On the second day of the stoppage, in the afternoon of 13th January 1905, 60,000 striking workers took to the streets in a demonstration of solidarity with the fallen and marched in a snowstorm through the streets of the working class Moscow district towards Old Riga at the heart of the city. When the marchers' forward columns reached the railway viaduct on the embankment of the river Daugava they found their way blocked by Russian troops ordering them to disperse. Nobody moved. Somebody on the bridge lazily tossed a snowball at the soldiers. As it landed a shot rang out from the crowd, wounding a soldier who later died. In the same instant the troops opened fire without warning — 73 people were shot dead, and over 200 wounded. The youngest to die was a 14-year-old boy. Many more drowned as they tried desperately to escape over the thin ice of the Daugava.

The final body-count was never established. Only the very seriously injured were taken to hospital; many of the wounded simply fled or were carried away. The names of only 64 of those killed are known.[7] The shootings marked the outbreak of the 1905 Revolution and the reverberations are felt in Latvia to this day.[8]

Present at the massacre were the poets Jānis Akurāters and Antons Austriņš. Deeply shaken by the bloodshed, Akurāters brought news of what had happened to a political meeting at a tailor's workshop in Dzirnavu iela that evening. Pale and angry, the poet shouted in broken sentences:

'Murderers, they are terrible murderers! My friend Anton is badly wounded, he might be dying! Dozens killed... hundreds wounded... The cruel Russian officer opened fire without any warning; they shot at unarmed people who were peacefully walking down the railway tracks. The white snow had turned red with blood, the bright red blood of innocent people... When the first horrible moments passed, sleighs appeared from nowhere, where the wounded were loaded to take them to hospital... some other sleighs were used to take the corpses to the morgue... The arms and legs of the corpses were hanging over the edges of the sleighs... The horror and pain frozen on the faces of killed comrades... Bright red blood, still seeping from the wounds, was dripping on the white road. Damn you! Damn you, a hundred times, executioners! We are not afraid! We shall win! The Tsar's crown will fall and the hour of revenge will come!'[9]

His horrified audience vowed to fight back even if it meant going to a certain death. At that moment Akurāters stood up and in a sad but defiant voice began spontaneously composing unfinished rhymes for what would become (when put to music by composer Jūliji Sproģis) the revolutionary Latvian song of mourning and battle, *Ar kaujas saucieniem uz lūpām* (With Battle Cries on Their Lips They Died).[10]

The bodies of the 'January martyrs' lent weight to the arguments of those who pushed for more resolute action. The funerals of those killed in Riga turned into enormous demonstrations of up to 20,000 people, often ending in confrontations and fighting with the Cossacks and police. When news of the shootings reached Liepāja the strike quickly spread throughout the city, bringing 25,000 people out onto the streets. The general strike lasted for a whole week after the shootings and grew in intensity throughout Latvia. It was followed immediately by a wave of local trade strikes, which swept the country, demanding a nine-hour day and a minimum daily wage of one rouble. As the strikes spread, clashes between strikers and police became daily occurrences. Frequently they were armed. Under the impact of the massacres in St. Petersburg and Riga, the workers' movement began to find ways of defending itself from attack.

The answer to the mystery of what Jānis Žāklis was doing in Riga from the autumn of 1904, while still officially restricted to Sabile, was now revealed; he was preparing for the inevitable armed escalation of the struggle. At the beginning of 1905 Jānis Žāklis (Mērnieks), Ferdinands Grīniņš (Burlaks) and Jānis Lencmanis (Ķencis) were elected as members of the Technical Commission of the LSDSP Central Committee; with Žāklis as Chairman. Their job was to organise and coordinate all military operations of the Party. Žāklis was given authority over all money collected to buy arms. He was also in charge of all 'conspiratorial flats' (safe-houses) and the military training of all Party members who volunteered to become fighters. Training sessions in arms and explosives were conducted by Žāklis on Sundays in the forest outside the city[11]

Under the auspices of the Riga Federative Committee, Žāklis set up a Fighting Organisation (*Kaujas organizāciju*) of 200 members, bringing together the fighters of the LSDSP and Bund, with himself as leader.[12] Fighting groups were organised in all of the city's factories. Their brief was simple: defend demonstrations and meetings from police attacks, execute spies and provocateurs, and organise the escape of any comrade arrested by the police. To equip themselves they carried out raids on gun shops and systematically disarmed police and army patrols. Bomb factories were established secretly in four Riga metal works (the Etnā, Fēniks, Poles and Felzer factories), and workers began manufacturing improvised firearms. A fighting organisation of similar size was also formed in Liepāja, and smaller fighting groups appeared in other towns. Effectively, Jānis Žāklis had become the military leader of the Latvian revolution.

That Žāklis was appointed to such an important position at such a crucial period, directing not only the armed operations of his own Party but also those of the Bund, prompts the question, *why?* What had Žāklis done that persuaded the Riga Federative Committee to place such trust in him? Most likely, as the organiser of an important rural section of the Party and someone who had proven himself as an effective conspirator – able to withstand police interrogation, imprisonment and surveillance – Žāklis had done enough to demonstrate his talent for organisation and leadership. His fluency in Yiddish would have been an added bonus when it came to working with the Jewish socialists of the Bund. He also had the ear of Jūlijs Kažemirs, his comrade from Talsi, who was now on the Central Committee of the LSDSP.

This is an example of where Soviet historians of the period have done their best to edit Jānis Žāklis out of the history of the 1905 Revolution, while exaggerating the role played by less important figures that more faithfully portray a "correct" Bolshevik image. A case in point is Jānis Luters-Bobis, who took over as Chairman of the Fighting Organisation from Žāklis at the end of 1905, after Žāklis incurred the Party's disapproval by displaying "anarchist tendencies". But Luters took over the post at the *end* of the revolution, when most of the significant guerrilla operations in Latvia had already taken place. It was Jānis Žāklis in whom the Riga Federative Committee put their trust when the need for action first arose in January 1905.

Although based loosely on the conspiratorial 'cell' system of the LSDSP, the practical infrastructure of the Fighting Groups relied heavily upon overlapping friendship networks. Žāklis found no shortage of able recruits, eager to hit back against the regime which had fired upon unarmed workers. One of the most capable was thirty-seven-year-old Pēteris Lapsa, a blacksmith at the Riga rail-wagon foundry. Žāklis made Lapsa his assistant and entrusted him with putting together a fighting group in Riga. Lapsa surreptitiously purchased arms through an intermediary at a central Riga gun shop and established a bomb-making laboratory at the Fēniks (Phoenix) factory, where he instructed workers at the plant in their use. But the manufacture of explosives was chiefly the responsibility of Ferdinands Grīniņš, an educated young man and the son of an industrialist from Ventspils, who lived unobtrusively in a respectable flat in Dzirnavu iela, and Jānis Priedītis, a Professor of Analytical Chemistry at Riga Polytechnic Institute. Outwardly respectable and unknown to the police, Grīniņš and Priedītis trained specially selected fighters in the manufacture of explosives in the building of the Riga Polytechnic Institute Chemical Faculty, at 4 Kronvalda boulvard, and in the cellar of a pharmacy at 109 Dzirnavu iela.

Another pivotal figure was Kristaps Salniņš (known as Griška); a former art student, and draughtsman at the Fēniks factory in Riga, then still only nineteen years old. Despite a rather unprepossessing physical appearance ('slightly more than average height, very skinny, blond, stammers, wears shoes size 14')[13], Salniņš was a physically strong and quick-witted character, renowned for being a crack shot and keeping a cool head in the tightest of corners (and a weakness for posing for photographs). He appears in one of the few photographs taken of Jānis Žāklis to have survived, taken in 1906 (see image 13). Salniņš was already a revolutionary of some experience, having set up his own fighting group in Riga's Moscow district the year before. After the January massacre he had gone underground and moved to Liepāja. Now Žāklis recruited him for a mission to Jelgava, to establish a fighting group there.

Žāklis and Salniņš arrived in Jelgava in the spring of 1905 and contacted Rūdolf Lemkins (Štāls), a close friend from Liepāja who had been sacked from his job in Jelgava for leading the January strikes. Lemkins introduced Žāklis and Salniņš to an energetic young art student called Ģederts Eliass; one of three sons belonging to an influential family, all of whom were entirely devoted to the revolutionary cause, that lived on a large farm called Zīlēni in Platones parish. Eliass, though aged only seventeen, already belonged to a local resistance network, had been a member of the Jelgava Workers' Committee since 1904, and had helped to organise the strike movement in the area. He was to become one of Jānis Žāklis' closest friends and comrades in the coming insurrection. Now the men set about organising an armed resistance network in the Jelgava area.

* * *

Mayday 1905 was more than symbolic to a country pregnant with revolution. In Latvia it was celebrated by a general strike lasting two and a half days. In the run up to the strike the Jelgava Fighting Group, around Salniņš, Lemkins, Eliass and Žāklis, carried out sabotage operations, cutting the Riga-Jelgava railway and telegraph lines, to ensure the disruption of all communications with the capital.

In Riga itself, fearing action by the Cossacks, the LSDSP refrained at the last minute from taking part in the workers' demonstration. Despite this, at the Vērmanes Park and Grīziņkalns areas of the city, several Cossack and police patrols came under fire and were driven off with bombs. In the Vērmanes Park incident an evening concert was in progress inside the park when a bomb hurled at a mounted Cossack patrol bounced off the leg of one of the Cossacks and rolled into the street, injuring two horses in the explosion. Concert-goers in the park reportedly shouted 'hurrah!' and applauded the attackers. At midnight another bomb was thrown at three policemen outside the Apollo Theatre, killing two of them outright. The third policeman, wounded in the explosion, pursued the bomb throwers and was shot dead.[14] The attacks were directed by Žāklis and Lapsa.

In matters of this sort, Social Democrats faced something of a dilemma. Caught between an ideological commitment to orthodox Marxism, militating against resort to "individual terror", on one side and the violent realities of the situation in Latvia on the other, the LSDSP hedged its bets. The *Resolution Concerning Armed Uprising*, passed in June 1905 at the Party's 2nd Congress, stated that the Russian workers were not class-conscious or organised enough to begin an open rebellion; and that, 'in isolated parts of the empire, with the proletariat of other parts not participating', an armed uprising would be violently crushed. Consequently, the Congress deemed it inadvisable to invite 'such a hasty step'. Instead, it saw the Party's chief task as being, 'to stir up the workers' class consciousness', and organise and lead the struggle. Since government repression made this impossible, the Party advised the workers:

'…ever to be prepared for an armed uprising parrying each violent act of the government with an armed fist, and turning skirmishes with the tsar's henchmen into never-ceasing guerrilla warfare.'[15]

This acceptance of guerrilla methods, forced upon them by practical considerations but nonetheless brilliantly exercised, was something that sharply distinguished the Latvian Party from its Russian counterpart. It was also one of the things which most attracted the attention of Lenin, who was struggling (without much success) to turn his fledgling Bolshevik Fraction into a *fighting party*.

Hardly had the 2nd Congress pronounced armed insurrection inadvisable and cautioned against hasty action than sailors of the Baltic Fleet garrisoned at Liepāja and Kronstadt mutinied. In Liepāja the sailors threw up barricades and fought troops sent against them, but it was a lost struggle. Without leadership, and with only weak contacts with the workers in the city, the revolt quickly collapsed. The Party was surprised by the revolt and had no chance to help the sailors. One hundred and thirty seven mutineers were arrested, and the LSDSP launched a vigorous propaganda campaign in their defence. The agitation added greatly to the militancy sweeping the country. On 26th July, six months to the day after the Riga massacre, factory workers in Riga and Liepāja launched a new wave of strikes, after the gains won in January and February had been withdrawn.

* * *

In the countryside, with political meetings outlawed, village churches became a natural focus for revolutionary agitation. The Lutheran Church was widely reviled by the Latvian peasants as a bastion of German oppression. The priests were mostly Germans, who could not even speak good Latvian. Typically, an agitator would ascend to the pulpit before the religious service commenced and deliver a political tirade in place of the usual sermon. One such agitator was Maija Cielēna, the younger sister of Ģederts Eliass. On some occasions the whole congregation would get up and walk out the moment the parson began his usual prayer for the tsar, and hold a political meeting outside. This was usually followed by a collection for the LSDSP, and the destruction of portraits of the tsar, army recruitment lists, and other symbols of oppression.

Sometimes the peasants marched out of the church behind a red banner and went in a body to the landlord, to press their demands for improved conditions. These church demonstrations sometimes met with success and a landlord would agree to the peasant demands. More usually they ended in physical clashes or strikes. At the height of this movement the authorities were forced to close churches by the dozen in a desperate attempt to crack down on subversion. At one of these church demonstrations a local baron, incensed by the revolutionary speeches, pulled out a pistol and opened fire on the congregation. And when a socialist in the audience took the gun off him to stop him shooting anybody else, the man who *disarmed* the baron was arrested and received four years in prison, where he died. The baron walked away scot-free.

Jānis Žāklis too played an active part in this agitation. He was one of the principal speakers sent by the Party to lead church demonstrations in Lielvārdes and Madliena, just outside Riga, during *Līgo* (the summer solstice holiday) in June 1905. Accompanying him as bodyguards were Kārlis Krieviņš (a close friend who would shortly join Žāklis in defecting to the anarchists) and Jānis Lencmanis (later a minister in the short lived Bolshevik Government of Latvia in 1917/18, the *Iskolat*). Lencmanis says:

'Mērnieks (Žāklis) was the speaker, and Krieviņš and I served as assistants and bodyguards in case of confrontation with the Black Hundreds [the popular name for the Union of Russian People, a virulently anti-Semitic terrorist organisation under the patronage of the tsarist secret police] or the police. The demonstrations in both towns were very successful (shining, outstanding), even though in the church at Lielvārdes the Black Hundreds had organised themselves and were awaiting our demonstration. Already then Krieviņš showed himself as a real fighter'.[16]

At the beginning of July, a three-day general strike halted the wheat harvest in Courland. 30,000 peasants joined demonstrations in front of town halls, burning pictures of the tsar, passports, and official papers. Fighting groups of the LSDSP seized Crown moneys and carried out attacks on police patrols.

The landlords reacted by hiring gunmen to attack the peasants and tenant farmers. Groups of Black Hundreds, to whom the onset of revolution was proof of a sinister alien conspiracy, started anti-Jewish pogroms. On 19th August, martial law was declared. Cossacks and dragoons were stationed on the estates. The Baltic barons formed a special police force to make sorties into the peasant farms and carry out reprisals against those who had joined the strike. In the midst of all this the LSDSP Fighting Organisation launched one of its most famous actions.

* * *

In September 1905 the Riga Federative Committee gave Žāklis his biggest challenge to date, the freeing from Riga Central Prison of two important prisoners who were facing imminent execution.

Jūlijs Šlesers and Jānis Lācis both belonged to the Fighting Organisation. Lācis, a carpenter who was also one of the leaders of the Federative Committee, had made the bombs used in the Mayday explosions in his carpentry workshop. A member of the Bund betrayed him to the police. When they came to arrest him he managed to struggle free and grabbed a pistol but was overpowered and hauled off to gaol.[17]

Riga Central Prison was a tough nut to crack. A new model prison only recently opened, constructed on 13,000 square metres of land between the

Matīsa cemetery and the Riga-Orel Railway, it was the most modern prison in the Russian Empire; it even had central heating.

The whole facility consisted of an administration block (a four-storey brick building), a main cell-block with 24 common cells for 598 prisoners, three churches (Lutheran, Russian Orthodox and Catholic), a solitary confinement block of 55 single cells and 48 'night isolation' cells, a hospital block, a women's block (with two departments for common and single cells), a workshop block, a power station with a bathhouse and a laundrette, an outhouse with an ice cellar, stables with flats for horse-drivers, a guards' cabin at the main gate, a firewood store, a wooden apartment block for the clergymen, a guards' block with store-houses near the main gate, a chapel and fences (a brick wall surrounding the whole complex, and wooden fences between the buildings inside). It was built to house 1,360 prisoners (1,082 common cell places, 96 single cell places, 48 night isolation cells and 130 hospital beds), but the majority of its 2,000 prisoners in 1905 were political revolutionaries.[18]

A first attempt to free Jūlijs Šlesers and Jānis Lācis in August failed, when a seven-man group led by Kristaps Salniņš (dressed as the prison governor) trying to bluff their way into the gaol disguised as a night patrol, came under fire from an alert prison guard.[19]

The second attempt was prepared more thoroughly. According to Eduards Medne, who took part: 'It was not difficult to draw a plan of the central prison, because most of us had recently spent some time there.'[20]

Keys to the prison gates and to the doors of the solitary confinement block were obtained with the help of workers in the prison maintenance department.

The size of the prison, together with the increased surveillance, frequent patrols by Cossack guard units and the proximity of the Izborsk Regiment barracks, meant that the success of the operation depended upon the preparations being kept strictly secret and the attack being conducted swiftly and decisively.

At eleven o'clock on the night of 6th/7th of September, a group of 52 armed fighters from the Federative Committee (members of the LSDSP and Bund) gathered at the Matīsa cemetery opposite the prison. Medne says their leader was Jānis Žāklis, 'a brave comrade with a lot of fighting experience.' Žāklis split the fighters into four groups. The first, largest group placed themselves near the wooden fence opposite the gates to the administration block, in order to prevent prison guards and dragoons from getting out of the building. The second group took up positions on both sides of the road leading to the prison, to prevent Cossack patrols and other soldiers from coming to the assistance of the prison guards. The third group, of five men, cut all telephone wires to isolate the prison from the city. The fourth group (which included Medne, because he knew the layout of the prison), under the leadership of Žāklis himself, had the task of getting into the prison.

Before the action began Žāklis asked the fighters if anyone had any doubts about the operation or was afraid to take part; nobody had. Then, says Medne, 'Comrade Žākle announced the time when the operation was due to begin. I don't clearly remember if he said it was 1 or 2 a.m. All the group leaders synchronised their watches'.

As soon as the first three groups had taken up their positions, the insertion group led by Žāklis went into action. Medne takes up the story:

'We unlocked the gate of the inner stone wall of the prison. We saw the solitary confinement block, brilliantly lit up by searchlights, and the prison guards walking around it. Until this moment everything was done in complete silence, without a noise.

'The distance between the gate and the block was about 50-60 metres. We had to reach it as quickly as possible. We dashed forward as fast as we could. The guard fired a shot, we shot back and he fell. We were already by the door to the block. We quickly unlocked the outer door and entered the building. The guards had already scattered. Some of the fighters stayed behind to guard the outer doors. Some climbed the stairs to the upper level to guard the door leading from the solitary wing to the main block, through which guards could attack us from behind.'

Unfortunately for Žāklis, the keys he had for the cells were useless. He told Fēlikss Cielēns afterwards that the prison administration had changed the locks on all the cells the day before the attack and it was necessary to shoot off the locks to open the cell doors.[21]

The attackers managed to free Šlesers and Lācis, but had no time left to open any other cells. Medne says:

'By that time the guards had recovered from the first shock and started shooting at us. We started to retreat, shooting back. When we got out into the courtyard they started shooting at us from the windows.

'The shooting had alarmed the whole of the prison force. When the guards and dragoons ran out of the administrative block, Comrade Snipe's group opened fire on them. Having lost several men they ran inside again and didn't dare to come out.

'Our group with the freed comrades hurriedly left the prison...

'The fighters had no losses – no killed, no wounded. The second group did not even manage to take part in any action – no Cossacks, police or soldiers came up the road.

'A signal was given to the fighters to scatter to predetermined destinations. Together with Comrade J. Lācis, I had to first hide in a flat not far from the Central Prison and later take him to a safer place, where he could lie low for a longer time.'[22]

Medne took Lācis to a flat in Matīsa ielā. When morning dawned and the streets were filled with people going to work, Medne and Lācis ventured out to the flat of another comrade, who dressed them up to look like gentlemen, called a posh cab and took them to a rendezvous in the forest not far from Riga, where Lācis was handed over to other Party contacts.[23]

The success of the operation was unprecedented in the history of revolutionary activity in the Russian Empire and caused a sensation in the European press.

Lenin, writing in the Bolshevik newspaper *Proletary* a week later, was jubilant, hailing 'the Heroes of the Riga Revolutionary Detachment' as the embodiment of what revolutionists should aspire to:

'See how successful the venture of the Riga revolutionaries was... Our trophies are two revolutionary leaders rescued from prison. This is indeed a brilliant victory!! It is a real victory, scored in a battle against an enemy armed to the teeth. It is no longer a plot against some detested individual, no act of vengeance or desperation, no mere "intimidation" — no, it was a well thought-out and prepared commencement of operations by a contingent of the revolutionary army, planned with due regard for the correlation of forces...'[24]

The 'revolutionary leaders' thus freed were smuggled secretly to London, from where Lācis (as Mr J. Zarins, 505 Commercial Road, London East) wrote a letter, intercepted by the *Okhranka*, describing how he and Šlesers had left Riga in the cold hold of a ship, where they had hidden for eight days. He wrote that if he was not able to return to Latvia he intended to go to Boston in America, where there was lots of Latvians:

'But let us hope that we'll be able to go back soon, because it's better to die in your own country than to roam around the world.'[25]

Most of the London LSDSP group (of 12 members) had returned to Latvia after the tsar's *October Manifesto*, Lācis noted, and only four comrades remained:

'It was very difficult to get used to life here, but the hope to go back helps me to withstand everything, and had I gone to America as it was planned I would not have been able so easily to return. The friends with whom I came to London have all left already. I am left here alone. Šlesers went back a week after his arrival in London'.[26]

Lācis complained that he found living in London hard – more difficult than prison – and was ready to return to Latvia any day, 'but I am forced to remain here for a while longer, until all the books that are being printed abroad have been despatched'; something the *Okhranka* underlined in blue pencil.[27]

For the chiefs of the Riga Criminal Intelligence Department, Greguss and Dāvuss, the attack on Riga Central Prison had been a humiliating personal blow. The effectiveness of their work against the revolutionists depended to a large degree upon fear of their supposed omnipotence. Dāvuss later claimed in his self-published memoirs to have discovered the true identity of the organiser of the raid, named as a certain Bārdiņš (Little Beard),[28] but the truth is that the police were completely in the dark before and after the escape. It was an intelligence failure of monumental proportion; the mysterious Comrade Mērnieks had pulled-off the impossible.

Notes

1   *Latvijas revolucionāro cīnītāju piemiņas grāmata* (The memorial book of revolutionary fighters of the 1905 revolution). I. Sēj: 2. Daļa. (Riga, 1980), p. 42.

2   Latvians speak of having gone through three historical periods of national *awakening* (*atmoda*). The first was from the mid-19th century until 1881, when Tsar Alexander II was assassinated. The second began with the 1905 Revolution and ended in 1918, with the declaration of Latvia as an independent nation. The third awakening began in the Gorbachev years and ended in 1991 when Latvia regained its independence.

3   'Revolucionārās kustības apskats Baltijā' (A review of the revolutionary movement in the Baltics), *Melnais Karogs* No. 2, August 1911, p. 108.

4   Set during the Great Terror of the French Revolution, Baroness Orczy's novel *The Scarlet Pimpernel* (London, 1905) told the story of Sir Percy Blakeney, an English fop who leads a double life as a swashbuckling rescuer of aristocrats. The book created the blueprint for the "masked-avenger" genre and inspired several films in which the outwardly unassuming hero risks his life to rescue strangers from peril, torture or tyrannical government.

5   LVA 4568/15/225, #66: Head of the Vidzeme guberna Gendarmerie, 4th October 1912.

6   *Ibid.* #63a: Head of the Kiev *Okhranka* to the Head of the Special Department, 20th July 1912.

7   According to the Latvian TV documentary *Latvijā, Mosties!* (Wake up, Latvia!) (Riga, 2005), five soldiers and a policeman were also shot by provocateurs in the crowd.

8   In 1930 the scene of the shooting, Karla Street, was renamed 13th January Street, and in 1959 a monument to the fallen, sculpted by A. Terpilovsky, was unveiled on the embankment near the railway bridge. It is one of very few statues from the Soviet period left in place after Latvia resumed independence in 1991.

9   Fēlikss Cielēns, *Laikmentu mainā*, (At the turn of the century) vol. I (Stockholm, 1961), p. 151.

10   Ibid.

11   *Latvijas revolucionāro cīnītāju piemiņas grāmata* (The memorial book of revolutionary fighters of the 1905 revolution). I. Sēj: 2. Daļa. op. cit. p. 83.

12   Interview with Andris Puļķis, Riga 28th August 2003.

13   LVVA, 4569/1/373, File of 1907, List No. 27 of the Courland Gendarmerie.

14   LVVA, 4568/1/678/1, Police report on the 1st May 1905 bombing at Vērmanes darza. The police investigation into the two attacks named 24-year-old Karlis Legzdens (Kenins), a worker at the Tilava wire factory and organiser of a fighting group in Pardaugava, as the bomb-thrower. He was arrested in 1906, after taking part in several other armed actions, and executed. A second man, 20-year-old Oskars Liepins, a worker from the Fēniks factory, was arrested a few weeks after the Mayday attacks and sentenced to 15 years in Siberia.

15   Ernest O. F. Ames (ed.), *The Revolution in the Baltic Provinces Of Russia — A Brief Account of the Activity Of The Lettish Social Democratic Workers' Party By An Active Member*, (ILP, London, 1907), pp. 16-17.

16   *Revolucionārās cīņās kritušo piemiņas grāmata* (The memorial book of those fallen in the revolutionary struggle. Prometejs, Moscow, 1933), p. 154.

17   LVVA, 4621/1/24. #13.

18   Dace Ekerte, 'Uzbrukums Rīgas Centrālcietumam: (Ne)iespējamā misija' (An attack against Riga Central Prison: Mission (im)possible), *Agora* No. 4 (University of Latvia, Riga 2006), pp. 188-201. In the year of punitive expeditions 1905-1906, over 200 political prisoners were executed in the Riga Central Prison.

19   *Latvijas revolucionāro cīnītāju piemiņas grāmata* I. Sēj: 2. Daļa. op. cit. p. 42.

20   Ibid. p. 42-43:

21   Fēlikss Cielēns, *Laikmentu mainā*, (At the turn of the century) vol. I. op. cit. p. 217.

22   *Latvijas revolucionāro cīnītāju piemiņas grāmata* I. Sēj: 2. Daļa. op. cit. pp. 42-3.

23   Ibid. p. 50.

24   Lenin, 'From The Defensive To The Offensive', *Proletary* No.18, 13 (26) September 1905

— *Collected Works*, Vol.9, pp. 282-5.

25   LVVA, 4621/1/9, #14: Letter from Janis Lacis , London, 29th December 1905.

26   Ibid.

27   Ibid. In fact Lācis remained in London, where he worked as a joiner for a Whitechapel cabinet maker, and carried on political work with the Latvian immigrants in the East End until 1910, when he moved to Philadelphia, USA, becoming a founder member of the Communist Party of America in 1919. Lācis returned to Latvia in 1931, and after the Soviet occupation of 1940 joined the Russian Communist Party. When the Germans invaded Latvia in 1941 he was arrested and sent to Salaspils concentration camp outside Riga, where he perished in 1942 or 43.

28   Jānis Dāvuss, *"Slepenpolicista Dāvusa atmiņas" – Par savu darbību un 1905g. revolūciju Latvijā* (Riga 1925), p. 22.

3

October to December 1905
A Rough School

It was a rough school in which the Lettish proletarian graduated, in the winter of 1905-06…

M. N. Pokrovsky[1]

The situation in Latvia was critical. On 13th October 1905 Riga ground to a halt under the impact of another general strike. Railways, telephone and telegraph, and supplies of electricity and water ceased to function. Confronted by a wave of similar strike action throughout most of Russia, the tsar panicked and by a Proclamation of 17th October, granted freedom of conscience, speech and association, ordered the freeing of political prisoners, and promised a Constitution and the calling of a Parliament (the Duma) to share power. It was too little, too late. In Latvia, far from acting as a brake upon popular discontent, the small degree of political freedom granted by the *October Manifesto* provided a launching pad for open insurrection.

The power of the authorities began to evaporate. On the 19th October 60,000 people gathered on the left bank of the Daugava to listen to revolutionary speeches, and as many again came out onto the streets in the east of the city. The next day 100,000 people gathered in the working class district of Grīziņkalns to listen to more speeches and songs, delivered by 30 agitators in Latvian, Yiddish and Russian. The audience at Grīziņkalns rose to 150,000 on 21st October and smaller meetings continued for a further two days. Top of their list of demands was the release of political prisoners. The Governor of Riga swallowed his pride, met the Federative Committee and gave in to their demands. Victorious, the Federative Committee halted the strike on 24th October.

For the next three months an uneasy dual power existed in Rīgā and Liepājā. The army and police still tried to keep a presence on the streets, but with only 2,000 troops in Riga they were incapable of enforcing the civil administration. Real power rested with the Federative Committees. What had begun as a strike movement, struggling for better pay and conditions, was now transformed into a national and social revolution that embraced the whole Latvian people. *Latvija, mosties!* (Wake up, Latvia!), a popular song written by Fricis Roziņš (sung to the tune of the English socialist hymn *England Arise!*), became the battle hymn of the Latvian revolution.

The disgruntled police and supporters of the tsar responded by organising gangs of Black Hundreds to stage "patriotic" demonstrations, directed primarily against socialists and Jews. Bank managers in the city openly boasted of the large donations they made to fund pogroms, and distributed leaflets headed 'Kill the Jews!' Anti-Semitism had never been strong in Latvia, and unlike other parts of the Russian Empire there was no history of pogroms. Latvian and Jewish workers were united under the umbrella of the Federative Committee. When a mob of Black Hundreds, armed and encouraged by the police, invaded the predominantly Jewish Moscow district of Riga, Latvian workers joined Jews in fighting them off. Voldemārs Skare says that the mob was organised by the district police chief, Vasiļevskis, 'in order to wage an armed struggle against socialists, students and intellectuals. The Moscow district police handed guns to the Black Hundred bandits, who consisted of déclassé working-class elements, caretakers, etc.'[2] Skare tells us that, 'Comrade Mērnieks (real name Žākle)... was particularly active in October, November and December 1905 in the struggle against the Black Hundreds, police and spies.'[3]

On the afternoon of 22nd October, the third day of the huge meetings at Grīziņkalns, a crowd armed with revolvers, clubs and stones moved into the Moscow district and began breaking into and looting Jewish shops, and attacking passers-by. The focus of the attack was the Jewish *Asyle* at Ludzas (Jaroslavļas) ielā 41/43; a refuge for the poor, invalids and orphans. Jānis Žāklis and his fighters set up a field headquarters in the New Riga Theatre (opened in 1902) in the centre of the city, at Lāčplēša (Romanova) ielā 25, from where they were able to keep in telephone contact with events in the Moscow District, and dispatched militia patrols from the Federative Committee to break up the mob near St. John's Church in Lielā Kalna ielā. No sooner had the militiamen got there than Cossacks arrived and opened fire on them.

News of the pogrom was immediately dispatched to Grīziņkalns, where the revolutionary speeches were interrupted by an urgent announcement of what was happening. Everybody who had weapons was asked to come forward to one of the platforms, where fighting groups were hastily assembled. One of those who volunteered was Fēlikss Cielēns: 'As I had a Browning pistol, which I had recently acquired, I hurried to the designated place. There I met several young men I knew; some of them were still students of secondary schools. All in all, about 200 armed people came together, who subsequently divided into groups of 10 men, elected their commanders and set off to the Moscow district to instil peace and order. Also my group under the command of a "real school" student Žanis Amatnieks, hurried to this district, which was predominantly populated by Jews and Russians. We didn't manage to have a fight with the Russian bandits – on hearing our first warning shots, they immediately dropped everything and scattered to all sides, leaving behind 7 murdered and about 30 wounded Jews and dozens of burgled shops.'[4]

Cielēns and his group were assigned to guard the Jewish shops overnight. In the middle of the night, he and another comrade, Ernest Ozoliņs who later became the Latvian State Controller and Director of the State Bank in the time of Latvian independence, were standing in Marijas ielā when they heard the sound of a gunshot close by: 'We hurried there and saw a man walking. We shouted: "Stand still! Hands up!" The man didn't obey, stuck his hand into his pocket and mumbled something in Russian. We grabbed him and pulled a large Nagant revolver from his pocket.'

Cielēns and his friend took the detained man to the headquarters of the Federative Committee at the New Riga Theatre. The building was teeming with life. Couriers from every part of the city were coming and going, bringing news of what was happening on the streets and around the Russian army barracks; dozens of armed fighters were also present, ready to be despatched to wherever trouble broke out. The Federative Committee representative directing operations that night was Ģederts Eliāss: 'There were two pistols on the table in front of him – a Browning and a Mauser. I had not even finished telling him the whole story about the suspicious man we detained, when a buoyant young man rushed into the room and placed three round metal objects the size of a large orange on the table in front of Eliāss, saying in a grave voice: "These three bombs are ready for use!" Having searched the detained man, we found a visiting card in his briefcase, which identified him as a high-ranking officer of the secret political police. The bloody enemy had dared to disturb the new revolutionary order, firing shots from his revolver! The political police butcher! Death to the bastard! Exclamations like this resounded all around.'[5]

The secret policeman was locked in the cellar, awaiting a decision on what to do with him, but allowed to receive food from a nearby restaurant. When the Federative Committee met the next morning it was decided to hold a people's tribunal. Three judges, a prosecutor and a defence attorney were all elected. But before matters could proceed further two dozen Cossacks appeared and stormed the entrance doors of the theatre, on the orders of the District Police Chief. The captive had used the opportunity of receiving food from outside to send word of his predicament to the police. Ģederts Eliāss and the other fighters inside had to flee, leaving their prisoner behind. The group of thirteen LSDSP members found a ladder in the yard behind the theatre and escaped over the roof of an adjacent factory into Ģertrūdes ielas. The last man over was Voldemārs Skare, who barely managed to lift the ladder onto the roof before the Police Chief appeared in the courtyard and threatened him with his revolver. Luckily the policeman didn't shoot. When the fighters emerged at the other side of the factory, workers there mistook them for a gang of Black Hundreds and were about to beat them up until they recognised Ģederts Eliāss, who had spoken at a meeting in the factory the day before, and they were allowed to proceed unharmed.[6]

That morning, 23rd October, the Black Hundreds killed a worker and a woman returning from shopping at a house at Mazā Kalna ielā 15. A patrol of workers tried to disperse the mob, but a policeman arrived with troops and began to arrest the workers and passers-by. Later in the day, about noon, another mob of a thousand Black Hundreds waving icons, portraits of the tsar and Russian flags gathered near the church in Lielā Kalna ielas again. They moved off down Ludzas iela, singing the Russian national anthem, to attack the Jewish Refuge and this time succeeded in breaking in. Two people inside were killed and ten injured. In Maskavas ielā one of the Black Hundreds killed two more Jews, one of them an eighteen-year-old student.[7]

In response, Jānis Žāklis organized and lead armed attacks against the Black Hundreds' meeting points. Skare says that Žāklis, 'played an active part' in all of these actions.[8] The attacks launched by Žāklis in the area of Daugavpils, Kazaku (Abrenes) and Maskavas ielas stopped all attempts at further marches, but seven LSDSP Fighters were killed in the clashes. Black Hundred losses were even higher; over thirty killed. Altogether the Black Hundreds were liquidated in the course of three or four days. The defeated vigilantes returned some of their weapons to the police department but others were seized by Žāklis' fighters. Some of the Black Hundreds even tried to sell their guns to the fighters for three roubles a piece.[9]

Žāklis' men also detained several notorious police agents; amongst them Baron Engelhart and a well-known informer called Teihman. A contemporary account says that: 'Arresting them the socialist representatives made an investigation with the assistance of several witnesses from the inhabitants and then transferred them to the Governor who liberated them. Later the spy, Mr. Teihman repented his deeds and wrote an apology to the Federal Committee. He was then dismissed by the Governor General and later even arrested.'[10]

* * *

When martial law was extended beyond Courland to cover the whole of Latvia in December, the Riga workers launched another four-day general strike and began to manufacture arms in all of the factories. The Governor desperately appealed to the government to send troops and gunboats.

While the workers in Riga and Liepāja were in effective control of the cities but refrained from launching an all-out insurrection, the situation in the countryside was far less restrained. The propaganda of the summer church demonstrations had spilled-over into frequent armed clashes and by the late autumn assumed the proportions of a popular insurrection, encompassing the whole of Courland and parts of Livonia.

The insurrection in the Latvian countryside dwarfed anything seen in the cities, and went far beyond anything seen in Russia proper. An illegal Congress of Baltic Peasants' Delegates called for revolutionary councils in every parish to take over control of all local institutions, and to defend themselves if necessary with arms. Within two weeks of the congress, councils of revolutionary peasants were elected in nearly all the villages. They took over all public administration, telephones and telegraphs, formed a people's militia, demanded the immediate release of imprisoned peasants, and occupied the estates of the barons who had fled. The peasants claimed the forests and estates of the German landowners as collective property, raided the great manor houses for arms (frequently burning the houses down), and fought pitched battles with Russian dragoons and bands of *Selbstschutz* (Self-defence Units of gentleman vigilantes) garrisoned on the estates. One anonymous member of the LSDSP who took part in these events encapsulated their distinctive character:

'Whilst the success of an armed rising in the towns was so doubtful, the rising in the country districts, thanks to the provocation of the nobles, was already an accomplished fact. It was not a rebellion after the manner of Moscow's revolt. The peasants did not erect barricades; they simply dismissed the local officials, and refused to recognise the authorities, and, only when necessary, defended their institutions with arms.'[11]

The battles fought in the Riga district, south-east of the city around Lielvārde, Koknese and Skrīveri (the area Žāklis had toured as a speaker in the church demonstrations during the summer), were particularly fierce. Hatred of the German barons and the feudal regime they presided over, exacerbated by harsh treatment meted out to suspected revolutionaries, ensured that few among the peasants were disposed to show compassion when the tables were turned. The part played by Jānis Žāklis in the action was decisive and completely ruthless.

During the night of 23rd/24th November, Jānis Žāklis and Pēteris Lapsa arrived in Skrīveri by train with a group of fighters from Riga. Gathering together the local revolutionary militia of a hundred men, Žāklis surrounded the manor house of Baron August von Henning, junior assistant to the Governor of the Riga district, not far from Skrīveri railway station. The baron was a particularly loathed figure in the region, notorious for his cruelty. After an intense gun battle the manor house was set alight and von Henning and a dragoon officer in the building were captured and disarmed. Žāklis granted no quarter – both of the prisoners were shot. One of the fighters from Riga who witnessed the action says, 'The capture and shooting of von Henning... happened under the direct leadership and with the participation of Lapsa and Mērnieks (Žāklis), and the Mauser which was taken from von Henning was kept by Lapsa or Mērnieks as a trophy.'[12]

The death of von Henning was a grim portent of what was to come.

Realising that his forces were too weak to defeat the rebels, the local dragoon commander, Captain Štern, summoned all army units in the region to Skrīveri Castle. On their way to Skrīveri during the evening of 25th November a group of barons, dragoons and *Selbstschutz* from outlying parishes captured two peasants from Lauberes. The peasants were tortured at the castle in an attempt to find out the plans of the rebels. The next day, dragoons returning from von Henning's funeral at the Aizkraukles Cemetery went on the rampage, murdering more peasants in revenge. That evening, revolutionary militia surrounded Skrīveri Castle and subjected it to rifle fire.

The same evening, the priest of Vestiene and seven members of the *Selbstschutz* arrived at Koknesē railway station hoping to travel to Riga. The railwaymen were on strike and there were no trains, so the party were forced to stay overnight at the manor house of the local priest, who had fled. They were immediately surrounded by revolutionary militia, who demanded that 'the gentlemen should disarm'. The besieged priest tried to bribe the revolutionaries with a large sum of money but his offer was turned down, and the militia laid siege to the manor house all night. In the morning the *Selbstschutz*, some of whom had been wounded, finally gave in and surrendered their weapons: seven Mausers, Brownings, and a lot of ammunition and sabres. The priest and *Selbstschutz* were taken hostage and placed under guard in the basement of Koknesē Castle, while the militia waited for instructions from the Riga Federative Committee

Back at Skrīveri, the besieged Captain Štern saw that his only hope of escape was to withdraw along the Daugava highway to Riga. At 10 a.m. on 27th November the Captain and his dragoons, together with 17 barons and their families (36 people), set out for Riga. But militia units from surrounding parishes had already gathered in Rembatē, north-east of Lielvārde, blocking their escape route. The railway was completely in the hands of the rebels, and militia units from Skrīveri and Koknese arrived on the scene by train. One militia group barricaded themselves in the Ēbeļs pub, while another detachment took cover in a ditch running along the cemetery. At around 2 p.m. Captain Štern's detachment arrived in Lielvārde, where it came under fire from the pub and the ditch. Along the railway, at about 400 metres distance from the pub, a train full of armed fighters chugged back and forth. One dragoon was killed and four others wounded (including the Captain), but the front of Štern's squadron managed to break through and escape to Riga. The wounded Captain Štern and his remaining twenty dragoons, together with the barons and their families, were driven back by gunfire and taken prisoner. They were all disarmed and taken to Lielvārde Castle.

The battle of Lielvārde proved a pyrrhic victory. When the revolutionary militia occupied Skrīveri Castle they found two of their comrades inside who had been kept as hostages, one of whom was dead. The castle was burned down to deny a garrison point to any further troop reinforcements.

Now the insurgents had to decide what to do with their prisoners. The terms of surrender imposed by the Lielvārde militia were extremely mild given the circumstances; the hostages were even allowed to keep their revolvers. But in the evening Žāklis and a group of twenty armed fighters arrived from Koknese. Žāklis annulled the terms of surrender, disarmed the barons and escorted von Peterson (junior assistant to the District Chief), Maksimovich (scribe to the late von Henning), and three estate managers back to Koknese.

On 28th November the people of Lielvārde held a meeting at which it was agreed to keep the prisoners hostage until further instructions were received from the Riga Federative Committee. In response to a telegramme from Koknese, the female captives were freed and the remaining men were put aboard a train to Koknese. At Skrīveri Station the hostages were led out and paraded in front of a large gathering of people, where they were each identified by name, title and estate, to the jeers of the crowd. The prisoners were then placed under guard in Koknese Castle, while a people's forum discussed what to do with them. Votes were cast and it was decided to shoot them. But then news arrived that troops were advancing from the direction of Daugavpils. The hostages were allowed to write letters to the collegium of the regional government (the Vidzemes Landrat). Baron von Peterson pleaded: 'I beg you to recall all army units and lift the state of martial law, otherwise not one of our houses will remain standing and we shall all perish; I beg you – there is no sense in all that. The dragoons together with Štern have surrendered, as well as the Cossacks... Scheinvogel, I and other gentlemen are incarcerated in Koknese Castle and we shall die the moment military forces arrive here — as well as Stoll and all the rest. Save the land and all of us — nothing else can be done otherwise.'[13]

The final confrontation began the next day, on 30th November, when an army unit advanced up the railway line from Stukman Station in Daugavpils to Koknese. Local insurgents tore up the railway tracks and derailed the train, killing one soldier and wounding 35 more. The survivors came under heavy fire from militia fighters hidden in concealed positions in the surrounding fields. The troops hurriedly retreated back to Stukman Station, where they were attacked again by militia during the night. The soldiers managed to repel the attack, but did not dare go any further.

The victory of the peasants was short-lived. On 1st December fresh army units arrived in Skrīveri and arrested many of the participants of the uprising. But faced with something of a stalemate the Vidzemes Landrat sent two barons, Rozen and Wulf, to Lielvārde Castle to meet with representatives of the Riga Federative Committee, Jānis Jansons-Brauns and Ansis Buševics, to plead for the release of the hostages. The German emissaries conveyed promises from the Barons' Convention to lift martial law, withdraw troops from the estates and disband the *Selbstschutz*. Taking off his hat in front of the public gathering in Lielvārde, Baron Rozen swore solemnly that the barons would keep their promise. It was agreed to free the arrested barons the same day (1st of December).

But regardless of what the Riga Federative Committee might have agreed, the local insurgents had other ideas — von Peterson, Maksimovich and three estates managers, who were particularly hated were taken by Koknese militiamen to the Pērses bridge and shot by Žāklis and Lapsa.[14] On the surface such cold-blooded ruthlessness appears shocking. But the intransigence of Žāklis, Lapsa and the Koknese militia can only be understood by setting it alongside the general policy of cruelty, torture and massacre perpetrated by the Baltic barons against the peasants. In his own eyes Žāklis was the dispenser of social justice; holding individuals guilty of violent crimes against the peasants directly responsible for their actions. Žāklis also knew that the promises of the German barons would be worth nothing once they regained the upper hand.

The peasants did, in fact, have cause to regret freeing their other captives. When "order" was restored, the released barons lost no time in pointing out the participants of the uprising to the police and the punitive expeditions. Those not summarily executed were brought before a court martial. The case of 63 participants in the Lielvārde-Skrīveri-Koknese uprising came before a Military Court in Riga on 5th September, 1907. Nine people were sentenced to death by hanging, later changed to a firing squad, and at 4.30 a.m., on 11th September 1907, all nine revolutionaries were shot.

Comrade Mernieks was not among those executed — he had disappeared the day after the shooting at Pērses bridge.

* * *

While Žāklis was still occupied at Koknese-Skrīveri in late November 1905, a military formation led by the Baron von Reke of Durbes raided peasant farms and mills at Slokā near the rural town of Tukums. The soldiers carried off 5,000kg of flour. At the same time the inhabitants of Tukums were subject to daily assaults and whipping by dragoons stationed there. Peasants coming into town were ill-treated by the soldiers. No heed was paid by district police chief Baron von Radens, to the complaints of the townspeople. Finally in desperation the people rose and attacked the dragoons. From positions in the town's school, the insurgents fired on seventeen dragoons billeted in a small hotel across the street. Forced out of the wooden hotel by a hail of bullets, the dragoons took cover in stables behind the building, only to have their retreat spotted by observers posted in the Church Tower by the rebels. The townspeople set light to the stables and burned their quarry out. Abandoning their horses, the dragoons fled on foot to sound the alarm.

For three days (13th-15th December) the people of Tukums fought an army of 2,000 men commanded by General Horunshenko. On the side of the rebels was a local LSDSP membership estimated at between 300 to 500, with its own fighting group, and a hastily summoned band of fighters from Riga led by two experienced guerrillas. More than 24 dragoons, and several soldiers of other regiments died in the fighting and the insurgents lost several men. By 15th December the battle had reached stalemate. Unable to subdue the town without completely destroying it, and short of ammunition, General Horunshenko allowed the revolutionists to leave the town with their arms and banners on the understanding that no reprisals would be taken against the civilian population. As soon as they had left, Baron von Reke cold-bloodedly executed over 60 peaceful inhabitants, among them several women and children.

Afterwards, in a report to the tsar, General V. A. Bekman explained that the soldiers had refrained from razing the town because the residents had assured him that they had driven all the rebels out, that they had greeted the troops with the traditional bread-and-salt, had turned over the bodies of an officer and a dragoon who had been killed, and surrendered sixty-two guns and forty-five revolvers. The tsar noted in the report's margin: 'This is no reason. The city should have been destroyed.' The complaint, about what he saw as unnecessary leniency, is typical of the tsar's callous attitude to the use of terror against a civilian population. On a different occasion, hearing news of the punitive expeditions, Nicholas is reported to have commented, '*Cela me chatouille!*' (This tickles me!).[15] When another report about summary execution in the Baltic provinces, by a certain Captain O. Richter, reached him, the tsar noted on the document: 'What a fine fellow!'[16]

The dead dragoons were taken to Jelgavā, where the Governor of Courland ordered that the bodies be mutilated and photographed.[17] The photographs of the mutilated dragoons were then distributed amongst the military as "proof" of the revolutionist atrocities, to incite the soldiers against the Latvian population. General Horunshenko's army avenged their defeat at Tukums by bombarding and pillaging the small town of Talsi.

In mid December 1905 the tsar sent Prince Alexander Orlov and the Life Uhlan Regiment into Latvia to direct a programme of "pacification". At Orlov's disposal was a Russian military force totalling 19,000 — composed of three infantry regiments, fourteen cavalry squadrons, four heavy guns, and twenty machine guns.[18] Placed under the command of those same Baltic barons who had been chased away by the insurrection, this expedition took on a punitive character.

Burning, torturing, and carrying out mass executions as it went, Orlov's expedition swept through Latvia without pity. Armed with *proscription lists* (death lists of *proscribed* persons) drawn up by the barons, the soldiers killed all those named without trial. Members of Peasant Councils and all suspected agitators were hanged from trees or telegraph poles along the roadsides. If the person listed was not at home, the soldiers would often execute his brother or father instead. Countless Latvians were whipped or beaten in public; women as well as men. At Ventspils, on 22nd December, four members of the local Social-Democratic committee were seized whilst asleep, carried on bayonets into the street and tortured to death. In Viljandi (now in southern Estonia), Baron von Sievers, chief of the local punitive expedition and landowner, arrested 49 persons and condemned them to death without trial. The prisoners were made to dig their own graves and kneel beside the edge before being shot in the head from behind. In Pļaviņās (Stukmaņmuižā) the local barons burnt seventeen peasant farms on Christmas Eve, saying it was the Christmas gift that the Latvian peasants deserved. In all, more than 300 farms were burned to the ground; their occupants prohibited from rescuing anything from the flames. Schools and social clubs were also destroyed. These incidents are typical of the atrocities carried out under Orlov. In the first 10 months of 1906 alone, 2,556 suspected revolutionaries were hanged or shot; another 4,533 were deported to Siberia, and some 5,000 fled abroad into exile.[19]

In the capital, Riga's wealthy Germans all feared that Orlov's men would burn down the theatres and cultural premises because they had all been used for revolutionary meetings. Wholesale destruction was only averted when the Mayor, George Armitstead (1847-1912), a member of a wealthy English family who had made a fortune in Latvia as jute merchants, persuaded the new Governor-General to keep the punitive expedition troops out of the city.

The peasant insurgents, unable to hold out against regular troops, escaped into the woods, where they formed themselves into irregular partisan bands of Forest Brothers (*Mežabrāļi*) and continued to wage a guerrilla war against the landlords, troops and tsarist administration. In the towns, groups of fighters operated as urban guerrillas. The early Soviet historian Mikhail Pokrovsky wrote of this period:

'Very many of them were shot on the spot of resistance. Executions without trial, which were the exception in Russia proper ... were the rule without exception in Latvia... The total number of those killed in the course of the "pacification" was 10,000. The barons displayed a particular hatred for the Lettish Social-Democratic Party; mere membership entailed penal servitude. It was a rough school in which the Lettish proletarian graduated, in the winter of 1905-06...'[20]

In the middle of this indiscriminate slaughter, directed by the local barons against the civilian population, came one of the most curious events in the life of the Žāklis family; explicable only by their unspoken connection to a member of the German nobility. In January 1906 the elder Žāklis brother, Kārlis, was accused of being a member of the revolutionary militia in Saldus during the preceding months of insurgency, and of stealing two guns from a neighbour. His name appeared on a list drawn up by the head of the Kuldīga district of persons to be handed over to the authorities for summary justice.[21] A search of the farm Klavini, where Kārlis Žāklis lived with his wife Lisa and their small children Marija and Jānis, found two guns.[22] Things looked bleak for brother Kārlis. The expectation was that he would be hanged or shot. But on 23rd February 1906, fate intervened in the person of Baron Keyserling, one of the leaders of the local punitive forces; a figure hardly renowned for his merciful impulses. All proceedings against Kārļis Žāklis were dropped at the insistence of the Baron. The name of Kārļis Žāklis was quietly taken off the list and he returned home to Klavini and his family.[23]

* * *

Attacks on the police and dragoon patrols increased in direct proportion to the atrocities committed by Orlov.

By December 1905 Jānis Žāklis was becoming increasingly estranged from the LSDSP. His penchant for taking independent action, coupled with his scorn for what he viewed as the timidity and over-inflated self-importance of the party leadership, made a clash inevitable. The execution of hostages at Lielvārde was in open defiance of directives from the Federative Committee; and back in Riga, Žāklis continued to operate with scant regard for sanction from the party leadership.

Voldemārs Skare mentions an episode after the Black Hundreds had been dealt with, when the Fighters in Riga, 'got short of work, but they still wanted to do something. And Comrade Mērnieks (Žāklis) got a wild idea to start shooting army officers... Mērnieks's anarchistic tendencies took the upper hand. Without informing the party, he went into the streets and started shooting at army officers.' The action caused Žāklis and four fighters from the Etna factory[24] to be strictly reprimand by the Party. Only then says Skare did Žāklis stop his 'crazy activities'. 'But one could notice that Comrade Mērnieks had anarchist tendencies and in the end he also became an anarchist.' [25] Žāklis, however, had still not learned his lesson.

Late in December 1905, as the state terror waged by Orlov's punitive expedition spread over Latvia, Žāklis launched a major urban guerrilla action against Russian troops garrisoned at the Provodnik rubber factory in the Sarkandaugavā region of Riga. Provodnik was the biggest factory in Latvia, employing 5,000 workers. A detachment of sixty Russian dragoons lived in a separate barracks in the courtyard of the factory, with stables for their horses a few metres away. According to Kristiāns Treimanis, who took part in the raid, the soldiers: '...systematically terrorised the workers. The dragoons even stole goods and there were several cases when young girls had been raped. During the fight with the striking workers, one of the dragoon riders trampled a pregnant woman under his horse. After that they killed one of our fighters who worked at the factory. We couldn't stand it any longer.'[26]

Fēlikss Cielēns, another participant in the attack, says: 'The HQ of the central fighters' organisation, headed by the chief organiser of the party fighters Mērnieks (Žāklis), decided to smash them and capture their weapons. Mērnieks decided to do this himself, without consulting the political committee. The plan of the attack was worked out in detail by Mērnieks and Brašais (Jānis Čoke), the leader of our fighting group: 30 armed fighters had to smash the dragoons within three to four minutes. The whole operation was based on surprise and perfect coordination of our actions. We had to act quickly, because a hundred Russian Cossacks were stationed about a kilometre away from "Provodnik": if we were slow in our attack, they could quickly come to the help of the dragoons and completely wipe us out.'[27]

At 6.30 in the morning of 20th December, the fighters entered the factory gates, mingling with workers going to work, and handed the guards tin pass numbers in order to be allowed on the premises. The fighters took up pre-planned positions in the factory, half of them gathering in the public toilet, nervously waiting for the signal to attack. The signal came as soon as the telephone cables were cut. The raiders included Jānis Žāklis, the brothers Jānis, Kārlis and Gustavs Čokes, Pēteris Lapsa, Rūdolfs Dēliņš, K. Legzdiņš, Līcis, and the Liepājas fighters Grīnvalds and Fricis Svars. The entrances to the barracks and the stables were guarded by only a single sentry each. A unit due out on patrol was dressed and preparing to groom their horses, but most of the dragoons were still in bed asleep. Two shots rang out, killing the sentries; then the fighters stormed into the corridors of the barracks. Fēlikss Cielēns says:

'Our sudden attack caught the dragoons completely unawares, only a few of them were in time to grab their rifles, which were stored in a separate room. Of course, all dragoons had their swords, but those were no match for our Mauser and Browning bullets. All the rooms and outside were reverberating with the deafening sound of shooting. I was among those fighters who were supposed to operate inside the makeshift barracks. A vivid picture of a dying dragoon has forever been etched in my memory: throwing his hands in the air, as if trying to catch hold of it, he gasped: "Mother, dear Mother!"'

'After three or maybe just under four minutes our operation was completed. Leaving behind 17 dead and 20 wounded dragoons; we took all 60 enemy rifles, and carrying with us two of our wounded, we all got into two previously prepared horse sleighs and disappeared in the pine-tree forests of Sarkandaugava under the cover of a winter morning darkness.'[28]

By 7 a.m. it was all over. It wasn't until an hour later that a military unit arrived at the factory, armed with rifles, machine-guns and two cannons. The Russian commander herded all the workers together in the courtyard and gave them ten minutes to point out the people who had taken part in the attack, threatening that if they did not carry out this order he would start bombarding the factory. The workers could not comply, because the fighters were unknown and had already escaped, so the bombardment commenced. A lot of the workers jumped over the fence and escaped over the river Daugava, but others who tried to cross the courtyard were not so lucky; rifle and machinegun fire ripped into them. Newspapers reported five workers shot dead and an unknown number wounded. In the end the managers of the factory managed to persuade the Russian commander to stop the senseless bombardment.

Treimanis says: 'The rest of the workers were searched and interrogated, but without any success. The police came and arrested a large group of workers, who were known by the *Okhranka* as "politically untrustworthy". No one was arrested from the organisers and participants of the attack.'[29]

For the fighters the raid was a huge success, but despite the retrospective acclaim accorded to it by Soviet historians (who credit Pēteris Lapsa and Jānis Čoke as the organisers but make no mention of Jānis Žāklis), the operation was mounted on the sole initiative of Žāklis, who organised and led the attack without the approval of the Party leadership. Voldemārs Skare makes it quite clear that the attack, 'in which Mērnieks (Žāklis) took an active part,'[30] was completely unsanctioned; further proof (if proof were needed) of Žāklis's "anarchist tendencies".

The Provodnik attack may have been a success for the guerrilla fighters, but it proved to be the last straw for the Riga Federative Committee and the LSDSP Central Committee. Their patience with Jānis Žāklis broke; he was unceremoniously removed as Chairman of the Fighting Organisation and replaced by Jānis Luters.[31]

Notes

1   M. N. Pokrovsky, *Brief History of Russia*, Vol. 2 (London, 1933), p. 281.
2   Latvijas Nacionālā bibliotēka (LNB), PA17/4/3/24.524/77-24.526. Voldemārs Skare, *Materiāli par 1905. gada revolūciju un tas darbiniekiem*. (Material on the 1905 revolution and its participants), p. 149. (Riga, 1950. Unpublished manuscript of 170 pages).
3   Ibid., p. 70.
4   Fēlikss Cielēns, *Laikmetu maiņa* (At the turn of the century) volume 1 (Stockholm, 1961), p. 218.
5   Ibid., pp. 218-19.
6   Skare, *Materiāli par 1905. gada revolūciju un tas darbiniekiem*, op. cit., p. 140.
7   Marger Vesterman, *The Jews in Riga* (Latvian Society of Jewish Culture, Riga 1991).
8   Skare, *Materiāli par 1905. gada revolūciju un tas darbiniekiem*, op. cit., p. 137.
9   Ibid., p. 150.
10 Ernest O. F. Ames (ed.), *The Revolution in the Baltic Provinces Of Russia — A Brief Account of the Activity Of The Lettish Social Democratic Workers' Party By An Active Member*, (ILP, London, 1907), p. 37.
11 Ibid., pp. 64-5.
12 *Revolucionārās cīņās kritušo piemiņas grāmata*. 1. sēj. (The memorial book of those fallen in the revolutionary struggle. Prometejs, Moscow, 1933), p. 140.
13 Ibid., p. 63.
14 *Latvijas revolucionāro cīnītāju piemiņas grāmata*. 1. Sēj. 1.daļa. (The memorial book of revolutionary fighters of the 1905 revolution). (Riga, 1976), p. 182.
15 Harrison E. Salisbury, *Black Night, White Snow — Russia's Revolutions 1905-1917* (Da Capo Paperback, New York, 1978. First published by Doubleday, New York, 1978), p. 167.
16 Abraham Ascher, *The Revolution of 1905 — Russia in Disarray* (Stanford University Press, California, 1988), p. 330.
17 Ernest O. F. Ames (ed.), *The Revolution in the Baltic Provinces Of Russia*, op. cit., p. 59.
18 Abraham Ascher, *The Revolution of 1905 — Russia in Disarray*, op.cit. p. 331.
19 Bruno Kalniņš, *Latvijas sociāldemokrātijas piecdesmit gadi* (Fifty Years of the Latvian Social Democratic Party), (LSDSP Ārzemju Komitejas izdevums, Stockholm, 1952), p. 333.
20 M. N. Pokrovsky, *Brief History of Russia*, Vol. 2, op. cit., pp. 280-1.
21 LVVA 5570/1/139, #22: List of persons to be given to the disposal of the state for their revolutionary activities in 1905. 'Karlis Janov Zhakle' is No. 6 on the list.
22 Ibid., items 14, 14a & 15, reveal that information about the activities of Kārļis Žāklis originated from Mikelis Sakne (a relative, who himself served with the revolutionary militia) and Fricis Alkne (a neighbour, who claimed Kārļis Žāklis robbed him of his gun).
23 Ibid., item 39, 23rd February 1906.
24 Skare, *Materiāli par 1905. gada revolciju un tas darbiniekiem*, op. cit., p. 138.
25 Ibid.
26 *Latvijas revolucionāro cīnītāju piemiņas grāmata*. 1. Sēj. 2. dala. (Riga, 1980), pp. 65-7.
27 Fēlikss Cielēns, *Laikmetu maiņa*, 1. Sēj., op. cit., p. 224.
28 Ibid., pp. 224-5.
29 *Latvijas revolucionāro cīnītāju piemiņas grāmata*, 1. Sēj. 2. dala, op. cit., pp. 66-7.
30 Skare, *Materiāli par 1905. gada revolciju un tas darbiniekiem*, op. cit., p. 150.
31 Kristiāns Treimanis, '*V* Bojevye *Gody*' (In the years of fighting): *Janis Luter-Bobis — Stranitsy zhizni revolutsionera-podpol'shchika — Sbornik statej I vospominanij. Sostavitel A. Luter*. (Janis Luters-Bobis — Pages from the life of an underground revolutionary — Collection of articles and memoirs. Ed. A. Luters. LVI, Riga 1962), p. 279.

4

January to March 1906
Dare to be a Daniel

I am humbly informing your Excellency [the Emperor of All Russia], that today, on the 17th of January, at 8:15 am, four armed criminals entered the Riga Police Department; went through to the Intelligence, attacked the guards of the Police and Intelligence Departments ... freed six prisoners and disappeared together with them. The matter is under investigation...

General-Major Narbut[1]

January 1906 was a month heavy with repression. In Riga the police operation against the fighters was in full swing. Mass arrests were a daily hazard. On 11th January the police picked up a man who gave his name as Kārlis Dūmnieks. Their prisoner was Fricis Svars; one of the 'boys from Liepāja' who took part in the big raid at the Provodnik factory in December 1905, and a man fated to die in London at the Siege of Sidney Street.

Fricis Svars had joined the LSDSP in Liepāja early in 1904, when the Party, though illegal, boasted a strong organisation in the city of around 600 members. Svars belonged to a cell in the shipbuilding yard[2] and probably first came into contact with Jānis Žāklis sometime in the spring of 1905, when Jānis Žāklis toured Courland, setting up fighting groups. Svars was a stout-hearted recruit.

Social Democrat Juris Daberts, who knew Svars as a worker of the Liepāja jute factory, a member of the party, who later became an anarchist, says: 'I remember my first meeting with Svars in the summer of 1905 near the railway station in Priekule, near Liepāja. Some gendarmes had arrested Svars, and an assistant of the District Chief, Baron Grothums, who came up to them, threatened him, asking whether he knew that he was facing death. Svars jumped up like he'd been stung, and shouted back at this hell's dog, known in the whole neighbourhood, in a terrible voice: "I am not afraid of death; it's only a question of who stands closer to it — you or me!" One had to see how all the anger of the cowardly Junker suddenly dropped down into his trouser legs — they started shaking, like an aspen leaf.'[3]

Svars obviously survived the encounter, because early in October 1905 he was arrested again, with four others[4]. They were all held on suspicion of taking part in a series of sabotage operations and expropriations during which a policeman and the manager of a state-owned monopoly shop (through which the government retained a state monopoly over the sale of alcohol) had been killed. Svars, accused of the policeman's death, enjoyed a formidable reputation in the revolutionary underground by that time. Working with the fighters, under the Party aliases Dūmnieks, Bobrikov, and Karpovičs, his tenacity earned him the nickname Bulldog amongst his comrades. In Grobin prison Svars and the others shared a cell with a legendary fighter known in the underground as

Bezvārdis (literally, no name — real name A. P. Berziņš), captured in September. On the night of 16th October, a group of fighters broke into the prison and tied up the guards, while Svars and his comrades sawed through the bars of their cell and escaped back into the guerrilla underground.[5]

Wanted now in Courland, Svars headed for the relative safety of Riga with two of his friends; Grīnvalds (Bahmuts) and Ans Ziediņš. At a conspiratorial meeting place at the knitting workshop run by Melnā Minna (Black Minna) in Marijas ielā, the fugitives made contact with Jānis Luters, who knew them well from his time in Liepāja. Luters made sure they were put up in safe-flats in Riga.[6] After taking part in the successful raid on Provodnik they were accepted as members of the fighting group of Pēteris Lapsa and the three brothers — Jānis, Kārlis and Gustavs Čoke — which regularly worked with Jānis Žāklis.[7]

On 31st December 1905 Svars carried out the expropriation of another monopoly shop in Riga with Ziediņš, Grīnvalds, Kārlis Briedis and Mārtiņš Imaks (Kundziņš). Luck was against them again. On the night of Wednesday 11th January 1906 they were all arrested in a flat at Krišjāņa Barona (at the time, Suvorova) ielā 106 and taken for interrogation to the notorious headquarters of the Riga police department, where Ziediņš began to talk. Whether he had already been recruited as a spy and *provocateur* by the police and had caused their arrests, or simply broken under torture is unclear, but now his efforts on behalf of the police were unrestrained; telling them everything he knew about the circle of fighters around Lapsa and the Čoke brothers. That same evening, acting on Ziediņš information, the police raided a flat at Rēveles (now Tallinas) ielā 59, looking for Pēteris Strazdiņš (Dzeguze). He was not at home but they arrested his older brother, Kārlis. Hidden under the floorboards, as Ziediņš had said, they found an arms cache of 30 rifles, 4 pistols and 36,000 rounds of ammunition. Pēteris Strazdiņš was arrested later that night at the flat of Black Minna.[8] The police also raided the home of Jānis Čoke; but found only his twelve-year-old brother, Arnolds. Not to leave empty-handed, the police took the boy into custody. Most crucially, Ziediņš betrayed one of the most carefully guarded secrets of all: the Canteen Austra.

Canteen Austra at Dzirnavu ielas 82 in Riga was a popular meeting and eating place for students and workers. Among its customers were the noted Latvian writers Kārlis Skalbe, Jānis Akurāters, Antons Austriņš, Kārlis Krūza and Jānis Jaunsudrabiņš, as well as numerous young actors and musicians. The cosy atmosphere of the canteen belied the fact it was a conspiratorial rendezvous for revolutionary fighters, and that the smiling and friendly owner, nineteen-year-old Austra Dreifogele, was an active supporter of the LSDSP fighting organisation.

A Latvian journalist who interviewed Austra's granddaughter, Rita Rotkale, in 2008 says: 'Austra and her sisters, and often even their mother, concealed weapons, leaflets and revolutionary literature on the premises, and ... one of the rooms where ordinary customers were never allowed, served as a meeting place for the fighters' conspiratorial get-togethers... Many years later, Austra's older sister Ženija wrote in her memoirs, that the police often made raids and searches of the canteen, and then the sisters hid guns in their boots, wrapped flags around their bodies under their nightgowns and lay in bed under the blankets pretending to be ill. The Dreifogele sisters often delivered Brownings, Mausers and ammunition to fighters, carrying them in buckets with piled-up vegetables or bread on top. It was a terribly dangerous way of life, where the smallest mistake could cost them their life. Ženija remembers that once, during a thorough search of the building, Austra's ingenuity and resourcefulness saved them from disaster. There were no fridges in those days, and in winter people often kept their food in buckets, hanging them outside their windows. That's where Austra hid the fighters' guns that time.'9

At two o'clock in the afternoon of Friday the 13th of January 1906, police and soldiers forced their way into the Canteen Austra and ordered everyone present to remain seated and not move. On a windowsill the police found a hastily abandoned Browning pistol and a pocket knife, and some leaflets and proclamations were found scattered on the floor. Unsurprisingly, no one volunteered ownership of the items.

The police began checking the papers of everyone present. All those who had the correct police stamp in their internal passport and whose appearance was not suspicious were allowed to leave. Anyone without papers or the police stamp to indicate their place of residence was detained. Two men caught trying to leave by the back door were stopped and guarded by four soldiers. Both carried false papers which they desperately hoped would hold up to close scrutiny, because both of them were high on the police wanted lists. Their real names were Teodors Kalniņš, a member of the LSDSP Central Committee, and Martiņš Grundbergs. Another fourteen customers whose papers or demeanour did not pass muster were guarded by two more soldiers.

The police now turned their attention to a well dressed diner, who had all the appearance of a respectable gentleman and carried a passport in the name of a flax-trader, Adolfs Karlsons. The respectable Mr Karlsons was Jānis Luters. Luters managed to answer all the questions thrown at him and might have escaped arrest and bluffed his way out, were it not for the traitor Ziediņš. Just at the point when it seemed Luters was about to be allowed to leave two soldiers walked into the room, one of them in ill-fitting army uniform. The sloppy looking soldier was Ziediņš; he had accompanied the police to point out anyone he recognised to detectives. He nodded in recognition at Karlsons; Luters was placed under arrest and put under guard with Kalniņš and Grundbergs. As the three prisoners were led out to the yard, Luters noticed another man had been detained, standing in the gateway, with soldiers on either side of him. It was Pēteris Lapsa (the assistant of Žāklis), who had been in the crowd of onlookers behind the soldiers' cordon, watching the raid take place when he was spotted by Ziediņš and arrested.

The two groups, of fourteen and four (Luters and company), were lined up in twos and marched off under heavy guard to the headquarters of the Riga police department in Teātra bulvāris (today Aspazijas bulvāris).

While the raid on Canteen Austra was taking place, Jānis Žāklis was in a meeting nearby, in the flat of August Riņķis, a bookseller who lived over his shop on the corner of Lāčplēša and Krišjāņa Barona ielas. Thirteen of the most active fighters in Riga (eleven men and two women) were assembled in the room when Austra Dreifogele burst in with the bad news, having come straight there after the policemen had left. The arrests of two members of the Central

Committee (Kalniņš and Luters), Žāklis' loyal assistant Pēteris Lapsa and Mārtiņš Grundbergs were a serious blow. Something had to be done, but the assembled fighters were not optimistic about the chances of success. The headquarters of the police department was a formidable target. Besides the detectives, and the policemen and soldiers guarding the prisoners, 160 soldiers of the Malojaroslavļas Infantry Regiment were garrisoned on an upper floor. The hotel opposite the building was headquarters to a squadron of dragoons, and a Cossack machine-gun unit and a police post were stationed at the nearby Central Railway Station. Voldemārs Skare says that: 'Even Comrade Mērnieks, who was a fearless fighter, when invited to take part in this operation, at first refused, because he considered it to be mission impossible. Still, he was later persuaded to take part in it.'[10]

Žāklis was not alone in viewing the operation as a suicide mission. Teodors Kalniņš's sister Anete says, 'some members of the fighting organisation were afraid to take part in the attack, but Comrade Made Frīdrihsone strictly reprimanded them, saying that they had to carry out this attack in any case — and in the end she persuaded them.'[11]

Various plans for a possible rescue mission were discussed, but no final decision could be reached. Then into the room came the tall, skinny figure of Jēkabs Dubelšteins (Jēpis); twenty-three years old, poorly dressed in a flat cap, scarf and overcoat, into which his hands were thrust (the overcoat pockets had been cut away to allow him to keep both hands on the two heavy Mauser pistols he invariably carried slung beneath his coat). In 1905 Dubelšteins worked as a telegraph mechanic at the Central Post and Telegraph Office in Liepāja, where he organised the tapping of telephone and telegraph wires and intercepted secret orders from the Governor of Courland, which caused great official embarrassment when published by the LSDSP. He was also the man who organised the attack on Grobiņ prison in October 1905 which freed Fricis Svars. Dubelšteins' arrival in Riga came after the collapse of the Liepāja organisation in the wake of the crushing of the armed insurrection in Aizpute. He had recently arrived to work with Luters. Now he placed himself in charge of the operation to free him.

It took only ten minutes to reach the Central Police Station from Canteen Austra. As they marched through the streets Lapsa, Luters, Kalniņš and Grundbergs were closely guarded by eight soldiers and an officer; he ordered them to look straight ahead, or be instantly shot. When they reached the police station the prisoners were bundled straight into the Detective Department and brought before the Chief, the notorious Emeriks Greguss, and his brutal assistant Jānis Davuss. The officer of the guard declared, 'These four were armed'[12] (only one pistol had been found, abandoned).

It had been a busy day for the police, all the cells were full. After brief questioning while their passports were studied again, Luters (Karlsons), Kalniņš (calling himself Mr Rozentāl) and Grundbergs were locked into a corridor in the Detective Department, where they found Fricis Svars and two other prisoners. Lapsa was locked up separately in a small anteroom, under strict guard. At 8 p.m. Grundbergs, Kalniņš and Luters were brought before Greguss, Davuss and two more detectives — Mihejevs and Sobeckis — and interrogated jointly about ownership of the Browning. The questioning was accompanied by threats of shooting if they refused to answer. All denied having known each other previously.

They were sent back to the corridor and recalled separately to a small office on the third floor. Grundbergs was tortured about the face. Luters was beaten and kicked and threatened again with a revolver. At midnight they were all interrogated again. Then at intervals throughout the night the four, together with Fricis Svars and another prisoner, Pēteris Strazdiņš, were, one by one, put through a series of savage interrogations in which torture and beatings alternated with remorseless questioning and threats of summary execution. The interrogation of each prisoner lasted several hours. Fricis Svars was terribly tortured. He later wrote to his sister Lisa that he got so many beatings that his head felt quite soft.[13] Strazdiņš was knocked onto the floor and flogged on the calves of his legs until they became so swollen that the meat started falling off the bone. Luters tried to bluff his way through the questioning by insisting he was an innocent trader, Karlsons. His interrogators stripped him, gagged his mouth with a wet towel, stuck a copy of his written interrogation to his bare back and beat it to shreds, using a thick rubber *nagaika* (whip); they poked him in the eyes with fingers and pencils and beat him again. Finally, they pretended to lead him out to be shot "whilst escaping", before taking him back to the corridor and locking him up.

The stubborn Lapsa also refused to confess. The soldiers guarding him had beaten him repeatedly with rifles; he was kicked to the floor and one of the policemen jumped onto his chest and kept jumping until his breast bone and ribs were broken. By morning Lapsa's condition was pitiful. He was unable to eat, and called feebly through the door for water. When it was brought his friends in the corridor saw blood pouring from his mouth. Young Arnolds Čoke, who was held in custody with the others for two days, told his brother Kārlis that even though Fricis Svars had been terribly tortured he could still smile when he saw the boy, but poor Lapsa was in such a state he couldn't even smile.[14]

Trials were a luxury at this period of the repression, and the captured guerrillas knew that the tortures were only a prelude to summary execution. Their only hope of survival was to escape.

* * *

At eight o'clock on Saturday morning Austra Dreifogele came to the Police Department, saying she was the fiancée of the prisoner Karlsons (Luters), and bribed the officers on duty into letting her visit her loved one. She brought with her a basket of food for the prisoners. After the visit Luters examined the crumpled newspaper the food was wrapped in and saw written on the top corner of the page, 'I will come'; and in the lower corner the name 'Jēpis' (Dubelšteins) — a rescue was being planned.

There was a break in the torture over the weekend. Policemen are people too, and need a rest. The prisoners used the respite to soften-up their guards, bribing them with oranges, cigarettes and cash. In return the guards allowed them to fetch wood from the cellars for the fire-places and prepare tea. Luters was allowed to move freely in the corridor, talk to his fellow prisoners and even walk into the 'big room' and look out of the window. Junior assistant to Greguss, Švābe, even asked Luters what he was arrested for — the prisoner seemed such a quiet man. That evening everything was quiet. Most of the interrogating officers had gone to the theatre, and the policemen left on duty all got drunk.

Early on Sunday morning, Austra Dreifogele and Anete Kalniņa (posing as the wife of Mr Rozentāl) returned to the police building to visit Luters and Kalniņš, bringing more gifts of food, and news that the escape was set for early on Monday morning, the 16th. Under the gaze of his gaolers, Luters innocently asked Austra to bring him some "sweets", code for small Browning pistols. "Relatives" had already thought of that, she replied, but they had not had time to get them yet. Leaving nothing to chance, Luters and Kalniņš kept the details of the plan to themselves.

That evening, four members of the fighting organisation met in a borrowed flat on the corner of Stabu and Marijas ielas, belonging to a comrade known as Rīgamāmiņa (Mummy Riga). The men were Jēkabs Dubelšteins, Kristaps Salniņš, Rūdolfs Dēliņš (Čoms) and Jānis Čoke (Brašais). They all agreed that the only way to free their comrades, irrespective of the danger, was by a direct assault on the police building. The final plan was for twelve people to take part in the raid: eight would take up defensive positions in the streets surrounding the police station, while four entered the building and freed the prisoners. For whoever was chosen to go into the building it would be like Daniel walking into the Lion's Den.

In Alberts Bels' fictionalised account of the discussion, Rūdolfs Dēliņš asks, "'Who, precisely? I hope the volunteer principle will be observed". Dubelšteins answers:

"No volunteer principles! I've already chosen the three to go with me – Brašais [Jānis Čoke], Straume [Ģederts Eliass] and Mērnieks [Jānis Žaklis]. Čoms [Dēliņš] will give full directions to the group outside. If anything happens you must cover our retreat at all costs. Let's go through it in detail."

"Why hasn't Mērnieks come?" asked Čoms.

Jēpis [Dubelšteins] did not reply.

"This isn't a station inquiry office", quipped Brašais sarcastically, glancing at Čoms."[15]

Dubelšteins and Ģederts Eliass would have to bluff their way past the sentry and enter the Detective Department, while Jānis Žaklis and Jānis Čoke stayed behind in the waiting room to deal with the sentry and any policemen on duty there and cover the staircase, to prevent any of the 160 soldiers upstairs from coming down. Two men against 160 soldiers! It was an audacious and virtually suicidal plan of action.

It had still not been possible to smuggle in guns to the prisoners, but Dubelšteins decided to go ahead anyway. At ten past eight on Monday morning the fighting group gathered one by one at the central post office near the police building. But the operation had to be aborted. There were so many soldiers deployed along Teātra bulvāris from the railway station that nothing could be done. The city seemed to have been transformed into an armed camp. When the girls visited the prisoners as usual bringing food, Anna Jansone leaned forward and whispered, 'tomorrow'.

At four o'clock that afternoon the questioning of the prisoners resumed. This time Greguss played the "good cop" routine. The prisoners were allowed oranges and the guards even brought pillows for them. The person the police seemed most keen to know about was their nemesis, the illusive Comrade Mērnieks (Žāklis). At 8 p.m. Luters was called back in to Greguss' office for a second conversation that night. This time he was ushered to a soft armchair. Greguss adopted a paternal tone and seemed to want a heart-to-heart. Still playing the innocent Luters told the police chief, 'I am sure intelligent people don't join the fighters' organisations'.[16]

'Don't say things like this', Greguss replied — 'there is a certain Mērnieks, who is a very intelligent and educated man. But I'll tell you, he is a real beast! It's not enough for him to kill a policeman. Afterwards he bashes the brains out of his head, kills his wife and children. It's just like snapping his fingers.'[17]

Luters feigned surprise at the existence of such a blood-thirsty creature (the man he had replaced as leader of the fighters) and said he was glad he had never heard of anyone like that.

Tuesday morning of 17th January was overcast and snowing. At 5 a.m. the "fiancées" of Karlsons and Rozentāls (Austra Dreifogele and Anete Kalniņa), together with Anna Jansone and Emīlija Volberga, arrived as usual at the police station with wicker baskets of food for their loved ones. While the other women flirted with the guards and created a diversion, Emīlija Volberga produced two pies from her basket and handed them to Luters. Hidden inside were two small Browning pistols. Bored, bribed or diverted by the women, the guards neglected to check the food.[18]

The prisoners held in the corridor were all going to and fro to the wash room when the Fighting Group entered the police station just before 8.15.[19]

Jānis Žāklis, Jānis Čoke, Jēkabs Dubelšteins and Ģederts Eliass marched inside the vestibule of the Police Department and up the stairs to the reception area on the first floor. They were all heavily armed with two Mausers apiece, concealed under their overcoats. Žāklis and Čoke stood around in the reception area with an air of looking lost, pretending that they had come into the building believing it to be the passport office. A stuttering Čoke turned to one of the two policeman on duty and asked innocently, 'C-c-c-c-could you p-p-p-please t-t-t-tell me w-w-w-where I am?'[20]

While Čoke engaged the policeman in bumbling conversation, Dubelšteins and Eliass strode past them, heading straight towards the Detective Department. The sentry at the door moved forward to stop them, and asked what the purpose of their visit was.

Adopting the tone of an irritated official Dubelšteins replied, 'We're going for a meeting with Kārkliņš (a common name); we're working in the interests of the secret police so don't waste time'. The soldier was so flustered by the bluff that he let the two men through.

On duty inside the Detective Department were two policemen, ten detectives and a soldier, armed with a rifle. The time was now 8.16 a.m. A policeman came forward and asked the two unexpected visitors who had just brushed past the sentry outside, 'Who are you? What do you want? Who let you in?' One of the detectives in an adjacent office looked up from the report he was writing. In the corridor, Luters and the other prisoners recognised their two comrades. 'We want to see the prisoner Kārkliņš', said Dubelšteins.

Attracted by the commotion, the soldier started to move forward with his rifle. From the corridor, Luters shouted in Latvian (because he knew the soldier spoke only Russian), 'Shoot the soldier!' Instantly, without removing his hands from his overcoat pockets, Dubelšteins shot the soldier. Luters and Kalniņš produced their two smuggled Brownings, Eliass had a Mauser in each hand. Everyone opened fire at once, wounding several detectives. The policemen scattered in panic and ran into an adjoining office. The detective who had been writing his report was so terrified (despite the Nagant revolver in his pocket) that he jumped headlong through the glass of an unopened window into the yard below, where he lay unconscious with a broken leg. Eliass and Dubelšteins rushed forward into the corridor and found Luters and Kalniņš together with Fricis Svars, Grundbergs, and two other comrades. Poor Lapsa was still locked-up in the ante room, and there was no time to open the door.

Outside in the waiting room, Jānis Žaklis had put the two policemen on the floor and was standing over them with his Mausers. Jānis Čoke ran after the sentry, who tried to escape up the stairs, and stabbed him with a knife. Then Žaklis sprinted over to the stairwell, and stood pointing his Mausers up the staircase, in case any of the 160 troops upstairs tried to come down. But the soldiers upstairs had no thoughts of coming to help the police. Instead they blocked the entrance to the stairs with a cupboard, afraid that the raiders would throw bombs and occupy the whole building. While Žaklis and Čoke acted as a rearguard, Eliass and Dubelšteins made for the exit with the six prisoners: Luters, Kalniņš, Grundbergs, Svars, Jānis Paegle and Pēteris Krastiņš.

'As I entered the waiting room', Luters remembered, 'I saw the policeman fall from a shot. In a few moments we were out in the street where the other friends secured our escape...'[21]

In his rush to escape, Fricis Svars had left his hat behind in the corridor. As they tumbled out of the building, Luters casually grabbed a bowler hat off an astonished passer-by and plonked it onto Fricis's head. The time was 8.20 a.m., the whole operation had only taken a little over five minutes. That evening the escapees were smuggled out of the city to safe houses near the seaside resort of Jūrmalā, while Luters and his rescuers left Riga by train for St. Petersburg.

The day after the escape, 18th January, fearing another attack to free Pēteris Lapsa and three other prisoners, left behind because there had not been time to open the locked anteroom, Greguss ordered that they be transferred to Riga Central Prison. Prisoners under transfer to the prison in this manner knew that they would never arrive alive. The move was simply an opportunity to shoot them. The four men were marched through the streets escorted by armed guards. They were approaching the Matīsa cemetery next to the prison when the guards shouted at them, 'Run!' Pēteris Strazdiņš managed to run across the railway tracks just in time, as a passing train covered his escape, but his brother Kārlis and the badly injured Pēteris Lapsa were gunned down where they stood — 'shot while attempting to escape'.[22]

* * *

After the attack on the Riga secret police, Žāklis, Salniņš, Eliass, Dubelšteins and Luters moved to Petersburg. They were amongst a large group of Riga fighters, escaping from Orlov's punitive expedition, which had collected in the Russian capital by the middle of January 1906 and established contact with the Petersburg fighting organisation of the Russian social democratic labour party (RSDLP). The Petersburg Latvians immediately made themselves busy, conducting a number of expropriations of banks and post offices.

Early in February the RSLDP Central Committee's fighting technical group (headed by Lenin, and entirely Bolshevik in composition), which oversaw all guerrilla activities and ensured strict Party control, gave the Petersburg Latvians an important assignment: to travel to Finland and organise the expropriation of the Russian State Bank in Helsinki. The operation, involving 25-30 fighters, was led by Jānis Luters, with the assistance of Žāklis, Salniņš, Lencmanis, Dubelšteins, Eliass and the three brothers Čokes, a stellar who's who of Latvia's most wanted guerrillas.

With the help of local Social Democrats, the group began making their preparations for the raid, hiding their weapons in the studio of the Finnish sculptor Alpo Sailo who lived near the bank in Mikhailov Street. Unknown to the fighters was the fact that the operation's secrecy had been compromised from the beginning. The *Okhranka* had skilfully infiltrated two of its agents, Treitmann and Ratsepp (each ignorant of the other's true identity), into the group.[23]

The *Okhranka*'s plan, devised by General Kurlov, was to allow the raid to proceed and afterwards arrest the attackers and recover the money. The General, however, was playing for higher stakes than the capture of a few bank robbers. Unlike the Baltic and the Caucasus, Finland enjoyed a degree of independence unique within the tsar's empire and had been comparatively undisturbed by the revolution. The regional authorities, sympathetic to Latvia's attempt to break free from Russia, generally tolerated the presence in Finland of Baltic insurgents and turned a blind eye to their activities, so long as they were directed at Russia. The Latvians, cherishing the *de facto* right of asylum which turned the area into a safe haven, reciprocated by leaving Finnish banks unmolested. The doubtful vigilance of the Finnish authorities was why Lenin had chosen the bank in Helsinki as a target, believing it to be easy pickings. Kurlov intended to take advantage of Lenin's breaking of the unwritten truce, to undermine the autonomy of the Finnish Parliament, drawing public attention to their laxity in matters of internal security and embarrassing the Finns into revoking their benevolent treatment of the Latvians. This all depended upon Kurlov keeping his intelligence of the raid secret. The *Okhranka*, not the Finnish police, must be seen to bring the expropriators to justice.

From Petersburg, General Kurlov despatched an experienced *Okhranka* officer (a certain Mednikov, chief of the investigation department of the Petersburg *Okhranka*) and eight detectives to Helsinki to keep in touch with his agents and to effect the arrests. In Finland, Mednikov was to reveal the plan only to Karl Lode, the Chief of the local *Okhranka*. Everyone else had to be kept in the dark about the real purpose of the detectives' visit. Lode inspected the bank himself, keeping its officials ignorant of the impending robbery, and made a careful study of its layout. What made Lode and Mednikov nervous, though, was that they knew neither the day or the time of the attack. Experienced conspirators, Luters and Žāklis worked on a need-to-know principle and the infiltrators Treitmann and Ratsepp, like the other fighters chosen, were not told when the raid would take place until the last moment. The *Okhranka* could only stake out the bank and wait.

A solid three storey building with tracery balconies (from 1921, home to the Swedish Embassy), the bank was located in the centre of the city, facing a noisy market square. The bank premises were on the first floor, with a cafeteria occupying the ground floor and grocery shops in a courtyard. No one would find the presence of large numbers of people there suspicious.

On the afternoon of Monday 13th February, 1906, the junior assistant of the city police, Lieutenant Bruno Yalander (later a General and Finland's Defence Minister), was passing the bank when he bumped into Lode standing with several men in the square. Knowing nothing of the *Okhranka* Chief's true purpose there, the policeman stopped and chatted before continuing on his way. Moments later, at 2 o'clock, the raid went ahead.

While some of the fighters took up defensive positions in the streets around the bank, 15-17 heavily armed Latvians strolled inside pretending to be customers. Amongst them was Ģederts Eliass. Interviewed in 1972 he remembered: 'The whole thing happened in broad daylight, and the market place was crowded with people. We freely entered the bank and did what we had come for.'[24]

A young employee of the nearby Union bank, Elza Ziliakus, had just gone into the building to change some roubles into Finnish marks. She was at the counter being served when she noticed a group of well dressed young men, talking in German and Russian, come in and stand behind her. The bank had few customers on Mondays so a doorman asked what business the men had. They replied that they wanted to change some money but were in no hurry and could happily wait. Ten of them were waiting quietly when the doorman saw several more men enter the doorway and stop. One of them (Jānis Luters) announced loudly, 'In the name of the Russian Revolutionary Committee we arrest the cash box — hands up!'[25] The ten patient "customers" all produced revolvers.

The safes were emptied. Luters calmly sat down and wrote out a receipt (the custom of Latvian expropriators who regularly announced in the Party press the sums of money taken), while packets of banknotes and heavy satchels of gold coins were packed into several parcels. Miss Ziliakus and the bank staff were locked in an office, with a bomb on the desk in front of them. Kurlov's secret agent, Treitmann, meanwhile carried out his part of the General's plan and pressed the bank's alarm button unnoticed. The alarm system connected the bank by cable to an army barracks 300 yards away, but no soldiers came running to surround the building. The *Okhranka* had underestimated their enemy. The Latvians discovered the cable and disconnected it before the operation began. With the detectives outside still unaware of what was happening, the raiders placed another bomb by the door and withdrew unhindered, taking with them 170,000 roubles (the equivalent then of £17,000 — a fantastic sum for the time). Lieutenant Yalander, returning from his stroll, paid no particular attention to a group of merry young men who passed him as he neared the bank.

Eliass thought that the operation must have taken place with the help of sympathisers amongst the bank's cashiers. The assistance of Finnish Social Democrats, he said, 'was absolutely essential for this action.'[26] According to him, a Soviet account of the raid (published in 1962) was wrong in stating that a police guard (the doorman) was killed. Eliass was adamant that nobody died in the action. There wasn't even any shooting in the bank. Everything happened as planned, quite peacefully and quietly. 'The Finns were delighted that the Russian Bank had been robbed', said Eliass, 'because Finland was greatly opposed to tsarist Russia.'[27]

Newspapers in Finland, Sweden, and Russia were filled for days with sensational stories about the 'Baltic bandits'. The bombs turned out to be ordinary sardine tins wrapped in paper. Police examination revealed fresh traces of fish.

Six of the Latvians were captured. Kristiāns Treimanis and the brothers Kārlis and Gustavs Čoke were traced by Lieutenant Yalander (not the *Okhranka*), and arrested at Kerana railway station after a gun battle. A third Čoke brother (Jānis) evaded a trap set for him by his "comrades" Ratsepp and Treitmann by climbing out of the toilet window of a restaurant run by another *Okhranka* agent. Jānis Čoke was picked up later at Tampere railway station and taken into custody. Producing a knife, he killed an Inspector, then seized a pistol from the table and used it to kill another policeman and wound a third. The other policemen fled. Čoke took over the police station and fought off a determined police assault for three and a half hours. Only after a fire engine doused the building with water and his ammunition was exhausted did he finally surrender. Some days later the police found Pēteris Siliņš. Emma Gailītis, in love with Jānis Čoke, decided to share the men's fate and gave herself up. Sentenced to two years, she was deported instead to Latvia as a vagrant. The five men were sentenced to long terms of hard labour. Jānis Čoke died four years later, aged only thirty.

Of the others, Eliass remembered: 'Some of us later left Russia via Sweden to Berlin. Luters — the chief organiser of this operation — joined us there later. I do not know how he reached Berlin, but I guess he had to sneak out as a stowaway on a heap of coal in a ship's hold.'[28]

The police found money from the raid on most of the men arrested, but the Latvians escaped with 150,000 roubles. Of what became of the money, Eliass said: 'The confiscated money was mostly smuggled abroad, for with this money guns and other weapons were bought from German and Dutch firms. Most probably, a part of this money stayed in Russia. The assertion of Anna Jansone that she had kept part of this money, and that she had this money in Riga, may be true. As it is, it had been decided earlier where the confiscated money should go, and I think the whole thing was connected with Lenin and other comrades. It goes without saying, that in those days we couldn't know the details of such things, and later I didn't bother to ask...'[29]

Eliass' guess was correct. Yelena Stasova — later famous as secretary to both Lenin and Stalin, and a well-known figure inside the Comintern — took 10,000 roubles to Petersburg for the RSDLP treasury.[30]

In July 1906 Ģederts Eliass was arrested in Riga and delivered into the hands of Greguss and Davuss. He was lucky to survive but never recovered emotionally from the experience. Feliks Cielens said, 'In the summer of 1907 in Terioki (Finland), Ģederts Eliass, who had just been released from prison, told me about the tortures he underwent in the Riga house of inquisition in 1906. Greguss ordered that Eliass be tortured until he admitted everything. He was repeatedly beaten with sticks and whips until he lost consciousness, brought to his senses by vinegar and water, and beaten again on his bare back. Greguss' menials would have beaten him to death, if one of the executioners had not taken pity on him — Davuss. Having noticed that the tortured man was a son of a rich farmer from Platones parish, he ended the beatings, adding in a grotesque way: 'I could have killed you like a mad dog, but because you are from my parish I will not do it, and you have enough with these deep wounds for the rest of your life.'[31]

Among those who went to Germany with the balance of the cash from the Helsinki raid was Jānis Žāklis. It was his first trip abroad and the beginning of a new chapter in his career.

Notes

1   *Janis Luter-Bobis – Stranitsy zhizni revolutsionera-podpol'shchika – Sbornik statej I vospominani.* Sostavitel A. Luter (*Janis Luters-Bobis – Pages from the life of an underground revolutionary – Collection of articles and memoirs.* A. Luters (ed.). LVI, Riga 1962), pp. 262-3.

2   Y. Pieche, 'Libau In 1905', *Proletarskaya Revolyutsiya*, No.11 (46), November 1925, pp. 174-93.

3   LVA, PA-36/5/198, Juris Daberts, 'SVARS Fricis, Fričelis'.

4   Files of the City of London Police, 'Houndsditch Murders', 534C/1.4, Confidential report No.7782, 30 October, 1911, from Baron Heyking, Russian Consul General in London, to Superintendent Ottaway of the City Police. London Metropolitan Archives.

5   LVVA, 35/12/213.

6   Kristiāns Treimanis, 'V Bojevye Gody' (In the years of fighting), *Janis Luter-Bobis – Stranitsy zhizni revolutsionera-podpol'shchika – Sbornik statej I vospominanij.* Sastādītājs A. Luters, op. cit., p. 279.

7   Latvijas revolucionāro cīnītāju piemiņas grāmata. I. Sēj: 2. daļa. (Riga, 1980), pp. 84-5.

8   Ibid.

9   Tekla Šaitere, 'Austra pret slepenpoliciju' (Austra versus the secret police), *SestDiena*, 22 (29), Riga, March 2008.

10 Latvijas Nacionālā bibliotēka (LNB), PA17/4/3/24.524/77-24.526. *Voldemārs Skare, Materiāli par 1905. gada revolūciju un tas darbiniekiem.* (Material on the 1905 revolution and its participants), p. 147. (Riga, 1950. Unpublished manuscript of 170 pages).

11 Ibid.

12 *Janis Luter-Bobis – Stranitsy zhizni revolutsionera-podpol'shchika – Sbornik statej I vospominanij.* Sostavitel A. Luter, op. cit., pp. 120-1.

13 Donald Rumbelow, *The Houndsditch Murders and the Siege of Sidney Street* (Revised edition, London, 1988), p. 59.

14 Latvijas revolucionāro cīnītāju piemiņas grāmata. I. Sēj: 2. Daļa, op. cit., p. 84.

15 Alberts Bels, *Saucēja balss* (Rīga 1973), pp. 144-5. English edition, *The Voice of the Herald* (Moscow 1980), pp. 124-5. The book was also turned into a film, directed by Olgerts Dunkers: *Uzbrukums slepenpolicijai* (Attack on the Secret Police, Riga 1974).

16 *Janis Luter-Bobis – Stranitsy zhizni revolutsionera-podpol'shchika – Sbornik statej I vospominanij.* Sostavitel A. Luter, op. cit., pp. 120-1.

17 Ibid.

18 *Voldemārs Skare, Materiāli par 1905. gada revolūciju un tas darbiniekiem,* op. cit., p. 147.

19 Twelve people took part in the raid: Jēkabs Dubelšteins (Jēpis); Jānis Žāklis (Mērnieks), Jānis Čoke (Brašais), Kristaps Salniņš (Grishka), Ģederts Eliass (Straume) and his brother Kristaps Eliass (Čipus); Rūdolfs Dēliņš (Čoms), Jānis Pieche (Auseklis); Aneta Kalnina; Anna Jansone; Made Fridhison and Emīliju Volbergu (Sarkana Cilpa). Dubelšteins, Eliass, Čoke and Žāklis went inside the building, while Dēliņš controlled the door to the street; the others were positioned outside in the streets around the building.

20 Alberts Bels, (English edition), op. cit., p. 153.

21 Ernest O. F. Ames (ed.), *The Revolution in the Baltic Provinces Of Russia – A Brief Account of the Activity Of The Lettish Social Democratic Workers' Party By An Active Member,* (ILP, London, 1907), p. 79.

22 *Latvijas revolucionāro cīnītāju piemiņas grāmata.* I sejums 2.dala, op. cit., p. 79.

23 Valentines Šteinbergs, 'Drāma Somija' (Drama in Finland), *Zvaigzne* (Star) No.23 & 24 (Riga, 1980).

24 Valentines Šteinbergs. Unpublished interview with Ģederts Eliass, Riga, 16th December, 1972.

25 *Latvijas revolucionāro cīnītāju piemiņas grāmata.* I sejums 2.dala, op. cit., p.81; N. E. Burenin, 'Bobis v Finlyandii', *Janis Luter-Bobis – Stranitsy zhizni revolutsionera-podpol'shchika – Sbornik statej I vospominanij. Sostavitel A. Luter,* op. cit., p. 293.

26 Valentines Šteinbergs. Unpublished interview with Ģederts Eliass, op. cit.

27 Ibid.

28 Ibid.

29 Ibid.
30 Valentines Šteinbergs, 'Drāma Somija', op. cit.
31 Feliks Cielens, *Laikmentu maina*, (At the turn of the century), I Sej. (Stockholm, 1961), p. 232.

5

April to December 1906
The Same, in Word and Deed

> Shot through with contradictions, fragmented into varieties and sub-varieties, anarchism demanded, before anything else, harmony between deeds and words.
>
> Victor Serge[1]

The two months after the attack on the state bank in Helsinki, until the spring of 1906, brought Jānis Žāklis his first glimpse of life outside the Russian Empire.

After the bank raid a number of the Latvian fighters (according to Ģederts Eliass) went via Sweden to Berlin, where money from the robbery was used to buy arms from German, Dutch and Belgian firms. The shopping list included 500 Mauser pistols, 1,000 kilograms of dynamite and three million rounds of ammunition. The leading part in this arms buying spree was played by Ferdinands Grīniņš, but his companions on the trip included Jēkabs Dubelšteins and Jānis Žāklis. Their mission fits in with the assertion by the *Ohkranka* that Žāklis provided arms to the revolutionaries, and a report in an American newspaper that 'Peter the Painter was one of the chief organisers of the revolution … whose chief business was to smuggle arms into Russia'[2]

On their way back to Latvia the trio stopped off briefly in Switzerland — at Castagnola, a suburb of Lugano — where the celebrated Latvian writers Jānis Rainis (real name Jānis Pliekšāns, 1865-1929) and his wife Aspazija (Elza Rozenberga, 1868-1943) had settled after the uprising of December 1905 failed. To the young urban guerrillas who had robbed the Helsinki bank and spent the money on arms, Rainis was a figure of veneration, the Latvian Revolution's great poet and man of letters. Rainis makes no mention of Žāklis, but he does recall that in March 1906, 'A young hero Ferdinands Grīniņš visited us in our little room in via Circonvallazione. He was a tender and exquisite, deeply educated and intelligent young man, with a reserved manner, quiet and full of a rich content of soul. I seldom met anyone as likeable as he was after that, a person so sincere and sensitive. And this tender, beautiful soul was the soul of a hero and a martyr for a great idea; it turned this young man into a fearless soldier for Latvia and revolution, who was hard as steel. He was that type of hero whom I was always searching to portray in my plays — an exquisite, spiritual force, which wins also in the real, rude battle… he thirsted for struggle, and after a brief but dazzlingly bright career he died a martyr's death so heroically as almost nobody else from the many beautiful heroes of 1905. I am happy that I have seen in real life something I could only imagine in my dreams.'[3]

The martyr's death of Ferdinands Grīniņš, executed in Koknesē on 18th January 1907, after being horribly tortured, was far from unique among the beautiful heroes of 1905, but of those who survived none acquired more notoriety outside Latvia than Jānis Žāklis — the real Peter the Painter.

* * *

Whatever influence this first taste of Europe had on Žāklis (and whether or not he met Rainis), one thing is sure: Žāklis left Latvia as a Social Democrat but came back to it as an anarchist.

For a long time Žāklis had been growing uncomfortable with the idea of Social Democracy. Out of step with the party and impatient with talk of suspending the armed struggle in favour of entering the Russia Duma, Žāklis was looking for something that would reignite the flames of revolution and free Latvia once and for all. Žāklis may have been familiar with anarchism already, but the events of the 1905 revolution in Latvia would have appeared as self-evident confirmation of some very basic anarchist ideas. The use of direct action (strikes) rather than political action; the strategic linking of the general strike and armed insurrection; the largely spontaneous mushrooming of peasant councils as organs of genuine self-management, all were practical examples of what anarchists had been arguing in favour of since the Russian anarchist, Mikhail Bakunin, clashed with Karl Marx in the First International, over whether it was possible to proceed directly to a classless society without the need for a "transitional" period of proletarian dictatorship.

The verbally theatrical Bakunin had extolled the notion of 'an invisible network of dedicated revolutionaries', seeking 'to rouse, unite and organise spontaneous popular forces ...'[4], 'a sort of revolutionary general staff ... who are capable of serving as intermediaries between the revolutionary idea and the instincts of the people.'[5] Unlike Lenin's 'dictatorship of the proletariat', through which the Party would wield political power once the existing state machine had been destroyed, Bakunin's 'invisible dictatorship' existed to abolish political power altogether, and to ensure that no new state machinery was constructed that would limit the 'popular anarchy' of the people. Bakunin's organisation would be 'free from all official character'.[6]

Peter Kropotkin attempted to put the ideas of Bakunin onto a scientific basis, by arguing that Anarchism was the social practice of mutual aid, a natural phenomenon that constituted the culmination of human evolution.[7] Anarchist Communism would replace the state with a society organised in more or less the same way that the Latvians had adopted during the 1905 Revolution: federated councils of workers and peasants, *free soviets* in modern parlance.

After famously escaping from St. Petersburg's Peter and Paul prison fortress, and being imprisoned and deported from France, Kropotkin settled down to write his major anarchist works in England, where from the 1890s onward he was closely associated with a number of important figures in the early Latvian socialist movement. With the events of 1905 in the Baltic seeming to confirm the validity of Kropotkin's ideas, his influence among the younger generation of revolutionaries coming out of Latvia was considerable.

One Latvian anarchist has hinted that Žāklis may have found what he was looking for while on his trip around Europe, that it was Latvian revolutionaries who had become acquainted with anarchists abroad who first introduced anarchism to the Baltics, when they returned to Riga in the spring of 1906.[8] If true, this was merely finding a name to articulate something that was already there. More than anything, it was their direct experience of the 1905 uprising which was chiefly responsible for radicalising disaffected social democrats like Jānis Žāklis and creating an organised Latvian anarchist movement.

An anonymous author, possibly Žāklis himself, in the anarchist journal *Brīvība* (Freedom) wrote:

'Anarchism existed in the Baltics before the first anarchist literature reached there. We can say it was born from life itself, and was created by the revolutionary people. When, in 1906, some comrades loyal to the revolution openly started calling themselves anarchists, many others who thought the same treated them in a hostile way because they used the name anarchist.

'The wider masses understood under this name all the horrors of which they were accused by the press of those days. And that's why the first Latvian anarchists often suffered misunderstanding from their comrades, who had the same opinion only a different name. Many carried out anarchist activities, stood up for anarchist ideas, but were enraged when they were called anarchists.

'Now many comrades say, "I haven't changed my views; I have always thought and done so before". And they are right, only their name has changed.

'The anarchist idea was not brought to the Baltics from outside. It was created there. Its author is the people, and its school is the revolution... The history of the revolution in the Baltic region can prove that the genius of the people can create new ideas and new forms of society.'[9]

For the young LSDSP activists who followed Žāklis into the new anarchist movement it was a powerful experience. The Russian revolutionary Victor Serge (Kibalchich), who became an anarchist in France at around the same time, has described the impact: 'Anarchism swept us away completely because it both demanded everything of us and offered everything to us. There was no remotest corner of life that it failed to illumine, at least so it seemed to us... Shot through with contradictions, fragmented into varieties and sub-varieties, anarchism demanded, before anything else, harmony between deeds and words.'[10]

Quite appropriately, Žāklis chose *Pats — vārds un darbs* (The same — in word and deed) as the name of the anarchist affinity group he formed in Riga on his return from Europe in April 1906.

* * *

According to his critics in the LSDSP, Žāklis had always been sympathetic to anarchism; he had been reprimanded for displaying "anarchist tendencies", and finally had been removed from his post of chairman of the Fighting Organisation for carrying out unsanctioned operations. By the time Žāklis returned to Riga he made no bones about why he was so out of step with his own party — he was an anarchist. Now he believed that what at first he assumed were the shortcomings of social democracy were in fact the very essence of it, that the LSDSP was incapable of carrying through a real revolution, and that all genuine revolutionaries should leave the party and create an independent, unashamedly anarchist organisation. The defection of Jānis Žāklis, with his considerable reputation as a guerrilla leader during the 1905 Revolution, produced a haemorrhage of LSDSP members to the anarchists and made him an acknowledged leader in the young movement. As well as Žāklis's own *Pats — vārds un darbs*, a number of other anarchist groups were founded in Riga, and an attempt was made to unite them in a federation.

To some degree, the wave of defections is explained by the LSDSP's abrupt change of policy towards the *First Duma*. The Latvians had been bitterly critical of the tsar's *October Manifesto* which had brought the Duma into being, and the LSDSP had campaigned strongly for a boycott of the Duma elections in February 1906. The RSDLP abandoned the boycott policy at its Fourth (Stockholm) Congress in April, and decided to form a parliamentary group within the Duma. The Latvian party had followed the change in line, but many of its members radicalised by their experience of armed insurrection, in which Federative Committees and Peasants' Councils had taken over the running of daily life, could not make the shift away from anti-parliamentarianism. It seemed logical for them to go over to the anarchists — traditionally the bitterest enemies of parliamentary politics.

According to Voldemārs Skare, Žāklis left the party with ten other fighters and set up his own group, following what the anarchist journal *Brīvība* called 'a vehement exchange of words with the leaders of the Party'.[11] That was something of an understatement. The 'exchange of words' snowballed into a major argument which shook the party to the core and resulted in a mass of defections, expulsions and threats, some of them armed. The Party's version of what happened is provided by Jānis Zirnītis, the man in charge of the LSDSP printing houses, who knew Žāklis well and had taken part with him in the Helsinki expropriation. Zirnītis says that after he returned to Riga from Finland in April 1906, '...negative tendencies appeared within the movement — disillusionment with the revolution and the party organisation, contempt for its illegal activities, being carried away with anarchism, etc. — which also affected our ranks... A time came when a former party propagandist and fearless fighter Mērnieks went over to the anarchists, became their ideologist and leader, and boasted: "If I like, I will expropriate all the party businesses and will leave the party with empty pockets"...'[12]

Voldemārs Skare makes it clear that these threats were not empty rhetoric: 'One day the party learned that this group was preparing with the help of arms to take hold of an illegal printing press which belonged to the party. The party managed to evacuate the printing press, which printed *Cīņa* (The Struggle), just in time'.[13]

To add insult to injury, Žāklis had recruited two of the typesetters on the *Cīņa*, the LSDSP's main newspaper, Kaimiņš and Indriķis Rozenbahs (Bucītis). Bucītis was honest enough to say openly that his work in the party printing house was not compatible with ideological conversion to anarchism, and that it was better he left before he 'unwittingly let the printing house down' (by expropriating the party press). Bucītis told Jānis Zirnītis, 'I feel that the only way I can be useful to the revolution is with a "pipe" (Mauser) in my hand... it is better if someone else continues printing. I am joining the anarchists — they are more revolutionary than the Social-Democrats... Don't be afraid — I will not betray the printing press to the anarchists, even if they ask me the address... In case I fall [get arrested], the secret police will also not be able to get any information out of me, whatever tortures they may use – be sure about it.'[14] Kaimiņš and Bucītis were later tried by court martial in Riga: Kaimiņš was sentenced to four years hard labour; Bucītis was shot on 28 March 1907, aged only twenty-years-old.

Zirnītis nevertheless thought it prudent to move the printing press and typesetting office to different locations: 'I started getting very worried about the safety of the printing staff and materials. It wouldn't be difficult for Mērnieks or some other disorganizer to disclose one or other of our enterprises. It seemed suspicious to me, that no one from the other technicians and type-setters except for Bucītis acknowledged having been approached by Mērnieks or other anarchists, in order to persuade them to join the anarchists. At the same time, Mērnieks had tried several times to persuade me to leave the party, praising [flattering] me and abusing the Party, saying that the party was just using me and harming the revolution.'[15]

That it was 'the anarchist chieftain Mērnieks' who was leading this revolt was a particular worry for the LSDSP. As someone who had led the fighting organisations of both the Federative Committee and the Party, and the man who had organised and led all the major armed operations of 1905, Žāklis commanded a huge amount of respect among the Party rank-and-file. Worry turned to panic when, according to *Brīvība*, '…workers were leaving the social-democratic party *en masse* and going over to the anarchists… Propagandists were whistled in, and they, poor darlings, didn't know where to start. The powerful current of anarchism surprised them… The party had not expected that it would assume such huge dimensions. At mass meetings questions about anarchism were asked, and the party propagandists mumbled whatever came into their heads, because no directives from the Central Committee existed on this issue (those appeared only later). So at one meeting in the forest, one propagandist didn't know anything better to say to a question about who were those anarchists, than that those were thieves who stole women's pies from their baskets… Party circles began disintegrating "like snow under the sun". Scepticism and hatred towards the party even appeared within the ranks of the Central Committee, and a lot of diplomacy and wit were needed to win them over and back into the ranks of the Party.'[16]

Among those brought back into the fold were Ferdinands Grīniņš and Jēkabs Dubelšteins, close friends of Žāklis, both of whom according to *Brīvība*, 'had previously sympathised with the anarchists' but were co-opted into "cushy jobs" on the LSDSP Central Committee. Neither of them however was to enjoy a "cushy" future — both were captured by the police, horribly tortured and executed before the end of 1907.

Two other friends of Žāklis who had played important roles within the LSDSP fighting organisation, Kārlis Krieviņš (Keida, Krievs) and his companion Anna Caune (Milda), resisted the best efforts of the Party to keep them on board and threw themselves wholeheartedly into the activities of *Pats — vārds un darbs*. Rūdolfs Lemkins wrote bitterly that, 'Krieviņš was under great influence from Mērnieks, which explains the fact that in the summer of 1906 he left the Party and became one of the most fervent followers of the anarchist-communists.'[17]

On 15 August 1906, *Pats — vārds un darbs* outlined their views in a proclamation, announcing: 'We do what we ourselves consider right. We do not acknowledge the obligatory directives and rules set out by the Central Committee... *Pats — vārds un darbs* means that we have no commanders. We ourselves do what we say. We are not divided into committees that make decisions and organised comrades who carry them out. We shall also find our way ourselves, we shall find out how to implement our ideals in real life.'[18]

The proclamation made it clear that they rejected the notion, adopted by the LSDSP, of appealing to the Latvian middle class as well as the working class: 'We, exploited and oppressed, will have to fight ourselves and seek support among those, who are, like us, exploited and oppressed'.[19]

As anarchists they stated unequivocally that they rejected all forms of external authority in favour of workers control: 'We acknowledge neither the provisional legislation of the tsarist government [autocracy], nor the irrevocable constitution [laws] of the democratic republic, nor the obligatory [binding] directives and regulations [terms, conditions] of the Central Committee... The bourgeoisie is inviting the workers to make a political revolution... What good does it matter to the workers, if one tsar is replaced by hundreds of others? We don't need governments and their legislation... We need a workers' revolution! We have to appropriate all means of production, all factories and workshops, all land and all produced wealth... Everything belongs to us — let's go and take it!'[20]

In the summer of 1906, taking advantage of the temporary lapse in censorship granted by the tsar's *October Manifesto*, Jānis Žāklis published a thick 95-page pamphlet in Riga called *Liesmā. Rakstu krājums* (The Flame. A collection of articles); the first in a series of three volumes of anarchist writings edited by Žāklis to appear in Latvian.[21] The contents of *Liesmā* included seven articles by Peter Kropotkin (the first works of Kropotkin to appear in Latvian), an article signed by J. Kar, The Intelligentsia and Social Democracy, and a long article called *Satversmes sapulce* (The Constitutional Assembly), which was signed M–s, a thinly disguised way of writing Mērnieks, the conspiratorial alias used by Žāklis. The article was subsequently published separately as a 10-page hectographed pamphlet in November 1906 by the Riga Anarchist-Communist Group *Uz priekšu!* (Forward!), summarised in the files of the Riga police department as, 'a sarcastic attack on the Social Democratic idea of calling a meeting after the revolution to draw up the laws of a new society, and putting forward instead the anarchist idea of a society without laws (or private property, or private or state privileges, state power, etc)'[22]

The inspiration for Žāklis's article was the proposal of the LSDSP to turn away from open class struggle in favour of working towards the convocation of a Constitutional Assembly, which would stop short of social revolution, at the very moment when an armed insurrection in Latvia was being suppressed by a savage campaign of Russian state terrorism. Žāklis argued that Marxism, which espoused class struggle while pursuing a policy geared to achieving political power, contained an innate contradiction: no government, even when it claimed to be revolutionary, could abolish exploitation because all government rested on exploitation. The LSDSP deemed it prudent to follow the line of the RSDLP that a Russian Constituent Assembly should meet, at which the central bureau will convene the Latvian parish constitutional assembly in Riga, which will then work out definite plans for self-government. Žāklis argued that the notion of a constitutional assembly would put a brake on the revolution when the country was engaged in a desperate armed resistance against the Russian army. He proposed instead an intensification of the class struggle through the adoption of a dual strategy of the general strike and armed insurrection, with the final aim of social revolution and the establishment of 'anarchy'.

At the time of publication Žāklis was considered to be the chief ideologist and organiser of the anarchist movement in Latvia. Understandably the LSDSP, which in May 1906 affiliated to the Russian Social Democratic Labour Party as the Latvian Social Democracy (LSD), was incensed when the anarchist Pied Piper Žāklis followed the mass exodus from the party with the publication of his *collection of articles*. In August and September 1906 the Party published two large articles in its newspaper *Cīņa* attacking the Latvian anarchists, and in October that year issued a full-blown 38-page pamphlet, *Anarhisti-kompanjoni* (Anarchist Companions), focusing on the articles in *Liesma*, to try and negate the 'disorganising' influence of anarchism on the party rank-and-file. The pamphlet argued that with the revolution defeated, the sensible course of action should be to retreat, regroup and prepare the working class for a new mass struggle. It bemoaned the fact that anarchism was attracting support from people whose hatred was too great for retreat, who simply wanted revenge and immediate action: 'Burning with hatred, they were ready to go into battle alone, one against thousands. And they went... The number of separate anarchistic (unconnected, disorganised) attacks increased.'[23]

In an oblique reference to Žāklis, the pamphlet conceded that those who fought back against state terror as guerrillas were seen by the Latvian workers as defenders: 'The masses glorified certain fighters and sympathised with them — they were full of hatred and revenge, but they couldn't join in the fighting themselves.'[24]

And tipping the wink to Žāklis again: 'It was under such circumstances that those youths who fled Latvia as social-democrats, returned from abroad as anarchists. At the basis of their struggle they place the struggle of separate "heroic" individuals. Such were the circumstances that gave rise to these ideas, this is how the first impression of anarchism was crystallised and its first (but short-lived) victories were achieved. They found the sensitive chords within the hearts of many in the "guerrilla" and conspirators' ranks. Some of them enthusiastically joined the anarchists, because the latter had "theoretically" justified their means of struggle...'[25]

* * *

At the same time that Žāklis and the anarchists were fighting a war of words with the Social Democrats, they were also engaged in a real war with the police. The municipal police in Riga had quite a score to settle with Jānis Žāklis. Over the two-year period ending on 30th January 1906, they had lost 110 policemen to guerrilla attacks, more than a quarter of the entire police force.[26]

Now the mysterious Mērnieks, the man who started it all, was the prime mover behind the new anarchist peril that was emerging just when the police thought they were getting things back under control. The police were understandably ill-disposed to granting quarter to any anarchist found carrying arms. It was not the custom of Latvian anarchists to surrender when confronted with superior force. Knowing the fate that awaited them in police custody, the anarchists invariably offered armed resistance to the last. As one Riga anarchist put it: 'It was a deadly struggle. There was no thought of surrender and falling into the torturers' clutches, everyone was prepared to shut his own mouth with the last bullet. One act followed another in quick succession. Here a bomb explosion, there an infernal device — here directed against the fat bellies of *Selbstschutz*, there against the idiotic police representatives. All the supporters of the old regime were shaking with fear.'[27]

Gun battles between police and anarchists became common in the streets of Riga. One incident in particular was uncannily like the events at Sidney Street in London. On the night of 13th/14th August 1906, a large force of police and soldiers surrounded a flat at Stabu ielas 65 in Riga believed to be frequented by anarchists. Inside were two members of *Pats — vārds un darbs*, Kārlis Krieviņš and Anna Caune, both heavily armed with Mausers and bombs. Unbeknown to the police, members of the LSD were in another conspiratorial apartment on the floor above who had the good sense to stay quiet but who witnessed what followed.

In the stillness of the night the police knocked on the door of the anarchists' flat. There was a short conversation.

'Who's knocking?'

'The police, let us in.'

'Just a minute...'[28]

Before the minute was up the two anarchists fired through the door with their Mausers, wounding several policemen while others ran for cover. There was a brief moment in which to escape, but neither anarchist took it. Kārlis Krieviņš had earlier told one of his socialist neighbours upstairs, 'I'll never leave this flat alive.'[29]

The police action now did not allow for second thoughts. Barricading the door with furniture, Krieviņš and Caune held the police at bay with their Mausers. Several attempts were made to storm the building, but each time the policemen and soldiers were driven back by the anarchists' bombs (improvised hand-grenades). The doomed pair fought desperately and withstood the police assault all day, until 4 p.m., when they were both wounded and down to their last bullets.

The prolonged battle attracted a veritable garrison of soldiers from all over Riga. While still firing his Mauser, Krieviņš hung a red cloth from the window, like a banner, and the soldiers outside could hear the defiant anarchists inside singing revolutionary songs at the top of their voices. When the police finally burst into the flat, the wounded Krieviņš shot himself. Anna Caune, already mortally wounded, was shot dead by the police where she lay. An observer recorded that the anarchists' defiant struggle had left a great impression on the soldiers, who were heard saying, 'What a hero, shooting and singing...'[30]

The dialogue which preceded the Riga battle is reminiscent of the Houndsditch encounter, but the result on that occasion was quite different, because the London police did not understand the situation, and were not armed. The anarchists, though, behaved consistently. At the Siege of Sidney Street, where the London police response imitated the reaction in Riga, the anarchist intransigence is less baffling.

* * *

The net around Jānis Žāklis and his group was slowly tightening. On 11th December 1906, Emeriks Greguss, chief of the Riga police Detective Department, received information that two members of *Pats — vārds un darbs* would be arriving in the city by train that evening. A group of armed policemen were despatched to the railway station, where they assembled a reception committee of railway police to arrest the anarchists on their arrival. As the suspects left the train the police moved in to make their arrests, but the anarchists opened fire and tried to make a run for it. One of them managed to escape, but the other man, a seventeen-year-old anarchist called Jānis Pelcis, was captured and hauled off to the headquarters of the Riga police department for interrogation. Subjected to the usual tortures, the young Pelcis gave Greguss four addresses used by the anarchists. Greguss immediately assembled a raiding party of armed policemen and soldiers and set out in pursuit.

The upstairs flat at Artilērijas ielas 69, a simple two-story wooden building on the corner of Krāsotāja and Artilērijas ielas, was the family home of Jēkabs Leimanis and his wife and two children. Leimanis and two other members of *Pats — vārds un darbs —* Ansis Lintiņš (Leņķis) and a man whose name was unknown - were inside when the police knocked on the door at 1 a.m. Grabbing their Mausers, the anarchists opened the door and unleashed a fusillade of shots at the detectives outside, hitting a number of them. Another siege had begun. The anarchists resisted furiously, shooting from the windows and doors for two hours, before each was eventually cut down by police and army bullets, and a halt was called to the battle at 3 a.m. The three anarchists were all dead. Nine policemen and soldiers had also been wounded; among them Greguss, Davuss and the head of the district police, Birjukovičs, wounded in the yard where they were standing. Davuss later received a commendation for showing selfless courage and energy during the action. Leimanis's wife and two children, who were in the flat during the shooting but miraculously were unharmed, were taken into custody.

Inside the flat the police found a veritable arsenal — four Mausers, two Brownings, six Nagant revolvers, and a large amount of ammunition and dynamite — as well as rubber stamps for the The Anarchist-Communist Federation of Riga Groups and The Anarchist-Communist International. After it was all over and the victims taken away, some of the policemen and soldiers remained in the flat waiting for visitors, and by this device arrested several men who subsequently called there. The police also arrested Katrīna Liepiņa, a sister of one of the anarchists killed in the siege, at an address in Stabu iela given to them by Pelcis.

In a grim sequel to the siege, the Riga Military Tribunal dispensed summary justice to those in custody connected to the anarchists killed at Artilērijas ielas. Jānis Pelcis and Antons Bekmanis, believed to be the man who escaped when Pelcis was arrested at the railway station, were both shot by firing squad on 20th January 1907. And on 7th July 1907, the Tribunal handed out sentences to three people accused of being accomplices: 20 years for Anna Blūme; 13 years 4 months for Katrīna Liepiņa; and death for Artūras Dambis, commuted to 20 years hard labour by the Governor-General of the Baltics, Baron Mellers-Zakomelskis.[31] *Pats — vārds un darbs* seemed to be on an inexorable path to extermination.

On 11th September 1907, the police cornered another member of the group, Alberts Putniņš, a former member of the LSDSP, who worked as an apprentice at the Union factory. Putniņš was wanted for a wages snatch at the Sirius machine-parts factory in Riga, and for shooting a policeman. Betrayed by an informer, he and a woman called A. Zeļinskaja were besieged and shot dead in a flat at Aleksandra ielas 170. The police found Mauser and Browning pistols and two false passports on the bodies.[32]

* * *

With the revolution lost, those who fought on were branded criminals and bandits. Revolutionary Latvia became a killing ground. The summary executions of Orlov's expedition gave way to a systematic mass terror. Alexander Kerensky, then a young lawyer, saw the "pacification" in its later stages: 'After peasant and other uprisings had been crushed by punitive expeditions, it was a question of hunting out the remnants of revolutionary organisations — gangs, as they were called. The victims were handed over to military tribunals. It was a campaign of systematic judicial terror.'[33] At the end of February 1907, Kerensky was one of a team of lawyers called to Riga from St. Petersburg to defend 77 persons arrested after the Tukums rising. The judge, presiding over a special Military Tribunal which heard the Tukums Republic case, was General Koshelev; a sadist, Kerensky noted, notorious for his brutality: '...he had the habit of studying pornographic photographs in court during the hearing of cases in which the accused could be sentenced to death... At the trial it soon became obvious that Koshelev was not interested in trying to establish the truth, but only in selecting fifteen of the defendants to be hanged as a retaliation for the dead dragoons. The fifteen were hanged.'[34]

One by one the resistance fighters were hunted down and killed, thrown into prison, or forced into exile abroad. The prisons were full, and the courts working flat out sentencing those who had escaped Orlov's terror. The flow of revolutionaries choosing emigration in preference to hanging became a flood. After so many sieges and shootouts between the police and the anarchists of *Pats — vārds un darbs* it was only a matter of time before the net closed in on Jānis Žāklis.

Notes

1 Victor Serge, *Memoirs of a Revolutionary* (Oxford University Press, 1963), p. 18.

2 *The New York Times*, 5th February, 1911.

3 Jānis Rainis, *Kopoti raksti*, 17. sējums 'Ciemiņš F. Grīniņš'. First published 1928. Rīga, Zvaigzne, 1983, p. 27.

4 M. A. Bakunin, 'Programme of the International Socialist Alliance 1868'. First published in 1873. See, *The Hague Congress of the First International — Minutes & Documents* (Progress Publishers, Moscow, 1976), p. 630.

5 Bakunin, 'Letter to Sergei Nechaev, 2 June 1870', *Michael Bakunin — Selected Writings* (Arthur Lehning (ed.), London 1973), p. 182.

6 Bakunin, 'Programme and Objectives', *Michael Bakunin — Selected Writings*, op. cit., p. 635.

7 P. A. Kropotkin, *Mutual Aid — A Factor of Evolution* (Revised edition first published 1904. Penguin Books, London, 1972).

8 Brands, 'Baltija' (In the Baltics), *Briviba*, No. 4, April 1910, p. 49.

9 'Lasitaju ieveriba!' (To the attention of the readers!), *Brīvība*, No. 7, January 1911, p. 15.

10 Victor Serge, *Memoirs of a Revolutionary*, op. cit., p. 18.

11 Brands, 'Baltija' (In the Baltics), *Brīvība*, No. 4, April 1910, p. 49.

12 J. Žilinskis (J. Zirnītis, 'Arhivārs'), 'Veca nelegālista stāsts' (The Story of an Old Illegal), *Bez cīņas nav uzvaras* (Riga 1963), p. 109.

13 Latvijas Nacionālā bibliotēka (LNB), PA17/4/3/24.524/77-24.526. Voldemārs Skare, Materiāli par 1905. gada revolūciju un tas darbiniekiem, p. 151. (Material on the 1905 revolution and its participants. Riga, 1950. Unpublished manuscript of 170 pages).

14 J. Žilinskis (J. Zirnītis, 'Arhivārs'), 'Veca nelegālista stāsts', op. cit., pp. 109-10.

15 Ibid, pp. 110-11.

16 Brands, 'Baltija' (In the Baltics), *Brīvība*, No. 4, April 1910, p. 49.

17 *Revolucionārās cīņas kritušo piemiņas grāmata. 1. sēj.* (The memorial book of those fallen in the revolutionary struggle. Prometejs, Moscow 1933), p. 152.

18 *Pats — vārds un darbs* proclamation, 15th August 1906; cited in Julijs Daniševskis, *Anarhisti-kompanjoni* (Anarchist Companions) (LSDSP, Riga October 1906), p. 9.

19 Ibid.

20 Ibid.

21 Volume I — 'Rakstu krājums' (Collection of Articles) and Volume II — 'Kristiksu rakstu virkne' (A Number of Critical Works), both published in Riga 1906, are held by the Latvian National Library in the Misiņa bibliotēkā, Riga; Volume III — 'Kritisku rakstu krājums' (A Collection of Critical Articles), published in London, 1908, has still not been found.

22 LVVA, 4568/8/550, #30, 'Literature of Anarchist-Communist Group, 1906-1909'.

23 J. Daniševskis, *Anarhisti-kompanjoni* (Anarchist Companions), op. cit., p. 6.

24 Ibid., p. 7.

25 Ibid., p. 8.

26 Anna Geifman, *Thou Shalt Kill: Revolutionary Terrorism in Russia, 1894-1917,* (Princeton University Press, 1993), p. 28.

27 Brands, 'Baltija' (In the Baltics), *Brīvība*, No. 4, April 1910, p. 49.

28 *Latvijas revolucionāro cīnītāju piemiņas grāmata.* 1. Sēj: 3. daļa. (Riga, 1983), p. 31.

29 Ibid.

30 *Revolucionārās cīņas kritušo piemiņas grāmata.* 1. Sēj., op. cit., pp. 153-4.

31 Ibid, pp. 196-7

32 Ibid, pp. 218-19.

33 Alexander Kerensky, *The Kerensky Memoirs — Russia and History's Turning Point* (London, 1966) p. 76.

34 Ibid., p. 77.

6

1907 to 1909
Broken Pines

The towering pines, after breaking, will
Come up from the depths like great ships, and still,
Against all storms rise a proud-heaving breast,
Against all storms anew the fight press.

Jānis Rainis[1]

A story has passed down within the Žāklis family that around the end of 1906 Jānis Žāklis was somewhere in the Latvian countryside when he found himself surrounded in a 'shed' or outhouse by Cossacks of the punitive expedition making a sweep of the area. Besieged without hope of escape and facing certain death, Žāklis prepared to sell his life dearly in the inevitable shootout. At the most critical moment fate intervened in the shape of a farm girl who was working nearby. Seeing that the Cossacks were about to discover where Žāklis was hiding the girl ordered him to climb into a grain sack. Then, covering him in hay, she heaved the bulky sack over her shoulder and marched boldly out of the barn and through the line of soldiers to safety, as if innocently going about her work. The family say that Žāklis was so overwhelmed by the courage of this girl that he promptly fell in love with her and they were married, and that they left Latvia together.[2] The family in Latvia never heard from Jānis Žāklis again. All they knew was that he 'disappeared to America'.[3] The girl Žāklis married was called Lidija Schwarze (Švarce).

According to the Head of the Kiev *Okhranka*: 'In 1906 after the suppression of the revolutionary movement, Žāklis went to Pskov, from where he managed to escape abroad under the name Piatkov. In 1906, when still in Riga, he was very close to a girl called Schwarze, Lidija Maria (she also had another name)... At present this girl Schwarze lives in Russia near the border and probably has some connection with Žāklis.'[4] Exactly what her true name was is open to doubt, since *Schwarze* (Black) appears to have been an alias, but Žāklis was certainly in correspondence with an Anna Schwarze in Kiev when he lived in London in 1910 who sometimes signed herself 'your Black Girl', and in one postcard 'This is my picture... This is your old wife...'[5]

Up to this point quite a lot is known about Žāklis, from Soviet archive material and contemporary police reports. The problem in documenting his life begins when Žāklis goes abroad, the point at which the police lost tabs on the mysterious Mērnieks and Soviet historians lost interest because Žāklis had committed the unpardonable sin of leaving the party — and worse, of causing others to follow his example.

After escaping capture in the Latvian countryside, Žāklis and Lidija Schwarze moved to the city of Pskov, in north-west Russia, about 30 km east of the

Estonian border, on the Velikaya River. How long they stayed there is uncertain, but an informer in the London investigation into Peter the Painter told the police that 'Peter has been in Pskov several times — probably under the name of Piatkov', and that while there he worked at his trade painting street names and door numbers.[6]

With or without his new wife, Jānis Žāklis left the country sometime around the end of 1906 or start of 1907, saying he was going to America (according to the police in Riga, as Peter Piatkov; though there is no evidence that he used the passport in that name before returning to Europe in 1908). He was not the only one. An estimated 5,000 Latvians fled abroad in the first ten months of 1906 to escape the tsar's "pacification" of the Baltics; about half of them to the USA. Whether Žāklis left Pskov by choice or necessity, it is clear that the remains of his group *Pats — vārds un darbs* were active in the city at the time. The Latvian anarchist Ernsts Bonis (Mefistofelis), who in 1905 had been involved in the Mayday bomb attacks in Riga and had taken part in the attack on Riga central prison, was in Pskov in the autumn of 1907 with several others, preparing an expropriation. With depressing predictability, Bonis was surrounded in a flat by police and a siege ensued. Bonis shot several of the policemen dead, but when his ammunition was exhausted he exploded a bomb, killing himself and several more policemen.[7] Yet another anarchist who preferred death to surrender.

It is quite probable that Jānis Žāklis stopped off in London *en route*, and may have lived for several months in Bethnal Green and Shoreditch before crossing the Atlantic Ocean. 'A foreigner living in London' claimed in a press interview in 1911 that he had shared lodgings with Peter the Painter for two months eleven years previously (i.e. 1900), in Red Lion Street, Kingsland Road, before his fellow lodger 'went for quietness' to Queen's Buildings, Prince's Place, Bethnal Green. The anonymous informant said, 'Peter's real name is Straume. The name he most frequently used in the past ten years is Piatkow. He was born in Riga thirty years ago, and was brought up by his uncle, learning the trade of sign writer and scroll painter... Of very reserved manner, he was distinctly intellectual. Lettish was his native tongue, but he learned Lithuanian in London from immigrants. He spoke a little French, and quickly acquired English, which he could read perfectly and speak colloquially, but with a distinct accent.'[8]

The fixing of this first London episode to 1900 is not credible — Žāklis was then still at school in Kuldīgā and had not yet been abroad — but the interview contains enough verifiable detail about Žāklis to make the claim that he had lived in London some years before 1910 believable. The mention that he spoke 'a little French' at this period suggests it was before Žāklis moved to France in 1908, because he was subsequently (June 1909) complemented in court by a judge for speaking such fluent French, when he appeared as a witness to an accident

By September 1907 Žāklis was in the American city of Philadelphia. It was there that the famous wanted poster photographs were taken (see images 1, 14, 20), and it was the discovery of an *original* print in Riga in 1989 that first confirmed the identification of Peter the Painter as Jānis Žāklis. On the back of the photograph is the inscription, 'Žāklis in America as Tālbergs'.[9] Tālbergs was the maiden name of Žāklis's mother, Margarieta.

Whether as Piatkov or Tālbergs, Jānis Žāklis would have had little difficulty travelling abroad under an assumed identity. Latvian revolutionaries often escaped the country as seamen or hidden in the coal bunker of a ship going to Scandinavia or Britain. Once abroad they were free to travel under whichever name they pleased. Before 1914 travellers could move freely across Europe without the need to produce a passport, provided they had a valid railway or boat ticket for their journey (the only exceptions were Russia, Rumania and Turkey). America had no immigrant quotas and neither passports nor visas were necessary to gain entry. After the assassination of US President McKinley by the Polish-American anarchist Leon Czolgosz in 1901, the new president, Theodore Roosevelt, publicly denounced the 'anarchist peril' threatening America. The US Congress passed a law excluding from the country any person 'who disbelieves in or is opposed to all organised governments'[10] and suspect travellers were supposedly put under increased scrutiny. But entry into America was not difficult. One German immigrant asked on arrival whether he was an anarchist, answered with feigned naiveté 'I am a cabinet maker'. He was given a landing permit. In any case, American public opinion and the press, which carried detailed reports of the cruelties of the Russian government, tended to be sympathetic to refugees seeking sanctuary.

* * *

America was an important centre for the young Latvian anarchist movement. In addition to Žāklis, at least five of the suspects in the Houndsditch case had previously lived there before coming together in London (Svars, Hartmanis, Laiviņš, Dzirkalis and Celiņš); and the first significant Latvian anarchist journal of the emigration, *Brīvība* (Freedom), began publication in New York in December 1908, announcing itself as the 'publication of the American Latvian Anarchist Communist Group'. It was financed from the proceeds of expropriation.

It was in Philadelphia that Jānis Žāklis was reunited with Fricis Svars, whom he had not seen since rescuing him from the Riga secret police. Svars by this time had been expelled from the LSD[11] and now openly embraced the anarchist communism espoused by Žāklis. Fricis Svars kept running after being rescued by Žāklis in the attack on the Riga secret police. His cousin Jēkabs Peterss told the London police that Fricis had gone to America as a sailor at the start of 1906.[12] A passport used by Svars in the name of Peter Trohimchik recovered by the police in London indicates that he may have set sail for America on 14 May, 1907, after first travelling to Liepāja and Viļņius (in Lithuania).[13]

Whatever the date, Svars arrived in Philadelphia in the company of another Latvian anarchist, a friend of the family called Puika (Boy) Hartmanis. Well-built, five feet six inches tall, with a broad, handsome face, dark hair and a moustache, Hartmanis was a likeable, charismatic figure who displayed a natural aptitude for meticulous planning. An engineer by trade, he had worked in the railway workshops in Liepāja and been active as a fighter during 1905. Gravitating to Riga at the end of 1905, Hartmanis joined a group of fighters who were in contact with Jānis Žāklis. The group included fifteen-year-old Adam Čoke, younger sibling of the famous Čoke brothers (Jānis, Kārļis and Gustavs). As a member of this group Hartmanis had taken part in a gunfight in which several policemen were shot. He was also involved in the shooting of the *provocateur* Ziediņš, who had betrayed Fricis Svars and led the police to Canteen Austra. Hartmanis had sought to even the score further by trying, unsuccessfully, to assassinate the hated secret police interrogator Jānis Davuss, who had so cruelly mistreated Svars and his comrades before their dramatic escape.

But Hartmanis derives his real notoriety from his actions in London, where, as George Gardstein, he fired the fatal shots at Houndsditch. It was the accidental death of Hartmanis, abandoned at 59 Grove Street, which triggered the manhunt for Svars and Peter the Painter. Gardstein's real identity was never uncovered by the English police, and remained a mystery until the research for this book. Careful checking of material published in Moscow and Riga finally supplied the answer: 'Hartmanis (Puišelis, Puika). Liepāja fighter. Worked in the railway workshops; Anarchist-Communist. Emigrated to America. Took part in the same actions as 'Fričelis' – in America and London. Killed in a gun battle with the police in London December 1910, during an expropriation.'[14] 'Fričelis' (Fritzie), the diminutive of Fricis, is obviously Svars. That Gardstein really was Hartmanis is confirmed by the unpublished memoir of Juris Daberts held in the former archive of the Latvian Communist Party, now part of the National Archives in Riga: 'Being in emigration in England, together with Hartmanis, he (Svars) organised an "eksis" (expropriation) of some big jewellery shop in Houndsditch, London... Surprised by three English policemen, they shot them all, but at the same time... (Hartmanis was) accidentally seriously wounded ... (and) ... died later the same night from his wounds.'[15]

Few details about the life of Jānis Žāklis in America have so far come to light, but his purpose there was clear: he was reorganising after the liquidation of *Pats — vārds un darbs* and preparing to reactivate the anarchist struggle inside Latvia. Svars and Hartmanis were the kernel of the American end of that operation. The main focus of their activity was expropriation.

* * *

On the night of 6 February 1908, Officers Walsh and O'Neill of the Woburn (Massachusetts) police noticed three men crossing Woburn Common from the Unitarian Church on the corner of Winn Street. Sensing something suspicious about them, the officers called on the men to stop. They immediately ran off and the policemen gave chase. At the corner of Church Avenue the three men stopped and one of them started shooting, wounding both officers.

Unbeknown to the policemen, the three strangers had just robbed two businessmen in Billerica, near Pinehurst Park, and were heading back to the railway station to travel to Boston when they were called on to halt. With the officers down the men resumed their flight, but as they neared the tracks of the Boston & Maine railway one of them was grabbed by a local man called Bert Donohue. In the tussle five shots were fired and Donohue fell wounded to the ground. The shots attracted the attention of another policeman, Officer Murphy, who joined the chase. At this point the gunmen split up. One headed up Warren Avenue, while the other two ran off up Lexington Street, towards the West Side of town. Officer Murphy went after the man who had shot Donohue. As the fugitive reached the summit of Academy Hill on Warren Avenue a twelve-year-old boy, Sherwood Van Tassel, got in his way. Without hesitation, the man produced a semi-automatic pistol and shot the boy in the leg. Meanwhile, another policeman, Officer Keating, had commandeered a horse drawn wagon and set off with the driver, Edward Holland, up Lexington Street, in pursuit of the other two suspects. The men were in front of Dobbins and Shannon Farm when Keating shouted at them to stop. Their reply was a volley of shots, wounding the wagon driver in the back.

By now a crowd had gathered in front of Woburn police station and a call had gone out for volunteers from Company G, a local army unit, to join the manhunt. It was 3.30 in the morning by the time the men of Company G set off to Winning Farm, where their quarry had last been sighted. The soldiers and members of the Lexington and Arlington police combed a wide area. As dawn broke it was announced that two of the gunmen had been captured at Arlington. But the third gunman, who had shot young Sherwood Van Tassel, had escaped.[16] The two men in custody, it transpired, were both from Latvia. Their names are not recorded. They received sentences of 18 and 25 years in State Prison. No trace of the man who got away was ever found, but in 1911 the Boston police issued a reward of $500 for his capture and named him as 'Chris Zeltin'.[17]

In the spring of 1908 Jānis Žāklis returned to Europe as Peter Piatkov, to be better placed to direct operations in the Baltic. But the need for money was a constant imperative if the resistance was to continue.

On Friday 10th April 1908 three armed Latvians raided the Royal Bank of Scotland on Brandon Street in Motherwell, Lanarkshire, to the east of Glasgow. A few days before, one of the men had called at the bank asking to buy a postage stamp. The bank teller, John Kay Ferguson, told the stranger that they didn't sell stamps, but gave him a stamp from his own pocket and told him not to come back. At 12.30 on that Friday morning the man returned, accompanied by two others, and without uttering a word strode towards the opening at the end of the counter, behind which were safes containing £1,000. Ferguson blocked his path and struggled with the man. A second man strongly built and around six feet tall, came up behind the bank teller and put a gun to his head. Ferguson shouted for help. William King, the bank manager, who was in a meeting with an architect called Brown, rushed out of his office and caught hold of the gunman's wrist. The gunman reached over with his free hand, cocked his semi-automatic pistol and fired a shot into the air. Taking fright at the sudden appearance of King and Brown, the other two robbers promptly fled, leaving their comrade to struggle with the bank staff. The gunman wrenched himself free and ran out of the bank.

The struggle had lasted only a few seconds. Ferguson's hands were badly lacerated by the foresight of the pistol barrel, and King was bleeding profusely from a wound to his left cheek. Mr King rushed to the door, but the gunman had disappeared. Two boys told him they had just seen two men run away from the bank. King promised them a reward if they would follow the men and tell him where they had gone. The boys trailed the robbers for nearly a mile, before loosing sight of them on the outskirts of town. But at that point the boys met two policemen, Sergeant Mowat and Detective Walker, who were escorting a prisoner from Clydesdale back to Motherwell in a vehicle. The policemen promptly handcuffed their prisoner to the vehicle and took up the chase on foot. The robbers seemed to be making for the railway. The policemen chased them through the fields to the vicinity of Jerviston House, where one of the men turned and fired several shots at them, before making off towards the woods. The firing attracted the attention of a number of workmen from Clydesdale iron works; they joined in the chase too. Detective Walker managed to corner one of the fugitives in a farm yard. The man fired at Walker but missed and was overpowered. The second robber, who was unarmed, took shelter in the woods but was surrounded a few minutes later by the workmen and surrendered. The third man, rumoured later to be Peter the Painter, who had produced the gun in the bank and had escaped on his own, was never found.

The arrested men, Ludwig Bruno and Carl Smith, had been sharing lodgings at English Buildings, Craigneuk, a mining village in the suburbs of Motherwell near the site today of Ravenscraig steel works, 1.5 km from Motherwell town centre. Questioned through an interpreter at Motherwell police station, the prisoners said they had committed the crime because they were starving.[18] Smith had only been in Britain for four months and had worked as a farm labourer before that. In Scotland he worked as a labourer at an iron foundry, but had been unemployed for a week prior to the robbery. Bruno, according to one newspaper account, was 'a Socialist': 'His father was a well-to-do farmer, and gave his son a good education. He attended college at Moscow, and afterwards was surveyor on the Orel-Riga railway, but after its completion was out of work. He came to this country only three months ago.'[19] At their trial at the High Court in Glasgow, Bruno was sentenced to 10 years and Smith to 7 years. Both were sent to the notorious Peterhead prison, long regarded as the worst prison in Britain, to serve their sentences. Bruno died of tuberculosis of the lungs in Peterhead on 25th December 1909, aged only twenty-two. Smith survived his sentence and on release was deported. Nothing more was known about the men until the research for this book, when the real identity of Bruno was at last established.

Material collected in Moscow in 1936 shows that Ludwig Bruno was actually Ludvigs Putniņš. He arrived in London from Riga on 13 January 1908 and in the same year moved to Glasgow and died in 'Glasgow prison' (actually Peterhead) on 24th December 1909.[20] No indication of his political affiliation was given in the published account, but the membership records of the London Branch of the Latvian Social Democracy show that Ludvigs Putniņš (Bruno) was listed as a member of the Party. Entry No. 108 in the membership book confirms that he came to London from Riga and was admitted to the London Branch on 13th January 1908 and that he went to Glasgow. Alongside the entry someone at a later date added two notes: 'Died 24 December 1909 in Glasgow prison', and 'Expelled from the ranks of the branch 1908.'[21] No date is given for the expulsion but presumably it was as a result of him being arrested for an unauthorised expropriation — the Party banned expropriations in 1907.

Unusually for a bank robber, Putniņš was also a poet. His signed and dated poems, scrawled on scraps of paper and the backs of envelopes, make it clear that he was still in London on 18th February, but had moved to Glasgow by 17th March 1908, shortly before the bank raid. Of the various poems found on him (signed Ludvig Bruno), one is entitled *Krituśo varoņu piemiņai* (In Memory of Fallen Heroes) and dated Glasgow, 24th March 1908. He had also copied out poems by Jānis Rainis, one of which — *Lauztās priedes* (The Broken Pines, 1904) — is a famous revolutionary anthem, upholding the spirit of the oppressed Latvian identity; still sung as a choral piece at Latvia's National Song Festival.

Of various names and addresses found on Putniņš, two are probably his points of contact in London and Glasgow. The first, Robert Balad (Balodis — Pigeon — a very common name in Latvia) of Glasgow, is probably the same R. Balodis referred to in a Soviet book on the Latvian emigration of the period as a 'revolutionary emigrant in western Europe' (no other details given, but the implication is he was not a member of the Party).[22] The other, Jānis Austriņš (with an address in Tottenham Hale, London) is likely to be a Latvian Social Democrat.[23] Most of the material found on Putniņš is quite mundane, some comical, like the page of English phrases written in *as it sounds* English with the Latvian translation underlined beneath it, including such useful lines as 'Tu glass bier plis' (two glasses of beer please). The one significant item among his papers is a very rudimentary alpha-numeric cipher table that would be used to turn written messages into lines of numbers, which would be then turned back into "clear" by the recipient using an identical table. In practice any code-breaker (or crossword puzzler) would take about five minutes to crack the cipher! Not very effective, maybe, but it does indicate that Putniņš was interested in more than poetry or learning English.

Who the other two Motherwell robbers were is still a mystery. No Carl Smith (or Kārlis Schmidt) is listed in the membership records as belonging to the Latvian Social Democracy in London. If they were Social Democrats then the raid was (officially at least) an unauthorised operation, carried out on their own initiative. Alternatively, Bruno could have been drawn into temptation by anarchists linked to Jānis Žāklis. While there is no evidence to suggest Žāklis had been present during the robbery, and indeed the nervous behaviour of the three robbers suggests he *wasn't* one of them — he does appear to have been in London around that time, because he published the third instalment of his journal *Liesma* there sometime in 1908. Another indication of the presence of Latvian anarchists in England at this time is the appearance of an anarchist journal called *Naids* (Hate), which was edited in Manchester and published in Paris in 1908.

* * *

When Jānis Žāklis got back to Europe he seems to have had enough money to go to Switzerland, where he studied chemistry for a while, until for some reason he was forced to leave and move to Paris. From Paris Žāklis headed south to the port of Marseille.[24] Perched on the Mediterranean near the southern tip of France, Marseille was tailor-made to get lost in for a man on the run. The largest and oldest French city after Paris, Marseille was founded by Greek traders in 600

BC, and was a melting-pot of immigrants and cultures from all over Europe, Russia and North Africa. The city's revolutionary associations stretched back to 1792, when it despatched five hundred volunteers to defend Paris, proudly singing as they marched north *La Marseillaise*, the song adopted as the French national anthem. When the French Revolution soured the political prisoners from the Paris Commune of 1871 were brought to Marseille in chains and incarcerated in Le Chateau d'If, the offshore fortress-prison immortalised by Alexandre Dumas in *The Count of Monte Cristo*. The city was a magnet for artists and painters, and a home for political refugees and smugglers who worked the southern route into Russia through Odessa, Batum and Baku.

The hub of Marseille life was the Le Vieux Port (The Old Port), a fishing harbour renowned for its quayside fish market, guarded by the 12th-century Fort St-Jean on the north bank and the Fort St-Nicolas on the south. On the northern side of Le Vieux Port stretches the hilly district of Le Panier (The Basket), the oldest part of the city and traditionally the first stop for immigrants; a labyrinth of narrow streets, steep stairways and ancient, pastel-coloured houses, flanked on its western edge by the commercial docks of Joliette. On 16 April 1908, six days after the Motherwell bank robbery, Žāklis (using the name Peter Piatkov) found lodgings at 11 Rue d'Aubagne; a small street on the eastern edge of Le Vieux Port.

Initially Žāklis seems not to have been over-burdened with the need to find work, spending a good deal of time mixing with Russian students, and apparently studying medicine. The primary sources of information on Žāklis at this time are two reports from the *Sûreté* in Paris and Marseille, and some pencil notes from a police informant. Piatkov first came to the notice of the French police on 23 May 1908, when he was among five "suspected refugees" questioned during a house search at an address in Le Vieux Port. No arrests were made, but Žāklis disappeared shortly afterwards. The *Sûreté* noted that he came back to Marseille from Oran (French Algeria) on 7 June, 1908, and rented a room at an address in the Arab quarter of Belsunce: 'According to the keeper of the furnished house, 37 Rue des Dominicaines, Piatkov was a very violent character and often disappeared with his Russian friends, and finished by separating from them.'[25] The house where Žāklis stayed is still there, known today as the Hôtel Edward. But he only lived in Rue des Dominicaines for a month. His stay in Marseille was marked by frequent and sometimes prolonged absences; the French police recorded four different addresses for Piatkov from April 1908 to January 1910.

Another of those questioned in Marseille was a certain Yosselevitch, who allowed Piatkov ('of whom he speaks very highly')[26] to use his address for correspondence. Yosselevitch admitted knowing Piatkov 'very well' and said he had 'often eaten with him in 1908 as a student' (of medicine). Piatkov had 'abandoned his studies to work as a painter'. Yosselevitch last saw him about the end of 1909, when Piatkov left for Evian-les-Bains (on Lake Geneva), he did not know what had become of him since. The French police noted: '...Yosselevitch appears to ignore the Houndsditch tragedy, or at least the search for Peter the Painter. According to him, Piatkov, nephew of a Russian Colonel, is a Socialist, convinced, and not using his real name...' Yosselevitch was the source of the famous "wanted poster" photographs of Peter the Painter. The Marseille police bragged that they had 'managed to deceive him for a short time' while they had the pictures copied without his knowledge, 'for he would not have consented to this operation'. One of Piatkov's former landlords ('the lodging house keeper of 8 Rue Chevalier Roze' — appropriately now an art gallery; the Galerie of Marseille) and his ex-employer Mr. Ebrard were shown copies. Both formally identified the man as Piatkov. Six copies of the photographs (three of each pose) were enclosed with the report.[27] The pencil notes on Piatkov in the files of the City of London Police are clearly taken from an interview with someone who lived with him in France, quite possibly Yosselevitch.

The informer told the police that Piatkov had escaped from prison after being jailed 'for acts committed in the Revolution'. He studied chemistry in Switzerland and had gone to Paris before arriving in Marseille. His father died in 1908, but his mother and sisters lived on a farm somewhere in Courland, in the vicinity of Talsi. An uncle, 'a Colonel in a regiment in a town in central Russia' used to write to Piatkov and told him 'if he would go to Paris to study — not politics — he would send him money each month'. In Marseille Piatkov 'used to have his letters addressed to the name of a Spanish Anarchist in the next street to where he lived'. He arrived in Marseille from Oran 'shortly after the King of Portugal was assassinated' (Lisbon, 1st February, 1908). England was never mentioned, but Piatkov had been to Sweden, Denmark, Germany, Switzerland. 'Said he knows nearly all countries in Europe'. All of the details above fit neatly with what we know about Jānis Žāklis: he had spent time in prison, his father died in 1908, his mother and sisters lived on a farm in Talsi district, he had a benevolent uncle who was a Colonel in 'a town in central Russia' (Bobruisk). According to this informant, Piatkov arrived in Marseille with 'a little Polish man'.[28]

More interestingly the notes give us a glimpse of how Žāklis lived in Marseille: 'Whilst in Marseille did not go out (with) girls or drink — only smoked and played cards — worked on a new building outside Marseille — Estaque the name of the place — liked to work and worked hard. He was a vegetarian whilst in Marseilles. Used to earn a Franc more than the others.'[29]

Now absorbed into the edge of Marseille's northern suburbs, L'Estaque (Connection) was then a small secluded fishing village, and a favourite haunt of artists from the impressionist, fauvist and Cubist movements such as Cézanne, Renoir and Braque. When Peter the Painter arrived in London, Fricis Svars introduced him to Luba Milstein saying that Peter was studying art. She told the police: '[Peter the Painter] had no trade qualifications; he was only studying to paint pictures — it was not his profession. Peter and Fritz had known each other in Russia, and they were friends. Fritz told me that Peter's parents sent him money from Russia, and that he lived on this money. He did not do any work.'[30] Was his focus on art one of the reasons Žāklis gravitated to Marseille and L'Estaque in particular? That he was also working hard on a building site at L'Estaque is attested to by a photograph taken there (found by the police in London after Peter the Painter fled, see image 24). It shows Žāklis striking a serious pose in the midst of a group of laughing workmates, some clutching wine bottles, surrounded by huge blocks of stone. His frowning demeanour is at odds with the general gaiety of his mates, suggesting a rather self-conscious relationship with the camera. Except for his shabby work clothes, the pose (right arm forward across his body, left arm akimbo) is very like that of the "wanted poster" pictures taken earlier in America.

Besides the building job at L'Estaque, Žāklis also worked at various jobs in Marseille as a painter, first of doors, then for a painting and tapestry company, for a Mr. Ebrard at 37 Rue Consolat (for 5 Francs per day), at the Docks and at an Exhibition of Electricity. He clearly enjoyed hard work, and was paid more for being a good worker, but was never too proud not to work when he didn't have to.

But the main focus of Žāklis' attention, as always, was the resistance in Latvia.

* * *

While Žāklis was in Marseille and the Scottish police were questioning the two Latvians captured at Motherwell, the authorities in Riga were still trying desperately to identify the mysterious Mērnieks, whom they suspected was behind the new wave of anarchist activism. The first round in the new bout of resistance began at the end of 1907, with the appearance of a new anarchist fighting group in Riga.

On 5 November 1907, an anarchist called Vilhelms Zavinskis arrived in the Latvian capital from America, after first stopping off in London where he met the anarchist ideologue Kropotkin. Operating under the nickname Mazais (Shorty — a nickname shared with Alfred Dzirkalis) and known to the *Okhranka* watchers as Boris, Zavinskis had previously carried out expropriations with Žāklis' old friend Kristaps Salniņš, with whom he had visited London earlier in 1907 'to steal guns and send them to Riga'.[31] Zavinskis smuggled the arms into Latvia from Sweden, established an anarchist printing press in Estonia, and gathered sufficient comrades together to reconstitute the Riga Group of Anarchist-Communists. But operating in a climate of skilful police surveillance and harsh repression was not conducive to remaining at liberty for long. When the group was rolled up by police and liquidated on 13th May 1908 it was established that Zavinskis was 'in correspondence with Mērnieks'.[32]

Three days later the police in Riga carried out a search of a flat belonging to Katrīna Rudzīte, secretary of the Anarchist Red Cross organisation which organised support for imprisoned comrades. The police found four passports in the flat, together with 'a letter from Mērnieks, in which he asked Rudzīte to give him addresses in America and to give him money'.[33] Shortly before that, on 24th April 1908, an investigator of the Riga District Court had asked the head of the Riga *Okhranka* to inform him urgently about the identity of Mērnieks, who 'belongs to a party of Anarchist-Communists'.[34] The *Okhranka* replied that according to the executed Jēkabs Dubelšteins the name Mērnieks was used by Nikolajs Ivanovičs Laivinieks, and that in 1906 Mērnieks organised a group of Anarchist-Communists in Riga, and in 1905-06 was a member of the Riga Federative Committee.[35] Dubelšteins knew very well that Mērnieks was Žāklis, having worked closely with him in the fighting organisation, but was clearly protecting his friend to the last. In another report, the *Okhranka* agent Leepa says, 'Mērnieks is just as well respected as Mazais' (Zavinskis). 'An intelligent man, a former Social Democrat, and now since two or three years, has gone over to the anarchists'.[36] The vague rumours of their anarchist nemesis continued. On 10th October 1908 the Riga *Okhranka* filed a report on an anarchist called Eduards Kārkliņš, whom they described as 'one of the fighters of the "Afanesia" gang of Mērnieks, who is now abroad'.[37]

Of overriding concern to the Latvian anarchists in exile was bringing material support to their imprisoned comrades and organising escape attempts. Jānis Žāklis is chiefly remembered in Latvia as the organiser of the successful raid on Riga Central Prison in 1905, and as a participant in the spectacular attack on the Riga secret police at the start of 1906. This spectre of Comrade Mērnieks, the man who never left anyone behind, came back to haunt the *Okhranka* in November 1908, when they began to pick up scraps of intelligence which indicated that he was preparing a daring new operation to free Vilhelms Zavinski and another imprisoned anarchist, Kārlis Krapšs.

Krapšs had been a member of the LSDSP in January 1905 but in April crossed over to the Socialist Revolutionaries (SR),[38] taking with him 20 pistols belonging to the Party, and organised a fighting group in the Torņkalns district of Riga. In November and December 1905 he and his group carried out half-a-dozen burglaries of flats in Riga to steal guns. In August 1906 he became a member of the Latvian Social Democratic Union (the Latvian equivalent of the Russian SR Party)[39], joining their fighting organisation Red Terror, and in September 1906 took part in a series of expropriations of pubs and monopoly shops for money and guns. At the end of 1906 he changed his affiliation again and organised an anarchist-communist group in Riga, before finally being arrested in July 1907 and charged with a total of sixteen expropriations.[40]

Krapšs was admired as a hero by the anarchist movement and plans were soon mooted to free him, but unbeknown to his admirers outside, the young activist, only twenty-two-years-old, had cracked under police pressure and was telling his interrogators everything he knew. According to the protocol of his interrogation on 27th November 1908 by Rotmeister Chleborodov, Kārlis Krapšs claimed that while he was accused of offences from January 1905 to November 1906, he had not been active after that date, and since his arrest he had co-operated fully with the police, even going so far as to act as an informer against other prisoners, notably the anarchist Eduards Rostaks. Krapšs told the policeman, 'I know that in December of this year 1908 anarchist-communists are going to spread leaflets in Riga, under the title "The New and the Old Bourgeoisie", and that in 1909 the leader of the anarchist-communist group is going to come to Riga…'.[41] The anarchist "leader" so imminently expected in Riga could only have been Jānis Žāklis.

The day after Krapšs's confession the *Ohkranka* received a report from another of its agents, warning them that there were '872 armed anarchists' in Riga who were all led by 'The same man who led the attack on Riga Central Prison'; and that he was planning to free the anarchists Zavinskis and Krapšs from prison.[42] The report was based on an intercepted letter smuggled in to

Krapšs by a female friend or relative ('your Zelma'), who consoled him not to feel sorry for himself: '… you are going to be liberated when they are going to take you to court. Last Sunday the Executive Committee of the Fighting Organisation held a meeting to discuss your situation, and all the comrades have unanimously decided to free you, however much it would cost. Every comrade is ready to lay down their life for you. The comrades' total force will consist of 872 armed persons. The operation will be led by the same man who took part in the attack on the Central Prison. It is at the moment impossible to say when the operation is going to be carried out — on the way to the courthouse or on the way back.'[43]

In the event the expected rescue attempt never materialised. Despite his abject cooperation with his captors, Kārlis Krapšs was executed in Riga Central Prison on 3rd January 1909.

The intense interest of the authorities in Mērnieks is significant, not only for the fact that he was clearly perceived as a major adversary, whom they believed was behind the plans to free Zavinskis and Krapšs, but also as testimony to the skill of Žāklis in keeping his real identity concealed. Even in 1911, when the *Okhranka* informed the City of London Police that the wanted Peter the Painter was Jānis Žāklis, they had still not closed the triangle and made the connection between Piatkov-Žāklis and the notorious Mērnieks, and in fact they never did.

* * *

Three months after the ill-fated raid at Motherwell, in an incident directly linked to the Siege of Sidney Street, Latvian expropriators hit the headlines again, this time across the Atlantic in Boston.

'Seven men were sitting in the Winterson & McManus saloon at 3171 Washington Street, near the corner of Boylston Street. It was just before 11:00 p.m. on Tuesday, July 21, 1908. Thomas Winterson, the proprietor, … John Carty, the bartender, … and five customers were having a last drink. Just before closing, three unfamiliar men entered. As one jumped over the bar and threw the cash register to the floor, his two companions drew pistols and began firing. Winterson took bullets to the base of the skull and the left arm. Customer Patrick Doran was struck in the left side and the spinal column. A second customer, Frank Drake, was hit in the right lung. While one of the men picked up the money from the register, bartender Carty escaped to the back room and called police station 13. With their take of $90 the three men ran into the street.'[44]

The three robbers, and possibly a fourth, went to ground in Forest Hills Cemetery, where they spent the night. Two of the men left the cemetery the next day (22nd July), but were challenged by a policeman at 7 o'clock in the evening and a running gun battle through the streets of Jamaica Plain ensued, during which a policeman and six other people were wounded. At the entrance to Forest Hills Cemetery the fugitives came upon watchman Herbert Knox. They were overheard to ask Knox if he was a policeman. When he answered, 'No, I am a watchman,' one man said, 'Take no chances,' and the other man shot him, mortally wounding him in the abdomen. Knox died later at Emerson hospital.[45]

By 8 p.m., 250 policemen had surrounded the cemetery, but with darkness approaching, no attempt was made to search the grounds. Instead, every street around the cemetery was patrolled by armed men. Automobiles equipped with searchlights patrolled the adjacent streets. At 8.15, one robber was seen approaching the fence, but police drove him back with shots from their revolvers. At 9.20 p.m., Patrolman Edward McMahon, keeping watch on the west edge of the cemetery, heard a noise at the cemetery fence. When he came out into the light to investigate, he fell with a gunshot wound to the abdomen. His fellow officers returned fire in the direction of the shots, but with no apparent effect. The rest of the night was quiet.[46]

At 4 a.m. the next morning, 23rd July, the police entered the Cemetery and saw to the left of the main entrance a man running over a hill toward a dry ravine. The man fired a whole clip from a 7.65mm semi-automatic pistol at the police, inserted a fresh magazine and began firing again. 'The police returned fire as they advanced, but he continued into the gully, firing as he ran. He sought cover from one tree to another, settling behind a fir tree. As police bullets rained down on the man's location, a single shot came from behind the fir, and a puff of smoke, but no further answers to the police fusillade.'[47] A frenzied melee followed as the crowd of armed policeman fought their own senior officers to get at the dead man, crying, 'Kill him', 'Finish him up', 'Make an end to him.' The brawl lasted several minutes before discipline could be restored, and a doctor announced the outlaw was dead.[48]

While the police were busy brawling among themselves the other two robbers, seemingly forgotten, climbed over the cemetery wall at an unguarded spot and disappeared. The only trace police found of them were their coats, one with a bullet hole in one sleeve and the lining saturated with blood (suggesting one of the fugitives had been wounded). Unbeknown to the police the robbers entered the house of one Christopher Sprūdes at 48 Jamaica Street and exchanged their coats for two coats Mr. Sprūdes and his brother had left in the kitchen the night before.[49]

The dead gunman was identified as Edward Gutman, a Latvian who had come to the United States within the previous two years. Gutman was well known in the Latvian communities in South Boston, Roxbury and Jamaica Plain. After arriving in America he worked in a mica mine in New Hampshire, before moving to Massachusetts. In Boston he had worked for the metropolitan park force, killing gypsy moths in Middlesex Fells Reservation and had been promoted to foreman. Two of his friends in the gypsy moth crew Peter Plaude and Andrew Jekapson were fellow Latvians, and it was assumed they had been Gutman's accomplices in the saloon heist. A note written in Latvian found near Gutman's body in the cemetery was addressed to a Miss L. Mauren, at an address not far from the saloon that was robbed.[50] The woman, Leontine Mauren, was traced to 43 Union Avenue, Jamaica Plain, but was not to be found.

One of the two associates of Gutman had recently traveled to Philadelphia. Police discovered that on his return he and Gutman stayed in Jamaica Plain at the home of a local Latvian, John Walter. A Latvian newspaper called *Patiesiba* (Truth) was published from the same address. Police interviewed Walter, and learned that the men had no money, and had spoken of going out and committing highway robbery. According to Walter there had been five men present at the meeting.[51] The police concluded that Peter Plaude and Andrew Jekapson were the men who shot their way through the streets of Jamaica Plain. Plaude was 'the big man' who witnesses said did the shooting, and Jekapson resembled the other, who reloaded the pistols for his partner. Both men were Latvians, both in their twenties, with sandy hair. Both had spent time in Philadelphia.

The three men and Leontine Mauren were all said to be members of a Latvian anarchist organization that held meetings in Roxbury. Gutman was described in the press as the leader. Mauren was 'a believer in a violent form of anarchism',[52] who addressed their group, 'denouncing the treatment of the workers, and counseling murder when expedient.' Peter Plaude had come to the United States with his brother, and the brothers had lived in Jamaica Street, opposite the home of Christopher Spruhde, where the saloon robbers' coats were found. Eventually they and Leontine Mauren had moved into another address together. Peter Plaude and Andrew Jekapson started work on the Middlesex Fells Reservation and became friends with Gutman. As well as all being anarchists, the three men began raising money through long-shore scams, defrauding installment stores, buying furniture and clothing and reselling it without first paying the full amount. When the creditors demanded payment Plaude fled to Philadelphia and Leontine Mauren returned to her parents, before moving back to Jamaica Plain and moving in with her sister. Plaude returned from Philadelphia early in July 1908, and he and Jekabson were found rooms in Roxbury by Gutman.[53]

On 28 July 1908 the police announced in the press that there had been a fourth man at the raid on the saloon, standing guard outside. He was named as Peter Svare, 'a known associate of the three bandits, though not a member of the gypsy moth crew. Svare did not have the reputation for violence the others did, and police said they sought him as a witness rather than as a definite suspect...'[54]

The four had been 'expelled from their association several months earlier for their bloodthirsty views, and the fear that they would bring disrepute upon the law-abiding members.'[55]

In October 1908 Boston Police detectives traced Leontine Mauren and her sister Elizabeth to a lodging house in New York City, where they were working as dressmakers. Somewhat anti-climatically, given the lurid tales of violent anarchism printed in the *Boston Globe*, police issued a statement saying they were confident that the sisters had no information to provide regarding the case, and the matter was quietly dropped. Peter Plaude was reported to be in Russia, and Andrew Jekapson and Peter Svare were assumed to be there as well. The *Boston Globe* concluded sadly, 'it was likely that no arrests would ever be made in the case.'[56]

The investigation came to a halt but was re-opened five years later, when the Boston police announced that two fugitives involved in the Jamaica Plain shootings were dead. The events in London at Houndsditch and Sidney Street had happened three years before, but the Boston police had only recently been alerted to a possible connection. Acting on a tip from Boston's Latvian community, Inspector Thomas Lynch was dispatched to London to investigate the possibility that two of the three men who escaped from Boston were identical with the man accidentally shot at Houndsditch in 1910 (Hartmanis) and with Fricis Svars who had died fighting the British Army at Sidney Street. Lynch knew that both men were Latvians and anarchists, and both were known as criminals with many deaths on their hands. Lynch's investigation in London convinced him that Svars had killed Herbert Knox, the cemetery watchman, and that Gutman was not killed by his own hand or bullets fired by the Boston police, but had been killed by Hartmanis before he and Svars fled. Gutman had told his comrades that he could not keep up their pace, and Hartmanis killed him out of fear that Gutman might be captured and talk, though how he did so unnoticed by eighty-nine policemen in the cemetery is a mystery.

The source of Lynch's information was reported to be 'a woman who was associated with both men in London'.[57] According to her, Svars and Hartmanis had boasted of the raid on the saloon and the running shoot-out through the streets. She could not say where the crimes had occurred, but the details she gave were such that Inspector Lynch was confidant that the crimes she described and those that took place in Jamaica Plain were the same.[58] The woman in question was probably Lonny Jansone, whose husband Teodors Jansons told the City of London Police in February 1911 that 'about two years ago a reward of $20,000 was offered by the American police for the arrest of Fritz Svars for participation in a shooting outrage in Pennsylvania, USA'.[59] Clearly, the interest of the American police related instead to the events in Boston.

That Svars and Hartmanis were involved in the Jamaica Plain episode is corroborated by August Svinks, in a rather jumbled account collected in 1933 for the *Memorial to Fallen Fighters* but not included in the published book: '...they appeared in America (in Boston), but here they... didn't find any support (that's why they had a crisis), and then they decided to carry out one more expropriation in Jamaica Plain. This expropriation was successful, as earlier, one can say "with big leaves but small onions". The sum of money was small, but they made a lot of noise. They shot some policemen, a tram conductor, and five onlookers. The expropriators returned to Forest Hills Cemetery, where the wounded Hacen-ģeģeris [Gutman] ended his life himself. After that the remaining two managed to reach Beverley [a city in Essex County, Massachusetts]. There again they were surprised by the police when they were sleeping in the forest. The cleverness of the police did not exceed the ingenuity of the boys. The policemen went to sleep forever (they were killed). But Svars with his comrade left for Chicago... After that there were widespread arrests in Boston.'[60]

Next stop for Svars and Hartmanis was London, where they would be reunited with Žāklis, who was then in France, and where unbeknown to them they would reach the end of the line. But London in a way was also the place where it had all begun.

Notes

1 Janis Rainis, 'Lauztās priedes' (The Broken Pines), 1904 (*Kopti raksti*. I. sēj. Riga: Zinatne, 1977, p. 137).

2 Interviews with Ira Gruntmane, granddaughter of Anna Žākļe (Sakne) and Līvija Rēfelde, granddaughter of Kārļis Žāklis, Saldus, 5th June 2004.

3 Interview with Malvina Sakne (then aged 94) and Ira Gruntmane, Saldus, 30th May 2004.

4 LVVA, 4568/15/225, 'Letters from agents', #63a: Letter from the Head of Kiev *Okhranka* to the Head of the Special Department, 20th July 1912.

5 Files of the City of London Police, 'Houndsditch Murders', 534C/1.4, London Metropolitan Archives.

6 Ibid., Box 1.21/1a, b & c, op. cit. Pencil notes of information from an un-named informant, possibly Yosselevitch in France.

7 *Latvijas revolucionāro cīnītāju piemiņas grāmata.* I. Sēj: 2. daļa. (Riga, 1980), p. 133.

8 *New York Times*, 5th February, 1911.

9 The Žāklis photographs were first collected in the late 1920s by the Latvian Historical Society; originally a group of amateur enthusiasts, which in 1936 became a state institution, the *Latvijas vēstures institūts* (Latvian Institute of History). In 1927 one of its founders, Kārlis Beirebahs, published a book on the events of 1905.

10 The US Immigration Act of 1903, also called the Anarchist Exclusion Act, added four inadmissible categories to previous immigration regulations: anarchists, people with epilepsy, beggars and importers of prostitutes. The provisions relating to anarchists were expanded in the Immigration Act of 1918.

11 Interview with Dzidra Paeglite, Riga June 1989.

12 'Houndsditch Murders', Box 1.5a, op. cit. Statement of Jacob Peters, December 1910,

13 Ibid., Box 1.21.

14 *Revolucionārās cīņās kritušo piemiņas grāmata. 1. sēj: 1905. gada revolūcija* (Prometejs, Moscow, 1933), p. 267.

15 Juris Daberts, 'SVARS, Fricis, Frichelis', LVA, PA-36/5/198.

16 Marie Coady, *Unmasking the "Yeggmen".*

17 Ibid; Marie Coady, *Woburn: Hidden Tales of a Tannery Town* (Arcadia Publishing, 2008)

18 *The Scotsman*, 11th April 1908.

19 *The Motherwell Times*, 11th April 1908.

20 *Revolucionārās cīņās kritušo piemiņas grāmata. 2. sēj: 1907-1917* (Prometejs, Moscow, 1936), p. 397.

21 LSD Londonas nozares biedru grāmata (Membership book of the LSD London Branch). Glabājas LVA.

22 Līga Dūma & Dzidra Paeglīte, *Revolucionārie latviešu emigranti ārzemēs, 1897-1919,* (Rīga 1976). (Latvian revolutionary emigrants abroad, 1897-1919).

23 LSD Londonas nozares biedru grāmata, op. cit.

24 'Houndsditch Murders', Box 1.21/1a, b & c., op. cit. Pencil notes of information from an unnamed informant.

25 Ibid., 534C/1.2. Report from the Chief of the Marseille *Sûreté* to the Commissioner of the City of London Police, 20th January, 1911.

26 Ibid.

27 Ibid.

28 'Houndsditch Murders', Box 1.21/1a, b & c., op. cit. Pencil notes of information from an unnamed informant

29 Ibid., 534C/1.21. Pencil notes.

30 Ibid., Box 1.5 (b), Statement of Luba Milstein, 23 January 1911

31 LVVA, 4621/1/99 & 4621/1/69.

32 LVVA, 4621/1/99, #15.

33 LVVA, 4621/1/69, #93.

34 LVVA 4568/8/58.

35 Ibid.

36 LVVA, 4621/1/99, #10.

37   LVVA, 4621/1/69, #30.

38   The Party of Socialist Revolutionaries (SR), established in 1902 on a programme of democratic socialism, distinguished themselves from Marxist Social Democrats by looking to the rural peasantry rather than the industrial proletariat as the revolutionary class in Russia. The SR advocated the division of land among the peasants rather than collectivization under state management. A distinctive feature of SR tactics until 1909 was their tactic of assassinations of individual government officials.

39   The Latvian Social Democratic Union (*Latviešu sociāldemokrātu savienība* (LSS)); established in exile in the autumn of 1903 by Mikelis Valters and Ernests Rolavs. The LSS distinguished itself from the LSDSP by a more radical and nationalist program; demanding full autonomy for Latvia and proposing that the Russian empire be transformed into a federation of autonomous republics, and advocating the expropriation of Baltic German estates. The LSS affiliated themselves to the Russian SR in 1913, as the Latvian Revolutionary Socialist Party.

40   *Revolucionārās cīņās kritušo piemiņas grāmata. 1. sēj.* (Prometejs, Moscow, 1933), p. 257-8.

41   LVVA, 4568/8/60/127: Protocol No. 127.

42   LVVA, 4568/15/196, # 50.

43   LVVA, 4568/8/60/151.

44   *Boston Globe*, 22nd July 1908.

45   *Boston Globe*, 23rd July 1908.

46   Ibid.

47   *Boston Globe*, 24th July 1908.

48   Ibid.

49   Ibid.

50   *Boston Globe*, 25th July 1908.

51   *Boston Globe*, 26th July 1908.

52   *Boston Globe*, 27th July 1908.

53   Ibid.

54   *Boston Globe*, 28th July 1908.

55   *Boston Globe*, 29th July 1908.

56   *Boston Globe*, 30th October 1908. In a bizarre twist to the story, the Boston suspect Peter Plaude and his brother are likely to have been Pēteris and Alberts Plaudis, two notorious journalists from *Rīgas Avīze* who worked for the *Okhranka* in Latvia and London. In April 1908 the Plaudis brothers arrived in England and joined the London branch of the LSD, but were expelled from the group on 8th May 1908 after being exposed as spies. They returned to Riga but apparently moved to the USA. On 20th September 1911, *Rīgas Avīze* published a lurid article, 'Anarchists in Riga', reporting a meeting in the city of 16 social democrats who formed themselves into an Anarchist-Syndicalist group called *Liesma* and distributed copies of *Melnais Karogs* and a pamphlet by Kropotkin. An investigation by the *Okhranka* established that chief among the organisers was Pēteris Plaudis.

57   *Boston Globe*, 6th February 1914.

58   Ibid.

59   'Houndsditch Murders', ibid., 534C/1.4. Statement of Theodore Janson, 8th February 1911.

60   LVA, PA-36/5/198, #14: 490, Pencil notes by A. Svinks: 'Svars/Svarelis, Frichelis, Piter Painter, Peters'. August Svinks (born 1884) was a member of the LSDSP fighting organisation in 1905; in 1907 he emigrated to the USA, where he was reacquainted with Fricis Svars. His archive account, written 20 years after the event, rather bizarrely confuses the chronology of events and claims that Svars did not die in Sidney Street in 1911, but escaped to America where he carried out the expropriation in Jamaica Plain in 1908.

7

1897 to 1908
Foreigners, Anarchists and Vegetarians

They've got foreigners over there, Sir; and anarchists — and vegetarians, Sir; vegetarians!

Pub Barman[1]

In 1893 the Riga Mutual Aid Society of Lettish Handicraftsmen founded the newspaper *Dienas Lapa* (The Daily News), edited by Rainis, Pēteris Stučka and Jēkabs Kovaļevskis. The newspaper was the mouthpiece for what became known as the New Current (*Jaunā strāva*) movement. Believing that national consciousness alone was insufficient to improve the conditions of the industrial workers in Latvia, the New Current espoused a radical creed of socialism and internationalism that was heavily influenced by the ideas of Karl Marx. The Russian imperial government was nervous at the growth of the movement and in 1897, following strikes in all of the factories in Liepāja and Riga, cracked down and arrested 138 people. It was Latvia's first major political trial. Forewarned of the arrests, those most at risk fled abroad. From that point on London became the main focal point for Latvian emigration.

The decision to move the centre of agitation abroad was first considered in 1896, at a secret meeting of the New Current leadership held at the country house of Jēkabs Kovaļevskis in Zemgale during the summer solstice celebrations. As the situation in Latvia worsened in 1897 two representatives of the movement, Hermanis Punga and Dāvids Bundža, were dispatched abroad with instructions to set up a printing press in London. After a difficult journey across Lithuania and Germany the two men arrived in Hamburg and boarded a crowded steam ship for London. Punga describes their arrival in London:

'On the fourth day the steam ship enters the mouth of the Thames, ahead we can see a thick cloud of fog — the seamen say that it is London. Only in the evening we reached London. It became clear that we shall be allowed to leave the ship only the next morning. The ship is still moving. A terrible, heavy mood. We went to bed. In the morning we were woken by a terrible noise. Screams, whistling and the screeching of chains. We quickly wash our faces and rush on deck. It is cloudy and drizzling. All around we can see sombre grey buildings, the ship has cast anchor in the middle of the river. At a distance we can see several bridges, among them one with big towers at both ends — the famous Tower Bridge. We watch the banks of the river for a long time. We are amazed at the multitude of people and traffic. A little steam boat takes us ashore. Once on the ground, we don't know in which direction to go. We only have seven shillings, which we received after exchanging our last ten German marks on board the ship. In our pockets we have recommendation letters to Polish socialists in Beaumont Square, Mile End Road. But we have no idea where this square is and how to find it. We turned to a grey-haired old man. This man pointed at some

85

lifeless statue in the middle of the street, next to a big street lantern. We approached it and it turned out to be a policeman. We asked again for Beaumont Square. But he didn't understand, stretched out the palm of his hand and made as if he was writing on it with a finger of his other hand. We guessed that we should write the address down. I pulled out the recommendation letter and gave it to the policeman… Taking the letter, the policeman waved to us to come along with him — we became uneasy, thinking he was taking us to the police department. We trudged along with him for a couple of blocks, until we came across the same man in dark uniform also standing in the middle of the street; that man receives the recommendation letter and leads us further. Thus we were led for over an hour and passed on from hands to hands by at least ten policemen, while the last one stopped in front of some building and knocked on the door with a metal tube which was hanging next to it.

'The door opened, the letter received from the policeman, and then we heard in clear Russian: "Vy iz Rossii? Zachodite!" (Are you from Russia? Come in!)

'The English policeman said a smiling good-bye and we go inside the chief publishing house and representation of the Polish Socialist Party.'[2]

As the first recorded meeting between Latvian revolutionaries and London policemen, this quaint encounter stands in marked contrast to the violent confrontation at Houndsditch thirteen years later; two episodes separated by the revolution of 1905 and the savage repression which followed. The corresponding change in attitude towards uniformed police officers is not difficult to appreciate in this context.

Punga and his comrade were made welcome by the Poles, who were eager to hear about the Latvian movement and did their best to help them; but when news arrived from Latvia about the mass arrests which had taken place after the men's escape their plans seemed to be in ruins: 'The organisation was demolished, and we could forget about receiving money for the printing press. We had to start looking for work.'[3] Punga found work in a factory, but Dāvids Bundža fell seriously ill. Doctors diagnosed tuberculosis and advised him to leave London as soon as possible. With the help of the Poles, who collected the money for his travel costs, Bundža left for America. He settled in Boston, where his health recovered and in 1898 Bundža became the editor of the first Latvian Marxist monthly, *Auseklis* (The Morning Star), before dying in 1901. Punga remained in London, living in Hanbury Street, Whitechapel, and working as a typesetter for the Polish Socialist Party printing house. In his free time he visited the London Docks and got to know some sailors who regularly travelled to Riga, through whom he began sending socialist literature into Latvia.

The smuggling was boosted by the arrival in London of Ernest Minka, a worker from Liepāja, who seemed especially adept at persuading sailors to take on the role of courier. The Latvians also received help from the small group of émigré Germans who ran the Communist Working Men's Club and Institute (the Communist Club) in Charlotte Street, not far from the British Museum. More assistance was forthcoming from the older Russian émigrés grouped around the *Fond Vol'noj Russkoj Pressy* (Fund of the Free Russian Press) in Hammersmith, who Punga says 'on many occasions were very obliging to Latvian refugees, as well as helping to send literature to the Baltics before we developed our own well-organised, working "transportation apparatus".[4]

The Friends of Russian Freedom and the Free Russia Press, founded in London in 1890 by Sergius Stepniak (Kravchinski) and Felix Volkovsky, was the focal point for all of the prominent exiles in the early Russian revolutionary movement; not least the anarchist Peter Kropotkin. 'Which one of us had not read Stepniak's *Underground Russia*', says Punga, 'in which he in such a breathtaking way depicted Peter Kropotkin and his daring escape from a prison hospital in Petersburg…'[5] Punga says that he first saw Kropotkin in 1898, at an anarchist event at the Athenaeum Hall:

'Emigrants had turned out in large numbers. When Kropotkin appeared on stage, he was greeted with loud applause. He was accompanied to the stage by a small grey-haired old woman — the well-known communard of the Paris Commune in 1871 Louise Michel, and an Italian anarchist leader Malatesta. The public was carried away by Kropotkin's speech; it left a great impression on the audience. Official speeches were followed by an informal tea reception in the evening. Our Latvian group attracted special interest of the old Russian revolutionary, who in a special table address greeted the young comrades in the battle against tsarist autocracy. I got to know Kropotkin closer at the house of a well-known Tolstoy admirer Chertkov, to which I later moved. Kropotkin often visited Chertkov to listen to the latest material produced by Tolstoy, which he received directly from Tolstoy for publication and filing in the Tolstoy archives. Kropotkin greatly admired Tolstoy's talent, but he was also a great opponent of Tolstoy's theory of non-violence (non-resistance to evil). Chertkov tried to counter Kropotkin's criticisms and unflinchingly defended Tolstoy's teachings of Christian anarchism. Often the discussions of these two heart-felt friends ended in furious conflicts, which threatened to put an end to their personal relationship, and a lot of effort was required from everybody who was present, to calm down these old, excessively fervent opponents — until the next theoretical discussion and a clash of views.'[6]

The small group of Latvian émigrés around Punga, swelled by the arrival of fresh political refugees from Latvia, attracted sympathisers from among the English socialists too, including J. Ramsay MacDonald (a future Prime Minister), and Ben Tillet and Tom Mann, two leaders of the London dock workers strike in 1899. But it was the 'Tolstoy admirer', Count Vladimir Chertkov, who played the crucial role in realising Punga's dream of a Latvian press in England.

A millionaire and distinguished cavalry officer in the Life Guards, Chertkov met Leo Tolstoy in Moscow in October 1883, and thenceforth devoted his life to promoting the moral self-improvement of the Russian people, organizing and financing a publishing house that offered cheaply produced books on art and moralizing literature. In 1896 he was forced to leave Russia on the orders of the Minister of Internal Affairs and the Procurer of the Holy Synod, for the crime of being a signatory to a letter, to which Tolstoy had added a supporting postscript, protesting at the treatment of the Dukhobors (a pacifist religious sect that rejected secular government and refused to perform military service), which was delivered to the tsar. Chertkov was first exiled to Estonia, but after the intervention of his influential mother, Elizaveta (born the Countess Chernysheva-Kruglikova), he was allowed to go to England, where his mother lived in Bournemouth, and was appointed as Tolstoy's literary executor. At first Chertkov settled just outside Croydon, on Duppas Hill, before moving to Hill Farm in Purleigh, near Maldon, close to a Tolstoyan land colony at Cock Clarks in Essex. At Purleigh, Chertkov established a printing press to continue his work, the Free Age Press, producing cheap English language editions of Tolstoy and illegal unabridged Russian editions, which were smuggled into Russia where Tolstoy's writing was otherwise subject to strict censorship. Needing Russian-speaking typesetters for this work, Chertkov recruited Punga (then still working at the Polish printing house) and brought him to Purleigh. Chertkov and Punga became good friends, and the Latvian soon managed to arrange for his comrade, Ernests Rolavs, to be employed as a home-teacher with the Chertkov family. More importantly, Chertkov offered to lend Punga money for the purchase of Latvian type and the setting up of a Latvian printing press.

In 1899 a new wave of strikes engulfed Latvia. All the Liepāja sea port workers were on strike, as well as the workers of the jute factory in Riga, and many other enterprises. The measures taken against the strikers produced another exodus to London, including Fridrihs Vesmanis and Fricis Roziņš: 'I met them both at the flat of our Latvian circle [in Walthamstow]; they were both absolutely exhausted by their difficult escape journey. Latvian sailors had hidden them under the main boiler on board some English steamer in the Port of Riga, where they had to lie several days in impossible heat, surrounded on all sides by coal and without any food. Only when the coal in the boiler room had been used up, there was an opportunity to transfer and hide them in the coal bunker. When they arrived in London, they were literally 'black like devils'.[7]

Their arrival brought Punga the necessary editorial staff to begin setting up the printing press. Punga brought Vesmanis to Purleigh to meet Chertkov, who coughed up the money to order Latvian type from Leipzig. Then he wrote to the Latvian émigrés in Switzerland and agreed to start publishing an organ of the Latvian Social-Democratic Union of Western Europe *Latviešu strādnieks* (Latvian Worker).

Fricis Roziņš in Purleigh was elected as editor, but the Swiss group insisted on also electing an editorial collegium, consisting of themselves, to oversee all theoretical articles before publication. The arrangement led to bitter conflict between the Londoners and the Swiss group, as well as causing a split among the social-democrats in Latvia. Punga and his group viewed the Swiss collegium's control over articles as censorship, and complained that corrections made in Switzerland were unacceptable in London, where they had to be corrected again and sent to Switzerland for a second time, producing delays and hampering production of the paper. The whole thing escalated to the point of voting on whether to give a free hand to the editor and leave the printing press in England, or move it to Switzerland. The Swiss group won the vote and the *Latvian Worker* ceased publication after its eighth issue. As the man financing the whole enterprise, Chertkov was forced to step in and inform the Swiss group that he had lent the money to the Latvians at Purleigh, not Switzerland. If they wished to take over the printing press they must repay the loan within six months. All the Latvian type was duely boxed-up and prepared for despatch to Switzerland. Punga's group were forced to take another loan from Chertkov and buy new type from Leipzig. When the new type arrived, they resumed publication under a new name, *Sociāldemokrāts* (Social Democrat).

At the end of 1899, Chertkov moved his printing house to Christchurch, near Bournemouth, where he had bought a number of houses. The largest of them, Tuckton House, housed the Free Age Press, and with twenty bedrooms became home to an odd colony of pacifist Tolstoyans, English socialists and Latvian revolutionaries, with as many as thirty people living there at any one time. The Tucton House community even had its own football team, Tuckton Football Club. Punga was entrusted with the management of the printing house, while a Polish socialist, Stanislav Vojtsehovsky (Punga's roommate at Purleigh, later the President of Poland) became the chief printer.

In 1901 the *Social Democrat* printing press transferred to London, where the Latvians entered into collaboration with a group of Russian socialists who produced a journal called *Zhizn* (Life). A congress followed at the beginning of 1902, with the impossible aim of uniting the warring factions within the Russian socialist movement. A platform was printed in thousands of copies, and the task of smuggling it into Russia was entrusted to Punga. Unfortunately for Punga, spies of the Russian government had kept everyone who attended the congress under surveillance. Travelling on an English passport under the name Jackson, Punga was arrested as soon as he arrived in Russian Poland and imprisoned in Warsaw. It took the Russian police six months to discover Punga's real name. He was then transferred to Riga prison and convicted to eight years' hard labour in eastern Siberia.

Thanks to the outbreak of the Russo-Japanese war, the exile of political prisoners to the Far East was suspended. Instead Punga was sent to Olonetsk province, where after two years in prison he was allowed to live in the forests of the province. His Russian comrades sent a considerable amount of money to the Riga organisation for his liberation, and with this help he managed to escape to the north of Finland. Resisting the temptation to cross over into Norway, Punga moved secretly to Riga and stayed there for a month, before a smuggler led him across the border to Germany. From there he went to Switzerland, where he met Lenin, who provided him with money to return to England.

In Punga's absence Chertkov recruited another Latvian to work at Tuckton House as a translator, a gifted linguist called Alexander Zirnis (Sasha). Zirnis was born in Limbaži (Lemsal), 90 km northeast of Riga, but left Latvia in 1903 to avoid conscription into the Russian army and because of weak health. On the advice of his doctor he went to America, where he worked (as A. Brady) on a ranch in the warmer climes of San Jose, on the outskirts of San Francisco. The offer of work from Chertkov brought Zirnis to England in 1904. As well as joining the staff of the Free Age Press, and in 1908 becoming manager of Tuckton House, Zirnis rather belatedly became a member of the Latvian Social Democracy on 29 December 1906. He was also active in English socialist circles, where he was much in demand as a journalist and translator, and in 1909 he married an English woman called Gertrude Stedman; he succumbed to tuberculosis and died in 1918, aged only 37.[8] Their eldest daughter, Melita "Letty" Norwood (born on 25th March 1912), was very helpful in the late 1980s during the early research for this book. She later achieved unexpected notoriety in 1999 when she was exposed by an article in *The Times* as a long-time 'atom spy' for the KGB.[9] Letty Norwood remembered that everything Tolstoy wrote was sent to Tuckton House, where the manuscripts were kept in a special room: 'At one stage they were put in boxes, by a window, with a ladder and folks handy. If fire broke out the first thing was to save these manuscripts. Then Chertkov got a special place built; keeping the temperature right, and a grill to get in — only certain folks were allowed in — and thick walls…'[10]

At the beginning of 1906, using another British passport, Punga went back to Riga, where he witnessed the repression at first hand. The city was surrounded by General Orlov's punitive troops, and Punga had to change flats almost every night to avoid arrest. In the end the 'passport bureau of the Riga organisation' provided him with a new internal passport and Punga moved to Petersburg. From there he set out for Helsinki, but when he crossed the Finnish border news broke about the sensational raid on the State Bank by Latvian fighters, and Punga wisely changed his travel plans and, with the help of Finnish revolutionaries, returned to England via Stockholm. In the 1920s and 30s Punga enjoyed a distinguished career as Foreign Minister and diplomat in the government of the Latvian Republic. He was arrested after the Soviet occupation of 1940 and died in Riga Central Prison on 12 April 1941.

Back at Tuckton House Punga drew on the experiences of his recent trip to Latvia to write *The Revolution in the Baltic Provinces of Russia*, the first and best contemporary account of the 1905 Revolution from a Latvian perspective. Published anonymously by the English Independent Labour Party in 1907 (with a forward by Ramsay MacDonald) as the work of "An Active Member", the book's authorship remained a mystery until 1988, when information from Letty Norwood, whose father, Alexander Zirnis, translated the book into English, confirmed Punga as the author.[11]

The collapse of the 1905 uprising produced a new diaspora, swelling the Latvian communities in Stepney, Tottenham, Walthamstow and Leytonstone. These new emigrants found work as seamen or in the docks, in the sweat shops of the East End, or the rubber factories of Tottenham and Poplar. In Christchurch, Tuckton House received a new influx of Latvians, among them Dāvids Birkmanis, Juris Daberts and Jēkabs Kovaļevskis, leading members of the LSDSP who were all actively occupied with sending illegal arms shipments to Latvia.[12]

The curious situation of this hard-core of Latvian gun-runners happily co-habiting Tuckton House with Chertkov's motley collection of vegetarian pacifists brings to mind a comical scene from the 1960 film *The Siege of Sidney Street*, where the plucky investigating detective on the trail of the Houndsditch gang is warned by a barman in the pub opposite the anarchist club: 'They've got foreigners over there, Sir; and anarchists — and vegetarians, Sir; *vegetarians!*'[13] The main player in the Latvian gun-running operation was Jānis Žāklis' comrade-in-arms from the attack on the Riga secret police and Helsinki bank robbery, Kristaps Salniņš (Grishka).

In May 1906, Kristaps Salniņš returned to the Baltic and resumed operations with the Forest Brothers partisans in the Grobiņ-Liepāja area. Salniņš was arrested but escaped after some days to Petersburg, where he represented the

Latvian fighters in the RSDLP fighting technical group. Most of the group's work was concerned with procuring and distributing arms. In the summer of 1906 two Lewis machine guns were stolen from the Petersburg Officers' School, one of which was sent to Riga but didn't arrive. In August Salniņš sent the Riga fighting organisation a consignment of dynamite and 30 Japanese grenades for use with a launcher.

In the autumn of 1906, the fighting technical group despatched Salniņš back to Riga, but once there he came under police surveillance and had to move to Liepāja. There he narrowly escaped capture again, in January 1907, when (according to the Russian Consul in London), '...in Liepāja researches were made by the police, during which a man escaped from that house. The police found in that house the stamp of the Liepāja section of the Social-Democratic Fighting Organisation. The escaped man was called Jan Sproge and had the nickname "Grishka".'[14] The wanted man was Kristaps Salniņš, a man the Courland police and Riga *Okhranka* were more than eager to apprehend: 'One of the most important revolutionaries in the Baltics... who has committed a whole number of murders and burglaries, and twice escaped from police.'[15] Salniņš, with his girlfriend, Otīlija Leščinska (Tija), and another comrade, Fricis Cirulis, went quietly by sea to Hamburg, and from there to Geneva and London. Tija Leščinska had known Salniņš since 1902, when they had both been students at the Benjamin Bluhm art school in Riga. Her family was wealthy (and rumoured to be descended from Katherine the Great) but socialist in outlook, and all of them supported the 1905 revolution. Tija had been in charge of a rented flat in central Riga which the Fighting Organisation used for conspiratorial meetings. But in the autumn of 1906 she was arrested by the police and subjected to prolonged interrogation and torture before eventually being released without charge. In London she earned a living by giving private art lessons, while working as a gun-runner with Salniņš until 1908.[16]

The trio returned to Petersburg in March 1907 and worked again with the fighting technical group.

One day in the spring of 1907 sympathetic railwaymen, sorting through rolling stock in the sidings near Petersburg, discovered a railway wagon full of rifles originally intended for use in the Russo-Japanese war. The wagon had been shunted to and fro so much that the authorities had lost track of it and the guns had lain overlooked until then. Salniņš quickly made sure they were unloaded and spirited away. The fighting technical group also maintained a bomb making school in the city. But persistent police surveillance forced the transfer of these activities to Finland: first to Kokkala, where Lenin was living as Erwin Veikov, then to a rented dacha just outside Kolomyag on the Russian border. Salniņš, whose cover had been blown in Petersburg, and other Latvians who had collected there, were enthusiastic students at the school, where they and Lenin also practised shooting in the woods. An incident in which a Finnish border guard was killed led to the capture of several of the Latvians, and an attempt to free them failed. The school had to be abandoned. Wanted now in Latvia, Russia, and Finland, Salniņš was on the move again: 'In summer 1907 on instructions from the FTG and with a mandate from the Central Committee, I became the representative of the group, and with Vladimir Ilyich Lenin's signature, I had to go to England and Belgium for arms. In England we were to get weapons from the Latvian Social-Democrats through their representative in England Kovaļevskis (Kundziņš).'[17]

Salniņš arrived in London in August. His first shipment of Mausers and Brownings was sent direct to Petersburg ('transported by our sailors').[18] But the second consignment went to his parent's address in Riga, aboard the steamship *Grand Duke Mikhail Aleksandrovich*. The navigating officer of the ship was a Latvian Social Democrat, Jānis Trautmanis, a swashbuckling figure renowned for his exploits as Captain of the *John Grafton* in an earlier, but ill-fated, gun-running expedition to the Baltic in September 1905.[19] In Riga, Salniņš' sister Katya was one of those who took charge of the weapons.

In December 1907 the arrest of almost all of the fighting technical group in Petersburg caused the group's activity to be suspended indefinitely. Salniņš was stranded in London, 'without work or means — all addresses have been "blown" and new ones haven't been set up yet.'[20] The group was also fighting for its existence within the Party. Salniņš, called to Germany for consultations, wrote at the time: 'From what I heard today, the C.C. has adopted a resolution regarding the disbandment. Thus the period of arming is over and all our great efforts, expenses and risks have gone to waste. It's sad, but what can we do. For a time I'll stick with the transportation of literature ... the Russians publish two newspapers in Geneva.'[21]

Without money, and with the Party now officially disavowing the fighting organisation, Salniņš, who in 1905 had not waited for the LSDSP to arm before forming his own fighting group in Riga, must have seriously considered the matter of resuming expropriations on his own authority. On 20th March 1908, he wrote from Brussels to a meeting of the Berlin LSD group: 'I can't be there personally but I ask the meeting to insert this separate point in the agenda about this year's 4 March lecture (on expropriations). Having been at this lecture I found something extraordinary. In this lecture the lecturer consciously or unconsciously provoked several group members in front of a wide audience. Not only that, but the lecturer in his summing up mischievously compromised the very group itself by saying "I know that in our group there are three to four times more members that support expropriations..." Taking into account the very varied cross section of the audience, and Germany's oppressive police conditions (especially against foreigners) I move that the Comrade lecturer be censured for careless behaviour, i.e. reckless compromising of other members of the group in front of people in the audience who are not members.'[22]

The 'careless behaviour' of comrades who talked too openly about expropriations was only one of Salniņš's problems. Writing from London, on the eve of a dangerous mission to Russia at the end of May 1908 (seven weeks after the Motherwell bank robbery), he steeled himself for what lay ahead: '... at this very moment they're after me in Riga. My father and mother have been arrested and have already spent five days with the secret police. My sister, who was in Petersburg, was picked up on the way back to Riga. We've been beset by great failures in Riga and Petersburg. I can't imagine how it will all end. Still one can't let one's soul cry. Now is the revolution, and the revolution knows no pity.'[23]

The desperate plight of Salniņš, hounded by the secret police and living a precarious hand-to-mouth existence abroad, was shared by all of the émigré Latvian revolutionaries in London. And desperate times produce desperate actions.

Notes

1   Dialogue from the film *The Siege of Sidney Street* (Monty Berman & Jimmy Sangster, 1960)

2   Hermanis Punga, *Revolucionārā kustība Latvijā, atmiņas un materiāli I* (*Latvijas Vēstures Pestīšanas Biedrības Raksti No. 1*), Rīga 1927, pp. 19-40.

3   Ibid.

4   Ibid.

5   Ibid.

6   Ibid.

7   Ibid.

8   Interview with Melita Norwood, London 28th June, 1988.

9   David Burke, *The Spy Who Came In From the Co-op*, (The Boydell Press, London 2008).

10   Interview with Melita Norwood, op. cit.

11   Ibid.

12   The activities of the Latvian gun-runners in England resulted in nine English and Scots socialists being prosecuted and fined for illegal possession of ammunition after 150,000 Mauser rounds were discovered in raids in Sunderland, Newcastle, Glasgow and Edinburgh in the spring of 1907. A mysterious 'German', most probably the Latvian Social Democrat Alfred Nagel, said to be the prime mover in the conspiracy, escaped.

13   Dialogue from the film *The Siege of Sidney Street*, op. cit.

14   Files of the City of London Police, 'Houndsditch Murders', 534G/3.15, Imperial Russian Consul General in London to Superintendent J. Ottaway, 1911, London Metropolitan Archives.

15   LVVA, 4569/1/373 , 'File of 1907, List No. 27 of the Courland Gendarmerie about the Revolutionary Movement in the Kuldiga area.'

16   In 1909 Otīlija "Tija" Leščinska (1884-1923) moved to Petersburg to concentrate on higher education and studied at the Art School of the Royal Society for Promotion of the Arts, specialising in painting and ceramics. Tija returned to Riga in 1917 and worked as a clerk and an artist. She died tragically and in mysterious circumstances, apparently by drowning in the Imatra rapids in Finland while on holiday in 1923. Her body was recovered from the river fully-clothed, on 14th September, after some days in the water; her face was unrecognisable and her hair gone. Her family always believed that Tija had gone to Finland, supposedly to meet a 'German engineer', to meet Kristaps Salniņš. Friends and family conducted a prolonged investigation with the Latvian and Finnish authorities, but nothing was ever proven. Information from Tija's niece, Silvija Freinberga, Riga, 19th September 2017.

17   Kristaps Salniņš , 'Deyatelnost latshkogo boevika v peterburge' (A Latvian Fighter's Activity in Petersburg), S. M. Pozner (ed.), *Pervaya boevaya organizatsiya bolshevikov* (The First Fighting Organisation of the Bolsheviks), Moscow 1934, p. 207.

18   Ibid.

19   This episode was the subject of a feature film, *Gaidiet „Džonu Graftonu"* (Waiting for the "John Grafton"), Rīgas kinostudijā 1979, directed by Andris Rozenbergs. See also Michael Futrell, *Northern Underground* (Faber & Faber, London, 1963), pp. 66-84.

20   LVA, PA-2/1/7/108, Letter from Salniņš.

21   Ibid, nr. 61.

22   Ibid, nr. 31.

23   Ibid, nr. 201.

CITY OF LONDON POLICE.

MURDER OF POLICE OFFICERS.

£500 REWARD

WHEREAS Sergeants Charles Tucker and Robert Bentley, and Constable Walter Charles Choat, of the City of London Police, were murdered in Exchange Buildings, in the said City, at 11.30 p.m., on the 16th December, 1910, by a number of persons who were attempting to feloniously break and enter a Jeweller's Shop, and killed the officers to prevent arrest, and whereas, THREE PERSONS whose descriptions, etc., are given below, are wanted for being concerned in committing the said crime, viz. :

FIRST. A MAN known as PETER PIATKOW, alias SCHTERN, alias "PETER THE PAINTER," age 28 to 30 years, height 5 feet 9 or 10 inches, complexion sallow, clear skin, hair and medium moustache black, otherwise clean shaven, eyes dark, medium build, reserved manner. Dress, brown tweed suit (broad dark stripes), black overcoat (velvet collar rather old), black hard felt hat, black lace boots, rather shabby. A native of Russia, an Anarchist.

PORTRAIT OF THE SAID PETER PIATKOW.

SECOND.— A MAN who gave the name of JOE LEVI, probably false, age 27 to 29 years, height 5 feet 6 or 7 inches, hair dark, supposed clean shaven, complexion somewhat pale, full round face, thickish lips, medium build, erect carriage. Dress, black overcoat, dark tweed cap. Foreign appearance, speaks fairly good English.

THIRD.— A WOMAN, age 26 to 30 years, height 5 feet 6 or 7 inches, fairly full breasts, sallow complexion, face somewhat drawn, eyes blue, hair brown. Dress, dark three-quarter jacket and skirt, white blouse, large black hat (trimmed black silk), light-coloured shoes. Foreign appearance.

The above reward of £500 will be paid by the Commissioner of Police for the City of London to any person who shall give such information as shall lead to the arrest of these three persons, or in proportion to the number of such persons who are arrested.

Information to be given to the City Police Office, 26, Old Jewry, London, E.C., or at any Police Station.

City Police Office,
26, Old Jewry, London, E.C.,
30th January, 1911.

J. W. NOTT BOWER,
Commissioner of Police for
the City of London.

WERTHEIMER, LEA & CO., Printers, Worship Street, London, E.C.

1. Wanted poster offering £500 reward for information leading to the arrest of Peter Piatkov, alias Schtern, alias "Peter the Painter". City of London Police, 30 January 1911.

2. The Žāklis family at Svites. (left to right): Peter the Painter's father Jānis Žāklis Sr. and older siblings Katrīna, Anna, Šarlote-Marija and Kārlis.

3. Peter the Painter's older brother, Kārlis Žāklis.

4. Peter the Painter's youngest sister, Milda Žākle.

5. Three generations at Svitēs:
Lote (Šarlote) Tālberga (centre),
with her daughter Margarieta
Tālberga-Žākle in the foreground
leaning on her lap on the right;
behind her granddaughters Anna,
Katrīna and Šarlote-Marija; in the
foreground on the left,
granddaughter Milda.

6. Peter the Painter's uncle,
Juris Žāklis in Bobruisk.

7. Jānis Žāklis after his arrest
in Bobruisk on 28 May 1904.

Въ Курляндское Губернское Жандармское 116.
Управленіе

Политическаго поднадзор-
наго Ивана Иванова Жакл

Прошеніе.

Въ виду того что по дорогѣ изъ г. Минска въ г.
Вольмарь я простудился и болѣзнь моя осложни-
лась, такъ что ѣхать туда нѣтъ у меня фи-
зической возможности, а проживать тамъ
я не могу за неимѣніемъ средствъ; въ виду
также этого что по дѣлу, возбужденному
Минскимъ Губернскимъ Жандармскимъ
Управленіемъ, назначенъ мнѣ залогъ и я из-
бралъ мѣстомъ жительства, въ чемъ и далъ
оному Жандармскому Управленію подписку,
арендуемую отцомъ усадьбу "Абель" Курлянд-
ской губ, Тальсенскаго уѣзда Бринкъ—Педва-
ленской волости, прошу Курляндское Жандармское управленіе учредить надо мной
надзоръ у полиціи Мѣстечка Цабельнъ, ко-
торое отстоитъ отъ усадьбы Абель на шесть
верстъ

Иванъ Ивановъ Жакл.

усадьба Абель
октября мѣсяца 7го дня 1904 года

8. Letter (in Russian) from Jānis Žāklis to the Directorate of
Gendarmerie for Courland Province, 7 October 1904.

9. Kristaps Salniņš (Grishka) and Otīlija Leščinska (Tija),
Riga, *c.* 1905.

10. Kārlis Gertners, the son of Jānis Žāklis'
sister, Šarlote-Marija. At the end of WW2,
Kārlis joined the *Mežabrāļi* (Forest Brothers)
to fight against the second Soviet
occupation of Latvia. He disappeared
without trace.

11. Ģederts Eliass.

12. Riga central police station in 1906.

13. Fighting group, 1906 (left to right): Kristaps Salniņš, Kārlis Čoke, Gustavs Lackis and Jānis Žāklis.

14. Jānis Žāklis in America as Tālbergs.

15. "From the family album in Australia": Jānis Žāklis, Mērnieks, c. 1905-1906.

16. Anna Caune (Amalija Grosvald, alias Milda).

17. Stabu iela 65, 1906.

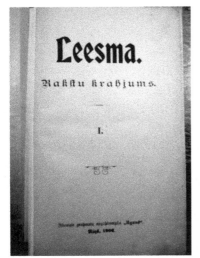

18. The first volume of the anarchist journal *Liesma* — *Rakstu Krājums* (The Flame — Collection of Articles), Riga 1906. The journal was edited by Jānis Žāklis, Mērnieks.

19. Confiscated arms and literature, Riga 1906, including volumes I and II of *Liesma*.

20. Jānis Žāklis in America, 1906. The famous
studio pose which appeared on the London
wanted poster in 1911.

21. Another Jānis Žāklis, the son of Peter the Painter's brother Kārlis, seen here in Latvian army uniform, 1936. After the first Soviet occupation of Latvia in 1940 he was arrested and sent to Siberia, where he died.

22. Fricis Svars in London, 1910.

23. Jānis Žāklis (centre) surrounded by workmates on-board ship, Marseille c.1908-1909.

24. Jānis Žāklis (middle row, second from the right) striking a serious pose in the midst of a group of laughing workmates at L'Estaque (Marseille).

25. Hermanis Punga (in white hat) and Aleksandrs Zirnis at Tuckton House, Christchurch, near Bournemouth, 13 May 1907.

26. Jānis Palamieks (Bifšteks) and Jānis Celiņš (John Rosen).

27. Aleksandrs Zirnis with Tolstoy's grandchildren, Lulu (Ilya) and Sonia, sitting on his knees. Around them, visiting Latvian Social Democrats from London (left to right): Juris Daberts, Jēkabs Kovaļevskis, Davids Birkmanis and Jānis Ozols (Zars). Tucton House 23 September, 1907.

29. Juris Laiviņš (George Dubov).

28. Jānis Celiņš (John Rosen) in
London, 1911.

30. Juris Laiviņš (George Dubov)
after his arrest in London, 22
December, 1910.

31. Alfrēds Dzirkalis (Karl
Hoffman) after his arrest in
London, 17 February, 1911.

33. Nina Vasiļjeva (Minna Griķīs, or Griķītis) after her arrest in London, 17 February, 1911.

32. Jēkabs Peterss in London, 1910.

34. Hartmanis in the mortuary, December 1910.

35. Hartmanis. Mortuary photograph of "George Gardstein" used by the City of London police on a wanted poster, 22 December, 1910, when they were trying to identify him.

36. Issue No. 5 of the Latvian anarchist-communist organ *Brīvība* (Freedom, 1908-1913), published in August 1910, was edited by Jānis Žāklis in Paris and Fricis Svars in London.

37. *Melnais Karogs* (Black Flag; 1911-1914).

CITY POLICEMEN MURDERED BY ALIEN BURGLARS.

THE TERRIBLE MIDNIGHT SCENE IN EXCHANGE BUILDINGS, HOUNDSDITCH, WHERE THREE POLICEMEN WERE MURDERED AND TWO WOUNDED BY REVOLVER SHOTS FIRED BY FOREIGNERS, WHO ARE SUPPOSED TO HAVE BEEN ATTEMPTING A BURGLARY ON NEIGHBOURING PREMISES.

Sketched by a " Daily Graphic " Artist from materials supplied by an eye-witness of the outrage.

38. A contemporary artist's impression of the Houndsditch shootings. *The Daily Graphic*, 19 December, 1910.

39. Exchange Buildings the morning after the shooting.

40. Fricis Svars' last letter to his father, written in Sidney Street, giving his carefully couched account of events prior to the siege.

41. The last resting place of Fricis Svars and William Sokolov (Joseph): grave 42311, square 338, lying close to bed 2092 in what is now part of the memorial garden at the Corporation of London Cemetery, Manor Park.

42. The son of Fricis Svars. Alfred Driscoll
with his mother, Luba Milstein, in America.

43. Alfrēds Dzirkalis (Mazais)
in America.

44. Alfrēds Dzirkalis with stepson Alfred Driscoll (the son
of Fricis Svars) in Peekskill, Westchester County, New
York., USA.

45. Jānis Celiņš (John Rosen) with his wife Rose in Australia, sometime in the 1940s or 1950s.

46. John Rosen's hairdresser and tobacconist shop (today a Pizza parlour) on Ford Street, Beechworth, Australia.

47. Funeral notice: 'Veteran of the 1905 struggle, Jānis Rozens (Celiņš), born in Riga on 12 October 1884, died in Beechworth on 9 October 1956'. Underneath is a verse from the Rainis poem, *Lauztās priedes* (The Broken Pines). Published by the Beechworth Latvians in *Austrālijas Latvietis*, October 1956.

48. Jēkabs Peterss with his English family on the eve of his departure to Russia, 1 May, 1917.

49. Jēkabs Peterss with Lenin in Red Square at the funeral of Yakov Sverdlov. Moscow, 18 March, 1919.

50. "Extraordinary Commissar fulfilling special assignments". Jēkabs Peterss in his office during the defence of Petrograd, June 1919. Note the pistol resting next to the telephones.

51. Jēkabs Peterss with Mikhail Kedrov (third person unknown) relaxing on the
Pulkovo Heights during the defence of Petrograd, May 1919.

52. Jēkabs Peterss and members of his defence staff on the Pulkovo Heights
outside Petrograd, May 1919.

53. Antonina Zakharovna Dmitrieva,
Jēkabs Peterss' second wife, April 1920.

54. Jēkabs Peterss with his son Igor.

55. Jēkabs Peterss talks to news correspondents from *Pravda*, 19 November, 1929.

56. Antonina Peters, Moscow 1980.

57. Igor Peters. When the NKVD arrested Jēkabs Peterss in 1937 they confiscated all photographs in which he appeared. Igor's mother was forced to cut the image of her husband out of family photos, like this one, in order to save some pictures of her son.

58. Facing death. Jēkabs Peterss after his arrest by the NKVD in 1937.

59. Igor Peters after his arrest by the NKVD, 6 November, 1947.

61. Maisie Peters after her release from the Gulag.

60. Maisie Peters after her arrest by the NKVD, 17 January, 1949.

62. Kristaps Salniņš and Ivan Vinarov in Moscow, 1930.

63. "Christopher Lauberg". Kristaps Salniņš in Beijing, 1925.

65. Kristaps Salniņš after his arrest in April 1938. Shot on 8 May 1939; buried in mass grave No. 1, Donskoe cemetery, Moscow.

64. Kristaps Salniņš wearing the Order of the Red Banner.

66. Svites. The Žāklis family farm, 1910.

67. Svites in 2004. Originally 63 hectares, the farm is only 47 hectares today.

68. Svites, birthplace of Peter the Painter.

69, Juris Žāklis, the owner of Rednieki farm, 30 May 2007. The resemblance between Juris and the 1904 mugshots of Jānis Žāklis is uncanny.

70. The Žākle family gathered at Svites in 1908. Numbered on original print: 1. Kārlis Žāklis; 2. Margarieta Tālberga-Žākle; 3. Katrīna Žākle; 4. Milda Žākle; 5. Lote (Šarlote) Tālberga; 6. Herman Sakne; 7. Anna Žākle-Sakne; 8. Jānis Sakne; 9. Kārlis Sakne; 10. Lize Žākle.

8

January to October 1909
Alien Robbers Run Amok

> A rough looking man, very unshaven, a revolver in his right hand …
> was firing at the police and they at him.
>
> Charles Rolstone[1]

'Alien Robbers Run Amok', was how *The Times* for Monday 25 January 1909 began its report of what became known as the Tottenham Outrage.

Two days before, at Schnurmann's rubber factory in Chestnut Lane, Tottenham, the company car bringing the Saturday morning delivery of the weekly payroll for its 150 workers had been held up as it reached the gate and robbed of £80 (equivalent to £8,800 today) by two men armed with semi-automatic pistols. The robbery was not a smooth affair. There was a struggle. Shots were fired. Passers-by decided to "have a go". Schnurmann's was situated directly opposite Tottenham High Road Police Station. A general hue and cry went up immediately and the hold-up men found themselves forced to flee (first on foot, then by hijacking a succession of vehicles — a horse drawn milk float, a cart, and an electric tram), pursued by an angry mob of hastily armed police, do-gooders, and passers-by, in what turned into a running gun battle.

The chase lasted for nearly two hours, covered some six miles over north-east London to the edge of Epping Forest, and ended in the deaths of both robbers; a policeman, PC William Tyler; a ten-year-old boy, Ralph Joscelene; and a horse, name unrecorded. Seventeen other policemen and civilians were wounded. Near the end of the chase, one of the robbers, later identified as Paul Hefeld, shot himself in the head to avoid capture, after failing to scale a fence at Ching Brook, just as his pursuers caught up with him. He was taken, critically wounded and under constant police guard, to the Prince of Wales Hospital, where he died on 12th February, without ever properly regaining consciousness. His comrade in arms, a certain Jacob Lepidus met his end in the upstairs bedroom of a coal-porters' cottage at Oak Hill, Hale End, on the edge of Epping Forest, now the site of 59 Hale End Road, behind the Chingbrook Arms pub. Surrounded, he put a Bergman pistol to his head as a policeman, PC Eagles, armed with a service revolver burst into the room. Both men fired in the same instant, and it was not until the inquest that it was established that Lepidus had been killed by his own bullet. He was buried with his comrade, Hefeld, in an unmarked grave in Walthamstow cemetery.

Clearly these were no ordinary hold-up men. The pair had fired over 400 rounds at their pursuers. When police visited their lodgings they discovered so much revolutionary literature that a removal van had to be called to take it away. Investigations soon established that both men were Latvians who were known to work as sailors, engaged in smuggling revolutionary literature to the Baltic. Hefeld and Lepidus were believed by Special Branch to be aliases. The press referred to them as 'anarchists'. Members of a Latvian SR club in Tottenham, said to be frequented by the robbers, repudiated the action and said they belonged to the Communist Club in Soho and were Bolsheviki.[2] Neither of the men was listed as members of the London Branch of the Latvian Social Democracy, which issued vigorous public denials that Hefeld and Lepidus were officially sponsored expropriators, citing the Party's 1907 decision banning expropriations, but no one seriously believed that the robbery had been anything other than political.

According to *The Times*, Jacob Lepidus first arrived in London from Riga four years before, in 1905, 'when he distributed literature on behalf of the secret society to which he belonged.'[3] His former landlord, Stanislaus Kolensky, said he had lived at Ashley Road, Tottenham, from December 1907 until March 1908. Lepidus had worked briefly at a furniture factory in Tottenham but lost his job and was evicted by Kolensky for not paying the rent. At the time of his death he was living in the next street, Station Road. He was also known to have lived in the East End and, significantly in view of the possible association with the Motherwell robbers, had spent time in Glasgow.[4] Paul Hefeld was known to have first rented a room in Ferry Lane for two weeks, then moved to 51 High Cross Road, just around the corner from Chestnut Road where the robbery took place. He had worked briefly at Schnumann's as a labourer (16th to 29th December 1908), where he was entered on the timesheets as *Elephant*. *The Times* claimed Hefeld was wanted by the Russian police and, in a reference to the Motherwell bank robbery the previous April, was 'supposed to have been associated with Schmidt, who took part in a raid on one of the Scotch banks some time ago.'[5] According to his landlord, Hefeld had spent four years 'in a certain country' and one year in Britain. 'He had travelled widely in Britain, including Scotland, where he had been just prior to the robbery. He had come south with an unidentified man who was a cabinet maker.'[6]

What happened to the money from the robbery was a mystery to the police, and it took eighty years for a probable explanation to come to light. *The Guardian*, in an anniversary article on the robbery published in January 1989, mentioned that a serving policeman, PC Peter Lawrence, had, twenty years before, interviewed Charles Rolstone (a boy of six when Lepidus burst into his parents' cottage at Oak Hill). Rolstone remembered, 'A rough looking man, very unshaven, a revolver in his right hand. He bolted the door. He was firing at the police and they at him. He tried to go up the chimney and I believe that's where he hid the money. Some years later they found some in the ruins of the cottage when it collapsed.'[7]

The disappearance of the £80 payroll convinced the police at the time that at least one other person had been involved in the robbery at an early stage, to whom the money bag had been passed. Special Branch believed this 'third man' to have been a certain Jacob Fogel, described by the Russian Consul in London as a 'well known anarchist and thief ... who gave himself out in London as a Social Democrat'.[8] Fogel was the old friend of Jānis Žāklis, Kristaps Salniņš. The trade by which Salniņš earned his living just happened to be that of cabinet maker, but his real profession in Britain was as chief organiser of an extensive arms and literature smuggling network based partly in Scotland, from where his consignments were shipped to the Baltic.

The suspicions of Special Branch about Fogel's involvement at Tottenham surfaced again during the Houndsditch investigation, in a letter from Special Branch Commissioner Sir Melville Macnaughton to Sir William Nott-Bower at the City Police, and then in a note by Inspector MacNamara of the City Police in the case papers: '...discreet enquiries were made last night to ascertain Fogel's whereabouts, but without success, as he is not known to have any fixed abode. Being of a roving disposition he generally stays at lodging homes and with comrades when in London... Fogel came under notice in connection with the late Tottenham Murders.'[9]

Salniņš's reference in his memoir to 'our sailors' acting as couriers in his arms and literature smuggling network suggests that Special Branch suspicions about him were not without foundation. Both of the men killed after Tottenham were known to be sailors and were in possession of a large quantity of revolutionary literature. Were the men two of his couriers, and the Tottenham robbery an expropriation carried out to fund the smuggling operation? The links of all three men to Scotland and the alleged connection of Lepidus and Hefeld with the Motherwell robbers seem unlikely to be mere coincidence. Salniņš certainly knew one of the Motherwell robbers, Ludvigs Putniņš (Bruno); both were members of the London Branch of the LSD. Alternatively, were they all (Salniņš included) disaffected Social Democrats who had come under the influence of Jānis Žāklis and been working with the anarchists? Ilga Apine, a Latvian Professor of History specialising in the 1905 Revolution, agreed it was possible that Salniņš could have ignored the Party's ban on expropriations and organised something in 1909, when I put the proposition to her.[10]

Mortuary photographs of the Tottenham Anarchists are held today at Scotland Yard's Black Museum. Strangely, one of them — that of Jacob Lepidus — appears also in a Latvian Communist Party history of the period,[11] purporting to show one Ozoliņš (Little Oak Tree — ironic, given that Lepidus met his death in Oak Tree Cottage), said to have been killed in Riga on 4 February 1908. This is clearly impossible. It would be foolish to deny that the picture may simply have been incorrectly filed or labelled in Riga, either before or after such *Okhranka* material fell into Bolshevik hands. It seems unlikely, however, that the photograph was not easily identifiable as from an outside source, namely, the London police, who probably sent it with its companion, in a letter seeking to identify both men.

Rather more probable is that the editors of the Latvian work, which was published in Moscow in 1933, wanted to obscure the fact that a loyal Social Democrat (or a disloyal one who had gone over to the anarchists) had taken his own life in the course of an expropriation such as had been officially repudiated in 1907. If this man was Ozoliņš, his death in such circumstances would be too much of a political embarrassment. One indication that this may have been the case is that a similar process was applied to Ludvigs Putniņš in the second volume of the same book (published in 1936), where the circumstances which resulted in his prison sentence in Scotland and the reason for his expulsion from the LSD are omitted. Anarchists were not considered relevant by Soviet historians, and those who left the LSD virtually disappear from the record at the same point — as Jānis Žāklis did.

* * *

The house in Whitechapel, 29 Great Garden Street (now Greatorex Street), where Kristaps Salniņš lodged at the time of the Tottenham Outrage was owned by another political refugee, Charles Perelman. Perelman, who earned his living in London as a photographic enlarger, told the City Police that he came to England with his family from Saratov, on the river Volga, in July 1906.[12]

Curiously, a Kārlis Perlmanis is listed amongst the names of those who died from injuries sustained in the reprisals at Tukums in 1905. It seems rather a coincidence that a Charles Perelman should subsequently appear in London as the landlord not only of Salniņš, but at various times most of the main suspects in the events at Houndsditch and Sidney Street. Could they have been the same man? When interviewed in London years later by Donald Rumbelow, Perelman's son insisted that his father had considered himself a revolutionary, and could not return to "Russia" on pain of death. He confirmed that the Perelman family arrived in London in 1906 without any possessions.[13] Their arrival in such circumstances (and at that date) is consistent with their having fled from the repression that swept over Tukums after the rising.

Though the house was owned by Perelman, the person who brought the Latvians together there was one of Perelman's lodgers, Jānis Palamieks, nicknamed Bifšteks and Sosonov, who was wanted by the police in Latvia.[14] A singularly handsome man, with a thick mane of brushed-back hair and pencil-moustache, Palamieks first appeared in London at the end of 1906, and his membership of the London LSD branch was recorded on 12th January, 1907. He doesn't appear to have stayed a member for long though, leaving later the same month to go to sea as a sailor. Membership records show that he was never subsequently readmitted to the branch, and he appears to have become an anarchist.[15]

In August 1908 Palamieks became friendly with Perelman's sixteen-year-old daughter, Fanny, at the Workers' Friend anarchist club in Jubilee Street, Stepney, which served the émigré community, not just the anarchists, as a social forum. When Fanny brought her boyfriend home to meet her parents, Palamieks told them he worked as a sailor on a cargo ship to America. For the next six months he regularly visited the house whenever he was in dock. In the sailor's hostel in Poplar, where he was then living, Palamieks became friendly with two young anarchists from Latvia, John Rosen (real name Jānis Celiņš), a former member of the LSDSP in Riga, who worked in London as a barber, and Karl Hoffman (real name Alfrēds Dzirkalis), a seaman from Liepāja who worked as a painter and decorator when ashore. Palamieks introduced the pair to the Perelman family, and they struck up a common friendship. They were also friendly with another anarchist painter and decorator called George Dubov, real name Juris Laiviņš.

Born in Alsviķi in the Alūksnes region of Livonia on 3rd December 1886, Laiviņš had been an agitator for the LSDSP in Alūksnes prior to 1905. On 20th November 1905, Juris Laiviņš and his younger brother, Alfrēds, had taken part in an anti-government demonstration in a church at Zeltiņs. When the Priest, Plamšs, began his prayer for the tsar a group of young people from the choir started shouting 'away with the tsar; away with autocracy'[16] and began singing revolutionary songs, raised a red flag and handed out leaflets. The priest and his parishioners started to sing hymns, but the demonstrators' singing was much louder. Some of the people who took part in the demonstration were afterwards shot by the authorities and others sentenced to prison terms. Juris Laiviņš, who was then only nineteen, was held in the cellar of Alūksnes palace — The Wolf's House (*Vilku nama*) — and given 100 lashes; afterwards serving two months of a four month sentence in Valka prison before managing to escape.[17]

Information held by the Riga *Okhranka* states that Laiviņš was due for call-up into the Russian Army in 1908, but went abroad instead in 1907.[18] He first appeared in London in June 1907, but stayed only four days before moving to New Jersey, USA. By April 1909 he was back in London, where he lived with his brother Alfrēds in Whitechapel, but eventually (January 1910) moved in with the Perelman household at the suggestion of Jānis Palamieks.

When the Perelmans moved to a larger house at 29 Great Garden Street at the end of 1908, Palamieks (who told Perelman he was on shore leave) joined them as a lodger, occupying the ground floor front room. Two weeks later he brought another Latvian into the house to share his room, whom he introduced as Grishka Sander. The new lodger was Kristaps Salniņš. The Tottenham Outrage took place ten days afterwards.

The pair remained at Great Garden Street for about two months before Perelman, apparently sharing the Special Branch suspicions about Salniņš, asked both him and Palamieks to look for alternative accommodation. But before they left Salniņš was visited by a friend who stayed the night: Fricis Svars. Svars said he had come from America and worked in the West End of London as a locksmith. The next day, Perelman rented him the front room upstairs. Shortly afterwards Palamieks left, saying he was going to America on a ship. Two or three weeks later Svars brought George Gardstein (Puika Hartmanis) into the house to share his room.[19] Hartmanis was clearly also an associate of Palamieks, whose photograph was found in his wallet by the London police. Another photograph of Palamieks, discovered by the police in the lodgings of Fricis Svars and Jānis Žāklis, showing him with two other anarchists linked to Žāklis, Krišjānis Rēdlihs and Ernsts Bonis, strongly suggests that Perelman's lodgers were linked together by more than friendship.

Svars and Hartmanis had only recently returned from America, having narrowly escaped from the shootout at Jamaica Plain, and seemed to have become inseparable. Juris Daberts, who had known them in Latvia, recalls meeting them again in London; where he had politely to decline their offer of Mauser pistols as a means of settling an industrial dispute: 'I remember meeting Svars and Hartmanis, who already at the end of 1909 offered their armed assistance to the strike committee at some London East End factory in their fight with the factory administration and the strike-breakers. I happened then to turn down that offer.'[20] The 'boys from Liepāja' had been conditioned by the workers' struggle in Latvia to see the class war as literally just that: *war*. The inability (or refusal) to accept that different social conditions require different methods of struggle contributed in no small measure to the tragic outcome of the events that lay ahead of them.

Svars and Hartmanis stayed at Great Garden Street as lodgers for about three months before Perelman asked them to move on. During the time they lived there they were visited by Alfrēds Dzirkalis, Jānis Celiņš and Juris Laiviņš, all three of whom had previously been in America, where they may all have known one-another already.

These five individuals were the nucleus of the group of Latvian anarchists who came together in London as *Liesma* (The Flame). But the focus of their operations, as always, was Latvia.

* * *

By the summer of 1909 the efforts of Jānis Žāklis to reinvigorate the armed resistance in Latvia were beginning to bear fruit.

The first clue to what the anarchists were up to came on 18th July 1909, when the police in Riga arrested Jānis Lapiņš on charges of shooting a certain Mr. Štāl with a Browning pistol ten days previously. Lapiņš confessed under interrogation that he had left Riga in 1906 and worked abroad as a sailor. Over the Christmas of 1908 he had become friendly in London with Edvards Klebais (Bifelis), Fredriks Riters (Afrikānis), Jānis Alprozītis (a friend of Fricis Svars) and Alfrēds Dzirkalis (Mazais), all of whom, he told the police, had organised an Anarchist-Communist Group in London under the leadership of an émigré called Alexei Teplov. Teplov was one of the older generation of Russian *Narodniks* exiled in London; he ran a Russian lending library in the East End and had been deeply involved in the smuggling of arms into Russia and the Baltic from London during the 1905 revolution. Lapiņš said that the group was preparing to operate in Riga. Ahead of their departure the group smuggled anarchist literature, arms and ammunition to Riga by ship. The consignments were received in Riga by an anarchist named Augusts Dakars. The group planned to reactivate the anarchist struggle inside Latvia through attacks on the police and expropriations. Teplov in London had supplied them with pistols, seven bombs and a quantity of explosives. One-by-one the group came to Riga as stowaways, hiding in the coal bunker on board the merchant ship *Sergei*, helped by the crew of the ship. The first man to arrive in Riga, in February 1909, was Lapiņš himself. Then at the start of May came Klebais and Riters; then Dzirkalis, Ivanov, and some others whose real identities were unknown to Lapiņš. They all brought with them Mausers, ammunition, explosives and illegal anarchist literature. On arrival in Riga this material was left on board the ship, in the safe-keeping of the senior stoker, Jānis Ruļļis (named as wanted, but who managed to escape arrest), until it was deemed safe to collect a couple of days later. Soon afterwards, with the help of the same stoker on board the *Sergei*, Teplov sent five more bombs over from London, which were collected by Klebais and Dakars. Lapiņš confessed that at the end of May 1909 he went to the flat of Johan Sprontis with 16 kilos of anarchist literature, which had been brought over to Riga from London by Alfrēds Dzirkalis. Sprontis agreed to keep the literature in his flat.

Armed with this information from Lapiņš, the police arrested Klebais, Riters, Dakars and Sprontis, and combed Riga looking for the other members of the group. The police operation unearthed ammunition, bombs and a copy of the Russian Anarchist-Communist journal *Khleb i Volya* (Bread and Freedom). Buried near the flat of Riters, the police dug up a rubber stamp for the Group of Anarchist-Communists of the Baltic Federation — "Avenger" (*Baltijas federācijas anarhistu-komunistu grupas "Atriebējs"*).[21]

The interrogation of Riters and Klebais brought forth the information, 'that while in London they had connection with the Anarchist-Communists in Paris, from whom they got instructions that if any of them went to Riga they should visit Jānis Bišentrops and pass the literature to him; whose address the Paris group provided. Bišentrops was searched and arrested. During the search a letter from Paris written in Latvian was found. Klebais and Riters admitted their guilt, but Bišentrops denied the charges and all knowledge of the Paris group. Klebais and Riters said that in May and June 1909 they had held several meetings in the forest with the aim of forming an Anarchist-Communist group in Riga, to organise propaganda and armed actions. At one of those meetings it was decided to assassinate the head of the Detective Department, Greguss. Riters admitted taking part in a string of expropriations in Riga in 1906.'[22]

The Riga police asked the police in London to put three named ships under surveillance. But at least two of the wanted men had already managed to slip the net and escape back to London, Alfrēds Dzirkalis and Juris Laiviņš. Laiviņš later testified in court, during the Houndsditch trial, that he went to Riga from London in June 1909 and returned in January 1910, but prudently did not volunteer the purpose of his visit or the reason for his swift return.

What is interesting about this episode, apart from the facts that London was the base of operations and that two of the future Houndsditch defendants (Alfrēds Dzirkalis and Juris Laiviņš) were involved in it, was that the *Atriebējs* (Avenger) group received their instructions from anarchists in Paris — where Jānis Žāklis was a regular visitor during the frequent disappearances from Marseille that were noted by the French police. Žāklis needed to be in Paris so often because he had taken over direction of the monthly anarchist journal *Brīvība* (Freedom), following a dispute over money with the editor in New York, Jānis Līdumnieks (a participant in the raid on Riga Central Prison). The second issue of *Brīvība*, published in New York in March 1909, announced that it would henceforth appear as the publication of the Latvian Anarchist Communist Federation, under the editorship of a new group based in Paris; and that all money, letters and articles should be sent to it c/o the French anarchist paper *Libertaire*, at 15 rue d'Orsel in northern Paris. The third issue of *Brīvība* duly appeared in Paris in June 1909.

At the end of 1909 Jānis Žāklis finished his job as a painter at the Exhibition of Electricity in Marseille, and left for Evian-les-Bains on Lake Geneva. By 15th January 1910 he had settled in Paris, where he lived at 4 Rue Danville, a small side street near Montparnasse cemetery in the 14th *Arrondissement*. An *Okhranka* report records that Žāklis was occupied there working 'for the left-wing party newspapers',[23] confirming his editorship of *Brīvība*. The fourth issue of *Brīvība*, published in April 1910, acknowledged financial contributions from C. Lamberts (a name that figured in the Houndsditch trial as an alias of Juris Laiviņš), Fricis, Buldogs (an alias of Fricis Svars), and Mazais (Alfrēds Dzirkalis).

In October 1909 Fricis Svars had an unexpected visitor in London; his cousin Jēkabs Peterss (Jacob Peters). Peterss was born on 3rd December 1886, on the Briņķi estate of Baron Hahn at Nīkrāces, in the rural district of Aizputes. His father, Kristaps Peterss, who worked on the estate as a labourer, had married a girl from Liepāja called Līze Svare. The couple called their new son Jēkabs after Līze's brother, Jēkabs Svars, the father of Fricis Svars, who had been born the year before. Not much is known about Jēkabs Peterss' childhood. He had two brothers and three sisters (Ilze, Trīne, and another; the names of the brothers are not known), but few other facts about them (even their ages) have survived. As the son of a farm labourer Peterss received only a brief education at the parish school. 'Starting at the age of eight,' he remembered in 1928, 'I had to earn my own living working as a shepherd for neighbouring farmers.'[24] By the time he reached fourteen he had become a farm labourer like his father. But the conditions in which he grew up at Briņķi could not fail to breed a hatred of privilege. 'It seems to me that there is no other place in the world', he wrote, 'where a rich man with the title of Baron or Graf had such an unlimited power over the fate of hundreds of men as Hahn in the Briņķi estate'.[25]

Early in 1904, the eighteen-year-old Peterss left Briņķi and moved to Liepāja where his cousin Fricis Svars was already secretly a member of the LSDSP. In Liepāja Peterss first found work as a grocer's assistant, then got a job in the harbour as a dock labourer, working at a goods lift. Peterss confessed later that he knew nothing about socialism before his move to the city: 'Already in school I became interested in the struggle against landlords, but at that time I had no idea of the socialists or the social democracy. Only in 1904, having moved to Liepāja, I met some of my former schoolmates, who already at that time were members of various organisations, and in May I myself entered a circle of the Latvian Social Democracy in the harbour.'[26]

By his own testimony, Peterss worked in the docks for only a month, before the 1905 revolution took hold of Latvia. Peterss was always reticent to acknowledge the extent of his activity during 1905, preferring to give the impression that all his energies had gone into working as a 'voluntary agitator (unpaid) in the army and the working classes.'[27] More difficult to understand is the curious vagueness on this score of Soviet historians, who say only that Peterss toured the countryside as an organiser and propagandist, helping to organise strikes among farm labourers and establishing 'committees'.[28] Only one fleeting reference draws attention to the fact that in 1905, 'whilst engaged in propaganda work among landless peasants, *he formed fighting detachments*.'[29] (italics added). This claim however is hard to accept at face value. Peterss is notable by his absence in the encyclopaedic *Memorial Books to the Fighters* of 1905, where the careers of those who occupied important positions in the Soviet Union are given great prominence. The inescapable conclusion is simply that Peterss was rather a minor figure during the 1905 Revolution, certainly in comparison to his cousin Fricis Svars, and was only drawn into serious revolutionary activity later. The *Brief Autobiography*, written to support his admission into the Society of Old Bolsheviks in 1928, offers only a glimpse of Peterss' activity: 'In 1905 I changed my work for a job at a creamery... I almost continuously travelled from farmstead to farmstead in the Kurland province, visiting different organisations of the revolutionary power. After the repression of the insurrection I remained at work at the creamery ... till 1907. During this period I was drawn to active revolutionary work in the Liepāja organisation, and also ... became attracted by the acute fractional struggle, in which I chose the position of the Bolshevist fraction.'[30] This propensity for 'acute fractional struggle' (not always to his credit) was to contribute in no small measure to Peterss' importance to Lenin, who was trying hard to inject the quarrels of the Russian Party into the Latvian Social Democracy, which had hitherto ignored the Bolshevik/Menshevik split. It also made it unlikely that Peterss would have anything to do with anarchists.

On 14th January, 1906, three days after Fricis Svars was picked up at the start of the roundup in Riga, Jēkabs Peterss was amongst a group of revolutionaries held by the punitive expedition in Siguldā. The detachment shot three of them out of hand. Peterss and four more were flogged (Peterss getting twenty-five lashes) and released. Two of the four flogged with Peterss, Cers and Bezvārdis, had both broken out of Grobiņ prison with Fricis Svars on 16th October 1905. Bezvārdis was now an important organiser with the Forest Brothers (*mežabrāļi*) in the area around Liepāja and Kuldīga. The Bezvārdis group was noted for its audacity. To acquire arms, they twice successfully attacked the mansion of a Baron at Snēpelē, where guns were being stockpiled for use against the peasants; and, to fund their resistance activity, used the weapons taken in the first raid to rob the Post Office at Lielrenda on 11th December. Eventually Bezvārdis was forced to emigrate to England, and worked in London as a tailor. Letty Norwood still remembered him fondly in 1988 as Mr. Bezbard, coming to stay with her father Aleksander Zirnis near Bournemouth during the First World War.[31] Until the research for this book, it was assumed that Bezvārdis had subsequently emigrated to Australia, where he had disappeared from view. But Letty Norwood's sister, Gertrude Noyes, maintains he died in England whilst undergoing heart surgery and was cremated at Golders Green in London.[32] Peterss and Bezvārdis evidently worked together again in London, though not without disagreement.

In March 1907, Peterss was arrested again. This time things were more serious. He was charged with attempting to murder the owner of the Liepāja creamery he worked in. The newspaper *Latvija* reported that together with Fricis Urbekalns, Peters was accused of attacking 'the engineer of the Vezuves factory' Kārlis Māls on 12th March, shooting him several times in the neck with a revolver and wounding him.[33] In Liepāja prison Peterss saw at first hand the inhuman treatment given to captive revolutionaries. He was especially appalled by the fate of one young comrade, tortured by Baron Brēdrihs to compel him to divulge the names of his comrades. The twenty-three-year-old youth had lost his hearing, his hair turned grey, and his hands and legs were mutilated. Peterss was tortured too, and had his fingernails ripped out. Sir Robert Bruce Lockhart records that Peterss showed him the scars, still visible on his hands, in Moscow during 1918.[34]

In the autumn of 1907 Peterss and his fellow prisoners went on hunger strike, demanding that the public prosecutor be called to visit the prison. The prosecutor, a young man, was perplexed when he arrived to hear that the prisoners wanted to be chained whenever they had to be transferred to the country parishes for identification. The reason was that on the way most of the prisoners had been shot, and the charge recorded that they had been 'attempting to escape'. After nearly two years in prison, during which they were kept in solitary confinement, Peterss and Uberkalns were finally put on trial in front of a Military Tribunal in Riga. Luckily for them, public indignation against the summary treatment of prisoners had reached such a pitch by this point that the hearing was conducted according to the book. No evidence could be brought against them and on 1st September 1908 Peterss and Uberkalns were acquitted.[35]

Peterss returned to Nīkrāce and stayed with his father, hoping to escape the vigilance of the *Okhranka* in the Courland forests, where he worked as a logger at a sawmill. But it soon became evident that the police would not leave him alone, when they began to follow him. The unpublished memoirs of his cousin Ēvald Roze, kept at the Kuldīga Museum in Latvia, say: 'In the late autumn ... the police again started searching for him with the aim of arrest. Jēkabs happened to be away from home, probably visiting Rozentāls in Zilbārži. When Jēkabs was coming home, his aunt, his father's brother's wife, was in time to warn him about the police ambush in his house. Jēkabs quickly escaped to Lēģernieki, where his sister Ilze was employed as a servant. For some time he was hiding there, but later, when the police again caught trace of him, he hid at another place and was not found. One of the night-guards of the local bakery secretly took him away to Lithuania, to a small place called Piķeļi, where on Thursdays they organised bazaars. It was just Thursday then. My father met Jēkabs there and took him to his house, where he was hiding him for some two weeks. But nobody was looking for Jēkabs. Enķūzis lived not far from Piķeļi. He helped Jēkabs cross the border with Germany for forty roubles.'[36]

Peterss' second wife, Antonina Peters, disputes this. She says that Peterss was smuggled to Hamburg in the hold of a ship, where he lay hidden in the coal.[37] Peterss went to Hamburg intending to emigrate to America, but he lacked the money and so found a job instead. He also renewed his contact with the Party, through the local LSD group, and visited a cousin, Līze Svare (Fricis Svars' sister), who worked in Hamburg as a teacher. Peterss moved next to Denmark, but was unable to get work there. In October, 1909, he arrived in London and went to stay with Fricis Svars, at the house owned by Charles Perelman in Great Garden Street, and was officially listed as having joined the London branch of the Latvian Social Democracy on 25th November, 1909.[38]

The two cousins, Fricis Svars and Jēkabs Peterss, had not seen one another for almost four years. In that time Svars had transferred his political affiliation to the anarchists, and was wanted in America for expropriations. For a passionate sectarian like Peterss, the conversion of Svars to anarchism must have seemed like betrayal. The two cousins argued incessantly about their conflicting views. When Peterss finally left Great Garden Street a month later, it was because they could not agree to differ.

The year 1909, which had opened so dramatically with the Tottenham Outrage, appeared to be closing on a deceptively domestic note. But the gradual coagulation of individuals around Fricis Svars was set to shatter the tranquillity of London in the most sensational of ways.

Notes

1   Julia Hagedorn, 'Death Stalks the Streets', *The Guardian*, 31st January, 1989.
2   *The Times*, 26th January, 1909.
3   Ibid.
4   *The Times*, 27th January, 1909.
5   *The Times*, 26th January, 1909.
6   Donald Rumbelow, *The Houndsditch Murders and the Siege of Sidney Street* (Revised edition, London 1988), p. 44.
7   Julia Hagedorn, 'Death Stalks the Streets', op. cit.
8   Files of the City of London Police, 'Houndsditch Murders', 534G/3.15, Russian Consul in London to Superintendent Ottaway, London Metropolitan Archives.
9   Ibid, 534G/3.15: Inspector Thomas MacNamara, December 1912.
10 Interview with Ilga Apine, Riga, 3rd September 2003.
11 *Revolucionaras cinas kritusha pieminas gramata*, 1 sejums, (Prometejs, Moscow, 1933), p. 268.
12 'Houndsditch Murders', 534G/3.15, Statement of Charles Perelman, 20th February, 1910, op. cit.
13 Interviews with Donald Rumbelow, 13th/14th January, 1988. The death of Karlis Perlmanis, described as a 'house owner', was reported in *Dienas Lapa* No. 267 and *Rigas Avize* No. 266, December 1905.
14 'Houndsditch Murders', 534G/3.15, Information from the Russian Consul in London, 1911, op. cit.
15 *LSD Londonas nozares biedru grāmata* (Membership book of the LSD London Branch). Glabājas LVA.
16 Reports in *Dzivtsnes Albass* No. 11, 31st January 1914, and *Jaunais Vārds* No. 43, 2nd February 1915.
17 Ibid.
18 LVVA, 4569/7/342/1
19 'Houndsditch Murders', 534G/3.15: Statement of Charles Perelman, 20th February, 1910, op. cit.
20 LVA, PA-36/5/ 198.
21 LVVA, 4568/8/118/10, #54.
22 Ibid.
23 LVVA, 4568/15/225, #63, 'Letters from agents', Jan Janovich Krauze in Kiev to the Riga *Okhranka*, 3rd July 1912.
24 Jēkabs Peterss, *My Brief Autobiography*, unpublished manuscript written for the Society of Bolshevik Veterans, Moscow, 21st December 1928.
25 Jānis Mende, 'Jēkabs Peterss 1886-1938', *Karogs* No. 4, Riga, 1967, p. 122.
26 Jēkabs Peterss, *My Brief Autobiography*, op. cit.
27 *The Times*, 9th May 1911.
28 Jānis Mende, op. cit.
29 *Geroi Oktiabria* (Heroes of October), Vol. II, pp. 234-5 (Leningrad, 1967).
30 Jēkabs Peterss, *My Brief Autobiography*, op. cit.
31 Interview with Melita Norwood, 28 June 1988, and unpublished typescript memories of her father, Aleksander Zirnis, October 1988.
32 Letter from Gertrude Noyes and Melita Norwood, 23rd November 1988.
33 *Latvija* No. 203, 2nd September 1908. Peters himself, in his *Brief Autobiography*, says he was arrested with two other comrades, Mirkau and Stepe, at the flat of the Sudmalis brothers. Nikolajs and Arturs Sudmalis were both prominent expropriators, known to have been responsible for a string of daring attacks in Liepāja with Janis Cirulis. All three were hanged in Riga Central Prison on 4th February, 1909.
34 Sir Robert Bruce Lockhart, *My Europe* (London 1952), p. 48.
35 *Latvija* No. 203, 2nd September 1908, and *Dzimtenes Vestnesis* No. 303, 8th September 1908.
36 Ēvalds Roze, Atminas (Jēkabs Peterss), No. 28.519. Unpublished oral memoir of Ēvalds Roze about Jēkabs Peterss, transcribed by Livija Feldmane, 9th August 1976. Kuldīga

museum of local history and art.

37 Interview with Valentines Šteinbergs, 1988 (Prof. Šteinbergs interviewed Antonina Peters in Moscow, 1985).

38 *LSD Londonas nozares biedru grāmata*, op. cit.

9

October 1909 to December 1910
The Flame

There is a special committee organised in London for the purpose of collecting, keeping and distributing money to fund the affairs of the anarchists.

Riga *Okhranka*[1]

As well as Svars and Hartmanis, Charles Perelman had two other lodgers when Jēkabs Peterss turned up in October 1909: William Sokolov and Nina Vasileva.

Sokolov, known as Joseph, was a twenty-nine-year-old Jewish watchmaker, anarchist and crook who had come to England from Moscow in 1898. The London police, who interviewed him in October 1909 in connection with the burglary of a jeweller's shop in Old Street, Moorgate, where he worked as manager, suspected Sokolov of being involved in a string of break-ins at jewellers' shops up and down the country. According to Nina Vasileva, Sokolov had been put on trial in the Crimea with Max Smoller, a frequent visitor at Great Garden Street.[2]

Nina Vasileva, who occupied the ground floor back room, claimed to have been born in Ekaterinoslav (today Dnepropetrovsk) in 1891, and to be the daughter of a Chef in the tsar's palace in Petersburg, but available evidence suggests that she was in fact Latvian.[3] At the time of her arrest Vasileva was in possession of a passport in the name of 'Minna, daughter of Indriķ Griķīš', a peasant resident in Courland. Jānis Celiņš told the police that besides Russian, Yiddish, and some English, Vasileva spoke Latvian — unusual for someone from Ukraine who claimed only to have mixed socially with Latvians for a couple of years. Vasileva is also alleged to have told her landlord, Isaac Gordon, that she had been sentenced to death in "Russia" and could not return there. Perhaps, then, she had participated in the activities of the Latvian fighters in 1905. While held on remand in Holloway Prison, Luba Milstein told the police that she only knew Vasileva by sight, as someone who frequented the anarchist club in Jubilee Street, but 'Fritz told me that he knew her and that she came from one of the Lett (Latvian) Provinces... Nina never visited... In fact, Fritz told me that he did not like her.'[4]

Sokolov's associate Max Smoller was less of an enigma. Apparently wanted in the Crimea for jewel and fur robberies, Smoller lived with his wife and two children at 147 Stepney Green Dwellings. By bringing together members of the Latvian anarchist group *Liesma* with two Jewish criminals from the Crimea, the house at 29 Great Garden Street became the birthplace of the Houndsditch gang. The suspicions of the London police in October 1909 about Sokolov's earlier role in setting up a string of jewellery shop burglaries, together with the arrests at Motherwell and the question mark over the Tottenham Outrage, make it clear that the group was active in Britain well before Jēkabs Peterss' arrival.

The inclusion of Peterss in the Houndsditch case is warranted only by his being the cousin of Fricis Svars, with whom he had broken off relations. Sokolov and Smoller were instrumental in bringing local intelligence and professional skill to the mix; affording the Latvian expropriators an opportunity to operate in England as they had done previously in Latvia and America. The series of jewellery shop burglaries which ended with the Houndsditch attempt, the proceeds of which would have gone in part to support political prisoners in Latvia, provided the means to continue funding the resistance in the Baltic. The role played by Jānis Žāklis was not one of direct participation, but of strategic co-ordination of the overall plan of campaign.

* * *

J. E. Holroyd, who looked for signs of previous robberies bearing the hallmarks of the Houndsditch expropriation, concluded in 1960, 'There had been several similar burglaries during the preceding eighteen months'.[5] The first had taken place in the summer of 1909, when gold and silver plate was stolen from premises in High Holborn by burglars who bored a hole in the wall and removed a fireplace. In June 1910 there were two more robberies. In the first, foreign burglars rented a vacant shop below a diamond cutters' workrooms in Maddox Street and bored through two ceilings to get at the gems; in the second, thieves took over a vacant shop in New Bond Street and took silver goods to the value of £1,000 from an adjoining stationer.[6]

By June 1910, Fricis Svars was intent only on sending for his wife, still living in the Baltic, and emigrating to Australia. But one mid-summer evening at the club in Jubilee Street, Alfrēds Dzirkalis introduced Fricis to a young anarchist from Kiev, nineteen-year-old Luba Milstein. For Luba it was love at first sight. Svars left his new love for two weeks at the end of July. When he came back, with Hartmanis and Smoller, Milstein noticed that all three sported gold watches, which they frequently exchanged.[7] The timing of this incident coincides with a robbery in Birmingham in August 1910 that had all the hallmarks of the Houndsditch gang: foreign looking men took premises adjoining a firm of jewellers; bored a hole through a wall eighteen inches thick (big enough to admit a man) and used an oxygen cylinder and blowpipe.[8]

At the end of August 1910 Svars, calling himself Peter Trohimschik, rented a room at 35 Newcastle Place. His landlady, Esther Goodman, described her new lodger to the police as, 'age about 28, 5ft 11, fair complexion, bushy hair and moustache fair, well built with broad shoulders, usually wore a brown suit, dark mackintosh, dark American slouch hat, and very large grey bow tie.'[9] By the end of September, Luba Milstein had moved in with Svars. Their regular visitors included Dzirkalis, Celiņš, Laiviņš, Hartmanis, Sokolov and Smoller. Since returning from Riga in January 1910, Juris Laiviņš had taken lodgings with Charles Perelman (who had moved to 74, Wellesley Street, Stepney) and found work as a painter and decorator. When the work ended he went to Switzerland and returned again to London on 20th September 1910, living at 20, Galloway Road, Shepherd's Bush; again finding various painting jobs.

* * *

Though it was Fricis Svars, with his considerable reputation in the movement as a fighter, who was the *Liesma* group's leading light (and something of a "star" in the social scene in which he moved), Hartmanis was the prime mover of the Houndsditch robbery. Somewhat less abrasive than Svars, Hartmanis shared a reluctance to talk about his past. But the Latvian anarchists nevertheless mixed freely with their European counterparts. Hartmanis first became known in London anarchist circles after being introduced by 'a Russian comrade' to the Austrian anarchist Siegfried Nacht: '… as a man who had been active in the movement in Lettland, and had to flee when the big repressions started in the Baltic provinces. Nacht had found Hartmanis a taciturn, uncommunicative person, who seemed unwilling to lift the veil over his past.'[10] Nacht, in turn, introduced the Latvian to the Italian anarchist Errico Malatesta (then the most important theoretician of Anarchism next to Peter Kropotkin) in the Jubilee Street Club.

Interestingly, Siegfried Nacht's brother, Max Nomad, admits to having met Hartmanis in Paris during 1910: 'Speaking fluent Russian, he showed me a piece of paper on which my brother in London had written my name. That was sufficient introduction. What name he gave me I no longer remember… He had come from London, where he had been a member of a revolutionary group, to see the sights of Paris, but now he was in trouble and wanted me to help him out. He had taken a room in a small hotel and had, according to his custom, put his automatic under his pillow at night. Only about an hour after having left for the Louvre, he noticed that his gun was not in his pocket. He returned immediately, but his bed was already made, and there was no gun under the pillow. As he did not speak French at all, he could only look questioningly at the room servant, who just smiled without saying a word.

'Nomad advised the worried Latvian to buy another gun.

'"They're very expensive," he replied. "They cost about seventy francs. Couldn't you go to the hotel and ask the servant for the gun? After all, you speak French."

'Nomad politely declined, but offered to write a note in French to the servant. He advised Hartmanis that should the police have been informed in the meantime, he should explain that as a stranger to France he didn't know that the carrying of weapons was prohibited.

'"Nobody is ever going to have a chance to arrest me", the Latvian replied.

Nomad never met Hartmanis again, but he recognised him immediately from the picture of the dead burglar when he read about the Houndsditch shootings in the newspapers a few months later.'[11] Colourful as this story is of Hartmanis taking a holiday in Paris to look at the pictures in the Louvre, the timing of the visit ('a few months' before the Houndsditch shootings) more reasonably suggests that he was in the city to see Jānis Žāklis. A letter sent to Peter Piatkov at 4 Rue Danville in Paris and returned to sender undelivered, prior to the arrival of Jānis Žāklis in London, was found on the body of Hartmanis at Grove Street after the Houndsditch shootings.

* * *

In the last week of October 1910 Jānis Žāklis arrived in London and made his way to call on Svars at Newcastle Place. Fricis introduced him to Luba Milstein as Peter Piatkov, Peter the Painter. Žāklis was clearly eager to be reunited with Svars, whom he visited every day, but because Svars' room at Newcastle Place was too small, he slept at the lodgings of Alfrēds Dzirkalis. On Friday 4th November, Svars and Milstein left Newcastle Place and moved into more spacious lodgings at 59 Grove Street, a typical terraced house in Stepney. Žāklis and Dzirkalis helped them push the handcart carrying their few items of furniture.[12] At Grove Street, Svars and Milstein occupied the small upstairs back room. Jānis Žāklis took the larger room, overlooking the street at the front of the house.

How many members of the London *Liesma* group had met Žāklis previously, besides Svars and Hartmanis, is unknown, but Svars was the person who made the introductions. Juris Laiviņš described how Svars had introduced Peter Piatkov to him at the anarchist club in Jubilee Street: 'I sit in one chair. Peter sit in other chair. He say "Nice." I say. "All right." He ask me, "What I work." I say, "Painter." He say, "I am painter also, and got a £30 job for shipping company".'[13] After his job came to an end, Laiviņš visited Žāklis at Grove Street on 13th December to discuss the painting of 'some decorations at a balalaika performance which they were going to give'. Afterwards he spent the evening drinking with friends at Millwall Docks, getting so drunk he had to return to Grove Street to sleep it off in Žāklis' room: 'I had had a good bit to drink and my head was aching, so I went back to Grove Street and stayed there all night'.[14]

London was looming large in the ambitious plans that Žāklis was brooding over; his arrival was for more than a brief visit. He intended to use London as a base for a complete overhaul of the Latvian anarchist movement. In a 'Secret' report dated, 6th April 1910, the Riga *Okhranka* noted, 'Received information that anarchists living abroad, who up to now have not had an organised connection between groups, only a loose federation — each group of which could work independently — now have the intention to hold a congress of all the anarchist groups, and the aim of this congress would be the creation of The Main Anarchist Organisation with a centre in London and local branches in Russia and abroad in the form of small group organisation. This wish to create a centre is explained by the fact that up to now anarchists have not been able to stand up and defend their general as well as group interest because they did not have a co-ordinating organisation. The anarchists are also intending to carry out a general re-organisation. They are going to review their programmes, the ways they carry out propaganda, etc. Besides, they are intending to intensify agitation in Russia, where they are going to intend to increase the transport of illegal literature, of increasing help to their comrade prisoners and financial campaigns (gathering money).'[15]

On 14th April 1910 the file notes that the London conference had taken place, and that the anarchists had decided to publish large amounts of literature for distribution in Russia: 'There is a special committee organised in London for the purpose of collecting, keeping and distributing money to fund the affairs of the anarchists, and to create a London anarchist library. A special committee was collecting anarchist publications for the library'.[16]

The 'special committee' in charge of raising finance was headed by Jānis Žāklis. London was to be his new base of operations; the means by which money was collected was expropriation. When the fifth issue of *Brīvība* appeared in August 1910 it acknowledged receipts of money from the *Liesma* group in London. The November issue (number six) included a short report on the back page signed by Mērnieks (Žāklis), as the treasurer of the London Group *Liesma*. The item was duly noted, translated into Russian and kept on file by the ever vigilant *Okhranka* in Riga. It was the last issue of the journal to appear before the Houndsditch expropriation.

Žāklis clearly intended to stay in London for some time. His reorganisation of the Latvian anarchist movement was based on the premise that London was ideally suited as his main base of operations. Most of the previous smuggling of arms and literature into the Baltic had emanated from Britain, anarchist literature could be legally printed there, and apart from the disasters at Motherwell and Tottenham the Latvians had successfully conducted expropriations for more than two years, with minimal interference from the British police.

Žāklis was also looking forward to being reunited in London with his wife Lidija, or Anna Schwarz ('your black girl'), who wrote to him from Kiev that she would be joining him by 1st March 1911, 'no matter what happens'.[17]

The shooting at Houndsditch changed everything.

* * *

On the afternoon of Friday 16th December, 1910, Fricis Svars hosted a social gathering at his flat in Grove Street. One of those present was a balalaika player called Nikolai Tokmakov. Tokmakov had become friendly with Svars at the anarchist club in Jubilee Street eight months before and had been teaching him to play the mandolin, visiting Grove Street for that purpose every day. Describing the event later at the Old Bailey, Tokmakov said that the gathering had been in the large room at the front belonging to Peter the Painter and that he had also seen there Fricis Svars, John Rosen (Celiņš), Josef (William Sokolov), Osip Federov, Luba Milstein, Marx (Max Smoller), Gardstein (Hartmanis), Dubov (Juris Laiviņš) and Hoffman (Alfrēds Dzirkalis). Peter the Painter and Celiņš played chess; Smoller and Svars were busy mixing paint for a theatrical production Svars was involved with. (Svars was to have played the role of police sergeant Gamba, in a production of the play *Mateo Falcone* that was due to be staged at a meeting hall in Wilkes Street, Spitalfields, on Boxing Day evening, 1910. He was expected to attend a rehearsal there on 18th December. Jānis Žāklis helped paint the scenery for this production and was to have taken on the job of prompter during the performance). Tokmakov played the mandolin and chatted to Sokolov, Federov and Laiviņš (who told him 'he knew of a factory where he would ask for work for me'). After an hour Tokmakov went home, leaving the mandolin behind. He was the first to go. He 'saw absolutely nothing suspicious there', but said that Fricis Svars had a Mauser pistol and bullets for it; and that a fortnight before Svars had visited him at his lodgings and showed him a Browning pistol'.[18]

Juris Laiviņš explained his presence at Grove Street by saying he had gone there to see Peter the Painter, who had offered to help him find some decorating work, taking with him a watercolour he had painted as a gift. 'Peter the Painter had told me that he would have some other painting work, to paint a certain house'. Afterwards he returned home to Shepherd's Bush and had not gone out again that night.[19] According to Luba Milstein, Marx (Max Smoller) had arrived 'about three o'clock that afternoon bringing in a long narrow packet done up in paper'.[20] Fricis Svars and Josef Sokolov left Grove Street together about five o'clock in the afternoon, after all the other guests had left; Fricis telling Luba that he would be gone overnight and to expect him back around eleven the next morning. When Luba Milstein and her friend Sara Trassjonsky went out to the cinema, only Peter the Painter remained at home, playing the violin in his room.

At 11.30 that evening the police blundered into Exchange Buildings and met a hail of gunfire. Three officers were dead and two more badly wounded. 'City Policemen Murdered By Alien Burglars', *The Daily Graphic* announced over a lurid sketch which filled the front page, showing the unarmed officers being mown down by bowler hatted gunmen.[21] Puika Hartmanis had been found dead at Grove Street and Sara Trassjonsky arrested, but the police had few clues as to who were responsible, or where the killers were now. But from the papers left in the flat it was apparent that they were dealing with Latvian anarchists.

According to the information of the Special Branch in 1911, 'The so called "Liesma" (Flame) group ... came into existence within the past two years and consisted of eight or nine members. They had no regular place of meeting and were almost unknown to members of recognised groups. None of the persons concerned in the Houndsditch crimes were known as Anarchists although some of them frequented Jubilee Street and other meeting places. They appear to have formed part of a section of foreign criminals who used the term "Anarchy" to cover their otherwise nefarious callings. Their real object, it would appear, was not the furtherance of an anarchical movement or conspiracy, but plunder and robbery for personal gain.'[22] Despite this official pronouncement, Superintendent Quinn of Special Branch was reported in *The Times* of 1st January 1911 as saying that Special Branch, 'have little doubt that these men were "expropriators"' The 'eight or nine' members of *Liesma* included Fricis Svars (the group's secretary), Jānis Žāklis (treasurer), Puika Hartmanis, Jānis Celiņš, Alfrēds Dzirkalis and Juris Laiviņš.

When the police searched Svars' lodgings at Grove Street they found correspondence between two Latvian anarchist groups in London (*Liesma* and *Censonis* (Zealot) probably the same people under different names) and the *Brīvība* group in New York. The Grove Street letters give a small insight into the activities of the Latvian anarchists in exile. They were trying to form an international federation amongst the émigré groups in London, Paris, New York, and Philadelphia; and had contacts also in Zurich, Baku, Liepāja and Rīga. The paper *Brīvība* (smuggled back into Latvia) was appearing at two-monthly intervals, and had reached number six by the time of the Houndsditch shootings. They were also active in support of their comrades inside prison. Much of the correspondence was concerned with the prisoners in Riga Central

Prison. In this work they were in close touch with the *Melnais Karogs* group in Paris and maintained links with the Anarchist Red Cross organisation, a Committee for Impartial Prisoners (revolutionaries belonging to no particular group), and with the Socialist Revolutionary Party in Baku. All of this helped clarify the motivation of the robbery, but the investigation was still nowhere near finding the culprits.

* * *

On Sunday afternoon, 18th December 1910, Luba Milstein walked into Leman Street police station with her brother Jack. 'This is my sister Luby', he told the desk sergeant. 'This is the young woman the police are looking for. She lived at 59 Grove Street.'[23] Unaware of what Fricis Svars and his friends were doing until their dramatic midnight appearance at Grove Street, Milstein was still in shock. Her respectable Jewish family had insisted that her only option was to tell all to the police. Milstein made a statement saying she didn't know if Svars was at home or not before the wounded Gardstein (Hartmanis) was brought to Grove Street: 'Fritz had left me about five o'clock on Friday afternoon to get some money which had been sent him by his parents. I do not know that any money had been sent to him, very likely he was making a fool of me.'[24]

While Svars was away, Milstein left Peter the Painter alone in the front room and went to the cinema with Sara Trassjonsky. The two women left the pictures at 9.30 p.m. and returned home to have supper, not bothering to check if Svars had returned. Though in a subsequent statement, she noted that Peter the Painter was still in his room: 'I knew Peter the Painter was in the front room, as I had heard him playing the violin; I saw him at 10 o'clock but not afterwards.' [25] When Hartmanis was carried there after midnight, Milstein did not see the men who brought him: '… I was sitting in the back room. I remember two or three people running up the stairs after 12 o'clock. I think I was lying on the bed reading a book. I did not see anybody. I only heard men running upstairs. I went to look who it was. I knocked at the door of the front room. Fritz told me not to come in. I went back in the back room. After that some one opened the door of the back room. It was Max [Smoller]. He asked where Fritz was. I said "In the front room". Max went there. A few minutes later Fritz came to the back room. He didn't say much. He was very excited… I saw someone in the passage. It was Josef [William Sokolov].'[26] After a hurried conference Smoller handed Svars a Browning pistol and left, never to be seen again.

The presence at Grove Street of the mortally wounded Hartmanis made it impossible for Svars, Sokolov and Žāklis to remain in the flat without risking going to the gallows. Leaving instructions with Milstein and Trassjonsky to tend to the wounded man as best they could and to destroy any papers in the flat, the three men walked out into the night. Milstein couldn't stand the strain of being with the dying Hartmanis for long. Leaving him in the care of Trassjonsky, she left the flat and went in search of Svars at the only safe address she could think of: 'I went to Hoffman's 36 Lindley Street… Hoffman [Dzirkalis] was there. He was not in bed. Fritz, Peter the Painter, and Josef were there. Josef [Sokolov] had a revolver in his hand.'[27] Fricis told Milstein a story about having carried

Hartmanis 'like a baby' and brought him to Grove Street because he was crying out in pain, but he wouldn't say what had happened or let her stay. Cross examined during the committal hearings, Milstein said that her first statement to police after her arrest 'was not entirely true'; she had not told the truth because she was afraid of being charged with being involved, and of giving away Svars, Sokolov, Peter the Painter and Smoller.[28]

* * *

Since finding the address of Yourka Dubov (Juris Laiviņš) at Grove Street the police had been keeping the house in Galloway Road, Shepherds Bush, under careful surveillance. But on 20th December there was a leak to the press. A reporter from the *Evening News*, George Mumford, called at the house and spoke to the German landlady, Elsa Petter, saying that the police were offering a reward of £500 for the arrest of a man named Yourka, and didn't she have a lodger of that name? Laiviņš was called in and interviewed, though Mrs. Petter did most of the talking. No, Laiviņš assured the reporter, the names Fritz and Peter the Painter meant nothing to him. The next day the paper ran the story, 'Yourka — A Common Name Leads to Confusion. The Tale of a Painter. Yourka is Russian For George.' At two o'clock the day after that, 22nd December, Detective Inspector William Newell of the City Police led a raid on the Galloway Road address and arrested Laiviņš. 'You make mistake, terrible, gross', Laiviņš protested as he was led away.[29]

On the other side of London, Nikolai Tokmakov led Detective Inspectors Collison, MacNamara and Wensley to 48 Turner Street, Whitechapel, behind the London Hospital. Tokmakov played the balalaika in the emigrant clubs of the East End, and had been friendly with Fricis Svars. Now the prospect of claiming £500 reward money overrode personal loyalties. Svars had once lent him a guitar belonging to his cousin Jēkabs Peterss. He had only seen Peterss when he came later to collect the instrument, and briefly at a concert in the anarchist club in Jubilee Street. But he knew where Peterss lived. At 8.30 p.m., Jēkabs Peterss came home. Twenty-four-years-old, five feet eight inches tall, long brown hair and a slight moustache, dressed in his work clothes underneath a dark grey overcoat with a velvet collar. He was very tired after a hard day's work as a tailor's presser at Landau & Son in Spitalfields, and needed a rest and some tea. As he opened the door to the ground floor front room he rented, armed men suddenly surrounded him. A man whom he later discovered was an interpreter from the Thames Police Court, Casimir Pilenas, spoke to him in Russian and told him they were police officers. They searched him and told him he was under arrest. Something was said about a dead man being found in Svars' room. 'I don't care', said Peterss, 'I know nothing at all about it — I can't help what my cousin Fritz has done.'[30]

After their arrests, Jēkabs Peterss and Juris Laiviņš were put on a lineup, with thirteen other men, in the muster room of Bishopsgate police station. One after the other, the police brought in possible witnesses who might identify members of the Houndsditch gang. Solomon and Philip Abrahams pointed to Laiviņš. Isaac Levy and George Richardson identified Laiviņš and Peterss. Joseph Da

Costa identified Peterss alone. Ethel Millmore and E. J. Craighe thought Peterss was the man who had bought a sheet of asbestos from them on 10th December, like the ones found in Exchange Buildings. At 9.30 a.m. on 24th December 1911, Peterss and Laiviņš were charged with the murder of the three policemen at Houndsditch. Both men replied, via an interpreter, 'We deny all knowledge and we are not guilty.'[31]

Five days later, Peterss, Laiviņš, and a third suspect, Osip Federov (another friend of Fricis Svars', arrested late on the evening of 22nd December), were put on another identity parade at Guildhall Police Court. Henry Isaacs picked out Peterss and Federov as men he had seen with George Gardstein (Hartmanis) sometime in the middle of November, and Federov as being with Hartmanis again in Cutler Street on 1st December 1910. Ivan Bassinin pointed to Peterss as a man he had met at Jubilee Street anarchist club. Peterss protested, through the interpreter, 'I do not think it is fair as the photographs have appeared in the newspapers.'[32]

On the day Peterss, Laiviņš and Federov were arrested, the police issued a wanted poster showing a mortuary photograph of Puika Hartmanis (see image 35) and offering a reward of £500 for information leading to the arrest of Fricis Svars and Peter the Painter.

Notes

1   LVVA, 4568/8/187, Riga *Okhranka* file No.10. 1/1, N. 109400, 14th April 1910
2   Donald Rumbelow, *The Houndsditch Murders and the Siege of Sidney Street* (revised edition, London 1988), p. 64.
3   Interview with Richard Whittington Egan, Malvern, 19th March 1988. Richard interviewed Nina Vasileva at her flat at 99 Brick Lane, on 14th November 1960.
4   Files of the City of London Police, 'Houndsditch Murders', Box 1.5 (a), Statement of Luba Milstein, 17th February 1911, London Metropolitan Archives.
5   James Edward Holroyd, *The Gaslight Murders: The Saga of Sidney Street and the Scarlet 'S'* (London, 1960), p. 36.
6   Ibid.
7   *Rex vs. Peters and others*, CRIM.1/122, p.33, Testimony of Luba Milstein, 10th May 1911, National Archives.
8   James Edward Holroyd, *The Gaslight Murder*, op. cit., p. 36
9   'Houndsditch Murders', Box 3.15, Statement of Esther Goodman, 31st January 1911, op. cit.
10 Rudolf Rocker, *The London Years* (London 1956), p. 205.
11 Max Nomad, *Dreamers, Dynamiters and Demagogues* (New York, 1964), pp. 146-50.
12 'Houndsditch Murders', Box 1.5 (a), Statement of Luba Milstein (Holloway Prison), 17th February 1911, op. cit.
13 *The Times*, 25th January 1911.
14 The Proceedings of The Old Bailey, London's Central Criminal Court, 1674-1913, Ref. No: t19110425-75, Testimony of Dubov (Laiviņš), 9 May 1911: https://www.oldbaileyonline.org/browse.jsp?id=def2-75-19110425&div=t19110425-75
15 LVVA, 4568/8/187, op. cit.
16 Ibid.
17 'Houndsditch Murders', 534C/1.4, Letter from Anna Schwarz to K. R. Schtern [Jānis Žāklis] in London, 26th September 1910, op. cit.
18 Nikolai Tokmakov, evidence at the Old Bailey, 5th May 1911; The Proceedings of The Old Bailey, Ref. No: t19110425-75, op. cit..
19 *The Times*, 25th January 1911.
20 The Proceedings of The Old Bailey, Testimony of Luba Milstein, 10th May 1911, op. cit.
21 *The Daily Graphic*, No.6360, Vol. LXXXIV, London, 19th December, 1910,
22 'Houndsditch Murders', 534C/1.4, Assistant Commissioner of Police CID, Special Branch, Sir Melville Macnaughten to Nott-Bower, 30th January 1911, op. cit.
23 'Houndsditch Murders', 534C/1.1, Statement of Luba Milstein, 18th December 1910, op. cit.
24 Ibid.
25 'Houndsditch Murders', 534C/1.5 (b), Statement of Luba Milstein taken at the Guildhall on 23rd January, 1911, op. cit
26 *Rex vs. Peters and others*, CRIM.1/121, p.562-565, Testimony of Luba Milstein, 17th March 1911, op. cit.
27 Ibid., p. 566.
28 *The Times*, 18th March 1911.
29 Statement of Detective Inspector William Newell, 22nd December 1910.
30 'Houndsditch Murders', 534C/1.1, Peters, cited in the statements of Inspector John Collison and Police Interpreter Casimir Pilenas, 8th January 1911, op. cit.
31 *Rex v. Peters and others*, CRIM1/121, op. cit.
32 'Houndsditch Murders', 534C/1.1, op. cit.

10

January 1911 to December 1912
Retribution

I thought it better to let the house burn down rather than spend good
British lives rescuing those ferocious rascals.

Winston Churchill[1]

On New Year's Day 1911, the police got lucky. Tempted by the £500 reward
money, a mysterious informer came up with the whereabouts of Fricis Svars.
The man, whose identity was established only in 1973,[2] gave them a letter he said
Svars had asked him to post. Written to his father in Liepajā care of a family
friend, Jānis Sudmalis (two of whose sons had been executed in February 1909
for a string of expropriations),[3] it contained Svars' carefully couched version of
what had happened: 'I think there is no point any more in me telling you now
about London and the search for myself and others. I only want to tell you how
it all came about, and say that all of us who are on the run and who got arrested,
are completely innocent and didn't have the slightest connection with that
robbery, or the scheme for which we are hunted down. Matters stand as follows:
a short while ago I wrote to you that I would soon be going to that long
dreamed about land — "Australia". This would have happened between the 7th
and 10th of January, 1911. Also, by that time my wife would have been here, and
then both of us, along with three other men, would have left England.'[4]

Svars had enough money for the journey ('300 roubles from Russia'), and
from it had sent his wife 100 roubles (£10) and spent 160 roubles buying two
ship's tickets. But then, 'Some three weeks ago Puika (you remember him, the
shoemaker's son), who had just come from Paris, came to see me and asked me
to lend him 100 roubles for a short while, just for two weeks — he needed the
money badly, for there was a brilliant chance to get rich quick, in two weeks at
most. He showed me a telegram saying that his folks had also sent him 300
roubles.'[5] Svars lent Puika (Hartmanis) £6, leaving himself with £2. A week later
Hartmanis visited Svars again to say that after three or four days he would get
his money back with considerable interest: 'There was a prospect of getting a
couple of thousand pounds, in which case he would give me £100 (1,000
roubles). Of course, I was delighted.'[6]

That same Saturday night around midnight, two 'acquaintances' arrived at
Svars' flat carrying the wounded Hartmanis, who was unable to walk. 'I couldn't
stay in the flat a minute longer, because I was not sure if they had been seen
while bringing the wounded man into my flat — I would get arrested for
nothing and surely hung.'[7] The 'two acquaintances' fled immediately and Svars,
grabbing his gun and ammunition, went to 'some comrades' he knew. From
there he sent 'two girls' to go and bandage Hartmanis, fetch a doctor, clean out
the flat and burn all his letters and papers. The women returned three hours later
and told him that Hartmanis was dying. The doctor had been and said

Hartmanis must go to hospital but he had refused. Svars sent the women back to Grove Street to fetch his new clothes, photographs and ship's tickets. If Hartmanis should die they were to pour paraffin over him and set fire to the flat so that the police wouldn't know that he had been wounded, and any other evidence would be burnt. Hartmanis died and the police arrived before the flat could be set alight: 'One of the girls was noticed in the street, but managed to escape and brought me the ship tickets, but nothing else. I left at once and told her to keep the tickets safe. Immediately after I left, the police surrounded the house and arrested the girl. I don't know anything more about the ship tickets or anything else. Another lad had been staying with me, who also left.'[8]

The landlord had described them both to the police and they were looking for them as participants in the shooting: 'The whole of London is swarming with police. I know nothing about the other comrade, except that he still has not been arrested. If arrested he, as well as I, would most certainly be hung, because the real perpetrators are not known, and my landlord said that he didn't know if we were at home that evening or not. I am telling you, that if they capture us, they will hang us anyway, so I am going to resist them and then shoot myself.

'Jēkabs is arrested, who really is the last person to know anything about it, as well as two other comrades, only because they came to paint in my flat and were my friends... For two weeks now I have been on the run, I don't know how much longer I can manage. It is impossible to leave the city now; all the roads are closely guarded. I am not at all depressed, everyone knows that we all have to die, and what good can a man like me bring to mankind? It is not worth talking about it now.

'To you it wouldn't make a difference, either, because up till now I have not been able to help you — and in future, what luck would I have? So remain calm — if I get lucky and survive this, I will live and share with you the joys and sorrows; if not, then you will know that one day the same hour will come to you and you will be ashes the same as everyone else. Don't say anything to the shoemaker, she will find out herself soon enough. I kiss you all, and my dear friends. Send a kiss to Lisa also, because I am not allowed to write. Don't tell anyone — no one at all — about my whereabouts. Don't write before I contact you through comrades. Your Fricis'[9]

Some comment is required about the degree of candour in this letter. The affirmation of Jēkabs Peterss' innocence ('Jekabs is arrested, who really is the last person to know anything about it'[10]) is supported by other evidence, but Svars' protestation of his own innocence is at odds with the known facts. The letter is questionable on other grounds. What was the source of the 300 roubles, which Svars said he received from Russia? Who were the 'two acquaintances' who brought Hartmanis to the Grove Street flat? Svars' information about the movements of the 'two girls' (obviously Milstein and Trassjonsky) contradicts Milstein's statements to the police.[11] How can the mention of one woman ('noticed in the street') slipping away to bring him the tickets be reconciled with Svars' suggestion that he then visited Grove Street himself before the police arrested her in the flat? The reference to 'another lad', Žāklis, 'who also left' is ambiguous. Does this mean just that Žāklis fled, or that he returned to Grove

Street with Svars?

From the tone of the letter, and the fact that Svars was communicating with his family 'through comrades', implying that they were aware of his revolutionary activities and did not disapprove of them, the obvious inference is that Svars is telling his family what they should say (with the letter to prove it) when they received the inevitable visit from the Russian police.

News of Hartmanis' condition was first brought to Svars by Luba Milstein, tallying with her first visit to Dzirkalis' lodgings. Luba did what she was told, and, with Trassjonsky in tow, went in search of a doctor. Dr. Scanlon testified that two women roused him at 3.30, telling him only that 'There is a man very bad at 59 Grove Street'. As he followed them along Commercial Road to the flat one of the women (Milstein) 'disappeared down a street on the north side' (Settles Street, where Trassjonsky lived). Hartmanis refused to go to hospital, so at 4.30 the doctor took Trassjonsky to his surgery and gave her some medicine. On the way back Trassjonsky stopped at Settles Street to see Milstein and the two women went to consult Svars, confirming this part of his account (if we ignore the testimony of Milstein and Dzirkalis to the contrary). But this time Milstein's nerve gave way. Instead of bringing Svars his things as instructed, she went back to Settles Street, leaving Trassjonsky to tend to Hartmanis. This explains why Svars felt it necessary to return to Grove Street himself. When Dr. Scanlon visited Grove Street again at 11.15 he saw 'two young men' in the passage. 'They appeared to be English. I asked them "How is the man upstairs?" They replied that they knew nothing about him'.[12]

Hartmanis was dead. Nobody else was in the flat. Trassjonsky had presumably 'managed to escape' to speak to Svars and his companion. Scanlon went downstairs but the 'two young men' had gone. He returned to his surgery and called the coroner's office, who alerted the police[13]. Trassjonsky was busy burning photographs when the police arrived an hour later, narrowly missing Svars, and took her into custody.

The mysterious informer who betrayed Fricis Svars was Charles Perelman. Svars, he said, was staying with Yoshka (Sokolov) in Betty Gershon's room at 100 Sidney Street, Stepney[14].

* * *

Fricis Svars and William Sokolov had been in hiding for two weeks. Both of them were certain they would hang if captured. The police, who were bent on revenge for the deaths of their colleagues, made it plain by their actions that no quarter would be offered. The situation was simple, with five unarmed policemen shot their colleagues were out for blood, and the occupants of Sidney Street had discounted any idea of surrender. A peaceful resolution of the matter was never an option.

Despite their new intelligence, the police reacted with murderous ineptness. Perelman told the police that the fugitives planned to leave Betty Gershon's at 5 or 6 p.m. the next day to go to another hideout — kindly arranged by him. It would have been a simple business to arrest them without undue fuss when they walked into the trap. Instead, when Perelman returned to Sidney Street the next afternoon, two large horse drawn furniture vans filled with armed police were positioned outside in the street, ready to ambush the wanted men as they left. But nothing happened. Betty Gershon went to see Perelman at nine that evening and said that Svars would leave at nine the next night. Sokolov would want a coded message from Svars that he was safe, before leaving Sidney Street to join him. Apparently incapable of playing the game of cat and mouse with any subtlety, the police finally surrounded the house in the early morning of 3rd January with 750 officers (fifty of them armed), and evacuated the innocent tenants from the building. By a ruse, Betty Gershon was lured downstairs and taken into custody. But still no attempt was made to take Svars and Sokolov peacefully. The scene was set for a massacre.

At 7.30 a.m., seemingly at a loss as to what else to do, the police sent Detective Sergeant Benjamin Leeson up to the front of the house to throw pebbles at the windows. When this elicited no response from inside, he lobbed a brick through one of the second floor windows. This time he got an answer: a hail of bullets burst from behind the curtains, scattering the policemen opposite and wounding Leeson in the chest. The melodramatic Leeson is said to have uttered, 'I am dying. They have shot me through the heart. Goodbye. Give my love to the children. Bury me at Putney.'[15] Happily for Leeson, the bullet passed through his chest and come out the other side. He survived to write his memoirs. The Siege had begun.

For over an hour sporadic fire from inside the house kept the police at bay. Representations were made to the War Office, and the Liberal Home Secretary, Winston Churchill, was telephoned at home where he was in the middle of having a bath. Churchill, according to his own account, received the news 'Dripping wet and shrouded in a towel'.[16] He immediately telephoned the Home Office and authorised the use of troops from the Tower of London garrison. At 10.50 a.m., Lieutenant Hugh "Jock" Ross, two NCOs, and 17 men of the 1st Battalion Scots Guards arrived at the siege armed with Lee-Enfield rifles and took up positions at both ends of the street. Churchill himself, his 'strong sense of curiosity'[17] aroused, arrived at midday and took charge. It was an unparalleled event for a Home Secretary to participate so directly in a police operation of this sort.

Never a man for erring on the side of restraint, Churchill ordered that machine guns and artillery be summoned and placed in a state of readiness. Two 13lb field guns were despatched to the scene but did not arrive until 2.40 p.m., after the battle was over.

Churchill went far beyond his professed intention of merely observing the action. As he admitted himself, 'Some of the police officers were anxious to storm the building at once with pistols… It was not for me to interfere with those who were in charge on the spot. Yet … my position of authority, far above them all, attracted inevitably to itself direct responsibility.'[18] Which is a clever way of saying that he couldn't resist the urge to join in and take over when somebody sounded the charge. Plans were made to rush the building, get onto the roof and leap onto Svars and Sokolov from above. Churchill confessed that his 'own instincts turned at once to a direct advance up the staircase behind a steel plate or shield, and search was made in the foundries of the neighbourhood for one of a suitable size.'[19] But then, what Violet Bonham Carter calls 'these tactical problems'[20] (how best to attack Svars and Sokolov) were fortuitously solved. Just before one o'clock fire broke out in the upper storeys of the house, probably as a result of a bullet striking a gas pipe.

As the fire took hold, a fire engine arrived and an argument broke out between the police, who wanted the house to burn, and the firemen, who considered it their duty to put out the flames. Churchill personally settled the dispute by ordering the firemen to stand back and make no attempt to put out the fire until the occupants of the house were unquestionably dead. 'I thought it better to let the house burn down rather than spend good British lives rescuing those ferocious rascals',[21] he wrote later that day to Prime Minister Asquith.

Svars and Sokolov continued to move around the house, shooting at the troops and police from front and rear windows. A second detachment of fifty men of the 1st Battalion Scots Guards, led by Lieutenants J. C. Wickham and E. B. Trafford, joined the besiegers at 1.30 p.m., bringing with them a Maxim machine gun mounted on a tripod, but the machine gun was not used. It was shortly after this that Sokolov was struck in the head by a rifle bullet, from one of the soldiers posted behind the house. He was killed outright. Fricis Svars went on resisting bravely, forced down to the ground floor by the advancing flames. The last shots to come from inside the house were fired at 1.50 p.m. from the ground floor window near the front door. With all three floors above him now ablaze, Svars finally collapsed, overcome by smoke.

At two o'clock, with the roof and floors collapsing, the besiegers finally ceased firing and allowed the fire brigade to advance. Ironically, it was at this point that the forces of law and order suffered their only fatality of the day: a fireman was killed by falling masonry. The Siege had lasted for over seven hours.

The charred remains of Svars and Sokolov were recovered from the smoking ruins of the house. An inquest held on 8th, 9th and 18th January, concluded that Joseph had been shot through the head by a soldier whilst on an upper floor and had fallen through to the ground floor when the building collapsed. Svars died where he had been found, near to the front door. Cause of death: suffocation. A Mauser lay beneath his body, and another a foot away.[22] The remains of both men were buried on 23 January 1911, in unconsecrated ground at the Corporation of London Cemetery, Manor Park. Their plain coffins of unpolished elm bore brass plates, which read simply (and inaccurately): 'Fritz Svaars, aged 27'. 'Joseph, aged 25'. Fricis Svars was 25, William (Josef) Sokolov was 30. The man who betrayed them, Charles Perelman, was paid £166 13s 4d for Svars. To the General Purposes Committee of Aldermen who calculated the amount of the reward, Joseph was worth nothing.

* * *

The Central Committee of the Latvian Social Democracy in Brussels reacted to the shootings at Houndsditch, and the arrest of Jēkabs Peterss, by issuing a long disclaimer of any involvement in the affair (citing the Party's 1907 ban on expropriations).[23] The Party Foreign Committee, in a letter to the London LSD branch, declared Peterss innocent and called for a non-party defence. The

London members responded by persuading Aleksei Aladin, formerly a *Trudovik* (Popular Socialist Party, literally *Labour*) deputy in the *First Duma*, to organise Peterss' defence; and a Svanelis (Peterss' revolutionary nickname) defence fund was set up. On 21st April, Aladin wrote to Aleksander Zirnis that over £45 had already been collected. In America, the LSD paper *Strādnieks* announced on 12th May that $70.75 had been paid into the fund.

Aladin, a complex and abrasive character (who in 1917 went back to Russia as an agent of the British War Cabinet, and was instrumental in persuading General Kornilov to attempt the overthrow of Kerensky's Provisional Government and install a military dictatorship friendly to Britain), evidently quarrelled with a number of people concerned with Peterss' defence. In the letter to Zirnis, Aladin announces that he is breaking off relations with the old émigré A. L. Teplov, who ran a Russian lending library in the East End and kept the Houndsditch prisoners supplied with books; the same man whom the *Okhranka* says supplied guns and bombs to The Avengers (*Atriebējs*) anarchist group in 1909. According to Aladin the *Daily Express* had named Teplov as Peter the Painter. Teplov sued, and settled out of court for £100 plus costs. When Aladin telephoned asking how much of the money he might expect for the Svanelis defence fund, Teplov sent a £5 contribution. Two days later, Aladin discovered the £5 was money given to Teplov for the fund by another comrade.[24]

In London, the anarchist Errico Malatesta was briefly detained and questioned by police about his connection with Hartmanis. He told the police that he had been introduced to the man found dead in Grove Street ('a man whose name and address I do not know') about twelve months before at the anarchist club in Jubilee Street, and had allowed him to use his workshop at Duncan Terrace, Islington: 'He was I understood a Russian political refugee and an engineer. During the past 12 months he has used my workshop to do any little job he has had.'[25] Malatesta said that on 15th December he had sold the gas cylinder, and other apparatus found at Houndsditch, to a man called Louis Lambert for £5. Lambert spoke to him in French and paid a £1 deposit. The following day (the day of the shooting), 'an English looking lad' had come to collect the equipment, paying the balance of £4.

Earlier in the day a man giving his name as Charles Sommerfeld or Summerfeldt, and an address of 42 Gold Street, pawned a watch for £4. Hartmanis lived at 44 Gold Street, and had pawned a diamond ring in the same pawnshop on 1st November under the name Stenzel. Evidence produced in court showed that the man who pawned the watch and sent the money to Malatesta was Juris Laiviņš. The police checked the address given to Malatesta by Lambert (85 Dean Street, Soho) and found it was a pub. Nobody there had heard of Lambert. The police accepted Malatesta's story and released him.

Jānis Celiņš was already of interest to the police, having attended the social gathering at Fricis Svars' flat on the day of the shooting. On 31st January, 1911, he married Rose Campbell, someone he had been seeing for eight months, at the insistence of her mother who claimed he had seduced the girl, and possibly to gain the legal protection that a wife is not obliged to give evidence against her husband. Rose had told her mother, who told her son-in-law Edward

Humphreys, that on Christmas Eve, 1910, Celiņš had introduced Rose to Peter the Painter at an address in the East End. Celiņš was also alleged to have told Rose that he was a member of the gang, 'and that if any of them had been sick on the night of the murders he was the next one to be called upon to assist'.[26] He also claimed to know about the Tottenham Outrage and 'the Scotch Bank case' (the Motherwell bank robbery); and that a reward had been offered by the Russian government for the arrest of Gardstein (Hartmanis) for participation in 'an outrage in Russia.'[27] Rose denied the whole story when questioned, but her mother said she thought he might be connected with the gang.[28]

On 2nd February 1911, Celiņš was arrested at the barber's shop he worked at in Hackney. At first he denied everything put to him. Then on 5th February, he suddenly changed his story and made a new statement, naming names, and specifically identifying Karl Hoffman (Dzirkalis) as the man to whom Svars, Sokolov, and Žāklis had turned for help on the night of the shooting. He also named Nina Vasileva as having been at Houndsditch. Celiņš was not charged until 8th February, and then only with the lesser charge of conspiracy to break and enter.

Vasileva was already under police observation. Foolishly, she had told her landlord, Isaac Gordon that she had been at Exchange Buildings on the day of the murders, but that she had left before the shooting began. She entrusted Gordon with a parcel of books and photographs. Gordon went straight to the police and told all. On 18th December Vasileva was visited by Inspector Wensley (who missed bumping into Celiņš by only ten minutes), but she was not taken into custody until 7th February. The next day, Isaac Levy picked her out from a line-up at Bishopsgate police station as the woman he had seen with the men who had threatened him at Houndsditch.

The suspects in the Houndsditch case seemed plagued by loose-tongued landlords and acquaintances. Another informer, twenty-nine-year-old Teodors Jansons, had been feeding the police information since 23rd December, 1910, in a vain attempt to wheedle money out of them. Jansons told the police he had first met Fricis Svars at a concert at the International Seafarers Club in West India Dock Road sometime around the end of 1909, and they had visited each other occasionally since then. He had last seen Svars on 10th December, but said he could be contacted by writing to K. R. Schtern (a name attributed by the police to Peter the Painter) at 77 Whitehorse Street, Stepney. Jansons said that a man called Greenberg lived at that address who was very friendly with Svars and Peter the Painter, and he was of the opinion that he may be sheltering them there. He also identified the dead Gardstein (Hartmanis) as someone he had seen at the Jubilee Street club.[29] The police visited Whitehorse Street and interviewed Charles Greenberg, who said he was a locksmith employed by the London Electron Works in Stepney; not surprisingly he denied knowing Fricis Svars or Peter the Painter.[30]

In a further statement to the police Jansons reported a conversation on Christmas Day, in which he had asked Mazais (Alfrēds Dzirkalis), whether the three men then under arrest (Peterss, Federov and Laiviņš) were guilty. Dzirkalis had laughed and replied: 'No. There were nine men in the plot; none of them are yet arrested. It's a pity the man is dead [meaning Gardstein], he was the ablest of the lot and the leader of the gang. He also managed it that some members of the gang did not know the others'.[31] Dzirkalis also said that he thought one of the murderers had left the country aboard a ship. When Jansons asked about Whitehorse Street, Dzirkalis replied that the police had been there and it wasn't safe.[32] Jansons offered to find out where Gardstein had been living, if the police gave him some money, and returned the next day with the address (44 Gold Street) saying that 'a man' (Dzirkalis?) had asked him to collect three trunks from there. But the police had already raided the address. Jansons visited them again on 28th December, identifying a photo of Peter the Painter as someone that he had seen at the Jubilee Street club and a handwriting sample as belonging to Svars, and said he had not seen Dzirkalis since Christmas Day.

Despite his treachery Jansons was not playing entirely fair with the police either. Dzirkalis had fled to Antwerp after the Siege of Sidney Street, but when he suddenly reappeared on his doorstep, on 31st January, Jansons somehow neglected to inform the police. Unfortunately for both men, Dzrikalis' former landlord at 36 Lindley Street had told the police that mail for his former lodger could be forwarded to 114 Cannon Street (between Commercial Road and Cable Street), the address of Teodors Jansons.

The police raided Jansons' house at 2.15 in the morning of 8th February, only a few hours after the arrest of Nina Vasileva, and found Dzirkalis asleep in bed. In the pocket of a blue serge jacket hanging on a chair, Superintendent Ottaway found a passport in the name of Peter Trohimschik (the alias Fricis Svars had used when he lived at Newcastle Place).[33] Made of sterner stuff than the talkative Jānis Celiņš, Dzirkalis steadfastly refused to account for his movements, and made a token statement that is remarkable for its mixture of defiance, lies, and attempts at deliberately wrong-footing the investigation. Two days after his arrest Dzirkalis was confronted at Bishopsgate police station by Teodors Jansons, who told the police that he had seen him wear the jacket several times. But Dzirkalis remained defiant, protesting, 'That is not my passport. I know nothing about it. I never wore that jacket. Jansons may say what he likes, I never wore that jacket'.[34] On 15th February, Dzirkalis was finally charged with conspiracy to break and enter.

Teodors Jansons made one last feeble attempt to extract money from the police by telling them that, 'about two years ago a reward of $20,000 was offered by the American police for the arrest of Fritz Svars for participation in a shooting outrage in Pennsylvania, USA'.[35] Besides the fact the incident had taken place in Boston, the information was totally worthless, Svars was already dead.

* * *

At the end of December, Peterss, Trassjonsky, Milstein, Laiviņš and Federov had been brought to the Guildhall separately and in secret for a committal hearing. The public was excluded from the court, and a big crowd gathered outside the Guildhall to watch the prisoners driven away in two vans afterwards. The scene of good-natured curiosity at the Guildhall changed dramatically after the Siege of Sidney Street, which took place between hearings. Fearing that a serious attempt would be mounted to free the prisoners, the police put six armed warders aboard the van bringing Peterss, Laiviņš and Federov to the Guildhall from Brixton prison on 7th January. Large numbers of armed police watched over the huge crowds that waited to get a glimpse of the prisoners, and guarded every possible approach to the Guildhall. Proof of identity was demanded from all who entered the court, and armed Special Branch detectives kept watch inside.

On 23rd January, Archibald Bodkin opened the case for the prosecution against Trassjonsky, Milstein, Laiviņš, Peterss and Federov. The principal prosecution witnesses were Isaac Levy (who claimed to have seen the men escaping from Houndsditch after the shooting) and George Richardson, a jeweller's assistant in Houndsditch, friendly with Solomon Abrahams (who lived in Exchange Buildings and knew Hartmanis by sight). Hartmanis had once struck up a conversation with Richardson and tried to pump him for information about Houndsditch jeweller's shops, mentioning Harris's by name.

On 21st February, Luba Milstein was discharged on the grounds of insufficient evidence and allowed to go free. On 8th March, Sara Trassjonsky and Alfrēds Dzirkalis (whose non-co-operation had paid off) were discharged for the same reason. Trassjonsky was later to suffer a breakdown from the combined strain of tending the dying Hartmanis and the trial, and was admitted to Colny Hatch mental institution, where she eventually died, date unknown. Osip Federov, too, was discharged on 15th March.

The remaining defendants were committed for trial at the Central Criminal Court. Peterss and Laiviņš stood accused that they 'did kill and murder one Charles Tucker'; that, with Vasileva, they 'did ... harbour comfort and assist George Gardstein who ... had committed the crime of wilful murder, well knowing him to have committed the said crime'; and with Vasileva and Celiņš, 'did conspire ... together and with divers others to break and enter the shop of Henry Samuel Harris at 119 Houndsditch ... with intent to commit felony therein'.[36]

At the Committal hearing the defendants pleaded not guilty, and Prosecuting Counsel Archibald Bodkin began calling his witnesses. The prosecution's case was damning but circumstantial and badly prepared. All the defendants had been seen by neighbours, in or near Exchange Buildings before the day of the robbery attempt and shooting. Numbers 9 and 11 had been rented by Hartmanis (now dead) and Joe Levi (Smoller, who had escaped), plus a third man alleged to have been Fricis Svars. Vasileva and others had lived in Exchange Buildings in the days prior to the robbery to give the group's presence there an air of normality.

Louis Jonas, manager of J. Landau & Sons, the wholesale tailors in Spitalfields where Peterss worked, testified that he knew Peterss as Jacob Colnin. Peterss had worked at Landau's from around mid-July 1910 until 22nd December (from 7.30 a.m. until 7.30 p.m., with one hour for lunch). On Saturdays his hours were 8 a.m. until 2 p.m. with no interval. He had been paid 21 shillings a week and finished on 24 shillings. Peterss was away from work for only two afternoons during this whole period. On Friday 16th December, he had been paid in Jonas' presence at 8.30 p.m. and had then left to go home. He turned up for work again as usual the next day before 8 a.m. 'I noticed nothing different about his manner', said Jonas.[37]

Philip Abrahams, Peterss' landlord at 48 Turner Street said he knew the defendant as Jacob Peters and that he had come to lodge at that address four weeks before he was arrested. Peterss occupied the ground floor front room only. He usually left for work at 7.30 a.m. and returned in the evening around 8.30 p.m. On Friday 16th December he had gone out as usual. At 8.30 that night Abrahams was going out when Peterss came in. When he returned home around 9.30 p.m. there was a light on in Peterss' room. At 10 p.m., Abrahams said, he was asked by his wife to take Peterss a mousetrap he had asked for: 'I remained with him two or three minutes. The children were put to sleep and about 5 minutes afterwards I went out into the street. When I went out there was a light in Peters' room. I returned home at 11.30pm. Peters' room was dark then... Peters used to work in the wash house in the basement. In the morning I heard someone go downstairs about a quarter past seven. That was about his usual time. I heard the person come upstairs again into Peters' room and then I heard someone go out and bang the street door. The first time I saw Peters that day was the middle of the day... He remained in my house, keeping the same hours as usual, till he was arrested.'[38]

Alfrēds Dzirkalis gave evidence for the defence on 23rd March. He was in bed, he said, when Josef (Sokolov) came in around midnight and woke him up: 'He said Max had wounded Gardstein... He said they were somewhere — there was a fight and Max wounded Puika (Hartmanis). Josef had a Mauser pistol... In about two or three minutes Fritz came in alone. He had two pistols. One a Mauser and the other a Browning. In two or three minutes time Peter the Painter came also alone. Last of all Luba Milstein came — soon after Peter the Painter... [Fritz] said Max helped him to carry Gardstein to Grove Street and said that Max then gave him the Browning pistol and left and that he did not know where he had gone. Fritz said he had been carrying Gardstein [Hartmanis] like a baby. He said when they reached Commercial Road he intended leaving Gardstein there but Gardstein commenced to cry, so they took him to Grove Street... I began to dress. I asked them what was the matter with them when they came. Fritz and all of them said they intended to stay the night in my room. I would not let them and said I would leave if they stopped. So then they went away. I began to dress in order to leave. Luba went alone before the others. The others went all together. I have not seen any of them since.'[39] Dzirkalis was lucky that some of the material in the hands of the authorities was not introduced as evidence, otherwise he might not have been discharged from the case so easily.

Jānis Celiņš's statements to the police on 5th and 6th February caused a great stir amongst his co-defendants on remand. Not long before Dzirkalis was freed, the cleaner on 131 landing in Brixton's 'B' wing, Arthur Weeks (a criminal awaiting trial, who doubled as an informer for the prison officers), gave the authorities an exchange of secret notes passed, through him, between Dzirkalis and Laiviņš, in which they discussed Celiņš's admissions and adjusted their alibis accordingly. Remarkably, these notes were never introduced as evidence during the trial. If they had been, it is doubtful whether all of the people acquitted would have been. Amongst other things, the notes alluded to Celiņš having been involved in an expropriation in the USA: 'the American police will now take him for a similar case to this.'[40] Weeks also informed on Peterss, reporting a conversation he had with him whilst on exercise, when Peterss told him he expected to get five or six years.[41]

The Siege of Sidney Street opened up a way out for those in the dock. Taken together with the death of Puika Hartmanis at Grove Street, and the escape abroad of two other named suspects in the case, Max Smoller and Peter Piatkov (Jānis Žāklis), the judicial murder of Svars and Sokolov posed a problem of arithmetic for the court. The prosecution claimed that four men and a woman had been at Houndsditch. If the defendants were guilty as charged, then the men who died at Sidney Street must have been innocent. The political implications for Home Secretary Churchill were too catastrophic to contemplate. It could not be admitted that the savage overkill operation at Sidney Street was unnecessary, that it had been bungled, or that the wrong men had been killed for the sake of a moment of personal glory-seeking on Churchill's part. To cap it all, there was an added embarrassment: in the letter he wrote to his father and entrusted to Perelman, Fricis Svars claimed to be completely innocent, and the police must have known this before laying siege to the house in Sidney Street. If the chief suspects, who had all fled abroad or were now dead, were guilty then the people on trial could not be convicted.

* * *

The trial against Peterss, Laiviņš, Celiņš, and Vasileva opened at the Central Criminal Court at the Old Bailey on 1st May 1911, in front of Justice Sir William Grantham.

Jēkabs Peterss was identified as the man who had bought sheets of asbestos that were later found at the scene of the crime. Of the surviving police witnesses, PC Piper thought Laiviņš was one of the gunmen. D. C. Strongman said that Peterss was the man who had shot Tucker. The tobacconist, Isaac Levy identified Peterss, Laiviņš, and Vasileva as having carried Hartmanis away from Houndsditch. Unexpectedly, Justice Grantham stopped Prosecutor Bodkin from calling further witnesses and told him to save time; that on the evidence before him he could not recommend the jury to bring a guilty verdict on the murder charges against Laiviņš and Peterss. In his view it would be wiser to drop the murder charges and proceed with those of aiding and abetting, and conspiracy. The murder charges against Laiviņš and Peterss were dropped. The chief prosecution witness, Isaac Levy, was strongly attacked by the defence counsel, and Grantham directed that the charge against Laiviņš, Peterss, and Vasileva, of aiding and abetting Hartmanis, be dropped for lack of evidence. The trial against the four proceeded now only on the relatively minor charge of conspiracy to break and enter.

But before the trial continued Justice Grantham dropped his real bombshell. On 6th May, Grantham interrupted the proceedings to say that, in his opinion, three of the gang who had fired upon the police at Houndsditch had perished (Hartmanis, Svars, and Sokolov), and a fourth (Smoller) escaped abroad: 'There were three men firing shots and I think they are dead.'[42] This was echoed, for obvious reasons, by the defence case, which argued that there had been four conspirators: Hartmanis, Smoller, Svars and Sokolov. This was supported by Luba Milstein, who contradicted her earlier statement that she had not seen the men who brought Hartmanis to Grove Street, and said now (agreeing with Dzirkalis) that it had been Svars, Sokolov, and Smoller. On 12th May 1911, Peterss, Laiviņš, and Celiņš were found not guilty of the remaining charge and walked free from the dock. Nina Vasileva was convicted on fingerprint evidence (two bottles found in a cupboard at 11 Exchange Buildings), and she was sentenced to two years in prison. Five weeks later, the Court of Appeal quashed her sentence on the grounds of misdirection by Grantham, and she was released on 20th June 1911.

All the literature on Houndsditch portrays Vasileva as the "mistress" of Hartmanis, but she vehemently denied this to crime reporter Richard Whittington Egan in November 1960. She was not his "mistress". 'No', she said, 'I was never his mistress. No never... I introduced him to this other girl'[43] (a good friend of hers, who she claimed left the country after Hartmanis' death). The woman in question was Masha Sticking, who had lived at 40 Bromehead Street, Stepney, from September 1910. Police inquiries confirmed that both Hartmanis and Vasileva were constant visitors at the address. Masha was at home at the time of the shooting at Houndsditch, but afterwards was very upset and crying on several occasions, saying that she could not understand why Gardstein had not called to see her. Her landlady testified that Masha left at 7 p.m. on 25th December, saying she was 'going back to Russia'. She was last seen by the costermonger who wheeled her luggage to Liverpool Street Station in the company of an unknown man.[44] To Richard Whittington Egan, Vasileva said she had met the 'anarchist crowd' a long time before Houndsditch, when she lived at 29 Great Garden Street. Her room was the ground floor back. Upstairs, she remembered, lived Jēkabs Peterss and Fricis Svars ('a very charming man'). Max (Smoller) used to come and see them. Because her room was the only one with a fire in it, they all used to sit there to keep warm. Vasileva had never met Peter the Painter, and claimed to have met Trassjonsky for the first time in Holloway prison, but said she had known both Lenin ('a delightful person') and Kropotkin. Asked about Houndsditch, Vasileva said she was not at Exchange Buildings during the robbery, nor did she assist Hartmanis through the streets or at Grove Street.[45] 'I only came into it because I knew some of the men when I lived in the same house in Great Garden Street', she told James E. Holroyd in 1959, 'They couldn't prove anything at the trial.'[46]

* * *

The natural cynicism felt by the police towards the Old Bailey verdict ('English law maintained its great traditions, and the criminals went free',[47] City Police Commissioner, Nott-Bower) was indeed well founded, but for the wrong reasons. The release of Peterss and company was in part brought about by the need to justify Winston Churchill's unseemly conduct in personally directing the Siege of Sidney Street. The real irony of the outcome was that saving Churchill from further ignominy actually prevented a real miscarriage of justice, and allowed Jēkabs Peterss his later notoriety as mastermind of the Red Terror in

Russia.

Churchill's actions at the Siege of Sidney Street opened him to a fusillade of criticism. The Conservative opposition accused him of exhibitionism, play-acting, and interfering in matters he should have left to the police. In the Commons, the former Prime Minister Arthur Balfour stood up waving a picture of Churchill at Sidney Street and said, 'We are concerned to observe photographs in the illustrated papers of the Home Secretary in the danger zone. I understand what the photographer was doing, but why the Home Secretary?' Sir Harry Poland (a former prosecuting counsel for the Treasury) wrote in *The Times* that Churchill had, 'committed a grave error of judgement'. In his own Party too, many were disturbed by Churchill's melodramatic zeal for planning and directing military operations and indulging in overkill. A. G. Gardiner accurately summed up Churchill's state of mind: 'In the theatre of his mind it is always the hour of fate and the crack of doom'[48] The thirty-six-year-old Churchill loved every second of the Stepney battle. He dismissed his critics by attributing their adverse comments to, 'Sour grapes — they only wish they had been there to see the fun!'[49]

But Churchill's *chutzpah* was not enough to save him from the consequences of his action. The broad press coverage at home, which gave prominence to photographs of Churchill directing the operation, was echoed abroad where the French press in particular derided Churchill mercilessly. A newsreel in London cinemas showing Churchill issuing orders to the police was booed and mocked by the audiences, and he was referred to as 'the Napoleon of Sidney Street'. The Government hated this kind of publicity, and the King was said to have remarked that personally taking part in a fight in the East End was incompatible with the responsibilities of a Cabinet minister.

On 23rd October 1911 Churchill was moved from the Home Office to the Admiralty (where, during the First World War, he presided over the massacre of Australian and New Zealand troops on the beaches of Gallipoli). Austin Chamberlain remarked, 'Winston feels the Home Office is getting too hot for him.'[50]

* * *

The four men present at Houndsditch all died or escaped abroad, none therefore being among those brought to trial. Max Smoller fled to Paris by boat on the night of the murders. A bizarre twist to his escape is that the man who made it possible was Charles Perelman, the Sidney Street informer. Smoller sought Perelman's help after leaving Svars at Grove Street. As cover, Perelman loaned Smoller his ten-year-old daughter, Nettie, to accompany him on the voyage. Posing as her father, Smoller told the customs that the girl had diphtheria. When they arrived in Paris, Nettie was passed over to an aunt and Smoller disappeared. Perelman died in hospital three years later. Before he died he begged forgiveness of his son Carlusha, for betraying Svars and Sokolov.[51] On 26th February 1911 the police had information that Smoller was still in Paris, living at 9 Rue De Provence under the name Marks.[52] He was last sighted in Antwerp on 17th March, staying with a German couple who ran the St. Petersburg Café near the red light district at the docks.[53] On 25th April the police in London watched Smoller's wife and two children board a ship bound for Bremen in Germany.

All that was left was the mystery of Peter the Painter.

Edgar Allen Poe demonstrated that the best way to hide something was to put it in plain view. The trouble with mysteries is that the solution is often staring us in the face and we don't see it. Despite the confusion displayed in court, it is relatively simple to deduce from the evidence exactly who did what at Exchange Buildings after the police arrived.[54] The robbery had been planned meticulously by seasoned expropriators. Svars and Sokolov were positioned inside, armed with a Mauser apiece to protect the entry points to the buildings, while Hartmanis and Smoller retained the smaller Dreyse and Browning pistols while working outside in the back yard. Sokolov answered the door to the police at number 11; while Hartmanis scrambled over the back fences from number 9 and came in shooting through the back door of number 11. Jānis Žāklis was not present; he was playing the violin back at Grove Street. The police wanted posters bearing the famous photographs of Peter the Painter created a legend that took on a life of its own, but the only real mystery was how he escaped from London.

When Svars and Sokolov left Grove Street on the night of the murders, Jānis Žāklis went with them. Luba Milstein saw them together in Alfrēds Dzirkalis' room at Lindley Street. After Svars sent her away Žāklis left also. He sought refuge at 36 Havering Street, near the docks, the lodgings of Pavel Molchanov. The two men had been friends since September 1909, when they first met in Marseille. Svars had brought them together again in London after Žāklis' arrival. 'I did not recognise him', Molchanov told the police; 'he had a pointed beard in Marseille but was clean shaven when I met him in London'. Molchanov said that on the night in question Piatkov (Žāklis) knocked on his door at two o'clock in the morning: 'I opened the window to see who it was. I asked him why he came at that time, and he said "Can I sleep with you for the night?" I said "Certainly". He gave as his excuse that he was too late in getting to his lodging, to get in. He stayed until about 5pm.'[55]

Despite the impression of innocence which Molchanov tried to convey to the police he acted rather energetically on Žāklis' behalf. At 9.30 that morning Molchanov called on Alfrēds Dzirkalis at Lindley Street. He found Dzirkalis talking to Luba Milstein and Rosa Trassjonsky. They had just arrived with news that Hartmanis was dead, and were looking for Fricis Svars. Svars and Sokolov had already gone, probably around the corner to Betty Gershon's in Sidney Street (which Lindley Street ran into), but Dzirkalis either didn't know that or wouldn't say. Desperate and too afraid to return to Grove Street, Milstein appealed for help to Molchanov. He told her to go to his lodgings at Havering Street and that he would meet her there later, then accompanied Trassjonsky back to Grove Street. At Havering Street, Milstein found five men were 'talking in an excited manner' in the front room, so she went into a back room to wait for Molchanov, and came face to face with Peter the Painter. Milstein asked him what had happened, but he said he could not tell her anything about it. When she told him that Hartmanis had died: 'Peter became very excited, and started to walk up and down the room. I then asked him whether it would be better for me to leave England, and he then inquired if I had any money.'[56]

At that moment Molchanov entered the room, and announced that he had taken a half-sovereign from the dead man's pocket, which he handed to Milstein. 'Peter the Painter asked me to give him a few shillings, as he must get away. I gave Peter the half-sovereign and Pavel went out and changed it, and I gave Peter half a crown.' Molchanov also reported that the landlord at Grove Street had insisted that Trassjonsky remain there, and she had been found by the police. 'While I was talking to Pavel', says Milstein, 'a person called Ivan came in and talked to Peter in low tones, and I did not hear what was said — I was too excited to notice what they were saying. Peter the Painter asked what it would cost to get to Poplar, and he put on his coat and waistcoat. The above interview with Peter the Painter was at about 12 o'clock.'[57] Molchanov says simply, 'About 2pm ... Milstein called to see Peter, and stayed with him about 10 minutes. She gave him 2/6. He had no money except the half-crown'. Conveniently, Molchanov 'did not quite hear' their conversation, but said the word 'Paris' was mentioned.[58] Jānis Žāklis left at five o'clock and disappeared.

The police were completely in the dark as to the whereabouts of Peter the Painter. One theory was that he had escaped to Scotland and was being sheltered in Glasgow by local anarchists. Police in Glasgow called at the Clarion Club, the meeting place of the Glasgow Anarchist Group, and asked the caretaker for names and addresses. At the following meeting two plain clothes police officers masquerading as new members were exposed. They politely excused themselves and left.[59]

How Žāklis escaped was only established by the Security Service MI5 in 1932, in a report compiled by one of their informants among the Latvian émigré community in London: 'Peter hid for four days in the house of a man named Wagner in Dock Road, North Woolwich where there also lived a Lett named Veldi at that time connected with the group and later a member of the Canadian Mounted Police. The CID called while Peter was hidden there in a small box room but were fobbed off. Peter then escaped to Holland. He later called on the Social Democratic Party in Brussels, but received a cold welcome.'[60]

Bizarrely, the name of the interpreter who assisted the police in persuading the innocent occupants of 100 Sidney Street to leave before the Siege was Harry Wagner. Could he have been the same man who sheltered Žāklis in Dock Road when the police came looking for Peter the Painter? It is more probable that the Wagner in question was Jānis Vagners (1869-1955), a member of the Latvian Social Democracy who had taken part in the 1905 revolution in Bausk before leaving Latvia in January 1906. The man Veldi was Viktors Velde, a fighter from Liepāja and member of the Latvian SR, who had arrived in London in 1907 and emigrated to Canada in 1912. If the report by MI5 is accurate, then the date of Žāklis' departure from London must have been 21st December 1910, the day before the police arrested Juris Laiviņš, Jēkabs Peterss and Osip Federov.

MI5's claim that Peter the Painter went to Brussels is confirmed by Voldemārs Skare, who met Mērnieks (Žāklis) there unexpectedly, and saw 'photos of those arrested' in the Belgian newspapers the day after Žāklis left the city, on 23 December: 'While in emigration, he organised an attack on a jeweller's shop in Houndsditch, London... His plan did not succeed, a couple of attackers were arrested, but Comrade Mērnieks fairly quickly managed to escape from London to Belgium. In those days he was referred to as Peter the Painter (Pēteris Mālderis) in all London newspapers. On the same day as he arrived in Brussels, I accidentally met him in the street in front of the Latvian Folk House in Brussels. I was very much surprised to see him there. He didn't tell me anything about his attack on the jeweller's shop, but said that he urgently had to go to Paris. The same evening he left for Paris and from there to Switzerland, where he stayed. The next day after his departure all streets in Brussels were full of mobilised secret police who were looking for Mērnieks, or Peter the Painter. A number of criminal police spies were also stationed in the street where I lived, but Mērnieks was already gone. That day's newspapers were all writing about the attack in Houndsditch, London, with the photos of those arrested — so I immediately understood that Mērnieks was involved in this case.'[61]

Andris Puļķis, a historian at the Institute of History in Riga who studied restricted archive material on the Latvian anarchists, while helping to prepare the revised edition of the *Memorial Books to Fallen Fighters* of 1905 for publication in the late 1970s and early 1980s, is adamant that the expropriation at Houndsditch was organised by Jānis Žāklis.[62] And the memoirs of both Juris Daberts and Voldemārs Skare concur that it was the former party member Mērnieks (Žāklis), whom the English police called Peter the Painter, who was behind the robbery. Daberts claims no inside knowledge of the robbery, repeating only what appeared in the press. But his account insists that it was organised by Svars and Hartmanis, with the collaboration of Žāklis and the participation of Sokolov (whom Daberts says accidentally shot Hartmanis; he makes no mention of Max Smoller, who actually fired the shot): 'The English police accused the so-called Peter the Painter, a former party member [Mērnieks], of collaboration in the preparation of this expropriation, and were looking for him everywhere, but still did not manage to capture him... [Svars] Together with Hartmanis in emigration often dreamed about freeing the prisoners from Siberia, and undoubtedly the Houndsditch expropriation was meant to pay for the liberation of prisoners from Siberia'[63] Voldemārs Skare goes further and contradicts Luba Milstein's testimony (that Peter the Painter remained at home in Grove Street) by saying, 'Mērnieks [Žāklis] *took part* in the attack'. Skare knew Žāklis very well, having worked with him in Riga from 1904 to the end of 1905. When he met Žāklis again in Brussels after his escape from London, Skare says: '*In the fight with the police he was wounded in his arm* [italics added], but he still managed in a rush to escape to Brussels.'[64] This assertion that Žāklis was present at Houndsditch is completely unsubstantiated. If he was and was wounded, then the shot must have been fired by Smoller as he blazed away at the police and hit Hartmanis by mistake. The only support for this theory of a fifth man at the robbery is the claim by Augusts Svinks that *five* people took part in the Houndsditch robbery.

The Houndsditch shootings and the deaths of Hartmanis, Svars and Sokolov spelled disaster for the big plans Žāklis had for a major offensive in Latvia. Instead of being safely in London directing operations, Žāklis was on the run again, the most wanted anarchist in the world. The January 1911 edition of his journal *Brīvība* asked its readers to note that all money should now be sent to Mr. W. Spring in New York, because 'the former Paris address isn't valid anymore'.[65]

Žāklis no longer felt safe in Paris.

Interestingly, MI5 reported that Peter the Painter came back to England 'four months' after his escape from London, 'for a few days' (around April 1911), and elsewhere in the same document that it was '12 months afterwards, but [he] only stayed for 24 hours' (at the end of 1911).[66] If true, the notion of him coming back to London for such a brief visit suggests that Žāklis was *en route* to somewhere else.

In response to requests from the City of London Police for information on Peter the Painter, the *Okhranka* busied itself compiling everything they knew about Jānis Žāklis, which was communicated to London via the Russian Consul General. On 3rd July 1912 a police agent in Kiev, Jānis Janovičs Krauze, wrote to the *Okhranka* in Riga asking, 'if they are still looking for Jānis Žāklis an anarchist expropriator and revolutionary, who went abroad to Paris under the name Peter Piatkov, where he worked for the left-wing party newspapers and three years ago in London attempted an expropriation under the name of Peter the Painter. In 1905 he smuggled arms for the Latvian revolutionaries. After the London expropriation, in the St. Petersburg magazine *Ogunyuk* his photo was published with his description, saying that he was wanted. At present he is Germany, and if you think he should be arrested I can be at your disposal at any moment for your compensation.'[67]

The Head of the Kiev *Okhranka* followed up Krauze's letter by writing to the Head of the Special Department: 'Several years ago Žāklis took part in the London expropriation... At present his correspondence is probably forwarded to the following address: Geneva Central Post Office, 9, 13-3, c/o. But Žāklis himself lives in Germany. In the present year they are planning a congress of Anarchist-Communists in Geneva and Žāklis is going to it.'[68]

This intelligence was not followed up by the authorities in London and no attempt was made to apprehend Žāklis. The City of London Police by then had come to the conclusion that there was insufficient evidence to sustain a prosecution against Peter the Painter, and no further action was taken.

In the last report on file, the Russian Consul General in London informed Superintendent Ottaway on 16th December 1912, that the man Jānis Žāklis, who was identified as the suspect Peter Piatkov or Peter the Painter, was 'at present in Germany'. And there the trail ended. Peter had flown away, never to be found, or so it seemed.

Notes

1   Churchill, letter to Prime Minister Asquith.
2   Donald Rumbelow, *The Houndsditch Murders & the Siege of Sidney Street* (revised edition, London 1988).
3   The outer envelope was addressed in Russian to 'Mr. Janis Sudmalis, #64 Pastbishchna Street, Libau (Liepāja), Kurland'; the inner envelope was inscribed in Latvian: 'Please pass on to J. F. Svars, #8 Rožu iela.'
4   Fricis Svars letter to his father, Jēkabs Svars, 1st January 1911. Original in the possession of Donald Rumbelow; new English translation by Irene Ruff, London 2010.
5   Ibid.
6   Ibid.
7   Ibid.
8   Ibid.
9   Ibid.
10 Ibid.
11 Milstein claimed that after accompanying Rosa Trassjonsky to fetch Dr. Scanlon, she stayed at her friend's room in Settles Street until Rosa returned there at 7 a.m., bringing news of Hartmanis' worsening condition. They remained together in Settles Street for the next two hours, before going back to Grove Street at 9.15 a.m., to find that Hartmanis was dead. In a panic at what to do next, they went to see Alfred Dzirkalis at Lindley Street, looking for Svars, but he had gone. Files of the City of London Police, 'Houndsditch Murders', Box 1.5 (a), Statement of Luba Milstein (Holloway Prison), 17th February 1911, London Metropolitan Archives.
12 Colin Rogers, *The Battle of Stepney — The Sidney Street Siege: Its Causes and Consequences* (Robert Hale, London, 1981), pp. 48-9.
13 Ibid.
14 'Houndsditch Murders', 534G/3.15, police notes in pencil taken from informer on men at 100 Sidney Street, op. cit.
15 Inquest on the bodies of two unknown men found at 100 Sidney Street, Mile End (after a conflagration), one known as Joseph and the other known as Fritz or Fritz Svaars. Depositions taken on 8th, 9th and 18th days of January 1911 before Wyne E. Baxter, Coroner for County of London, (also Coroner's Summing Up). Deposition of Detective Inspector Frederick Wensley, 9th January 1911, p. 9.
16 Winston S. Churchill, *Thoughts and Adventures Through Stormy Years* (London 1932. Mandarin paperback edition, 1990), p. 43.
17 Ibid, p. 44.
18 Ibid, p. 45.
19 Ibid, pp. 44-7.
20 Violet Bonham Carter, *Winston Churchill As I Knew Him* (Pan Books, London 1967), p. 234.
21 Churchill, letter to Prime Minister Asquith.
22 Inquest on the bodies of two unknown men found at 100 Sidney Street, Mile End, op. cit. Verdict on Joseph, p. 28. Verdict on Svars, p. 30.
23 'The Lettish Social-Democrats and the Houndsditch Murders', Statement of the Central Committee of the Latvian Social-Democracy, Brussels 10th January 1911, *Justice*, London, 21st January 1911.
24 Letter from Aleksei Aladin to Aleksander Zirnis, from Melita Norwood.
25 'Houndsditch Murders', 534C/1.4, Statement of Errico Malatesta, op. cit.
26 Ibid. Box 3.15, Statement of Edward Humphrey, 28th December 1910
27 Ibid.
28 Ibid. Report by Det. Insp. William Newell, 12th January 1911.
29 Ibid. Statement of Theodore Janson, 23rd December 1910.
30 Ibid. Report by Det. Insp. William Newell, 27th December 1910.
31 Ibid. Statement of Theodore Janson, 26th December, 1910.
32 Ibid.

33   The Trohimschik passport, No. 2801, had been issued for a passage to Vilna (Vilnius, the capital of Lithuania) and stamped as having crossed the frontier at Liepajā on 14th January, 1907; then stamped at Vilnius as having left the country on 14th May 1907. Since the passport was originally in the possession of Fricis Svars, it is reasonable to assume that this is when he set sail for America after escaping from the Riga police.

34   'Houndsditch Murders', Box 3.15, op. cit. Report by Det. Insp. William Newell, 10th February 1911.

35   Ibid. Statement of Theodore Janson, 8th February, 1911.

36   *Rex vs. Peters and others*, CRIMI/121, The National Archives, Chancery Lane, London.

37   Ibid. Testimony of Louis Colman Jonas, p. 528.

38   Ibid. Testimony of Philip Abrahams, pp. 540-6.

39   Ibid. Testimony of Karl Hoffman (Alfred Dzirkalis), 23rd March 1911, pp. 587-90.

40   'Houndsditch Murders', 534C/1.28, op. cit. Note written on prison toilet paper by Karl Hoffman (Dzirkalis), 20th February 1911.

41   Ibid. Arthur Weeks, 24th February 1911.

42   Donald Rumbelow, *The Houndsditch Murders & the Siege of Sidney Street*, op. cit., p. 174.

43   Interview with Richard Whittington Egan, Malvern, 19th March 1988. Richard interviewed Nina Vasileva at her flat at 99 Brick Lane, on 14th November 1960.

44   'Houndsditch Murders', Box 3.15. Report by Det. Insp. William Newell, 28th February, 1911.

45   Interview with Richard Whittington Egan, Malvern, 19th March 1988.

46   James Edward Holroyd, *The Gaslight Murders: The Saga of Sidney Street and the Scarlet 'S'* (London, 1960), p. 246.

47   Colin Rogers, *The Battle of Stepney — The Sidney Street Siege: Its Causes and Consequences*, op. cit. p. 208.

48   A. G. Gardiner, *Pillars of Society* (London 1915), p. 58.

49   Violet Bonham Carter, *Winston Churchill As I Knew Him*, op. cit., p. 237

50   V. G. Trukhanousky, *Winston Churchill* (Moscow 1978), p. 101.

51   Donald Rumbelow, *The Houndsditch Murders & the Siege of Sidney Street*, op. cit, pp. 181-2.

52   'Houndsditch Murders', 534C/1.26, op. cit.

53   Ibid, 534C/1.20.

54   One of the key things to understand when unravelling who did what at Houndsditch is the ownership of the weaponry involved. The policemen Bentley, Tucker and Choate were all killed by bullets fired from the same 7.65mm Dreyse pistol. When the police discovered the body of Hartmanis the weapon was found beneath the mattress on which he lay. Identical 7.65mm ammunition was found in two magazine clips beside the pistol, and in Hartmanis' jacket and overcoat pockets. He also owned a C96 Mauser pistol; police found the wooden stock for it (but not the weapon itself) and 300 rounds of ammunition, when they visited his room at 44 Gold Street. According to Tokmakov, Svars too was in possession of a C96 Mauser pistol at Grove Street on the day of the shooting, in addition to the 7.65mm Browning pistol he had shown him two weeks previously. Typically, in the sort of urban combat situation experienced in Latvia, the Mauser was employed as a primary weapon (for its longer range and more effective stopping power), while the more compact 7.65mm pistol would be carried as a back-up weapon for close-quarter protection. Milstein testified that Max Smoller arrived at the social gathering at Grove Street with a long, thin parcel (suggesting a weapon). This could well have been the Mauser belonging to Hartmanis. The weapons recovered after the Siege showed that Svars' Mauser was attached to its wooden stock (for use as a shoulder fired carbine); the stock of the second Mauser (used by Sokolov) was not in evidence because Hartmanis had left it at home. Ironically, it was Svars's Browning (which he loaned to Smoller during the robbery) which killed Hartmanis. Smoller returned the Browning to Svars at Grove Street and escaped; witness testimony at the trial confirmed that Svars was then armed with a Mauser and a Browning (which he checked to see if it was loaded); Sokolov retained the other Mauser. These were the three weapons recovered from Sidney Street after the siege.

55 'Houndsditch Murders', 534C/1.4, Statement of Pavel Molchanov, December 1910, op. cit.

56 Ibid. Box 1.5 (a), Statement of Luba Milstein (Holloway Prison), 17th February 1911.

57 Ibid.

58 Ibid. 534C/1.4, Statement of Pavel Molchanov, December 1910.

59 Radical Glasgow History Project, http://www.radicalglasgow.me.uk

60 MI5 report KV3/39, 26th July 1932, The National Archives, Kew.

61 Latvijas Nacionālā bibliotēka (LNB), PA17/4/3/24.524/77-24.526. Voldemārs Skare, *Materiāli par 1905. gada revolūciju un tas darbiniekiem*. (Material on the 1905 revolution and its participants), p. 70. (Riga, 1950. Unpublished manuscript of 170 pages).

62 Interview with Andris Puļķis, Riga July 2003.

63 LVA, PA-36/5/198. Daberts, 'Savrs, Fricis, Fričelis' (unpublished manuscript).

64 Voldemārs Skare, *Materiāli par 1905. gada revolūciju un tās darbiniekiem*, op. cit. p. 70.

65 *Brīvība*, No. 7, January 1911.

66 MI5 report KV3/39, op. cit.

67 LVVA, 4568/15/225, #63, 'Letters from agents'.

68 Ibid. #63a.

II

1911 to 1917
Life After Sidney Street

Comrades, we'll not complain
Spring follows after frost!
We shall possess again
The heritage we've lost

Anonymous[1]

When Fricis Svars died in Sidney Street, Luba Milstein was pregnant with his child. In January 1912 she and the baby went to America and settled in New York. Luba's hurried departure from London was organised by Alfrēds Dzirkalis, after fellow members of *Liesma* warned him that 'she was at risk for her life, given she could not be trusted to remain silent.'[2] Dzirkalis, who had first introduced Svars to Luba, followed her to New York in 1913 as Sam Weinstein, and the two brought up Svars' son together. The son, Alfred Driscoll (an anglicised form of his step-fathers name), was unaware that his father was not Alfrēds Dzirkalis until he was thirty, when someone told him at a party. It was a tremendous revelation, and he spent the rest of his adult life battling against the secrecy that still gripped his family.

In 1988, Alfred Driscoll broke his silence for the first time to correspond with the author ('the first Englishman interested in the period who hasn't treated my father Fritz as some kind of degenerate'[3]), 'my parents, Mazais [Alfrēds Dzirkalis] and Luba told me nothing about Fritz. After I found out, from outsiders, that Fritz was my real father, they both had nothing but praise for Fritz, but still no details of what happened in London. This was in the '40s. I was married, had one child and was completely independent of them. I always resented this treatment and thought there was no logical reason for keeping information from me. They were both active revolutionaries in Europe and during the Great Depression we were all active politically. In the '40s some of the ardour had died but we shared the same opinions. I think the very 'cautious' attitude was unwarranted.'[4] One childhood memory, though, indicates that perhaps it was not: 'When I was 3-4 years old, someone left a suitcase full of money and literature in our apartment, and Mazais was relieved when it was finally picked up.'[5]

Of his parents in America and what they told him about Svars, he says, 'When my mother left ... [h]ospital with me in her arms, Mazais met us at the door and told her "Fritz told me to take care of you." ... My mother and I arrived in NY when I was six months old under my mother's maiden name. This facilitated our entry because her brother, an established businessman was able to come to Ellis Island and claim responsibility for us. Mazais arrived a year or two later under an assumed name. They remained married with and without documents for over 50 years until Mazais died. ... Fritz was older and more experienced when Alfred met him; but Alfred always referred to him as a good friend... Alfred introduced Luba to Fritz, probably by taking her to one of the meetings of the Latvian club. Alfred and Luba got acquainted in a chance meeting in some library.[6] Fritz never drank but was generous in treating friends. He edited a newspaper and was also a good artist. He was looked up to as a leader. Alfred admired his feats as an 'expropriator of the expropriators'. The money went to finance revolution in Russia and help free prisoners and get them out of Russia. 'Luba never wrote her love story but deeply loved both Fritz and Alfred... Neither one knew his complete background. Fritz once told Luba he had a married sister who was a teacher and lived in Hamburg. He gave her address to Luba and said his sister would care for her and the child if necessary... When the 1917 Revolution took place (I was six) they were Marxists and Bolsheviks — I think the change from Anarchists took place some time before the revolution... they were both enthusiastic supporters (of the Soviet Union) till they died.'[7]

Alfrēds Dzirkalis died in 1961, aged seventy-three; Luba Milstein died in 1973, aged eighty-one.

* * *

Jēkabs Peterss had no intention of leaving London. After his acquittal, he found work, according to Bruce Lockhart, 'in the transport firm of Gerhardt & Hey'.[8] Other accounts have him working variously as a clerk or presser at a wholesale tailors in the Holloway Road, Islington, and later at an export house. In 1913, Peterss described his occupation as 'Tailor's manager'.[9] One of the people he worked with was a young woman from Worcester in the English Midlands, Harriett Naomi May Freeman, known simply as May. The two fell in love and very soon were living together at 18 Canonbury Street, Islington, in North London.

Compared to the poverty-stricken East End, with its high concentration of foreign émigrés (all hopeful of one day making enough money to move on to America), Islington was then a relatively prosperous, attractive area of working class London. Despite some terrible poverty, it also boasted substantial enclaves of skilled workers and the middle class. Its housing was generally better than in East London, and its tree-lined streets, squares and parks contrasted favourably with the blackened back streets of Stepney and Whitechapel. For a man who had just cheated the gallows, and fallen in love with an attractive woman, Islington must have seemed to Peterss a blissful place.

Peterss' happiness was made complete not long afterwards when May became pregnant. On 3rd December 1913 (the day when Peterss himself turned twenty-seven-years-old), she gave birth at home to a daughter. The couple registered the child as Gertrude Winifred May Peters, but she was commonly called Maisie or Little May to distinguish her from her mother (though many people writing about the Peterss family confuse matters by referring to both women as Mary). Peterss doted on the child. Questioned about her husband five years later by a reporter from the *Daily Express*, May summed up this idyllic period of Peterss' life by saying, 'He was never happier than when spending his evenings at home with us.' She had not known Peterss at the time of the Houndsditch case she said, but he had told her everything during their courtship, 'so that I should not marry him in ignorance of his record.'[10] In fact, the couple did not marry legally, until 9th September 1916. The witnesses at the ceremony were Albert and Josephene Strautmalis, comrades of Peterss from the London LSD group.

Jēkabs Peterss always looked on himself as a man of the world. With an English wife, and a liking for English literature, it was natural for him to integrate himself into London life. Besides remaining active in the Latvian Social Democracy, he took an interest also (like many of the Latvians and Russians in London) in the English socialist movement. Peterss joined the Shoreditch Social-Democratic Club in September 1910, and the following month was admitted as a member of the Shoreditch branch of the Social-Democratic Party. At the time of his arrest, he was also a member of the (predominantly Jewish) Working Mens' Federated Union which existed then amongst the garment and catering trades of the East End. After the interruption of five months in Brixton Prison, he returned to the SDP and kept up his membership after it became the British Socialist Party (BSP) in December 1911.

Another focal point of revolutionary socialism which claimed Peterss' attention was the Communist Club in Charlotte Street, Soho. Frequented by English socialists and anarchists of every hue, as well as every nationality of political exile, the Communist Club provided an important international social centre for revolutionaries. Though otherwise bitterly sectarian, the anti-tsarist émigrés in London had since 1910 banded together in a single all-party welfare organisation, with Maxim Litvinov as its Secretary, and kept a separate room at the club as its office. Known as the Herzen Circle, after the 19th century revolutionary exile, the organisation held members' meetings, and put on amateur dramatics, lectures, and musical evenings in the club. It was the émigré cultural and artistic centre. In the words of the then Menshevik, later Soviet Ambassador to Britain, Ivan Maisky, 'the place where people of all parties and convictions, homesick folk eating the sorrowful bread of exile, could meet in a free and easy atmosphere, play chess or dominoes, have a cup of tea or a glass of beer together, find Russian books and papers and hear Russian singing and music. There was a fund from which assistance could be given to émigrés most in need of it… The Circle gave us émigrés much of the homely warmth we so sorely missed in the vast, cold stone labyrinth of London, and so it, or rather its quarters in the Communist Club, were always filled with Russian exiles drinking, eating, smoking, discussing the news, arguing, quarrelling and making it up again, planning the future — all amidst a cloud of tobacco smoke and a babble of tongues.'[11]

Other considerations notwithstanding, Jēkabs Peterss had an important political reason for staying in England. His release from prison coincided with the beginning of Lenin's attempt to "Bolshevize" Latvian Social Democracy, the RSDLP's largest single component. The question of Latvian support for Lenin inside the RSDLP became critical in January 1912, when the Russian Bolsheviks formally constituted themselves as a separate party. In London, the Secretary of the Russian Bolsheviks was Maxim Litvinov, Lenin's one time man in Riga. What

Lenin needed most, though, were people who could champion his cause within the LSD. Jēkabs Peterss, holding a position of authority in the London group, and one of the few real Bolsheviks within the Latvian Party, was naturally a figure who attracted Lenin's attention. The Latvian Central Committee condemned the founding Congress of the Bolsheviks and gave their support instead to the Menshevik-dominated August Bloc, which had formed an Organisational Committee of its own to replace the RSDLP's (Bolshevik) Central Committee.

Latvians who sought to stay clear of the factional squabbling, thinking that a panacea of 'organisational unity and organisational discipline'[12] could override ideological differences, were taken to task by the Menshevik Kristaps Eliass, brother of Ģederts Eliass. If the positions of neither Lenin nor the Organisational Committee were to their liking, he said, they should stop sitting on the fence and come forward with a plan of their own: 'To be neutral where there is a question of the Party's unity or schism means to be for the schism.'[13] By the summer of 1912, a Bolshevik centre had been formed in Riga to direct activity amongst groups inside the country, and a Bureau of the United Groups of the Latvian Social Democracy Abroad had been organised as an alternative to the LSD's Menshevik-dominated Committee Abroad. Jēkabs Peterss, who had already been carrying on a squabble with Lenin's critics inside the LSD Foreign Committee, now became a key member of the new (all Bolshevik) Foreign Bureau in London.

In May 1913, Lenin wrote a *Draft Platform* for his supporters to present to the Fourth Congress of Latvian Social-Democrats. Held in Brussels in January 1914, the Congress was the turning point in the Bolshevisation of the Latvian Party. Lenin was relentless in preparing for it, and went himself to Brussels to take charge of the Latvian Bolsheviks. Fortunately for Lenin, the entire Central Committee of the LSD were arrested in July 1913, and were unable to attend the Congress. Since they were all Mensheviks, some observers have gone so far as to suggest a Bolshevik conspiracy in the arrests. More probably, they are evidence of *Okhranka* manipulation of the RSDLP's internal differences. It is perhaps not coincidental that one of the men closest to Lenin in the Bolshevik Central Committee of the time was Roman Malinovsky, editor of *Pravda* and head of the Bolshevik faction in the Duma, who not long afterwards was exposed as a long-time agent of the *Okhranka*. The Congress was only a qualified success for Lenin. It voted in a new all-Bolshevik Central Committee, but the resolutions it adopted still put forward the position of Unionism, and specifically ruled out any organisational merger with the Russian Bolsheviks. This paradoxical situation was thanks to the confused voting of P. Augulis, delegate from Liepāja and an *Okhranka* agent. Lacking guidance from his police controllers, Augulis voted first for the Unionist resolutions. When his *Okhranka* instructions finally arrived he switched his support in mid-Congress to the Bolsheviks, barely in time to tip the balance (when the delegates were split 9 to 9) in electing the new LSD Central Committee.

On Lenin's insistence, the Latvian Bolsheviks ignored the resolutions of the Fourth Congress and six months later tried again to get a clear mandate for merger with the Russian Bolsheviks at the LSD's Ninth Conference. But they failed there also. Lacking a clear official mandate, the Leninist take-over of the Latvian Party had to rely now on denying their opponents a press, and gradually trying to take over the leadership of the district organisations. The coming of the First World War and the evacuation of Riga's factories interrupted this process, and the battle for control of the LSD focused once more on the organisation abroad. But Jēkabs Peterss was soon to prove his true worth to Lenin.

* * *

The Italian anarchist Errico Malatesta had not heard the last of Houndsditch. Though the police accepted the account he gave of his relations with Puika Hartmanis, there remained a lingering doubt about his connections with *Liesma*. The guilt by association was enough to get him sent to prison, facing deportation, a year later in a completely unrelated case. Malatesta's long career as an insurrectionist had made him a major target for police interest and, outside Britain, a fugitive 'wanted' by governments in Europe and South America. In London he was regularly under observation by not only Scotland Yard but also agents of half a dozen foreign powers. The Italian government deemed Malatesta so dangerous that it assigned two secret agents (code-named Dante and Virgil) to keep tabs on him around the clock, reporting directly to the Italian Prime Minister. The Central State Archives in Rome, where the files on Malatesta are the largest of any single individual, attest to their thoroughness. Despite such close surveillance, Malatesta maintained a relatively untroubled existence in England. His imprisonment in London was a consequence of an argument with another Italian exile, Bellelli. Malatesta had attacked Bellelli for supporting Italian imperialism in Libya during the Tripolitanian war of 1911/1912. Bellelli defended himself by accusing Malatesta of being a 'Turkish spy'. Malatesta in turn circulated a leaflet among the Italians in London declaring his willingness to clear his name in front of a court of honour, and dismissing Bellelli as someone, 'who used to call himself an anarchist ... but many look upon ... as an Italian spy.'[14] Bellelli sued for criminal libel. In the ensuing court action, much was made of Malatesta's connections with the Houndsditch gang. The judge sentenced Malatesta to three months in prison and recommended that upon release he be deported. More serious for Malatesta than going to prison, was the threat of deportation to a country where he risked assassination or faced more serious charges than criminal libel. A campaign demanding his immediate release and the lifting of the deportation order (culminating in mass demonstrations and a rally in Trafalgar Square on 9th June, 1912) drew such wide public support that on 17th June Home Secretary McKenna finally stepped in and the deportation order was lifted. When Malatesta left England a year later it was his choice.

Osip Federov, an innocent bystander to the robbery arrested solely because of his association with Svars, stepped back into obscurity. Nothing is known of his subsequent life. Of the other people caught up in the Houndsditch affair, Sara Trassjonsky died tragically, date unknown, still confined in Colny Hatch asylum; Nina Vasileva sent Sara a perfumed sachet during her confinement, in gratitude for her tending the dying Hartmanis in his last moments.[15] Vasileva never married nor had children. She worked as a cigarette maker at the Ardath Tobacco Company in Worship Street, Shoreditch. During the First World War she moved out of the East End to live at 63 Charlotte Street, north of Soho, near Goodge Street tube station, and at some point moved to leafy Hampstead. But the Metropolitan Police Special Branch had not forgotten her.

Whether or not Vasileva's pre-war acquaintanceships in London with Jēkabs Peterss and Kristaps Salniņš counted for anything (by the 1920s both men were important figures in the Soviet intelligence services), the British security services were careful to keep a watchful eye on her. Vasileva attracted their attention by getting a job with the Soviet trading company, Arcos, The All Russian Cooperative Society, whose Moorgate offices were raided by police in May 1927, on suspicion of being a front for espionage and subversion. What Vasileva's job was, and how and when she gained employment with Arcos, are not known; but on 20th May 1931 a Special Branch officer (PS Ernest Oliver) visited the City Police, 'on behalf of the Home Office', to make enquiries 'regarding Nina WASSILEWA, a Russian, residing at 23 Denning Road, Hampstead, and employed by Arcos Ltd., Bush House, Strand… A communication has been received at the Home Office alleging that she is an undesirable alien and that she was concerned in a notorious crime in London about twenty years ago.' The detective wanted photographs of Vasileva and any relevant records from the Houndsditch case.[16] But it was obviously Vasileva's connection with Arcos which was the real focus of the inquiry, and not the smokescreen of her being an 'undesirable alien'. Unusually, the Special Branch files on Vasileva were kept apart from the archives (in the SB office itself), suggesting that the investigation was ongoing, and she received sporadic visits by Special Branch for the rest of her life. At the height of the London Blitz during the Second World War (on 18th November 1940), Vasileva moved back to the East End; living first at 101 and then 99 Brick Lane. When Richard Whittington Egan interviewed her there in 1960, she was crippled with arthritis and walked with a stick. She described herself as 'apolitical' and a 'Greek Catholic'; and her small top floor room was cluttered with religious ephemera. Nina Vasileva died in St. Bartholomew's Hospital, after a heart attack on 24th February 1963. Her death certificate gave her official age as 70 (she was closer to 73).

* * *

Fricis Svars never made it to 'the blessed land Australia',[17] but at least one of his friends did: Jānis Celiņš. On 29th August 1911, Celiņš arrived in Adelaide as part of the crew of the cargo vessel *Caroline*, using the alias he used in London, John Rosen. In his own words, 'I worked my passage out from England'.[18] He left behind his wife Rose, who was three months pregnant with their first son (John Courtney Rosen, born in London on 28th March 1912). It was several years before they were reunited.

In the meantime, Rosen worked for six months in Adelaide and Port Piri, South Australia, before finding work in the mines of Broken Hill, New South Wales. He stayed in Broken Hill for eight years. During the First World War he was obliged to register with the police as an alien. His registration certificate noted: 'Applicant is a respectable man and nothing is known against him'.[19] Finally, Rose and their son were able to join the hard working Celiņš at Broken Hill, and a second son (Ronald Adolf Rosen) was born there on 15th April 1919.

Around 1920, the Rosen family settled down in the small gold-mining town of Beechworth, Victoria, on the overland route from Melbourne to Sydney, and Jānis Celiņš returned to his old trade as a hairdresser. Beechworth is best remembered for its association with the famous Irish Bushranger Ned Kelly, who once robbed the town bank. After the gold rush Beechworth became the administrative and commercial centre of north-east Victoria. It went into decline when the dominance of the gold fields diminished after 1856, but the town remains almost unchanged to this day, and is considered as the best preserved example of an original Australian gold rush town. John Rosen owned a small hairdresser and tobacconist shop (today a Pizza parlour) on Ford Street, and the family lived two blocks away in Finch Street, reputedly the most charming street in Beechworth.

Jānis Celiņš-Rosen led a mostly uneventful life in Australia. He was naturalised in 1925; his revolutionary activities were behind him in Latvia and London, and he concentrated on working hard to bring up a family of three sons (the third son, George Edward Rosen, was born on 19th June 1923). Only his passion for gambling on the horse races got him into trouble briefly with the Australian law. On 27th October 1928, Rosen and a local barman, Harold Davidson, were arrested and charged with 'having the care and management of a common gaming-house'.[20] The case was heard in the Beechworth Police Court on 29th November 1928, before police magistrate Williams. Rosen was found guilty of the charge and fined £30, with £18/16 shillings costs. Harold Davidson, answering the lesser charge of 'having conducted a common gaming house', was fined £20, with the same costs.[21]

Rosen appears to have had no further contact with Latvia or Latvians until after the Second World War, when a new wave of émigrés arrived in Australia from Displaced Persons camps in Germany, fleeing the Soviet re-occupation of the Baltic, and a group of them settled in Beechworth. The old revolutionary was adopted by the newcomers as a figure to be respected. When John Rosen died on 9th October 1956, three days before his seventy-second birthday, the Latvians in Beechworth published a notice announcing the funeral of, 'Veteran of the 1905 struggle, Jānis Rozens (Celiņš), born in Riga on 12 October 1884, died in Beechworth on 9 October 1956'. Underneath was printed a verse from the Rainis poem, *Lauztās priedes* (The Broken Pines). An obituary in the same newspaper spoke of the incredulity of 'old father Rosen' at hearing what the new émigrés told him about the Soviet occupation from which they had fled: 'He was like Tom Hillman in the novel "The Mountain of Loneliness" by Valdemārs Kārkliņš... [Who said], "It is so strange that now you have to flee from those, who in our time we called the fighters for freedom. At times it seems to me unbelievable". John Rosen started to consider it more believable when he found the name of his brother's son, Celiņš, on the list of Latvians deported to Siberia. And still he remained loyal to his convictions till his dying day. He could laugh about himself: "What a revolutionary I was in those days — I ran in front of it and got spanked." When the first Latvians appeared in Beechworth, Rosen with difficulty was looking for words in the Latvian language, but soon regained it quite smoothly. It was the old-fashioned Latvian that he spoke... At first when speaking Latvian he sometimes didn't notice how he switched back into English, but in later life it was the other way around.

'Often, when going fishing with other Latvians, he would address his son in Latvian too — and then he would wave his hand: oh, you don't understand anything. In earlier years he avoided speaking Latvian in his little shop, but later Rosen, seeing the strong Latvian men, explained to someone who was wondering what language he was speaking: "I am also one of those". Sometimes, when his wife was annoyed with him, she would say: "You are just like one of those Russians!" Once, after an 18th November (Latvia's Independence Day) celebration, she said: "Your people are still better than mine". They sang hymns with such fervour, and those hymns were not hers.

'When on his 70th birthday local Latvians came to congratulate Father Rosen and brought him presents, he said: "I thought I had become English, but now I see that I am still Latvian".

'On a rainy day in October in a soaked Beechworth cemetery, a grave appeared with three handfuls of sand on the coffin, with a wreath of pine branches and white flowers and a national Latvian ribbon. Next to the group of Latvian mourners stood the old Latvian's three strong sons, who could not speak a word of Latvian.'[22]

Fifty-four years later I asked the youngest of those sons, George Rosen (aged 87), about Jānis Celiņš's life in Australia. George says his dad stowed away on board ship from London. He had wanted to go to Canada or America on the first ship he could, but Latvian sailors simply smuggled him aboard the first boat leaving and he only found out afterwards that it was going to Australia. The Captain of the ship wasn't very pleased when the stowaway was found, but there was nothing he could do about it, he couldn't turn back; and because Rosen could cut hair and clean boots and make himself useful he was allowed to work his passage. When the ship got to Australia the Captain even paid Rosen some money as wages.[23]

When John Rosen worked in the mines at Broken Hill he was involved in a long strike. Afterwards he moved to Melbourne and called in at the office of the Hairdressers' Union. They told him about a vacancy at a barbers shop in Beechworth, so he went there and got the job, and eventually took over the business. Age had dimmed the memory of those times. George thought the shop was at 34 Ford Street, and the family lived at 31 Finch Street; he was not sure which number was which. The shop was on the corner of a lane-way (side street). It had a double swinging door, with a window each side, and two chairs for the customers to have their hair cut in, with a small room out the back. George Rosen says his dad never retired; he never stopped working, he just died of a heart attack one morning. He had a heart condition. One of George's brothers drove their father to work that morning and, as was his habit, he stopped off first to have a chat with his friend Mr Maton who ran the drapers. They liked to talk about the worlds' ills before beginning work, but that morning

John Rosen simply dropped dead at the counter.[24]

When I asked him what sort of bloke his dad was, George said, 'oh, excellent: excellent man, good worker, good family man, never took a holiday. His main hobby was fishing — and "a punt on the horses"...' About John Rosen's family in Latvia, George says there was a brother, Ādolfs Celiņš, and a sister. John Rosen corresponded with them but not so much in the early period in Australia, probably because he had entered the country illegally. But after John died the Latvian family wrote to his wife, Rose, and they corresponded. The Australian family used to send them things like medicine. John Rosen liked to study the newspapers, and George says he was good at predicating what would happen in the world. He once said that there would be no money in the future, everyone would be 'living on plastic'; he predicted credit cards. He liked to read, but just whatever came to hand. He read mostly light stuff, westerns; he had a broad outlook on reading.[25]

George says his dad used to refer to what had happened in London as, 'getting father's money back'. That was an expression that the members of the anarchist group used about their activities: 'oh we're just going to get a bit of father's money back...'[26] On another occasion, George remembered, his father had recounted that the gang in London had been knocking a hole through a floor or a wall as part of an attempted 'bank robbery', the attempt to get to the jeweller's safe at Houndsditch, but the police were called by a Jewish lad before the robbery was completed. George could not recollect whether his father had directly taken part in this or was simply recounting what other members of his group had done. It was all so long ago.[27]

John Rosen had mentioned knowing Peter the Painter, and he only referred to him by that name, but George had trouble remembering what had been said. His father had been somewhere meeting some friends one day, playing cards, and it was raining outside so Peter the Painter gave him his coat to wear. It must have been a very distinctive coat, George thought, because John Rosen got arrested wearing it. George didn't think his dad could have had any contact with Peter the Painter after leaving London; Beechworth was quite a remote place.[28]

* * *

Juris Laiviņš (George Dubov), the man accused with Jēkabs Peterss of the Houndsditch murders, slipped quietly back into Latvia in 1912. Though innocent of involvement in the Houndsditch robbery, Laiviņš was certainly a member of the group that carried it out. But *Liesma* now had ceased to exist. Hartmanis, Svars and Sokolov were all dead; Max Smoller and Jānis Žāklis escaped abroad and disappeared. Those who stood trial mostly settled back into obscurity. Only Juris Laiviņš walked out of the Old Bailey determined to continue the fight in Latvia.

Liesma may have been destroyed, but there were still Latvian anarchists in London and elsewhere in England who supported the armed resistance in the Baltic. In April 1913 the Paris based journal *Melnais Karogs* (Black Flag) acknowledged financial donations from the London group *Maize un Brīvība* (Bread and Freedom), and from someone nicknamed Rūķis (Dwarf) in West

Hartlepool.[29] At the same time, the *Okhranka* in Riga were beginning to notice a steady trickle of anarchists returning to Latvia from London. The first to appear was Alfrēds Laiviņš (Rūdolfs), known to the police as Zheleznyi, Juris Laiviņš's brother. The *Okhranka* noted that Alfrēds arrived in Riga from London on 20th February 1913, and lived at Matīsa ielas 45, Flat 52. They appear to have been unaware that brother Juris had preceded him. Surveillance of brother Alfrēds revealed that he met a certain Ozoliņš, and a known Riga anarchist called Albert, with whom he was thought to be preparing a large expropriation. But Alfrēds seems to have got wind that something was wrong after articles about the activities of anarchists in the Baltics appeared in the newspaper *Rīgas Avīzēs*. The *Okhranka* reported on 19th March that he was staying at home and had stopped meeting Riga anarchists.[30]

At the same time the police were also carrying out surveillance on 'a member of the Latvian anarchist group from London', twenty-eight-year-old Kārlis Glāzenap, a citizen of Tukums. Glāzenap, whose older brother Ernest had been killed by the barons in December 1905 after the Tukums uprising, was seen talking to five unknown men near the Riga Naval School and was suspected of having arrived in the city with the aim of carrying out another big expropriation.[31] But after following him around aimlessly for seven months, during which time nothing happened, the police appear to have got bored and gave up. The only interesting thing noted in seven months of boring surveillance reports was that Glāzenap had met Jānis Bišentrops, who had been connected with the *Atriebējs* anarchist group in 1909.

Then, at the beginning of May 1913, the Livonia Gendarmerie received secret information that two former expropriators had returned to Riga from abroad, both of them anarchists, and were living at Matīsa ielas 45. The two men were Juris Laiviņš and Jānis Vītums.[32] On 5th May two *Okhranka* agents, Nikolajs Bulajs and Otto Zīverts, were detailed to keep the suspects under observation and try to find out who they were. The agents followed Laiviņš and Vītums around Old Riga all morning but did not see anything suspicious; except that they seemed to spend quite a long time looking at the weapons displayed in the window of a gun shop. In the afternoon Laiviņš and Vītums returned to Matisa iela 45, and in the evening went out in the company of a woman to the Aleksandra Gate railway station. Agent Bulajs telephoned for back-up, and joined his partner Zīverts at the railway station, where they met a detective from the Secret Detective Department. They watched as the suspects bought tickets for the 8.40 p.m. train to Valka. When the train pulled out of the station agents Bulajs and Zīverts were also on board.

During the journey the train stopped at Sigulda, a beauty spot known as the Switzerland of Livonia, where one of the suspects got off and bought some postcards. On arrival in Valka, Laiviņš and Vītums went into the third-class hall, where one of them started examining the train timetable, but the other seemed to the agents to be on his guard and kept his right hand in his pocket all the time. Leaving Zīverts on watch, Bulajs reported to the local police and found they had already received a telegram from Riga, with orders to arrest the suspects. Bulajs later testified that he told the local Gendarme, Kornev, that the suspects were dangerous criminals and probably well armed, and that they had to be approached very quietly and arrested before they suspected anything.

Laiviņš and Vītums had already left the station building and were crossing the square, going towards the town, when Bulajs and Kornev approached them suddenly from behind and, according to them, shouted, 'Stop! Hands up!'[33] What happened next is a matter of dispute. At the subsequent trial at Riga District Court, in June 1914, Bulajs testified that the men turned around 'with a grimace', with pistols in outstretched hands. Kornev started struggling with Laiviņš, while Bulajs got hold of Vītums's hand holding the pistol and pushed it down. Two shots exploded and the bullets passed through the bottom of Bulajs's coat and trousers without wounding him. Two more shots were fired but missed, because Bulajs pinned the shooter's hand to the ground. Bulajs said he was convinced that the first two shots fired by Vītums were meant for him, but conceded that the last two shots could have been fired accidentally while they were struggling for control of the pistol. The shooting produced pandemonium. All the people near the station started running away. Laiviņš and Vītums put up a fierce fight, but were finally overpowered with the help of the other gendarmes at the scene and people working at the station.

The two men were dragged into a room in the station, where they were searched and found to be in possession of four pistols: two Brownings, one Mauser and one Mannlicher semi-automatic; they also had nineteen Mauser cartridges, a lot of Browning cartridges and a small box containing cyanide. Fearing that the prisoners might swallow poison, the gendarmes ordered them to get undressed, whereupon a new scuffle broke out and one of them, according to Bulajs, almost bit the top of his finger off. The postcards purchased at Sigulda were found to be addressed to people in Switzerland (where Jānis Žāklis was thought to be living) and 'other European countries'.

The next witness, Gendarme Kornev, told a different story. He testified that the suspects were arrested as soon as they were shouted at ('Hands up!'); both of them were seized from behind, before they had time to turn around. Kornev was fighting with Laiviņš, who had a pistol in his hand, but at the same time he could clearly see Bulajs struggling with Vītums. In this version gone were the 'grimace' and the deliberate attempt to kill a brave detective; Vītums was firing wildly without aiming, while Bulajs held his hands from behind. The other witnesses (among them agent Zīverts) only hurried to their assistance after the shots had been fired. The testimony of the local Gendarme Chief, *rotmeistars* Nesterov (read out to the court because he was not present), was that the Gendarme office in Valka had received categorical information that the aim of the anarchists Laiviņš and Vītums was to burgle the Valkas pawn shop. The accused themselves, understandably, offered an alternative account of their activities.

Vītums had left Latvia in 1904 to earn some money abroad, and had worked as a painter in Switzerland, London and other places. Laiviņš, also a painter, escaped to Switzerland after the events of 1905 because he 'was accused of something'. While abroad they mostly lived together. In April 1913 they heard that all political prisoners in Russia had been pardoned by a manifesto of the tsar. Shortly before their arrest they returned to Riga, and on 5th May were simply returning to their own district of Gaujeni to arrange their private matters.

They had no idea that they were under surveillance, and the sudden shouting in Valka ("Hands up!") had caught them unawares. Vītums said that he thought they were being attacked by robbers and instinctively produced his pistol from the pocket of his trousers, but he had no opportunity to point it and didn't even have time to turn around. All of the shots had been fired accidentally, when Bulajs caught hold of his hand, during the struggle for possession of the pistol. They had bought the guns and ammunition abroad and successfully brought them across the border, but wanted the guns just to give to 'some acquaintances', and had no thoughts of committing any crime.[34]

Their defence attorneys, advocates Shablovskis and Sokolov (from Petersburg), had little trouble in unravelling the story of deliberate attempted murder told by agent Bulajs. Under cross-examination, Bulajs undermined his own credibility by embellishing his story; saying that Vītums and Laiviņš had looked back and noticed they were being followed *before* he shouted at them to raise their hands, and that's why they had their pistols ready. Even the Chairman of the Court seemed puzzled as to why agent Bulajs had never mentioned this before during the investigation. Next, Bulajs was asked to take hold of the Browning and demonstrate the way in which the shots were fired. But his clumsy attempts to see if the gun was loaded or not so alarmed those in court that the Prosecutor took it off him, checked it himself and handed it back to Bulajs. The agent's clothes, with various bullet holes in them, were presented as material evidence. Bulajs was asked to put on his coat and climb onto the table of the judges, and advocate Sokolov pointed out that the holes did not correspond with the shots. Bulajs confessed that he had made one of the holes latter, after the arrests. He had only noticed the bullet holes in his clothes after his return to Riga, and only gave them to the Gendarmerie as evidence at the end of August.[35]

Then Bulajs came out with something else new: that the investigating magistrate had told him that four of the bullets in Vītums' pistol contained poison, and that even a little scratch from one of those bullets would have killed him, so 'only thanks to God' was he still alive. This fact had not been mentioned in the whole case, and Sokolov asked that the examining magistrate should be summoned for questioning. The court denied Sokolov's request.

An argument ensued between Sokolov and the Chairman of the Court. The Prosecutor ruled that the accusation had been proven. Both defence lawyers protested that the investigation was incomplete, and that the whole case was flawed because of the lack of expertise and the contradictory testimony of the main witnesses, and asked that the accused be acquitted. After a short deliberation the court came to the verdict: for the crimes of offering armed resistance to the lawful actions of government officials during their arrest, and of a premeditated attempt to murder the railway Gendarmes Kornev, Melikov and Shchupshkon, and an agent of the *Okhranka* Nikolajs Bulajs, the defendants Jānis Vītums (27) and Juris Laiviņš (26) should each be sentenced to ten years hard labour, with confiscation of all their rights.[36]

Even the newspaper *Jaunākās Ziņas* which reported the trial was moved to comment that the judgement appeared 'very politically tainted'.[37]

* * *

Juris Laiviņš returned to freedom three years later, in March 1917, after the gaols were emptied of political prisoners following the abdication of the tsar. Nothing more was heard of him until 1926, when he re-appeared living in Riga. He was photographed with Ģederts Eliass, Maija Cielēna and Voldemārs Skare at an official gathering held in honour of the 'participants in the 1905 Revolution', at the Dailes theatre in Riga on 26th January 1926.[38] Nothing is known of what he did in the intervening years, or of his subsequent life. Possibly he was involved in the Russian Revolution. His reappearance in Latvia in 1926 (then an independent state) coincides with the rise of Stalin in Russia and the first rumblings of the great purges. Whether Laiviņš remained an anarchist, and when he died, is not known. Conceivably, he survived like Ģederts Eliass into the 1970s, or else, more likely, he perished like so many other Latvians during the triple trial of Soviet-Nazi-Soviet-again occupation that afflicted Latvia from the 1940s onwards.[39]

But the imprisonment of Laiviņš and Vītums was not the end of the anarchist movement in Latvia. The files of the police and *Okhranka*, preserved today in the Latvian National Archives in Riga, testify to the resilience of Latvian anarchism. Long lists of anarchists under investigation belie the notion that the "anarchist peril" in Latvia ended with the break up of *Pats — vārds un darbs* in 1906 (or of *Liesma* in 1910). The tsarist authorities continued to be haunted by the spectre of anarchist resistance right up to 1917, when the autocracy collapsed and the *Okhranka* detectives found themselves out of work. In Paris, the journal *Melnais Karogs* continued to appear regularly right up to June 1914; the anarchist émigrés in Western Europe and America remaining in touch with a vibrant movement in the Baltic that was struggling to free Latvia not only from Imperial Russia, but from the oppression of *all* government. While proudly proclaiming themselves to be 'internationalist', the Latvian anarchists remained mindful that (as in the 1905 Revolution) the class struggle and the 'national question' were indivisible for a small nation fighting to be free: 'Waging an unceasing struggle against exploitation, its cornerstone — private property and its guarding bulwark — the State, we at the same time stand for the independence and free development of our people. There isn't, and cannot be, any other way of solving the national question.'[40]

In London, Latvian anarchists published a monthly journal, *Cīņas Balss* (The Voice of Struggle), from January 1915 until the end of 1916, which proclaimed itself *Rietumeiropas un Amerikas latviešu anarhistu-komunistu orgāns* (The organ of Anarchist-Communist groups in America and Western Europe); largely given over to articles debating anarchist attitudes to the war. It also printed contact addresses for Latvian anarchist groups in London, New York, Chicago and Philadelphia. But the isolation of the émigrés from their comrades in the Baltic, due to wartime disruption of communications, gradually became complete.[41] The death knell of Anarchism in Latvia, when it came, was rung by the double blow of the First World War and the triumph of Bolshevism in Russia.

It was the war, more than any manipulations by Lenin, which had the effect of pushing Latvian Social Democracy closer to the Bolsheviks. Latvians generally supported the war waged by Russia against Germany (the traditional enemy of the Letts). But the LSD took an internationalist position, opposed the war, and in doing so moved closer to Russian Bolshevism and away from the Western Social-Democratic parties that had now all opted for the defensist position of supporting their national governments in the war. Even as the Germans advanced into Courland, LSD leaflets were still proclaiming: 'War against war! Down with tsardom! Long Live the revolution and the international solidarity of workers!' In London too, as late as 17th July, 1917, Aleksandrs Zirnis could still note in his diary: 'Note from secretary that Lettish SDP branch still international socialists and against national defence.'[42]

Jēkabs Peterss was a member in London of what he calls in his *Autobiography* the Committee of Socialist Groups — whose task was to struggle against the war. This activity, he said, resulted in his being 'prosecuted again', but no details have yet been found of precisely what for or when. So many people were arrested for anti-war propaganda that it is unlikely to have been anything more than a minor charge, and Peterss certainly was not obliged to spend any time in prison as a result. His wife, May, worked in a munitions factory during the war, and had three brothers in the British Army (one, in 1918, at the front). She seems not to have involved herself in her husband's anti-war activity.

For the Latvians the question of what attitude they should adopt to the War had a particular significance. Latvia was in the front line of the fighting, and much of it was under German occupation. In August 1915, the tsar reluctantly gave permission for nine Latvian rifle battalions to be formed as part of the 12th Russian Army. Eight thousand Latvian volunteers flocked to enlist, eager for an opportunity to defend their homes, mindful in doing so of taking a step closer to Latvian nationhood. This goes a long way to explaining, for instance, why the Latvian riflemen (*Strēlnieki*) should have occupied such a vital role after the revolution. The mass desertions that weakened the Russian Army (whose troops wanted simply to get home to their villages in time to share in the redistribution of the land after the fall of the Tsar), never touched the Latvians, whose homes were under German occupation. They were fighting to free their families from a traditional enemy, and had nowhere to desert to — hence they were the only units who could be relied upon to fight.

The dispersal inside Russia of much of the Latvian population, fleeing from the German troops, brought with it an unexpected bonus in the eyes of Latvian Bolsheviks like Aleksandrs Zirnis: 'The Baltic Provinces are now devastated by war. Not only the economic but also the intellectual life of the provinces has been stifled by the fighting armies; Hindenburg's troops, on their victorious march — with the blessing of the official German Social-Democracy — have undone for the time being the party work of the Lettish Social-Democracy and have, for the most part, ruined all that our party has built up during long years of struggle… Be that as it may — the Lettish Social Democrats do not complain and do not despair. Since the forced evacuation of their country they are now reassured by thousands over the whole of Russia. And in the Russian industrial centres they will get into touch with the revolutionary movement now awakening. From their former field of action they will take with them the firm resolution to fight, shoulder to shoulder with the Russian proletariat, for the termination of the war and for the defeat of tsarism.'[43]

This is in fact exactly what happened. The Latvians in Russia, unable to return to their homes because of the German occupation, became, after the fall of the tsar, the most enthusiastic supporters of the Russian revolution. At the same time, with the retreat into Russia of Latvian Army units (containing many Latvian socialists), a situation was created in which Latvians were cast to play the decisive role in the next chapter of Russia's future.

Notes

1   Anonymous, 'Song of the Bog Brigade', A. G. Stock & Reginald Reynolds (eds.) *Prison Anthology* (London, 1928), p. 270.
2   Email from Melindria Tavoularis (granddaughter of Fricis Svārs and Luba Milstein) 10th September, 2016.
3   Letter from Alfred Driscoll, 7th April 1988
4   Ibid.
5   Letter from Alfred Driscoll, 26th June 1988.
6   Probably the Russian emigrants' library run by A. L. Teplov at 106 Commercial Road, an address where Luba Milstein received mail from Russia.
7   Letter from Alfred Driscoll, 7th April 1988.
8   Sir Robert Bruce Lockhart, *My Europe* (London, 1952), p. 48.
9   Birth certificate of G. W. May Peters, registered at Islington south-east, London, 13th December, 1913.
10 'Wife of the man of Terror — Moscow Murder Chief as Model Husband', *Daily Express*, 3rd October, 1918.
11 Ivan Maisky, *Journey Into The Past*, pp. 51-2 (London, 1962).
12 *Cīņa*, No.122-123, 21st June 1912.
13 Ibid.
14 *Daily Herald*, 20th May, 1912.
15 Vasileva admitted sending the sachet to Trassjonsky when she was interviewed by J. E. Holroyd in 1959, but curiously denied it when she was questioned by Richard Whittington Egan on 14th November 1960. She told him instead that she visited Trassjonsky twice in hospital and took her gifts of fruit, but that they had never met before being in Holloway prison together. Interview with Richard Whittington Egan, Malvern, 19th March 1988.
16 Files of the City of London Police, 'Houndsditch Murders', Report by Sgt. B. Nicholls, 'Subject Nina Vassilleva', 23rd May 1931, London Metropolitan Archives.
17 Fricis Svars letter to his father, Jēkabs Svars, 1st January 1911. Original in the possession of Donald Rumbelow; new English translation by Irene Ruff, London 2010.
18 National Archives of Australia (NAA). Naturalisation file of John Rosen: A1/1925/25764/Item 1615464 (Canberra).
19 Ibid. Alien registration certificate 476, 25th June 1917.
20 *The Argus* (Melbourne), Friday 2nd November 1928, p. 18
21 *The Argus* (Melbourne), Friday 30th November 1928, p. 18.
22 'Bīčvortas Toms Hilmanis' (Tom Hillman from Beechworth), *Austrālijas Latvietis*, October 1956.
23 Telephone interview with George Rosen, Mount Beauty (Victoria), Australia, 26th November 2010.
24 Ibid.
25 Ibid.
26 Ibid.
27 Ibid.
28 Ibid.
29 *Melnais Karogs*, issue 14, April 1913.
30 LVVA,4621/4/39, #8, 22nd February-19th March 1913.
31 LVVA, 4568/5/745, 'Diary of External Observation of Glāzenap, 14 March to 22 September 1913'.
32 *Jaunakis Zines* No. 177, 30th June 1914.
33 Ibid.
34 Ibid.
35 Ibid.
36 Ibid.
37 Ibid.
38 Klāvs Lorencs, *Kāda cilvēka dzīve* (Zelta grauds, Rīga 2005).

39   Members of the Laiviņš family were among the Latvian displaced persons who emigrated
      to the USA after WW2. Eduards Laiviņš, his wife Mirdza (Zanders), and their two young
      sons Juris and Uldis, arrived in America in 1951. The son Juris (born 1944) became a
      successful architect in Dallas, Texas. In March 2011 he provided the author with a partial
      family tree, which suggests that his grandfather, Hugo Laiviņš (born in Alsviki, 1882-
      1955), could have been a brother or cousin of his anarchist namesake Juris Laiviņš; of
      whom he knew nothing. Other members of the Laiviņš family were not so fortunate;
      they appear in the lists of Latvians deported to Siberia during the Soviet occupation.

40   'Dažas piezīmes tautības jautājumā' (Some notes on the national question) by 'Sampo',
      Melnais Karogs, issue 18, December 1913, pp. 274-6.

41   *Cīņas Balss* (1915-1916) was published in London by John Sandberg, 75 Jubilee Street,
      Stepney.

42   Diary of Aleksandrs Zirnis, copy from Melita Norwood.

43   Aleksandrs Zirnis, manuscript article in English, 'How The Lettish Social-Democracy
      Opposed The War', 26th October, 1915 (The Brotherton Collection, Leeds University).

12

1917 to 1939
No Time for Dreams

...the October days had not resolved the question of class struggle ...
the enemy was not sleeping ... there was no time for sentimental
dreams...

Jēkabs Peterss[1]

Jēkabs Peterss had been a rather minor figure in the revolution of 1905, and a completely peripheral figure to the Houndsditch tragedy, but now he was set to occupy centre stage in a series of events that would make him one of the most powerful and loathed figures in Russia, and end by devouring him.

Whilst a member of the Central Committee of the Latvian Social Democracy and a key Latvian Bolshevik, Peterss did not hold any position in the command structures of the Russian party. What gave him his authority in Russia was his direct relationship to Lenin, who valued Peterss as 'an important and extremely dedicated person'.[2] Peterss' service to Lenin in the crucial moments of seizing power in 1917, and his contribution to the consolidation of Lenin's dictatorship as one of the chief architects of the Soviet security service, has only partly been recognised. His career between 1922 and 1929 is a closed book; even in 1989 an officer of the KGB in Riga, Aivars Dombrovskis, protested that it was difficult to speak openly about Peterss' work, because 'all things started with him'.[3]

News of the tsar's abdication in March 1917 and the coming to power of a provisional government headed by Alexander Kerensky produced euphoria among the revolutionary émigrés in London. But the excited expectations of imminent socialism, an end to the war and the dismantling of the Russian Empire were not fulfilled. Kerensky sided with the Entente against Germany, kept Russia in the war and did everything he could to avoid power falling into the clutches of the people in the streets, who organised workers' councils (Soviets), and demanded 'bread, peace and land'. The uneasy standoff was labelled 'dual power'.

Jēkabs Peterss said goodbye to his English wife and four-year-old daughter and was among the first of the émigrés to return to Russia. He arrived in Petrograd (prior to 1914, St. Petersburg) via Murmansk at the beginning of May, 1917, and was immediately sent to Riga, to agitate among the soldiers of the Latvian rifle regiments. By the time Peterss arrived, Latvian troops had been fighting the Germans for two years, at a cost of 32,000 men, and 735,000 Latvian refugees were scattered over Russia and Siberia.[4] Courland was occupied by the German army. Behind the lines, politics in the rest of Latvia anticipated rather than imitated events in revolutionary Petrograd. With the tsar gone, civilian power in the unoccupied region of Livonia passed to a Provisional Land Council, nominally an arm of the Petrograd government but personified in a

Provincial Commissar whose sympathies were openly Bolshevik; and to the Latvian Soviets, the most important of which was in Riga. Military power rested with the Executive Committee of the Council of Latvian Riflemen, known by its Russian abbreviation *Iskolastrel*. In his first ten weeks in Riga Jēkabs Peterss delivered fifty-six speeches, arguing against the policy of national defence (fighting the Germans), to win over the Latvian riflemen to the Bolsheviks. By July 1917 Bolshevik membership inside the 12th Army had increased tenfold. For the first and only time, Bolshevism enjoyed genuine popular support in the Baltic.

What Lenin was to achieve in Russia by resort to arms, the Latvians gained by peaceful means. In August 1917 the Bolsheviks were voted into power in Livonia through elections to the Riga Council and the Provisional Land Council. But they chose instead to exercise power through the Executive Committee of Workers', Soldiers' and Landless Peasants' Deputies in Latvia, or *Iskolat* by its Russian acronym. For a brief period before Lenin seized power in Petrograd, the *Iskolat* presided over what was arguably the first Bolshevik republic in the territory of the former Russian empire. But almost immediately the German army launched an offensive against Riga, crossing the river Daugava to the south east of the city. Jēkabs Peterss was forced to leave Riga with the retreating 12th Army, to take charge of Party activity in the unoccupied towns east of the capital. Peterss represented the Latvian Social Democracy inside the Russian Bolshevik party, joined the editorial board of the LSD newspaper *Cīņa* (Struggle), and wrote for *Brīvajais Strēlnieks* (The Free Soldier), and *Laukstrādnieku Cīņa* (Farm Labourers' Fight).

At the end of August, Peterss was sent to Petrograd as one of the representatives in the elections to the Democratic Conference, and was elected as a delegate to the Second All-Russian Congress of Soviets. Lenin was secretly planning to launch an armed uprising before the Congress opened; before Kerensky could mobilise troops loyal to the Provisional Government to arrest the Soviet and move against the Bolsheviks. With the Latvian riflemen virtually the only dependable units in the Russian army, Lenin needed them on his side. Under cover of readying the Latvian Social Democracy for the Congress, Peterss came back to Latvia, in his own words, 'to prepare the military troops for the October Revolution'.[5] As it transpired, the Latvian riflemen, unwilling to leave the front, played no part in the Bolshevik takeover; they reached Petrograd only after the event. In those last autumn weeks before the revolution Jēkabs Peterss was constantly shuttling back and forth between Latvia and Petrograd, where he watched over the fugitive Lenin, who was forced into hiding after a series of armed demonstrations against Kerensky in July. Unable to reveal his presence in the Russian capital without being arrested, Lenin needed Peterss to look after his security and ensure that his instructions to the party had the appearance of having emanated from Finland, where he was officially supposed to be in hiding. Peterss had to keep Lenin hidden not only from Kerensky but also from the Bolshevik Central Committee, who opposed his plan for an armed coup and were unaware that he had returned to the capital. Peterss was assisted by two other Latvians: Bolsheviks Ivars Smilga and Mārtiņš Lācis.

* * *

On the first morning of the October Revolution, the American journalist John Reed bumped into Jēkabs Peterss near the Marinsky Palace, the meeting place of the Council of the Russian Republic: 'An automobile came by ... with armed soldiers on the front seat, full of arrested members of the Provisional Government. Peters, Lettish member of the Military Revolutionary Committee, came hurrying across the Square.

"'I thought you bagged those gentlemen last night", said I, pointing to them.

"'Oh", he answered, with the expression of a disappointed schoolboy. "The damned fools let most of them go again before we made up our minds..."'[6]

The Military Revolutionary Committee, to which Peterss belonged, was the general staff of the uprising. During the night MRC detachments, acting on the orders of Lenin and Trotsky, had successfully occupied almost all of the key points in the city except for the symbolically important Winter Palace. While the Bolsheviks waited for the order to advance against an unknown number of Palace defenders, Jēkabs Peterss used his American friends John Reed and Louise Bryant to secure the information which sealed Lenin's victory and created a Bolshevik myth. Leaving Peterss to his task of arresting government ministers, Reed and Bryant used their prestige as supposedly neutral foreign journalists to badger their way into the besieged Winter Palace. After spending three hours there, they returned to Lenin's headquarters at Smolny, bringing Peterss news of the morale, disposition and numbers of the troops inside the Palace. The defenders, they told Peterss, consisted only of a handful of military cadets and a solitary Womens' Battalion, who had no intention of offering serious resistance. A few frightened ministers were there, but Kerensky had already fled.[7]

The attack went ahead at midnight. But it was not the impassioned, charging, throng portrayed in Sergei Eisenstein's classic cinematographic epic, *October* (1928). After the cruiser *Aurora* had fired several blank rounds at the Palace, the Bolshevik Vladimir Antonov-Ovseyenko led a party of Red Guards up a narrow servants' stairway, disarmed the bewildered defenders, and arrested a small huddle of government ministers cowering in an interior room. A total of six people were killed in the whole October uprising. There were more casualties during Eisenstein's filming of the fictional "storming" of the Palace, in which the charging hordes of film-extras (real soldiers) fired off live ammunition, than in the real thing.

Lenin had seized power, but his position was precarious. Trotsky wrote that, only a few hours after the insurrection, Lenin 'demanded that one of the Latvian regiments, consisting almost entirely of workers, be posted to Petrograd.' 'If it comes to anything, the muzhik may falter', he said, 'and here we need proletarian determination.'[8]

When three trains finally pulled into the Baltic Station in Petrograd on 25th November, carrying 2,500 riflemen of the 6th. Tukums Regiment, the Latvian Bolshevik leader Pēteris Stučka and Vladimir Antonov-Ovseyenko were there to meet them. They were followed, at noon the next day, by a Special Battalion of 320 Latvian volunteers, hand-picked on Lenin's orders. The future Kremlin

Commandant, Pavel Malkov, recalled them as, 'workers imbued with the proletarian spirit, Bolsheviks almost to a man, and supremely devoted to the revolution. These were the glorious guard of the proletarian revolution.'[9]

But the arrival of the Special Battalion was a bit of a shambles. No one was there to meet them when they arrived at the railway station, and it was four o'clock in the afternoon before a guide came to show them the way to Smolny.

On the day that the first Latvians arrived, Peterss had been forced to bring in sailors from Helsinki to stop the looting of the Winter Palace's wine cellars. Wartime prohibition of alcohol meant that stockpiles were huge, and Peterss discovered 800 wine and spirit cellars in the city. Looting of them by mobs lost the new Soviet government huge foreign revenues (the contents of the Winter Palace cellars alone were valued at 30 million roubles) and threatened to produce serious disorders, as drunkenness reached epidemic proportions. Though brought from Latvia principally to provide security at Smolny, the Special Battalion were quickly pressed into service by Peterss to restore sobriety to the city. Peterss kept discovering new wine cellars; each time sending the Latvians to smash the bottles. In one place the soldiers smashed 300,000 bottles, and a fire engine had to be used to pump the wine out of the cellar into the river Neva. The operation took weeks. Inevitably the raids encountered trouble, and frequently ended in shooting. On 6th December 1917, a state of siege was declared in the city. Peterss imposed a curfew, and warned that looters of wine would thenceforth be met by machine-gun fire.

With the uprising over, the Military Revolutionary Committee deemed its job done. Responsibility for security matters was handed over to a new body, the All-Russian Extraordinary Commission for Combating Counter-Revolution, Speculation, Sabotage, and Misuse of Authority, more commonly known by its abbreviated Russian acronym ChK, or Cheka. Jēkabs Peterss and eight others were nominated as a Collegium (board), to direct the new security agency, under the chairmanship of Felix Dzerzhinsky. Urgent high-level decisions were the responsibility of a five-man Presidium chaired by Dzerzhinsky, with Peterss and Ivan Ksenofontov as his secretaries. Peterss also took on the job of Cheka treasurer, and was effectively Dzerzhinsky's Deputy. Sensitive perhaps to any suggestion that the former guest of Her Majesty's Prisons was now *poacher-turned-gamekeeper*, Peterss wrote of himself: 'It was distasteful to go out on raids and arrests, to see tears during the interrogations, especially when the comrades who had to do it had only recently gone through the same interrogations at the hands of the police.'[10]

The fledgling Cheka moved into a building at Gorohovaya 2, which had formerly housed the offices of the City Governor and the Department of Police, complete with its own gaol. Far from being an omnipresent secret police apparatus, the Cheka's entire records fitted into Dzerzhinsky's briefcase, and its finances, only 1,000 roubles at first, were kept in the drawer of Peterss' desk.[11] At the end of 1917, it still had only twenty-three personnel, and though that figure had risen to around 120 by the time it was evacuated to Moscow in March, 1918, all of them performed multiple roles.[12] Supplementing this embryonic security establishment, the Latvian Smolny Battalion, which took over as the Kremlin guard after the transfer to Moscow, doubled as a sort of

Cheka auxiliary, carrying out all the tasks of regular Chekists, including undercover operations.

In March 1918, Soviet emissaries concluded peace negotiations with the German government by signing the Treaty of Brest-Litovsk, and Lenin abandoned the Baltic Provinces, Finland, Ukraine, the Caucasus and Poland to the Germans. The Latvian rifle regiments, all of them now in Russia and unable to return home, accepted Bolshevik promises that non-Russian minorities would have the right of separation from Russia, something denied to them by Kerensky, and agreed on a voluntary basis to become transformed into units of the Red Army until such time as they could return to the Baltic. A Soviet Latvian rifle division of 19,340 men was organised under the command of Jukums Vācietis, a Latvian professional soldier formerly a Colonel in the Imperial Army. The Latvian Red Riflemen subsequently fought on every major battle front of the Civil War; but their initial deployment was on the internal front, where Lenin faced serious challenges to his drive towards a one party dictatorship.

With the German army so close to Petrograd, Lenin deemed it prudent to transfer the seat of government to the ancient Russian capital of Moscow. Late in the evening of 10th March 1918, Lenin and the Soviet government, accompanied by a 150-man detachment of Latvian riflemen, pulled out of the Nikolaevsky station aboard a train for Moscow. Jēkabs Peterss and the Cheka Collegium followed on the 30th March, establishing their new headquarters at Bolshaia Lubianka 11, formerly occupied by the Anchor Insurance Company and Lloyds Insurance.

The Muscovites, according to Peterss, reacted unfavourably to the Cheka. Two incidents in particular were to blame for their poor reception: 'immediately after our arrival from St. Petersburg, our comrades went to some tea-room to have a drink of tea (it turned out that you could also buy home-brew there) and drunken hooligan bandits jumped on our comrades and killed one of them. The bandits were caught, and seven of them were shot to death that very night. The second: our comrades once went to a circus where the clown Bim-Bom[13] was making nasty remarks about the Soviet authority. Our comrades, without thinking the matter over, decided to arrest him, and, moreover, to arrest him on the stage. With that decision, they moved in on Bim-Bom. When they approached him and declared that he was under arrest, the public at first thought that it was all part of Bim-Bom's act. Bim-Bom himself gaped at us in confusion but seeing that we were in all seriousness, started to run away. Our comrades opened fire. Panic broke out, and the Cheka was reminded of these two facts for a long time.'[14]

Irreverent clowns were the least of Peterss' worries. Lenin's escalating dictatorship was set on a collision course with an altogether more significant source of criticism: the anarchists. The quarrel in London between Peterss and his cousin Fricis Svars over irreconcilable political perspectives, mirroring the rupture in the LSDSP when Jānis Žāklis broke away from the Party in 1906, was set to assume a deadly significance for the future of the Russian revolution. Jēkabs Peterss admits that the real reason why Lenin was so concerned to move against the anarchists after the Cheka arrived in Moscow was that, 'two authorities existed there: on the one hand, the Moscow Soviet, and on the other, the Staff of the Black Guard.'[15] Lenin wanted to pre-empt any challenge by the anarchists to the Bolshevik monopoly of decision making, because they offered a credible alternative to the dictatorship of the proletariat and posed a serious threat to the whole notion of the leading role of the Bolshevik Party.

Between February 1917 and the spring of 1918, Russian Anarchism enjoyed a legal existence for the first, and only, time in its history. Though split on the question of support for the Bolsheviks, anarchists of all tendencies had taken part in the overthrow of Kerensky. They worked enthusiastically in the Soviets, and were represented in the All Russian Central Executive Committee (VTsIK). Many of them were captivated by Lenin's writings after April, 1917, particularly his famous work, *The State and Revolution*, which had re-examined Marx's theory of the state and concluded that the existing bourgeois state must be abolished (along with the standing army, police and courts) and replaced with a society modelled on the Paris Commune. Believing the Bolsheviks to be sincerely dedicated to this task, Soviet Anarchists were even prepared to temporarily bend their anti-statist principles, in the cause of seeing the revolution triumph, by supporting the dictatorship of the proletariat. As the Soviet state grew stronger, the contradictions between Bolshevik and anarchist aims became more irreconcilable. But the growing influence and numbers of the anarchists made it difficult to move against them openly. And among the burgeoning anarchist presence in Moscow were the Latvians.

* * *

The tragic events at Houndsditch and Sidney Street had broken up the London *Liesma* group, but at least one original member of the organisation was determined to rekindle the flame. Jānis Birze (Remus) was a Latvian anarchist who had taken part in the 1905 revolution, first as a member of the LSDSP then as a member of Žāklis's group *Pats — vārds un darbs*. In 1907 he was arrested and in 1908 sentenced to six years hard labour, which he served in Riga and Pskov prisons, before being exiled to Siberia. Freed after the fall of the autocracy, Birze made his way to Moscow, where he resurrected *Liesma* in August 1917.

Before then, Birze says, the Latvian anarchists in Moscow had worked independently of each other, as well as with Russian anarchist groups. But seeing the greater efficiency of communicating with the Latvian workers living in Moscow in their own language, they had come together as a permanent group, meeting once a week in a tiny flat, 'packed like sardines, to review and discuss the most important issues for the group.'[16] When the October Revolution began everyone in *Liesma* joined either the Red Guard or 'the anarchist fighting organisation' (Black Guard) and, in Birze's words, 'took the most active part in the October battles'.[17]

With Kerensky gone, the anarchists solved their problem of having no permanent quarters by deciding simply to squat in the houses of the rich. The house chosen was at 3 Presnensky Pereulok, a small and unfurnished property in need of repair. After two weeks, *Liesma* managed to transform it into the Latvian Anarchist Club, with public lectures every Sunday which attracted audiences of over a hundred people. On Wednesday evenings there were theoretical reading circles for members, where political issues were discussed. *Liesma* published pamphlets ('it was impossible to gather large masses of people in the tiny building — we had to give the masses something to read'[18]), and began organising communes as an example of anarchy in action, to instil in the workers a faith in creating a free social order. But confined in such cramped quarters *Liesma* needed more space, and in January 1918 took over a large house in Malaja Dimitrovka. The existing owner was allowed to remain living in one half of the building, while the other half became the new home of the Latvian Anarchist Club. The original squat in Presnensky Pereulok was turned into a commune. *Liesma* also organised its own Fighting Unit, which was supplied with ammunition and rations from the main Red Guard headquarters.

The Bolsheviks were deeply unhappy with initiatives of this kind. To counter the growing strength and influence of the anarchists, Bolshevik officials began to spread a fabricated story that Black Guard detachments had been infiltrated by bandits and former tsarist officers, who used *ideological* Anarchism as a cover for self-enrichment and counter revolution. Jēkabs Peterss says, 'The Staff of the Black Guard acted and issued orders as an authority, arranged round-ups on the streets, took away weapons and valuables, seized private homes belonging to members of the bourgeoisie, seized the valuables there, and handed out the bourgeois rags right and left to the population. By this method the bandits, themselves acquiring the valuables (silver, articles of gold, etc.), won the sympathy of the man in the street, who could not understand how the Bolshevik all-national equality differed from the "anarchistic" division of property...'[19]

The man in the street could be forgiven for seeing that the anarchists were doing no different than the Bolsheviks. The difference was that the Bolsheviks believed that their actions entitled them to be a government, the anarchists did not. The irritation of Lenin and Peterss with these *bandits* was caused by the fear that the man in the street actually might understand the difference between Bolshevik and anarchist ideas of equality.

In April 1918 *Liesma* was joined in Moscow by another Latvian anarchist group, which had arrived from the Ukrainian city of Kharkov. To accommodate the newcomers, *Liesma* and a Russian anarchist group, *Kommuna*, took over a manor house in Vedenski Pereulok (a side street), which had two out buildings. *Kommuna* occupied one of the buildings, while *Liesma* gave the other one to the Latvians from Kharkov. *Liesma* also established contacts with actors at the Moscow Latvian Theatre,[20] with a view to opening a Latvian Anarchist Theatre. A meeting of representatives of both theatre companies was planned to take place on 12th April 1918. But, as Birze says wistfully, 'man supposes and God disposes'.[21] Jēkabs Peterss and the Cheka had other plans for the 12th of April.

On the night of 12th April, 1918, Jēkabs Peterss launched an offensive against the Moscow anarchists, with raids against twenty-six anarchist centres in the City, and closed down the printing presses of the Moscow Anarchist Federation and its paper *Anarkhiya*. Caught by surprise, some of the anarchists were captured without a shot being fired, or put up only a token resistance. Elsewhere, the well armed Black Guard detachments were only overcome by full-scale military assault. At one of the target houses, a small two-storey building in its own grounds behind high iron railings set back from Bolshaya

Dmitrovka Street, Malkov and 200 Latvian riflemen of the Kremlin guard were met by rifle and machine gun fire. Blasting their way in with hand-grenades, they had to storm the house with fixed bayonets before the anarchists surrendered. As the prisoners were led away, Malkov and fifty of the Latvians were called upon to reinforce the Cheka group trying to capture Black Guard headquarters at number 6 Malaya Dmitrovka Street (The House of Anarchy, formerly the Moscow Merchants' Club, today the Lencom Theatre), where even fiercer resistance had been met. The anarchists kept their attackers pinned down with rifles and machine guns, and peppered the Chekists with shrapnel from a mountain gun, bombs and hand-grenades. The building was only captured after being bombarded by a three-inch howitzer mounted on the back of a lorry. At the end of the operation 100 anarchists were dead and, according to Malkov, 800 taken prisoner.[22] By 1 p.m. on the 13th it was all over. The Cheka had won 'in the course of a single night', says Peterss, 'the authority of the Black Guard in Moscow was liquidated.'[23]

The building occupied by *Liesma* was in the same street as Black Guard headquarters, but the Latvian anarchists apparently were given no opportunity to offer resistance. Jānis Birze says, 'we were woken up by a terrible noise, amid shooting and noise we could hear people screaming. In the first moments we couldn't ask anybody either. All rooms were overfilled with soldiers, who were on a horrible looting spree — they just went mad like beasts who broke out of cages — who were ready to tear you to pieces with their teeth for every word you dared to say.'[24]

Later in the day Peterss conducted Robert Bruce Lockhart, the unofficial British Diplomatic Agent in Moscow, round the scenes of the fighting. 'The sight was grim', wrote Lockhart: 'Typical of the times was the fact that Peters and our Cheka chauffeur wore exactly the same clothes as the dead bandits: breeches and belted brown-leather jackets with side pockets in which a revolver or a Browning could be held ready to fire.'[25] In his well known *Memoirs of a British Agent*, Lockhart describes the devastation he encountered on his tour with Peterss: 'we entered house after house. The filth was indescribable. Broken bottles littered the floors, the magnificent ceilings were perforated with bullet-holes. Wine stains and human excrement blotched the Aubusson carpets. Priceless pictures had been slashed to strips. The dead still lay where they had fallen. They included officers in guards' uniforms, students — young boys of twenty — and men who obviously belonged to the criminal class and whom the revolution had released from prison. In the luxurious drawing-room of the house of Gracheva the Anarchists had been surprised in the middle of an orgy. The long table which had supported the feast had been overturned, and broken plates, glass, champagne bottles, made unsavoury islands in a pool of blood and spilt wine. On the floor lay a young woman, face downwards. Peters turned her over. Her hair was disheveled. She had been shot through the neck, and the blood had congealed in a sinister purple clump. She could not have been more than twenty. Peters shrugged his shoulders. "Prostituka", he said. "Perhaps it is for the best." It was an unforgettable scene. The Bolsheviks had taken their first step towards the establishment of discipline.'[26] The scene that Peterss had arranged for Lockhart to witness was carefully calculated to justify the accusations made against the anarchists: 'officers in guards' uniforms', though Lockhart admits that everyone wore military tunics in those days; 'men who belonged to the criminal class' fresh from prison, most probably former political prisoners; and 'signs of an orgy', proof at least of a vivid imagination. The questionable morality implicit in Lockhart's acceptance that no further explanation was necessary for the death of the young woman 'shot through the neck', suggesting summary execution, simply because she was a 'prostitute', shows how the scenario resonated perfectly with the prejudiced attitudes of a foreign diplomatic observer eager to see law and order restored.

A special troika (three-man committee) of Chekists, led by an unnamed Collegium member (possibly Peterss himself), conducted the interrogations in Malkov's office at the Kremlin. The Chekists began by questioning the prisoners about their knowledge of Anarchism and, depending on their answers, sorted them into two groups: *ideological* anarchists, and *bandits*. Jānis Birze and his *Liesma* comrades were among those released: 'After several days of torture in the cellars of the Kremlin and behind the walls of Butyrka prison, we were recognised as "ideological revolutionaries" and were released with the following words from the high authorities: "we fight against bandits, but we leave ideological workers in peace". We were recognised as "ideological" workers, but only after our ideological work had been completely destroyed, the literature which had cost us so much effort and selfless work was burned, the printing press confiscated, all the capital looted. Rendered harmless, we were let off to go where we wanted. But it is possible to suppress a man, not an idea, and the "Liesma" group ... renewed its work again with twice as much dedication and energy. Pooling our last strength and means together, we started replacing our literature and started publishing our magazine.'[27]

The magazine *Liesma* was only to appear for one issue, in July 1918, before all trace of the group was lost. Of Jānis Birze's subsequent life all that is known is that he worked in the Soviet Union in the trade sphere during the 1920s and '30s. His last known place of work was Novosibirsk, where 'his life was ended' (according to a Soviet account written in 1962) at the end of the 1930s.[28]

Those who still dreamed of seeing Anarchy in their lifetime pinned their hopes on a *third revolution* against Communist dictatorship, based on the Makhnovist insurgency in Ukraine and the Kronstadt revolt of 1921, but by the end of the 1920s the anarchist movement in Russia was completely outlawed.

* * *

With the anarchists out of the way, the next obstacle to unfettered Bolshevik dictatorship was the Party of Left Socialist Revolutionaries (Left SRs, or LSRs), Lenin's coalition partners in the first Soviet government. Bitterly critical of Lenin's policy of appeasing the Germans, the Left SRs proposed instead a strategy of waging a 'revolutionary war'. When the Brest Litovsk peace treaty was signed they resigned from the government in protest, but still retained a sizeable presence inside the Cheka, to the extent that Jēkabs Peterss estimated that they made up half of the Cheka Collegium.[29]

Their continued membership of the Cheka afforded the Left SRs the means by which they hoped to disrupt the peace and provoke a resumption of hostilities, by assassinating German officials. At the top of their hit list was the German Ambassador in Moscow, Count William von Mirbach; a scion of the same family Mirbach to whom Jānis Žāklis was distantly related. At three o' clock in the afternoon of 6th July 1918 two Left SR Chekists, Nikolai Andreyev and twenty-year-old Yakov Blumkin, appeared at the German Embassy with forged instructions authorizing them to discuss a confidential matter with Ambassador Mirbach.

After exchanging pleasantries with Mirbach, the two Chekists drew pistols and fired. Their shots missed and the Ambassador ran out of the room. Blumkin tossed a grenade after him. Mirbach collapsed, fatally injured. The assassins escaped through the office's ground floor window to a waiting car and were driven to the Pokrovsky Barracks, headquarters of the Cheka Combat Detachment, commanded by the LSR, Dmitri Popov.

Hearing the news from Lenin, a deeply embarrassed Felix Dzerzhinsky rushed to the German Embassy, then stormed off to Popov's headquarters to arrest Mirbach's assassins. But it was Dzerzhinsky and his escort of three Chekists who found themselves disarmed and taken hostage. To add to the humiliation, Dzerzhinsky's own LSR deputy in the Cheka, Aleksandrovich, then went with the LSR leader, Maria Spiridonova, to deliver an ultimatum to the Bolsheviks at the Congress of Soviets in the Bolshoi Theatre.

Quite by chance, Jēkabs Peterss was attending that day's session of the Congress and bumped into Aleksandrovich, who told him that 'something interesting' was happening at the Pokrovsky Barracks, and that they must leave immediately.[30] Although unaware that Aleksandrovich was trying to lure him into a trap, Peterss was suspicious and refused. When Peterss reached the stage he was told that Trotsky was trying to get in touch with him by telephone. Trotsky broke the news that Dzerzhinsky had been arrested, that the Cheka Combat Detachment had mutinied and that Blumkin, on orders of the LSR Central Committee, had murdered Mirbach.

Peterss immediately summoned the Bolshevik members of the Cheka Collegium to a crisis meeting at the Lubyanka, and ordered troops to surround Popov's headquarters. Then he called the Pokrovsky Barracks by telephone, asking to speak to Dzerzhinsky. Aleksandrovich, whom he had just spoken to at the Bolshoi only minutes before, came on the line and said that Dzerzhinsky was under arrest. Peterss told Aleksandrovich that he had put himself outside the law and that the proper steps would be taken, then he hung up.[31] His immediate problem was that the guard at the Lubyanka consisted entirely of Left SRs, and Finns from Popov's Combat Detachment, who were ignorant of Russian and loyal to their LSR Commanders. As he started to review his options the telephone rang. Either Lenin or Trotsky, Peterss didn't remember which, told him to leave Mārtiņš Lācis at the Lubyanka, and take the other Chekists with him to arrest the LSR delegates at the Congress of Soviets. No sooner had Peterss left, than Popov's men occupied the Lubyanka and marched the unfortunate Lācis off to join Dzerzhinsky at the Pokrovsky Barracks.

When Peterss arrived at the Bolshoi he was summoned to the telephone again and given the bad news. All Bolshevik delegates were told to leave the theatre, and document checks were set up at the exits. Finally, at eight o'clock, Peterss went onto the platform and made an official announcement about the day's events. The theatre was surrounded by Latvians, he added, and no Left SR would be allowed to leave. All 450 LSR delegates in the building were now hostages. Peterss next lured the rebels out of the Lubyanka, by ordering the Cheka Secretary to send two truck loads of the Finns to Solkolniki Park, on the pretext of looking for buried weapons. When that was done, the men at the Cheka dormitory were instructed to report, one at a time, to the Lubyanka, where they were issued with weapons.

Peterss scraped together a force of 720 Latvian riflemen, 12 cannon, four armoured cars, 72 cavalry, and a machine gun unit of 40 men, which he placed under the command of Jukums Vācietis. The Left SRs had 1,800 riflemen, 80 cavalrymen, four armoured cars, 48 machine-guns and eight light cannon. What had begun as a limited action, centering on Mirbach's death, and intended to force a change in Lenin's policy, was transformed by Bolshevik intransigence into all out war.

As night fell, Left SR forces seized the telephone exchange, several railway stations and a number of newspaper presses. A small force also occupied the Central Post Office.

At 5 a.m. on 7th July, Vācietis opened his attack on the rebel positions. The LSRs replied by bombarding the Kremlin with a few desultory shells, but were quickly driven out of range. Around midday, the Latvians dragged one of their cannon to within 300 meters of the Pokrovsky Barracks, and started shelling the building. Under heavy covering fire from machine guns, the Latvians pressed home their assault with bayonets and hand grenades. The Left SRs fled in disarray, abandoning their prisoners, including Dzerzhinsky.

By the end of the day the uprising had collapsed. Aleksandrovich was arrested as he tried to board a freight train leaving Moscow, and taken to the Lubyanka. Jēkabs Peterss conducted the interrogation: 'Aleksandrovich was greatly agitated. For a long time I spoke to him alone and he could not find words to justify his behaviour, to explain how, as the Deputy of the VChK, he could betray the confidence of Dzerzhinsky, enter into a plot, and organize the uprising.'[32]

Aleksandrovich's justification, summarized by Peterss, was that he was bound by party discipline. His Central Committee had decreed that a war with Germany should be provoked, and that Mirbach should be killed. He was expected to implement that decree, and as a loyal party member had no choice but to obey orders. It was not an original defence, but Peterss, possibly recognizing that had Lenin asked him to do likewise he would not have demurred, was clearly moved: 'I got the impression that he was speaking sincerely, that he had been a member of the LSR Party who was exemplary from the point of view of discipline, and that his error lay in the fact that he subjugated himself to the discipline of that party when it made the most stupid, traitorous step. He cried. He cried for a long time, and it became hard for me to take, perhaps because, of all the Left SRs, he had left the best impression on me. I left him.'[33]

Aleksandrovich and twelve others were shot the same day, on Dzerzhinsky's orders, without waiting for a legal investigation or trial.

At his own request, Felix Dzerzhinsky was suspended and the Cheka Collegium was dissolved. Jēkabs Peterss was appointed as temporary Chairman of the Cheka, with orders to form a new Collegium. Peterss occupied the post until 22nd August 1918, when Dzerzhinsky took up the reins again. Dzerzhinsky took another break in October 1918 to visit his family in Switzerland. In his absence, Peterss took over as Chairman of the Cheka again, for nearly a month at the height of the Red Terror. It was a period in which he was responsible for some of the most important decisions made in Russia, not least of which the execution of the Russian royal family.

* * *

Officially, the decision to kill the Romanov family in Ekaterinburg on 17th July, 1918, was taken by the Urals Regional Soviet, and only approved after the event by the government in Moscow. Alarmed by the approach of Czech troops and fearing that the tsar would be rescued, the Soviet supposedly took the law into its own hands and shot the whole family. This remains the story put forward in Russia today. The KGB files on the executions remain closed, and are regarded as politically sensitive in a country where veneration of the tsar has undergone a revival since the collapse of the Soviet Union.

Lenin had wanted to stage a public trial for Tsar Nicholas, with Trotsky as prosecutor and the proceedings broadcast live to the nation over the radio, but the worsening military situation caused him to change his mind. In June 1918, he summoned his close friend, Fram Goloshchokin, the Urals Regional Commissar for War, for consultations to Moscow. Present at the meetings were Lenin (the head of the party), Yakov Sverdlov (the head of the government), and Felix Dzerzhinsky and Jēkabs Peterss (the heads of state security).[34] In the second week of July, with Dzerzhinsky officially on suspension, it fell to Peterss, as acting head of the Cheka, to attend a final meeting with Lenin and Sverdlov, at which the fate of the tsar was decided. As someone who had endured imprisonment and torture, and witnessed the atrocities in the Baltic after the 1905 revolution, when Russian troops laid waste to so much of Latvia on the personal orders the tsar, Peterss had few qualms about concurring with the decision to put Nicholas to death. On 16th July, a telephone call was made to Lenin's man in Perm, the Latvian Chekist Ivars Smilga, giving the final go ahead. Smilga conveyed the order to Goloshchokin in Ekaterinburg in a coded telegram. Goloshchokin instructed the firing squad to carry out the order. Trotsky first heard the news when he returned to Moscow from the battlefront, late in July. Sverdlov told him that the tsar and all his family had been shot. 'Who made the decision?' Trotsky asked. 'We decided it here. Ilyich believed that we should not leave the Whites a live banner to rally around, especially under the present difficult circumstances', said Sverdlov.[35] Lenin's wife, Nadezheda Krupskaya, says simply, 'We had him [Nicholas] and his family shot.'[36]

In an unlikely sequel to his part in condemning the Romanovs, Jēkabs Peterss subsequently went to great lengths to ease the captivity of another minor royal and facilitate her exit from Russia. Princess Elena Petrovna of Serbia, wife of Prince Ioann Konstantinovich Romanov, was the only member of the royal family to fall into the hands of the Urals Soviet and survive. As the wife of a Romanov and the daughter of the King of Serbia, she became a hostage to fate while high level negotiations for her release, brokered by the neutral government of Norway, stretched out until the end of 1918. In December 1918 she arrived in Moscow under the protection of a Norwegian diplomatic passport, but instead of the Norwegian Consulate her destination was the Lubyanka, where she was ushered into the office of Jēkabs Peterss. Much to her surprise, Peterss was respectful and even kind. He denied knowledge of her husband (a deliberate falsehood, Prince Ioann and his two brothers had been shot on 17th July), but he confirmed that the imperial family had been executed. Peterss promised to find out about her children, and soon afterwards reported that they were safe with their grandmother in Sweden. Instead of sending her to prison, Peterss had prepared rooms for the Princess in the Kremlin. He went out of his way to make her comfortable, sending her books from the Kremlin library, allowing her to walk outdoors, delivering an astrakhan coat to keep her warm, and allowing her former governess to share her daily walks. Returning from one such walk, Elena found Peterss waiting to impart some important news. She would be free to leave the next evening, in the company of the Norwegian Consul and his wife, but must be out of Soviet territory within forty-eight hours. There was one last surprise when the party boarded the train to Petrograd. An assistant of Peterss arrived with a bouquet of flowers, and apologies that Peterss couldn't be there to see her off in person.[37]

* * *

When the Romanovs met their grizzly fate in the summer of 1918, Jēkabs Peterss was preoccupied with outwitting the British secret agent Sidney Reilly and the foreign diplomats implicated in what the Cheka called the Lockhart Plot.

Outwardly the plot was a rather ham-fisted attempt to suborn the Latvian riflemen and use them to overthrow Lenin. In reality it was a clever sting operation, dreamed up by the Cheka, to draw the Allied representatives in Russia into a trap by telling them what they wanted to hear. The British secret intelligence service (SIS) was looking for an opportunity to bring down the Bolshevik government and drag Russia back into the war with Germany; the Cheka obligingly suggested the means to do so.

Two sympathetic Latvians called Shmidchen and Briedis, actually Cheka agents Jānis Buiķis and Jānis Sproģis, approached the British Naval Attaché in Petrograd, Captain Francis Crombie, asking for support for disgruntled elements among the Latvian riflemen. The gullible Crombie gave the Latvians a letter of introduction to Robert Bruce Lockhart in Moscow. Before delivering it, Buiķis took the letter to Eduard Berzinš, a Latvian artillery Colonel, who worked for Jēkabs Peterss. Berzinš and Buiķis called on Lockhart at the diplomat's flat on 14th August, 1918. Berzinš told Lockhart that he was the Commander of one of the Latvian units guarding the Kremlin and explained that while the Latvians supported the revolution, they were fed up with endlessly fighting the Bolsheviks' battles for them and wanted now only to go home. According to Jēkabs Peterss, Lockhart was keen to know the mood of the Latvian units, whether it was possible for the British to rely on them in the event of a move against the Soviet government, and hinted that the Latvians should take matters into their own hands. Money was no object, Lockhart emphasized.

More meetings followed. Lockhart introduced Berzinš to the French Consul, Grenard, and Mr. Constantine, (Sidney Reilly), an agent of SIS. Reilly wanted to use the Latvians to stage a coup in Moscow and install a provisional military government. Reilly reasoned cynically, 'The armed forces on which the Bolsheviks relied were Letts. The Red soldiers were deserting by hundreds of thousands. But the Letts could not desert. Latvia was in the hands of the Germans. The Letts were the only soldiers in Moscow. Whoever controlled the Letts controlled the capital. The Letts were not Bolsheviks; they were Bolshevik servants because they had no other resort. They were foreign hirelings. Foreign hirelings serve for money. They are at the disposal of the highest bidder. If I could buy the Letts my task would be easy.'[38]

Before the Cheka called a halt to the sting, Reilly paid Berzinš a total of 1,200,000 rubles. The final plan drawn up by Reilly was completed by 20th August. The Latvians would arrest Lenin and Trotsky, and parade them publicly through the streets bereft of their trousers, as figures of ridicule. Afterwards they would be executed. A simultaneous rising would take place in Petrograd, where Moisei Uritsky, the Chairman of the Petrograd Cheka, would be arrested.

Reilly and Berzinš went to Petrograd to meet members of a phony Committee which the Latvian claimed to represent, and to confer with British Naval Attaché Captain Crombie and Ernest Boyce, the SIS chief of station. But then two unexpected events forced the Cheka's hand and brought the game of cat and mouse to an abrupt halt. On Friday 30th August, 1918, a twenty-two-year-old member of the Popular Socialist Party, Leonid Kanegisser, assassinated Uritsky in Petrograd. At 7.30 that evening Lenin left a meeting at the Mikhelson factory in Moscow and was about to get into his waiting car when a woman handed him a petition and began to ask him some questions. Lenin had just started to answer her when she suddenly produced a Browning pistol and fired at him three times. One bullet pierced his neck and penetrated his left lung above the heart before stopping close to the breastbone, another bullet lodged in his left collarbone. The third shot glanced off, tearing his coat at the back. The woman who shot Lenin was brought to the Lubyanka, where she was interrogated by Jēkabs Peterss and Yakov Sverdlov. She was Fania "Fanny" Kaplan (born Feiga Roidman), a twenty-eight-year-old Right SR and former anarchist.

On Saturday 31st August, Dzerzhinsky brought two destroyers up the Neva to train their guns on the British Embassy building, and twenty Chekists broke down the doors. While Ernest Boyce and other members of SIS frantically tried to burn their ciphers upstairs, the foolhardy Naval Attaché Captain Crombie placed himself at the top of the stairs, with a Browning in each hand. Six Chekists advanced up the stairs, shouting 'Hands up, hands up!' Crombie opened fire, killing one of them outright and wounding three more. Crombie's fire was returned and he fell to the foot of the staircase, dead. Sidney Reilly, who had arranged to meet Crombie in a café that morning and had recklessly set off for the Embassy when Crombie hadn't shown up, arrived while the raid was still in progress and stood outside watching.[39]

At half-past-three the next morning, Robert Bruce Lockhart woke up in his Moscow flat to find himself looking down the barrel of Paval Malkov's pistol. Behind Malkov stood ten armed Latvians sent by Jēkabs Peterss. Lockhart was placed under arrest and driven to the Lubyanka with Captain Bill Hicks, who had been arrested in a separate raid. After a long wait, Lockhart was taken along a dark corridor by two armed guards, who stopped before a door and knocked: 'A sepulchral voice said: "Come in", and I was brought into a long, dark room, lit only by a hand-lamp on the writing table. At the table, with a revolver lying beside the writing pad, was a man, dressed in black trousers and a white Russian shirt. His black hair, long and waving as a poet's, was brushed back over a high forehead. There was a large wrist watch on his left hand. In the dim light his features looked more sallow than ever. His lips were slightly compressed, and, as I entered the room, his eyes fixed me with a steely stare. He looked grim and formidable. It was Peters.'[40]

Peterss was 'scrupulously polite', says Lockhart, 'but very serious'. Peterss asked Lockhart if he knew 'the Kaplan woman', and where Reilly was. When Lockhart replied that Peterss had no right to question him, Peterss produced the letter of safe conduct which Lockhart had given to Berzinš. 'Is this your writing?' Peterss asked. Lockhart refused to answer any questions. At 6 o'clock, Fanny Kaplan was placed in the same room as Lockhart and Hicks, in the hope that she might show some sign of knowing the men. Ignoring the Englishmen, Kaplan went to the window and looked out into the daylight, neither moving or speaking, apparently resigned to her fate, until the sentries came and took her away. Three hours later, Jēkabs Peterss came and told the two men that they were free to return home.[41]

Kaplan was transferred from the Lubyanka to a basement room in the Kremlin, where she was guarded by Malkov's Latvians. For the next two days Peterss continued to try to get Kaplan to tell the whole story, but she clung stubbornly to her tale of having acted alone, saying only that she had shot Lenin for betraying the revolution by making peace with Germany. On 3rd September 1918, Kaplan was tried in front of the revolutionary tribunal and sentenced to death. Latvian riflemen of the Kremlin guard escorted Kaplan out to a courtyard, where Pavel Malkov shot her in the back of the neck.[42]

On the day that Kaplan was executed, the Cheka picked up Robert Bruce Lockhart again, and started rounding up the foreign intelligence agents implicated in the plot to overthrow Lenin. Lockhart was held in the Kremlin and gently questioned by Peterss, the perennial "good cop". Peterss famously tried to persuade Lockhart to defect, using Lockhart's Estonian mistress Moura Budberg, yet another agent of the Cheka, as bait. Deeply compromised but admitting nothing, beyond putting the blame on the elusive Sidney Reilly, Lockhart was eventually released and, with a number of British SIS agents, exchanged for Maxim Litvinov, the unofficial Soviet representative in London, who the British had taken into custody as a hostage. Sidney Reilly escaped to conspire another day.[43]

The paradox surrounding Jēkabs Peterss is that privately he was so well liked, yet publicly was so reviled. Nothing typifies this so well as an article by the

Petrograd correspondent of *Le Monde,* M. Dosch-Fleuret, which appeared in the London *Daily Express* towards the end of September 1918. The dispatch set the tone for a flurry of western news reports that autumn, all presenting Peterss as the personification of Cheka cruelty. 'The most awful figure of the Russian Red Terror, the man with the most murder on his soul', said Dosch-Fleuret, 'is the present Extraordinary Commissar against Counter-Revolution and Sabotage, a dapper little blond Lett named Peters, who lived in England so long that he speaks Russian with an English accent.'[44]

'He was known and liked best by the American correspondents in Russia because he seemed more cultivated than the rest. Few of them had occasion to rouse him to fierce class hatred. They did not know the mean, crouched little man, with his pale eyes filled with venom, who now sits in the Kremlin signing away daily the lives of scores of men who he never saw. Let any one be declared a counter-revolutionary by a member of the Soviet and Peters orders him to be shot...' The journalist had known Peterss for more than a year, and found him 'kindly and considerate', until he asked him to help a Russian girl who needed a passport to visit her parents in England. Peterss at first agreed, but when he found out that the girl's father was an officer he refused to help. Dosch-Fleuret protested that the girl worked for her living, but Peterss was adamant: "No matter. She belongs to a class we must destroy. We are fighting for our lives. They are all enemies of the working classes." Seeing 'the fixed fanatical look' on Peterss' face, and fearing to be labelled a counter-revolutionary himself, Dosch-Fleuret let the matter drop. After a few minutes, 'when the fit passed', Peterss turned to another journalist present, a young American woman, with the request: "'Come, dine with me to-night. I feel I need a little Western civilization. I want to talk about books and art. I am sick of the sight of these untidy revolutionary men.'" Dosch-Fleuret concluded: 'Peters now has absolute power of life and death over anybody in Russia. A neutral who visited him lately on a number of occasions to plead for the lives of innocent people told me that Peters has become a mere furious little animal, signing death warrants all day, often not looking to see what he was signing. During one visit the neutral noticed he signed an order to shoot seventy-two officers without even glancing down at the paper.'[45]

Jēkabs Peterss was an obvious figure for the foreign press to focus upon. He cultivated British and American news correspondents as useful sources of information, and the fact that he had stood trial for murder in London was common knowledge to them. Their articles rarely failed to mention the Houndsditch murders. No matter that he had been found not guilty; the impression given was invariably that of 'Peters the terrorist'. His work in the Cheka was conveniently juxtaposed with allusions to Peter the Painter, to suggest an unbroken career of violence.

The reality was more mundane. A gap of ten years, between being arrested in Latvia for attempted murder in 1907 and taking up arms in October 1917, during which he took no direct part in any violent activity. Foreigners who knew Peterss in Russia found him congenial. Arthur Ransome, of the *Daily News,* described him as a person 'of scrupulous honesty'.[46] Even Robert Bruce Lockhart, who became Peterss' prisoner, was effusive in his praise of him. Far from being horror stricken by the harsh treatment meted out to the Black Guards in April 1918, foreign diplomats in Moscow had encouraged it. Shooting and imprisoning anarchists was something they understood and approved of. No foreign correspondent thought to telegraph indignant dispatches to London about revolutionaries being shot by the Cheka. Peterss was applauded for restoring law and order. The Red Terror only became an issue when it was turned against real opponents of the revolution. Dzerzhinsky's affable, hard working deputy was suddenly transformed into *Executioner* Peterss.

The *Daily Express*, eager to scoop its rivals, sent a reporter to interview May Peters at the Islington house where she still lived with her daughter: 'Mrs. Peters is a good-looking young woman who, before her marriage, was a Miss Freeman, of Worcester. Three of her brothers are in the British Army, one of them at the front. She refuses resolutely to believe that her husband can be a monster in human shape signing away hundreds of lives daily in Moscow. "It is unthinkable", said Mrs. Peters, producing letters from her husband... "He was a kind husband and father, and never breathed a word against Great Britain to me before he went away or since. As an Englishwoman I think it only just I say this."'[47]

May showed the reporter letters from her husband, all domestic in tone; the only references to Russia being allusions to the 'hard work' he was engaged in. 'Tell my darling baby that she will see me soon,' Jēkabs Peterss wrote in one letter, and in another, 'Look well after our darling, and the knowledge that she thinks of me will give me strength in my work. I cannot forget our darling, Maisie, in the midst of the hardest work.' 'Baby constantly speaks fondly of her father,' May said. 'He was never happier than when spending his evenings at home with us.' She explained that she had not gone to join her husband in Russia, when invited by Soviet diplomat Maxim Litvinov to leave with him when he was expelled from Britain, because there had been insufficient time to get ready. She had seen Litvinov on several previous occasions in regard to travelling to Russia with the child, but: 'Being English, it was never easy to make up my mind to go so far as things are at present.'[48]

'Some time ago Mrs. Peters worked at munitions, and thought she might have to go out to work again, as she received no money from Russia... Recalling the Houndsditch murders in 1910 and the Sidney-street affair in January 1911, in connection with which her husband was arrested and acquitted, Mrs. Peters said: "I did not know him then, and during our twelve months' courtship, in 1912-13, he told me everything, so that I should not marry him in ignorance of his record."'[49]

Jēkabs Peterss does not appear to have been unduly worried by his notoriety. If anything, it seems to have rather amused him. As he told Arthur Ransome, 'I have now got such a terrible name', he added smiling, 'that if I put up a notice that people will be dealt with severely, that is enough, and there is no need to shoot anyone.'[50] Peterss had sounded less flippant, three months before, when he spoke dispassionately to *Izvestia* at the height of the Terror: 'I am not a partisan of bloody terror except when it is absolutely indispensable, but I firmly and definitely maintain the necessity of systematic, planned and uninterrupted warfare against the bourgeoisie with a view to disarming it, rendering it impotent, and converting it into a working community.'[51]

* * *

On 11th November 1918, Germany signed an Armistice, ending the war. But in Latvia the German occupation forces were allowed to remain by the Allies, as a bulwark against Bolshevism. On 18th November a National Council of parties opposed to the Bolsheviks proclaimed Latvia an independent Republic, with Peasant League leader Kārlis Ulmanis as president of a temporary government.

Most Latvians though did not trust Ulmanis. The Latvian Bolsheviks denounced his government as having no mandate from the people. A month later the Bolsheviks launched an uprising in Valka, supported by 10,000 Latvian Red Riflemen from Russia, and in January, 1919, they entered Riga and formed a Soviet government headed by Pēteris Stučka. But unlike 1917, when the Bolsheviks had been genuinely popular, Stučka's government quickly alienated the Latvians by subjecting them to the terror of the Russian Cheka. The Ulmanis government fled to Liepāja, under British protection. The German garrison commander in Liepāja, General Rudiger von der Goltz, who had led the German invasion of Finland and conducted a White Terror there, had no intention of allowing a Bolshevik Republic to go unchallenged in Latvia. Dismissive of Ulmanis, whom he regarded as being dependent upon German and British support, von der Goltz staged a coup in Liepāja and installed a puppet government under the clergyman poet Andrievs Niedra. Ulmanis sought sanctuary aboard the ship *Saratov*. In the spring of 1919 Latvia had three governments: Latvian, Bolshevik and German. Backed by the Entente, the German forces rapidly took over Courland, and launched an offensive against the Bolsheviks in Livonia. Just as they had in 1906, the Germans inflicted terrible atrocities on the civilian population. Caught between the twin terror of the Germans and the Bolsheviks, neither of whom favoured Latvian independence, most Latvians switched their support to Ulmanis. As the Bolsheviks were pushed back to Latgale on the eastern border with Russia, the conflict became a fight between Latvians and Germans.

Bogged down in clashes with forces loyal to Ulmanis and under pressure from a British Military Mission led by Lieutenant-General Sir Hubert Gough, the German army was finally obliged to withdraw. The Ulmanis government was reinstated on 8th July, 1919. General von der Goltz circumvented the truce by enrolling German soldiers in the "Russian" Volunteer Army of Pavel Bermont-Avalov, though it was von der Goltz, backed by powerful financiers in Germany, who gave the orders. On 8th October 1919, the Bermont-Avalov army launched a massive attack on Riga. Faced now with a fight for the survival of Latvian independence, all Latvians, including the Social Democrats, put aside their differences and united behind Ulmanis. The decisive battle, which lasted until 11th November, ended in complete defeat for the Russian-German forces. Bolshevik forces in Latgale were finally crushed in January 1920. Ulmanis signed an armistice and a peace treaty with the Bolshevik government, and Lenin renounced all claims to Latvian territory 'for all time'.[52] Time ran out twenty years later, when Stalin occupied the Baltic States and Latvia was forcibly incorporated into the Soviet Union.

While the three-cornered fight in Latvia was going on, the White armies tightened their ring around Soviet Russia. Admiral Kolchak in the east and General Denikin in the south, pressed forward to Moscow. In the west, General Nikolai Yudenich, supported by Finnish and Estonian troops, got ready for an advance on Petrograd. Inside both cities the clandestine National Centre, which was based on the outlawed Cadet Party, backed by former industrialists and landowners, and directed and financed by British SIS agent Paul Dukes, was busy collecting intelligence of Red Army strength and dispositions, and began preparing uprisings to coincide with the arrival of the White armies. A British Naval squadron, commanded by Rear Admiral Sir Walter Cowan, took up station in the Baltic and the Gulf of Finland, to keep the Red Fleet bottled up in Kronstadt. In Helsinki, where Yudenich, von der Goltz and Gough all had their headquarters, the British Military Mission did its best to galvanize Yudenich to greater efforts.

In April 1919, Lenin made Jēkabs Peterss his troubleshooter for the duration of the Civil War, as Extraordinary Commissar fulfilling special assignments. First, Lenin packed Peterss off to Petrograd with instructions to rid the city and frontline areas of 'counter-revolutionary gangs'. At the beginning of May 1919, a massive offensive by General Yudenich against a Red Army composed mostly of conscripts prompted widespread desertions. Morale in Petrograd plummeted and there was widespread panic that the city was about to fall. Petrograd's political chief, Gregory Zinoviev, took fright, and without informing Moscow issued a series of ill-judged instructions which only made matters worse. Lenin responded to Zinoviev's inept handling of the situation, on 8th May, by making Jēkabs Peterss Commandant of the Petrograd Fortified Area, tasked with preparing the city for a last ditch stand. The key strong point in Peterss' plan of defence was the Pulkovo Heights, a line of hills dominating the southern approaches to Petrograd, only 20 km distant from the city centre. A team of Chekists from the Special Department for military security and counter-espionage led by Mikhail Kedrov supported Peterss' efforts by shooting members of the military intelligence staff of the Seventh Red Army.

On 19th May, Stalin arrived in Petrograd with special plenipotentiary powers, to bolster the sagging resolve of the city's defenders. Within days, though, a shift in the military situation made Moscow's position seem even more perilous than that of Petrograd. Jēkabs Peterss was recalled to the capital for an urgent meeting of the defence staff, leaving Stalin in command of Petrograd. On 28th May, Peterss sat down with senior representatives of the Cheka, Ministry for Internal Affairs (NKVD), and the Moscow Party Committee to discuss the threat to the capital posed by a pincer movement of the White armies of Kolchak and Denikin. The conference concluded by placing Peterss in overall command of a Special Combined Staff for Combating Counter-Revolution, to defend Moscow against the likelihood of any insurrection in support of the advancing White armies.

Peterss had hardly begun the job of galvanizing Moscow's defences when White troops captured Pskov, 242 km south west of Petrograd. The crumbling western front was immediately given absolute priority, and on 6th June, Lenin signed a new mandate, assigning 'Cheka Commissar Peters to take special action to cleanse Petrograd city and front area of White Guards, spies, and doubting elements'.[53] Instead of moving his staff into the Petrograd Cheka building, Peterss took over two buildings opposite, at numbers 6 and 7 Gorokhovaya Street, as his Internal Defence Headquarters. At Lenin's insistence, the Chairman of Petrograd's Trade Union Council, N. M. Antselovich, was appointed Peterss' deputy and a direct telephone link was installed between Peterss' office and the Kremlin.[54]

Peterss was immersed in planning a massive dragnet operation, to search the city looking for hidden arms and valuables, when the garrisons of Krasnaya Gorka (The Red Hill) and Seraya Loshad (Grey Horse), two artillery forts on the Gulf of Finland, commanding the southern entrance to the Bay of Petrograd, mutinied during the night of 12th/13th June. Peterss responded by seizing the wives and adult family members of the mutineers as hostages. The dragnet operation went ahead the next evening. A total of 12,000 men, mobilized by the trade unions, combed the residential districts of the city. Not surprisingly, in a city that was the birthplace of the October Revolution, large numbers of weapons were found. A search of the foreign missions, where people going abroad had deposited valuables to avoid them being confiscated at the border, yielded cash and jewellery valued at 120 million gold rubles. Peterss also ordered the disconnection of all private telephones. Anyone connecting subscribers to the city telephone network without the permission from the Head of Internal Defence was to be shot. The reason for the telephone ban became apparent when Red Marines stormed the rebel forts covering the entrance to the Bay of Petrograd, and retook them in hand-to-hand fighting.[55]

The feared White insurrection did not materialize, but Petrograd was still in danger of being overrun by the army of Yudenich; and White agents were in the city. One night a bomb exploded in the doorway of the Internal Defence Headquarters, blowing the door off, while Peterss was at work upstairs in his office. As the dust settled, Peterss' assistant dragged a heavy Maxim machine-gun into the room and defiantly poked the muzzle through the window next to his chief's desk. The machine-gun remained a fixture of the office for several days, supplementing the heavy service revolver which Peterss habitually kept on his desk.

In Britain, the *Daily Mail* reported, 'the horrors experienced in Petrograd in the past fortnight surpass the worst previously imagined. Eight hundred officers were massacred in one day and 3,000 hostages deported to Moscow. Wherever the slightest evidence of arms was discovered in a flat the whole family was shot.'[56] But according to Peterss the reported executions were a hoax, to encourage people to surrender their arms. In his report to the Central Committee, Peterss says that several June issues of *Petrograd Pravda* carried notices of mass shootings of people accused of carrying arms, but in fact, 'not a single person has been shot. Six men only were shot among the persons I had to give over to the Cheka. I did not carry out shootings, for I considered them absolutely inexpedient.'[57] Ruse or not, the effect was that hundreds of people queued up for several days outside the Internal Defence Headquarters to hand in their weapons. The final tally of arms confiscated amounted to 6,625 rifles,

150,000 cartridges, 665 pistols, plus machine-guns, bombs, grenades, and illegal telephone apparatus. Afterwards Peterss was recalled to Moscow to report to Lenin and Dzerzhinsky. Lenin was said to have laughed heartedly, when told about the fictitious shootings.

On his return to Petrograd, Peterss bolstered the city's defences by using the confiscated weapons to arm 5,000 workers. He mobilized another 12,000 men to construct defensive fortifications, and launched a fresh purge of military units. Some 200 Red Army staff officers, mostly military specialists, were arrested on suspicion of treasonable activity, and a number of Commissars, whose job it was to watch the specialists, were removed or transferred to other positions. Yudenich's White army reached the gates of Petrograd. Hand-to-hand fighting took place in the suburbs. But reinforced by the workers mobilized by Peterss, the Seventh Red Army held its ground. The White troops were forced back through the Pulkhovo Heights.

On 15th August 1919, Peterss returned to Moscow expecting to be sent back to Petrograd. Instead, Lenin had another job for him: Commandant of the Kiev Fortified Area. Peterss arrived in Ukraine on 23rd August, 1919, at the head of a Special Purpose Detachment (used by the Cheka for suppressing uprisings, giving combat support to the Red Army and organising partisan warfare behind the lines). As the personal representative of Lenin, Peterss was empowered to take whatever action he deemed necessary. First, the Ukrainian Cheka was unceremoniously dissolved, amalgamated with the All-Russia Cheka and placed under his own direct authority. Next, Mārtiņš Lācis, Klim Voroshilov and Yakov Naumov were drafted into a Military Council for the Internal Defence of the Kiev Area. Food supplies were strictly rationed and Peterss' publicly announced 'shooting' as the penalty for hoarding food. Peterss also devised an elaborate sting operation to trap those seeking to flee Red territory; opening a Brazilian Embassy in Kiev which sold visas for large sums of money, and then arresting everyone who took the bait. Peterss himself was widely believed (wrongly) to have acted the part of the Brazilian Ambassador, Count Pirro.[58]

The battle for Kiev was bitter and bloody. Peterss was wounded in the fighting and out of action for several days. The young nurse who looked after him introduced Peterss to a friend of hers, to cheer him up. The nurse's friend was Antonina Dmitrieva, an attractive, red-headed woman, still only nineteen years old, who had joined the Bolshevik Party in April 1917. Antonina had come to Kiev from Moscow while still a student to work as a teacher, but after her school was burned down by the Whites she volunteered for emergency hospital service, caring for the wounded brought back from the battlefront. Peterss had not seen his English wife, May, for more than two years, so the attentions of an attractive young woman who shared his commitment to the Bolshevik cause must have been compelling. He and Antonina would marry in 1920, without Peterss bothering to divorce May; Soviet law did not require him to do so. Less excusable, given the privations which Peterss subsequently forced upon his English family, is that it is doubtful whether he even wrote to tell May the news. On 29th August, after several days of bitter fighting, Kiev was evacuated. Peterss saw Antonina safely aboard a train to the north, then transferred his operations to Tula as head of the Military Council of the Tula Fortified Area.

By the autumn of 1919 the treat to beleaguered Petrograd had become critical. A fresh offensive by Yudenich, spearheaded by six British-manned tanks, had brought the White forces to Krasnoye Selo and Gatchina, only 48 km outside Petrograd. Lenin wanted to abandon the city, but was persuaded by Stalin and Trotsky to try and stave off the apparently inevitable. On 19th October, 1919, Trotsky and Zinoviev sent Lenin an urgent telegram requesting the recall to Petrograd of Jēkabs Peterss. Lenin responded by making his troubleshooter Commander of Internal Defence for Petrograd, for the second time. It was almost too late. When Peterss reached Petrograd on 20th October, the Whites had reached the Pulkhovo Heights, from where they commanded a prefect view of Petrograd, stretched out beneath them; the gilt dome of St. Isaac's Cathedral and the spire of the Admiralty gleaming in the autumn sunlight, and trains pulling out of the Nikolayevskaya station for Moscow, sending white plumes of steam trailing across the brown landscape. Finnish radio reported that Yudenich's army had occupied Petrograd. The Allied Ambassadors in Helsinki reported the news officially to their governments. Churchill was so certain that the Red citadel was about to fall that he ordered that a senior British General be sent to Yudenich's headquarters to ensure, 'a decent, enlightened, and humane administration'.[59]

Peterss and Trotsky divided the city into sections, each controlled by a staff of workers. Key points were surrounded by barbed wire. Artillery was positioned behind cover on the open squares and at important street crossings. Berthed in the Neva, the battleship *Sevastopol* trained its guns on the White positions. Canals, gardens, walls, fences and houses were fortified. Trenches were dug in the suburbs and along the Neva. Barricades were raised in streets and squares. The whole southern part of the city was transformed into a fortress. The few dozen motor cars still running were requisitioned for military use. Every available fighting unit was pressed into service: sailors from Kronstadt, Latvian infantry regiments hastily recalled from the Polish front, a Red Bashkir cavalry division. Despite his normally haughty disregard for irregular forces, Trotsky even ordered the resurrection of Red Guards. Detachments of Communist workers were organized. Women were armed with rifles and machine guns. Military cadets became frontline soldiers; the whole adult population of the city was mobilized. Peterss even swallowed his well known distaste for anarchists and re-armed his arch rivals. On 21st October, the Red forces along the Pulkhovo line stopped moving backwards and made their stand. Detachments of workers, marine units and military cadets attacked the British tanks with bayonets. They were mown down in rows by devastating fire, but the line held. Makeshift armoured cars and an armoured train were brought up to stop the tanks, and turned them back from the Pulkhovo Heights. The next day, the Red Army counter-attacked. By the evening of the 23rd, the Whites were finally dislodged from their positions in the suburbs and forced back towards Gatchina. When Gatchina fell, on 3rd November, the White retreat turned into a rout.

All through the Civil War Soviet Russia subsisted on a siege economy, cut off from its sources of grain in the Ukraine, coal in the Don Basin and oil in Turkestan and the Caucasus. This was the time of War Communism, gearing

Russian industry to the war effort at gunpoint. Winter snowdrifts and the ravages of war had brought things to the stage where the railways were threatened with a complete stoppage. The calamitous situation, Lenin thought, 'without exaggeration can be said to verge on catastrophe'.[60] On 12th November, 1919, Lenin appointed Jēkabs Peterss Chairman of a Special Committee for Introducing Martial Law on the Railways. On Christmas Day 1919, Peterss wired Lenin proposing the recall of skilled railways repair workers from the army. A month later he admitted that 'Arrests and commissions will not be enough here; more radical measures are needed'.[61] He demanded that the Special Committee for Introducing Martial Law on the railways be scrapped, and brought in a large group of Communists to work in the transport system. Peterss himself stayed at the front, as Cheka Plenipotentiary to Rostov-on-Don, Commissar of the North Caucasus Railway and Chairman of the Rostov Revolutionary Committee.

On 3rd March 1920, a report reached Moscow that Peterss was dead. Lenin telegraphed the Revolutionary Military Committee of the Caucasian Front: 'Is the rumour about Peters having been killed by the Denikinites in Rostov true?'[62] Peterss was indeed close to death, but not from a bullet. He had typhus. Rarely did anyone survive the killer disease which was plaguing Russia, but on 9th April Lenin received a telegram reporting the recovery of his special commissar. Peterss' American journalist friend, John Reed, was not so lucky: he died in Moscow on 17th October that year, after contracting typhus during a visit to Baku. When Reed's grieving widow, Louise Bryant, next saw Peterss he was in Tashkent.

Lenin's dream of a wave of revolution sweeping through Western Europe, bringing the proletariat of more technically advanced nations to the rescue of underdeveloped Russia, had failed to materialise. Now he hoped that Soviet support for national liberation struggle in India and China might weaken British imperialism in the east. Lenin had already rejected a proposal from Trotsky, for an outright invasion of India by the Red Army. After three years of civil war, the Soviet military machine was in no condition to sustain a prolonged foreign campaign. An alternative plan, suggested by the Bengali Communist, Manabendra Nath Roy met with more success. Roy proposed to raise, equip and train an 'army of Indian liberation' in Turkestan, which would invade and capture part of India, as the signal for a nationalist uprising throughout the sub-continent.[63]

The first stage of Roy's plan was to establish a secret Indian Military School in Tashkent, to train Indian Moslems as officers and NCOs, the liberation army's cadres. With the cooperation of the Amir of Afghanistan, Amanullah Khan, a headquarters would then be opened in Kabul and forward operational bases set up on Afghanistan's frontier with India. With Anglo-Soviet trade negotiations going on in London, keeping the venture secret was essential. Officially, Roy was to go to Tashkent as a member of the Comintern's Central Asiatic Bureau. 'Because of the fact that Turkestan was then the hot-bed of enemy espionage', says Roy, he was instructed to work closely with Jēkabs Peterss, whose job it was to oversee security for the operation.[64] The school itself was to operate under the auspices of the Comintern, allowing Moscow to disclaim all knowledge of its activities. Lenin introduced Peterss to Roy in Moscow during the Second

Congress of the Communist International in July 1920.[65] In August, Peterss was appointed to the Turkestan Bureau of the Communist Party Central Committee, and as Plenipotentiary of the All-Russia Cheka joined a special Turkestan Commission, which was being sent to Tashkent to rebuild the region's economy, enforce party discipline among the local Communists, and deal with the constant attacks from White troops and hostile tribesmen (Uzbek and Turkmen Basmachi). Peterss' new wife Antonina, who had been given a job in the People's Commissariat of Education, would accompany him as Extraordinary Commissar for fighting illiteracy among adults.

With the civil war in Central Asia still far from over, the 1,609 km rail journey to Tashkent was difficult and dangerous. Peterss took with him a detachment of Cheka cavalry, which soon saw action. Diverted to the Kazakh provincial capital of Alma-Ata, near the border with China, 805 km north-east of his destination, Peterss found the city occupied by White troops. With no other option but to fight, Peterss disembarked his cavalry and took the city back, before continuing his journey.

In Tashkent the Peterss family moved into a house which had belonged to a merchant who had fled to join the rebel tribesmen, before being taken over by the Cheka. They lived in a communal flat, together with another Latvian, Jānis Rudzutaks. It was there that Louise Bryant visited them in November 1920. She describes Peterss at this time as the Governor of Turkestan, who 'had even more sweeping powers than an ordinary governor, since he was the most important revolutionary official in a community not yet settled down to normal life. I also met the new Madame Peters ... a very pretty, red-headed Russian who had been a teacher and who still worked at the profession. They lived in a single room, shared a dining room with twenty others and were poorly dressed. When we discussed this point, Peters bitterly denounced several Soviet officials who, he said, were "living soft". "A revolutionist cannot expect to force privations on other people if he is not willing to be an example of self-sacrifice", he declared. He had become known almost as a conservative among the Left-Communists because he had refused to close the Mohammedan bazaars, saying these people were not ready for Communism. His public trials were attended by large crowds and proved of great educational value in a very unenlightened community. I found him much older. He seemed to have lived thirty years in three. He never mentioned the terror, nor did his wife, and I could not bring myself to. Only once did he indirectly refer to it. Then he turned to me [holding up a pistol] and said, "Have you ever used one of these?" I said, "Of course, I know how, but I've never had to." And then he exclaimed. "I wish to God I never had!" After all, what a story can be condensed into a single sentence!'[66]

Manabendra Nath Roy arrived in Tashkent around the same time as Bryant, in mid-November 1920. He brought with him two armoured trains, equipped with wireless sets and loaded with small arms, machine-guns, grenades, light artillery, a small flight of dismantled aircraft and an escort of two companies of Red Army soldiers.[67] His main task-force was to be recruited from thirty-thousand Indian Moslems who had been making their way to Turkey, to fight for Kemal Ataturk against the British, and who were then stranded in Afghanistan. The Red Army soldiers Roy brought with him worked as instructors, training deserters from the Indian Army in the use of machine-guns and light artillery. But the dream of setting the east ablaze was never fulfilled. On 16th March 1921, Lloyd-George and Leonid Krasin signed an Anglo-Soviet Trade Agreement in London; the first *de facto* recognition of the Soviet Government by any of the Entente powers. The agreement contained a clause, stating that both parties would, 'refrain from hostile action or undertakings against the other and from conducting outside of its own borders any official propaganda direct or indirect against the institutions of the British Empire or the Russian Soviet Republic respectively.' Specifically naming Roy, Lloyd-George called for an end to Soviet activity aimed at India from Tashkent, as an 'essential corollary' to signing the agreement. Lenin reluctantly ordered the closure of the Tashkent school and cancelled the "invasion". The offices of the official Soviet Trade Delegation, at 49 Moorgate Street, opened for business in London in April 1921.

At the same time that diplomatic relations were being normalized in London, the life of the Peterss family was also changing in Tashkent. On 3rd April 1921, Antonina gave birth to a son, whom they named Igor. Then, in January 1922, Peterss received a telegram recalling him to Moscow. He arrived there with his new family in the first week of February 1922. Summoning Peterss to Moscow was part of a radical overhaul of state security, prompted by the end of War Communism and the adoption of Lenin's New Economic Policy.

The Cheka, with its sinister reputation for dispensing summary justice, was set to metamorphose into the State Political Administration (Russian acronym GPU, reconstituted in the autumn of 1923 as the OGPU, or Unified State Political Administration; the beginnings of an ever changing alphabet soup that in 1954 evolved into the KGB); officially a "normal" state security agency, more limited in powers and subject to the law, though it didn't quite turn out like that. Peterss viewed the move as premature. On 1st March 1922 he dispatched a long letter to Lenin, outlining his reservations. He concluded by asking Lenin to 'find a few minutes to see me for a private talk. It is already three weeks that I have been in Moscow without anything to do'.[68] Terminally ill and undergoing treatment at a state-owned farm at Kostino, Lenin could only underline the salient points in Peterss' letter and decline the request: 'Comrade Peters! Because of illness I cannot unfortunately see you. As regards bribery, etc., the GPU can and should combat and punish by shooting through the law courts.'[69] Peterss was made a member of the GPU collegium, and appointed head of the new agency's Eastern Department, covering the Central Asian Republics.

* * *

There was a surprise waiting for Jēkabs Peterss when he arrived back in Moscow: his English wife and daughter were there. But his surprise was nothing compared to the shock that May Peters felt when she discovered that her husband had married a Russian wife. Their daughter Maisie says, 'In March 1921, my mother decided to join my father in Moscow, but when we came there it turned out that my father already had another family. My mother wanted to go back to England immediately, but my father refused to let me leave Russia, and thanks to father, mother also had to stay because of me.'[70]

Peterss installed his English family in a house next door but one to his own, in Bankovsky Lane (now Krivokolenny perleulok), a prestigious side street in old central Moscow, not far from the Lubyanka. Despite the emotionally fraught circumstances, the two wives and children got on well together. Maisie attended a Russian school, and quickly picked up the Russian language. Her mother also enrolled Maisie in the prestigious dance school of Isadora Duncan, something that Peterss was against, though to no avail. On 26th November 1923, Duncan and her students performed as part of the festivities of the Fifth Anniversary Congress of the Women's Department of the Communist Party. *New York Times* correspondent, Walter Duranty, was in the audience. Among the dancers onstage, he spotted the nine-year-old Maisie Peters, 'baby daughter of one of the most terrible of the Cheka zealots, her whisp of red tunic like blood in the spotlight.'[71]

May Peters was lonely and unwell. She didn't speak Russian and had trouble finding work. Because of the harsh conditions in Moscow after the civil war, she was forced to sell the contents of eleven trunks she had brought with her from London in order to survive. The only people she seems to have socialized with in Moscow were English-speaking Communists and Russians she had known in London, who all frequented The English Club. Harry Young, then a twenty-one-year-old British Communist working for the Comintern in Moscow (1922 to 1928), remembers being introduced to "Mary" (*sic*) Peters by his Russian wife, Esther Moray: 'At that time she [May Peters] was suffering a very unsavory reputation, as a sort of Communist "scarlet woman"… On various occasions when I was courting my wife, Mary Peters would turn up. I think the very first time I went to visit my wife on her own was probably at Mary Peters' flat… I don't think she consorted with many men. To me she wasn't all that attractive, quite honestly. But that's what she was supposed to be doing… I knew she had a kid; I remember my wife telling me.'[72] May's "reputation" had previously been noted with disapproval by Aleksandr Zirnis in London: 'Peters's … wife English – leaves little girl at home to go to theatres, etc.'[73] All that May and her daughter really wanted to do was to go home to England, but that never happened.

The work that Jēkabs Peterss was engaged in from 1922 to 1929 is still an official secret. But his membership of the GPU collegium would have involved him in all important matters of state security policy and decision making. All we know for sure is that his position within the Soviet hierarchy was in the ascent.

Though nominally charged with overseeing the Central Asian Republics, Peterss remained for much of the time in Moscow, where he seems to have been a major player in two important counter-intelligence games: the deception operations, Syndicate — 2, which successfully lured Boris Savinkov back to Russia in August 1924, and Trust, codename of a fictitious underground monarchist movement invented in 1921, which was the basis for a complicated six-year deception operation to lure anti-Communist émigrés back to Russia, culminating with the capture of Sidney Reilly in September 1925.[74] Former MI6 officer turned historian, Harry Ferguson says Peterss led both operations.[75] And another expert on British intelligence claims that Savinkov and Reilly were both interrogated by Peterss after their capture.[76]

On the tenth anniversary of the founding of the Cheka, Peterss was awarded the Order of the Red Banner, 'for active struggle against counter-revolution'.[77] In a separate ceremony on 18th December, 1927, he was presented with a special diploma from the OGPU, together with an engraved Mauser pistol: 'For relentless struggle against counter-revolution.'[78]

In 1928, while still a member of the OGPU collegium, Peterss began to devote most of his energies to political and administrative work, as Chairman of the Communist Party's Central Control Commission (of which he had been a member since 1923); as Collegium member of the Peoples' Commissariat of Workers' and Peasants' Inspection and its head for the Moscow Region; and as First Deputy Chairman of the Moscow City Soviet and of the Moscow Regional Soviet's Executive Committee. He retired from the security service, at his own request, on 31st October 1929.

At the end of November 1930, the *Daily Express* reported that Peterss had been called in to quell a serious mutiny in the Red Army, after two battalions of the Moscow garrison engaged in winter exercises at Izmailovo staged a protest over lack of food. OGPU troops were sent against the mutineers and a fierce gun battle ensued, in which many of the soldiers were killed or wounded. Some seven-hundred survivors were disarmed and arrested, and the government imposed a press blackout to try and keep the mutiny secret.[79]

The paper reported, 'Peters, the notorious executioner of the Soviet secret police, has been given authority to summon two batteries of artillery to Moscow to "cleanse the Red army of its disaffected element". He has been appointed to preside over a committee of three which is furnished with "special powers".'[80] And two days later: 'The fact that Jacob Peters, the Cheka chief of the committee which is "cleansing" the Moscow garrison, found it necessary to summon two batteries of artillery from as far away as Ivano Vosnessenks, is held to be highly significant. It shows that Peters does not consider the loyalty of the Moscow artillery sufficiently certain.'[81]

Peterss responded angrily to these reports on 1st January 1931, during a speech to the Central Committee and Moscow Committee of the Communist Party, denouncing the *Daily Express* as bourgeois, and 'a paper of the English Conservatives'. He pointed to a photograph of himself printed on the front page and called the paper's claims 'the craziest lies about what is happening here'. He had not been in England for ten years, he said, but still the English press wouldn't give him any peace. The newspaper was working with 'social-fascists', 'yellow press journalists' and 'White Guard officers', to prepare the psychological grounds for intervention.[82]

In 1932 Peterss moved to a new flat, apartment 369, on the second floor of the famous House on the Embankment (also known as Government House), at number 2 Serafimovich Street. The huge apartment complex was specially commissioned to house the Soviet elite. Built on an island in the Moscow River, facing the Kremlin, at a cost of 14 million rubles, it was considered the height of modernity and luxury. At the same time it was also a gilded cage, nicknamed 'the house of pre-trial detention', where the residents, including government ministers, lived in fear and kept a bag packed in anticipation of a knock on the door in the middle of the night. By 1941 one-third of its tenants had disappeared. Of the 505 families occupying the apartments, 308 of them were repressed in 1937 alone.

Peterss owed his power to Lenin. After Lenin's death, he retained his position by courtesy of Stalin. The two men were personal friends and their children grew up together; Igor Peters was Vasily Stalin's best friend. When in 1925 the Latvian delegates to the 14th Congress of the Communist Party gathered together for a group photograph they invited Stalin to join them; he is seated at the centre of the picture, with Jēkabs Peterss at his right-hand side. It would be comforting, in view of the fact that Stalin ordered his death, to think of Peterss as a critic of the policies that Stalin pursued throughout the 1930s. Sadly, Peterss' words and actions during those years are those of a loyal servant of "The Boss". His position in the Central Control Commission placed Peterss at the forefront of the campaign of slander and persecution of his fellow Old Bolsheviks. Ultimately, he was helping to dig his own grave.

Although they never applied for it, May Peters was granted Soviet citizenship in 1929, and daughter Maisie received Soviet citizenship in 1932. Both of them understood that the "honour" was the ultimate barrier to them ever leaving Russia. Undeterred, and without the knowledge of Jēkabs Peterss, they started visiting the British Embassy to solicit help in returning to London. In August 1937 a denunciation of Jēkabs Peterss was sent to Stalin, noting among other things the surreptitious visits to the British Embassy of May and Maisie; and suggesting that they were using the opportunity to pass on 'political secrets' gleaned from Peterss to the British.[83]

The sinister new chief of the NKVD, Nikolai Yezhov, forwarded the letter to Peterss for his comments. Peterss' reply was carefully couched to distance himself from the actions of his estranged wife and daughter: 'After the divorce Freeman categorically refused to give the girl to me. She also refused to send her to a boarding school. Against my will she enrolled the girl at Duncan's school, where the girl got spoilt. Because of a weak heart she had to leave this school. Her performance at the secondary school was very poor; she stopped attending in the fifth form. Then I suggested that she get a job in a factory, hoping that it would influence her in a positive way. She began to distance herself from me and refused to work in a factory. She got a job as a draughtswoman, sometimes she would phone, but visited very rarely.'[84]

A Russian friend who visited Maisie and May, noting their obvious poverty, once asked why Maisie didn't ask her father for help. Maisie said she refused to ask him for anything.[85]

The denunciation of Peterss for the actions of his English family was an ominous portent of the future.

* * *

According to a study by the Latvian State Archives, twelve punishment operations were organised in the USSR during 1937-1938 according to ethnic criteria. A total of 335,513 people were sentenced, of whom 247,151 (73.6%) were executed. Among these exercises in ethnic cleansing was a Latvian Operation of the People's Commissariat for Internal Affairs (NKVD). The operation was triggered on 30th November 1937, by means of a coded telegram

No. 49990, and continued until mid-November of 1938. During that time approximately 25,000 people were arrested according to "Latvian criteria", of whom 16,575 (74%) were sentenced to death. All evidence pertaining to the so-called "anti-Soviet activity" of those detained was obtained by means of torture.[86]

As a prelude to the Latvian Operation, the Latvian section of the Communist International was dissolved in 1936, and in the summer of 1937 the Latvian Communist cultural and educational association *Prometejs* was destroyed. In May 1937 the NKVD uncovered a "Latvian conspiracy". The leaders were said to be Jānis Rudzutaks, deputy chairman of the USSR Council of People's Commissars, who was godfather to Igor Peters; Roberts Eidemanis, chairman of the Central Council of the USSR Society for the Promotion of Defence, Aviation and Chemical Construction; and Jūlijs Daniševskis, the director of *Prometejs*, who in 1906 had penned the Latvian Social Democracy's attack on the Latvian anarchists. On 26th November 1937, four days before the notorious telegram No. 49990 was issued, Jēkabs Peterss was arrested on the personal orders of Yezhov and taken to Lefortovskaya prison. NKVD investigators Schneiderman and Iljitsky (who shot himself in 1938) interrogated Peterss at night. The questioning was prolonged and brutal. The prisoner was beaten and forced to stand facing the wall for long periods, while his inquisitors screamed their questions at him. During the daytime he was forbidden to sleep, and subjected to constant noise from aircraft engines that were kept running near the prison. As somewhat of an afterthought, on 14th December 1937, he was expelled from the Communist Party.

On 25th April 1938 the revolutionary tribunal passed judgment in the case of Jēkabs Peterss. His family, who had received no news of him since his arrest, believed he was sentenced to ten years. But the decision of the tribunal was quite different. That same day, Peterss was taken from his cell and driven to the NKVD Special Zone *Kommunarka*, a state farm 20 km south of Moscow city centre. The property was used as a country club by the NKVD, who maintained a firing range among the birch and linden trees that covered the estate. The sound of shooting at the range disguised the real purpose for the facility, an execution and burial ground for 6,500 victims of Stalin's repression. What his thoughts were in those last moments before Peterss was shot will never be known. His final resting place is a mass grave among the birch trees.

After Jēkabs Peterss was arrested, Antonina and their son Igor were evicted from the House on the Embankment. To avoid further attention from the NKVD, they adopted Antonina's maiden name, Dmitrieva, but in 1938 Antonina was arrested and sentenced to seven years in a labour camp. Seventeen-year-old Igor saved himself by publicly rejecting both of his parents as 'enemies of the people', and accepting work as an agent for the NKVD. He went to live with his half-sister Maisie and her mother, before getting married in 1940. Throughout the war years his home was a room at the Metropol hotel.

Maisie's first job after leaving school was as a guide for Intourist. She didn't like the work, possibly because it entailed reporting to the GPU on foreign visitors. After that Maisie had become a draughtswoman, first for *Mossovet*,[87] then at the architectural bureau of the Military Engineering Academy, but after her father's arrest she was dismissed. She found work at a knitting workshop, but lost that job in 1941, when the premises were turned into a munitions dump. Her mother, May Peters, died in 1942. Although a Soviet citizen for ten years, Maisie still retained her British citizenship, at least in the eyes of the British government. She found work at the British Embassy in Moscow — first as a nanny to the family of a British Attaché, then as a telephonist at the Embassy switchboard. As if her situation wasn't precarious enough, as the daughter of someone who had been "repressed" and who was under surveillance herself because of her job at the British Embassy, Maisie began a romantic affair with a member of the British Military Mission to Moscow. In February 1945 the Englishman introduced Maisie to a journalist from the *News Chronicle*, Paul Winterton. He had interviewed her uncle in London, George Freeman, and promised to do what he could to help reunite Maisie with her family in England. When British Foreign Minister, Ernest Bevin visited Moscow in December 1945, Maisie telephoned him and secured a meeting with him the following day. But nothing helped. The Soviet authorities refused to let her leave the country.

On 6th November 1947 Igor was suddenly arrested. So far he had remained at liberty by reporting to the NKVD on his friends among the Soviet elite, including Vasily Stalin and Andrei Sverdlov, the son of Yakov Sverdlov, the first president of the USSR. Now it was the same Andrei Sverdlov, a Captain in the NKVD under Beria, who helped interrogate Igor. He was tortured by being fed salted fish and denied water, and ultimately sentenced to ten years for espionage.

On 11th January, 1949, the State Security service (MGB) ordered Maisie to resign from her job at the British Embassy. She ignored the instruction. Six days later, she was arrested in the street, bundled into a car and taken to the Internal Prison of the MGB at the Lubyanka. Accused of being a British spy because of her relationship with the Englishman, Maisie was sentenced under Article 58 to 15 years corrective labour, later reduced to ten years. She served her sentence in Dubravlag, a labour camp for women near the village of Javas, in the Zubo-Polyanski region of Mordovia. She worked there, cutting timber, until she was released and rehabilitated in 1956, the same year as her brother Igor. After a life blighted by her father, and worn down by hard years in the Gulag, Maise succumbed to heart disease and died in Moscow on 1st February, 1965, aged 51. Her family in England requested that her ashes be sent to London, but they never arrived. The official explanation from the Soviet authorities was that they had been 'lost in the post'.[88]

When Peterss' widow, Antonina Dmitrieva, was freed she was not allowed to live in Moscow, and settled in Ryazan. On 30th May, 1955, she was rehabilitated and allowed to return to her old flat in Moscow's House on the Embankment. Her final years were made difficult by ill-health and blindness, but she still espoused a belief in the eventual triumph of Lenin's Communism. She bequeathed her few personal papers and photographs to the children of the Jekabs Peterss detachment of the Young Friends of the Militia (a cadet force teaching road safety), at Riga Secondary School Number 70. Antonina Dmitrieva died in Moscow on 11th November, 1988.

* * *

In 1912 Kristaps Salniņš emigrated to America as Alfred Laubergs and settled in Boston, where he worked for the Redville steamship repair company. In America Salniņš was one of the editors of the Latvian Social Democracy's newspaper *Stradnieks* (The Worker), and was secretary of the central committee of the *Amerikas latviešu koporganizācijas* (Latvian United Organisation of America), which had 2,000 members in USA and Canada, and was affiliated to the left wing of the US Socialist Party. He left behind him a history of derring-do that would defy belief, except for the fact that it was all true: bold guerrilla exploits in the 1905 revolution; running guns into the Baltic for Lenin; suspected by the British Special Branch of involvement in the Tottenham Outrage of 1909; and, despite his friendships with Jānis Žāklis and Fricis Svars, narrowly avoiding the guilt by association that befell Jēkabs Peterss in the Houndsditch Murders case of 1910. Any flirtation he may have had with *Liesma* was behind him. But the apparent calm of his life in America proved only to be an interlude in a remarkable secret career.

Soon after the fall of the tsar, in April 1917, Salniņš travelled to Russia via Japan and found work in a rail wagon repair workshop in Vladivostok. But his proven talent for underground activity marked him out for more secret work. In October 1917 the Bolshevik Maritime Committee sent Salniņš back to America. He found work with a steamship construction company in San Francisco, but his real job was to agitate among the lorry drivers in the port against the supply of military equipment to the White army of Admiral Kolchak in Siberia. It was while engaged in this activity in 1918 that Salniņš was enrolled in the newly formed Red Army, becoming the first agent of Soviet military intelligence to operate in the USA.[89] In June 1920 Salniņš left San Francisco, travelling via China to Siberia, with a shipment of medical supplies for Red partisans fighting against Kolchak. There he joined the Bolshevik 2nd Amur Army and was sent to Vladivostock for underground work.[90] Between 1920 and 1921 he was operating under cover in Shanghai and Harbin, posing as German businessman Christopher Vogel (recalling his London alias Jacob Fogel).[91]

On his return from China in 1921, Salniņš joined the Intelligence Directorate, or Fourth Department, of the Red Army (the *Razvedpur* of the RKKA), forerunner of the Chief Intelligence Directorate of the General Staff, known more commonly by its Russian acronym GRU (*Glavnoe Razvedyvatelnoe Upravlenie*). Salniņš worked first in the Intelligence Directorate of the Petrograd Military District,[92] before being posted back to Vladivostok, where he operated under the cover of working for a White Russian newspaper, using the name Zavadsky. The exploits of Salniņš were later used as the basis for a series of popular novels and TV serials about Soviet spies.[93] After the Red Army finally occupied Vladivostok in 1922, Salniņš was placed at the disposal of the 5th Red Flag Army Headquarters and sent to Harbin in China, posing as a White Russian businessman.

In 1923 Trotsky and Zinoviev came up with a plan for an armed revolution in Germany. Kristaps Salniņš was immediately transferred to Thuringia to establish a network of secret arms caches, and set up an underground fighting organisation of the German Communist Party, the so called Red Hundreds.[94] The uprising was timetabled to begin on 7th November 1923; the anniversary of the October revolution in Russia. But when 400 leaders of the German party gathered in Chemnitz to consider the call to arms, the enterprise was overwhelming rejected. Heedless of the decision, the delegate from Thuringia, Ernst Thaelman, took it upon himself to issue instructions to party organisations throughout Germany to go ahead with the revolution. The messengers were hastily recalled, but the courier to Hamburg had already left by train. The result was a fiasco. Two hundred Communists battled with police in Hamburg for three days, but the mass uprising of the German proletariat did not materialise.

In a similar attempt to export revolution, Salniņš appeared next in the south of Bulgaria under the pseudonym Osip, and spent four months there fighting government troops.[95] He also smuggled arms to the Bulgarian Communist Party, at the end of August 1924, with a young Bulgarian recruit to the GRU called Ivan Vinarov. Salniņš adopted the disguise of a Turkish sailor, complete with Turkish fez, and together they transported ten boatloads of light machineguns, pistols, hand grenades and munitions from Russia and Turkey.[96]

After Germany and Bulgaria, Salniņš spent the next two years at Military Intelligence Headquarters in Moscow, where he worked closely with the new head of the GRU, Jānis Bērziņš (real name, Pēteris Ķuzis), a fellow Latvian who had been arrested in 1907 and sentenced to eight years for killing a policeman; escaping execution only because of his young age.[97]

In 1924 Salniņš joined General V. K. Blucher's military mission to China, as a Soviet Military Attaché to the Chinese People's Army. And from January 1926 to April 1929 Salniņš was permanently stationed in China as the illegal GRU Resident (station chief), with Ivan Vinarov as his deputy and Vinarov's wife, Galina Lebedeva, a cipher clerk in the Soviet legations in Beijing and Harbin, as their cut-out.[98] But as well as directing Soviet espionage in China, Salniņš continued to operate in his familiar role of gun-runner and guerrilla. After the rupture of the uneasy alliance between Chiang Kai-shek's Kuomintang and the Chinese Communists in April 1927, Stalin decreed that the top priority in China was to establish a Red Army. In August 1927 Mao Tse-tung told an emergency Party meeting: 'Power comes out of the barrel of the gun'.[99] Kristaps Salniņš supplied the guns.

Salniņš set himself up in Shanghai as an American, Christopher Lauberg, a variation of the name he had lived under in America.[100] Behind the cover of an import/export company that traded in electrical equipment, sewing machines and spare parts from Europe, Salniņš and Vinarov transported the arms in specially constructed crates, hidden beneath layers of electrical tools and sewing machine parts.[101] For the most part they were British, French and Czech weapons, confiscated from the White army of Admiral Kolchak. Salniņš selected them himself from Soviet military bases in Khabarovsk and Vladivostok, where they were carefully concealed in consignments of "normal" goods from Berlin, Vienna, Prague and Belgrade. Salniņš and Vinarov often made trips to Europe to place new orders and to sell Far-Eastern goods: Chinese vases, crockery, figurines, ivory objects, wood carvings, silk pictures and other souvenirs. Their transit stops in Moscow allowed them to pick up new orders before they continued on to Vienna, Berlin and Prague to carry out their legitimate business.[102]

Vinarov's description of Salniņš in December 1927 is decidedly elegant: 'Dark sunglasses covered his eyes; the broad brim of his Italian hat threw shadow on his well-shaven face. He was wearing a stylish suit from England and fashionable black shoes. A thin Vietnamese walking stick with an ivory handle completed the appearance of this businessman.'[103]

But the stylish businessman could also be deadly. On 4th June 1928 Salniņš was responsible for the assassination of Marshal Chang Tso-lin, a notorious Kuomintang warlord who ruled Manchuria as Inspector General. Chang's private train was blown up as he approached Mukden. The attack was blamed on the Japanese Kwantung army and interpreted as the beginning of a Japanese plot to seize Manchuria. The effect was to drive a wedge between Japan and the Kuomintang forces of Chang Kai-shek. The man who planted the bomb was Naum Eitingon, who in 1940 oversaw the assassination of Trotsky in Mexico.[104] For his success in this operation, Salniņš was awarded the Order of the Red Banner.[105]

At the beginning of 1929 Salniņš and Vinarov were recalled to Moscow. The pair were concealing their activities behind the cover of legitimate businesses in Harbin, Beijing and Shanghai, which they handed over to a young German protégé called Richard Sorge — the legendary 'master spy', who was hanged in Tokyo in 1944. By April 1929 Salniņš was back in Moscow.

The intelligence work of Salniņš in the first half of the 1930s is obscured by a succession of inexpressive career postings listed in the official chronicles of the GRU. From 1930 to 1932, Salniņš was employed on special clandestine missions in Central and Eastern Europe, most notably Vienna,[106] where from 1930 to 1933 his friend Ivan Vinarov was the chief illegal resident of GRU.[107] During this time Salniņš also paid surreptitious visits to Britain, running agents.[108] In October 1932, Salniņš was promoted to Assistant to the Head of the Intelligence Department, Jānis Bērziņš.[109] Between 1933 and 1935, Salniņš was Head of the 3rd Sector of the 4th Department (intelligence) of the Special Red Banner Far Eastern Army (OKDVA) HQ, based at Khabarovsk.[110] From February 1935 to February 1936, Salniņš worked in Khabarovsk as assistant to Jānis Bērziņš. On 10th October 1935, Salniņš was awarded a gold watch, 'for exceptionally conscientious work in carrying out special tasks.'[111] And on 13th December 1935 he was promoted to Brigade Commissar (Brigadier General).[112] From February 1936 to June 1937, Salniņš was Deputy Head of Special Department "A" (Active Intelligence), at GRU headquarters in Moscow.[113]

The last arena of foreign operations for Kristaps Salniņš was the Spanish Civil War. Salniņš arrived in Spain in June 1937, under the unlikely identity of Colonel Victor Hugo,[114] as military intelligence advisor to the Spanish Republican government. The most senior Soviet military advisor in Spain was Jānis Bērziņš, who operated under the pseudonym, General Pavel Ivanovich Grishin, but Ivan Vinarov was there too, as Commercial Attaché Winzer (*Winzer* is the German-Austrian version of Vinarov's name; both mean a winegrower in English), working on the staff of Soviet Ambassador Rosenberg in Madrid. When Vinarov was reunited with Salniņš in Madrid he was surprised at how much his friend had changed. Wearing the uniform of a Spanish Republican officer, Salniņš had lost weight, looked tired and was hardly recognisable. They shared a bottle of wine in a small restaurant, while Salniņš talked wearily about the problems that existed in Spain between the Communist Party and the anarchists.[115]

In November 1937 Salniņš took over from Ilya Starinov (known in Spain as Rudolf Wolf) as chief military advisor and trainer of the 14th (Guerrilla) Corps based at Villanueva de Cordoba, 90 km from Cordoba city.[116] The unit had begun as a small group of guerrillas based on the outskirts of Valencia, but soon grew to battalion strength, and operated a sabotage and subversion school. The core of the unit was a group of Spanish Communists under the command of Captain Domingo Ungaria. As GRU specialist for Special Operations, Salniņš instructed his Spanish students in the use of improvised explosives and sabotage techniques, explained the organisation and methods of guerrilla warfare, gave basic training in small-arms and lessons in self defence. He also directed the unit's operations behind enemy lines. In December 1937, Salniņš was awarded the Order of Lenin for his part in storming the fortress at Teruel.

In March 1938, at the height of Stalin's Terror, Salniņš was recalled to Moscow. Boris Borisov, author of the screenplay for a Russian documentary about Jānis Bērziņš,[117] says Salniņš knew he was going to his death, but returned willingly. Salniņš felt guilty about some of his past actions and wanted to sacrifice himself, preferring death to dishonour.[118] But Stalin liked to toy with his victims before he did away with them. In Moscow, Salniņš was presented with his Order of Lenin and promoted to Deputy Head of the Military Intelligence Service. A month later, on 21st April 1938, he was arrested. After spending nearly a year in prison, during which he was doubtless tortured, he was sentenced on 14th March 1939 and shot on 8th May 1939, aged 54. Salniņš was posthumously rehabilitated on 25th July 1956. Despite his remarkable career, he remains a neglected and obscure figure in the annals of Soviet intelligence.

Jēkabs Peterss and Kristaps Salniņš, like a whole generation of Soviet Latvians, paid dearly for their belief in Bolshevism. Jānis Žāklis (Peter the Painter) had broken with the Party in 1906 over what he saw as the inherently authoritarian nature of Marxism, which he warned could only lead to a new form of slavery. He played no part in the Russian Revolution of 1917, and was not among those consumed in the Stalinist meat-grinder. When the lives of Peterss and Salniņš were extinguished at the end of the 1930s, Žāklis was living quietly, unnoticed if not quite forgotten, on the other side of the world.

Notes

1   Yakov Peters, *Vospominaniya o rabote v. VChK v pervy god revoliutsiy*, (Work In The Cheka
     During The First Year of The Revolution), *Proletarskaya Revolyutsiya*, No.10 (33), (Moscow,
     October 1924), pp. 5-32.

2   Lenin, 'To G. N. Kaminsky, D. P. Oskin, V. I. Mezhlauk', 20 October 1919, *Collected
     Works*, Vol. 35, p. 424.

3   Interview with Aivars Dombrovskis, Riga, 21 June 1989.

4   Figures from R. O. G. Urch, *Latvia — Country and People* (Riga 1935).

5   Jēkabs Peterss, *My Brief Autobiography*. Unpublished manuscript, written for the Society of
     Bolshevik Veterans, 21 December, 1928.

6   John Reed, *Ten Days That Shook The World*, (First published in London, 1932. Penguin,
     London, 1966), p. 91.

7   Louise Bryant, *Six Red Months in Russia*, (First published 1918. London 1982), pp. 79-82.

8   Trotsky, *On Lenin - Notes Towards a Biography*, (First published 1924. London 1971), p. 107.

9   Pavel Malkov, *Reminiscences of a Kremlin Commandant* (Moscow 1964), pp. 69-70.

10   Yakov Peters, *Jakobin proletariacki* (Proletarian Jacobin), first published in *The Battlefield*
     No.3, Moscow 1927. Translated from the Polish, *Towarzysz Jozef — Wspomnienia o Feliksie
     Dzierzynskim* (Comrade Josef - Reminiscences About Felix Dzerzhinsky), Ksiazka i
     Wiedzda, Warsaw, 1977.

11   Peters, *Vospominaniya o rabote v. VChK v pervy god revoliutsiy*, op. cit. pp. 5-32.

12   Ibid.

13   Bim-Bom was a celebrated Russian circus duo. 'Bim' was Ivan Semenovich Radunsky
     (1872-1955), and various individuals played 'Bom'. The act, which started in 1891,
     performed in Berlin, Budapest, Paris and Prague (1901-1904); as well as in films and on
     recordings. Radunsky had been a member of both the Bolshevik Party and the Futurist
     moment. After October 1917 the duo satirised the new Soviet government. In one skit,
     Bim appeared on stage with framed portraits of Lenin and Trotsky. Asked what he was
     planning on doing with them, he replied, 'I'll hang one, and put the other against the
     wall.' Nick Heath, *Bim-Bom, Bang Bang! Chekists and Clowns*,
     https://libcom.org/history/bim-bom-bang-bang-chekists-clowns

14   Peters, *Vospominaniya o rabote v. VChK v pervy god revoliutsiy*, op. cit.

15   Ibid.

16   Jānis Birze ("R" — Remus), 'No grupas Liesma dzīves' (From the life of the *Liesma*
     group), *Liesma* No. 1, Moscow July 1918.

17   Ibid.

18   Jānis Birze ("R" — Remus), 'No grupas Liesma dzīves', op. cit.

19   Peters, *Vospominaniya o rabote v. VChK v pervy god revoliutsiy*, op. cit. p.5-32.

20   On 3 February, 1938, at the NKVD shooting range in Butovo, 258 people were executed,
     of which 229 were Latvians. They included the Moscow Latvian theatre Skatuve (Stage;
     established in 1919) in its entirety, from the directors to the stage hands: director of the
     theatre Roberts Bancans (born 1891); directors Adolfs Vanadzinš (born 1884) and Karlis
     Kruminš (born 1897); actresses: Irma Balode (born in 1907), Zelma Zudraga (born
     1910), Lidija Berzina (born 1901) Marta Kalnina (born 1892), Zelma Boksberg (born
     1912), Marija Leiko (born 1887), Matilda Prince (born 1898); actors: Janis Baltaus (born
     1894), Karlis Baltaus (born 1904), Augustus Kruminš (born 1894), Vladimir Baltgalov
     (born 1911), Andrejs Osh (born 1899), Rudolfs Bancans (born 1898), Rheingolds
     Preymanis (born 1902), Alberts Zvaguls (born 1904), Eriks Feldmanis (born 1913),
     Oskars Zebergs (born 1905), Vilis Forstramnis (born 1894), Roberts Cirulis (born 1896);
     choreographer Nikolai Zubov (born 1904); artists: Karlis Veidemanis (born 1897),
     Arthur Rudzitis (born 1893), Alfreds Tikums (born 1895); secretary Alfrida Lesinya
     (born 1898), head of the production section Fricis Ulmanis (born 1899) and stage hand
     Robert Bredermanis. Altogether more than 6,200 Latvians were killed in the first half of
     1938 — more than 1,000 every month.

21   Jānis Birze ("R" — Remus), 'No grupas Liesma dzīves', op. cit.

22   Pavel Malkov, *Reminiscences of a Kremlin Commandant*, op. cit., p. 237.

23   Peters, *Vospominaniya o rabote v. VChK v pervy god revoliutsiy*, op. cit.
24   Jānis Birze, 'No grupas Liesma dzīves', op. cit.
25   Lockhart, *My Europe*, (London 1952), p. 51.
26   Lockhart, *Memoirs of a British Agent* (London, 1932), pp. 258-9.
27   Jānis Birze, 'No grupas Liesma dzīves', op. cit.
28   Latvijas revolucionāro cīnītāju piemiņas grāmata. 2. Sēj: 2. daļa. (Riga 1987), p. 42.
29   Peters, Vospominaniya o rabote v. VChK v pervy god revoliutsiy, op. cit.
30   Ibid.
31   Ibid.
32   Ibid.
33   Ibid.
34   Anthony Cave Brown & Charles B. MacDonald, *On a Field of Red — The Communist International and the coming of World War II* (London, 1982), p. 57.
35   *Trotsky's Diary in Exile 1935* (Havard University press, Cambridge, Mass., 1953), p. 81.
36   Nadezhda Krupskaya, *Reminiscences of Lenin* (Moscow, 1959), p. 478.
37   Charlotte Zeepvat, *Romanov Autumn — The last Century of Imperial Russia* (Stroud, 2006), pp. 279-95
38   Sidney Reilly, *Britain's Master Spy — the adventures of Sidney Reilly* (Dorset press, USA, 1985. First published, New York, 1933), p. 21.
39   Christopher Dobson & John Miller, *The Day We Almost Bombed Moscow* (London, 1986), p. 163.
40   Lockhart, *Memoirs of a British Agent*, op. cit, p. 318
41   Ibid., pp. 318-20
42   Pavel Malkov, *Reminiscences of a Kremlin Commandant*, op. cit., p. 181.
43   Lockhart, *Memoirs of a British Agent*, op. cit., pp. 326-31, 336-45.
44   'Leader of the Red Terror — Russian Fanatic Who Signs Away Lives', *Daily Express*, London 24 September, 1918.
45   Ibid.
46   Hugh Brogan, *The Life of Arthur Ransome* (Hamish Hamilton Paperback, London 1985. First published by Jonathan Cape, London, 1984), p. 136.
47   'Wife of the man of Terror — Moscow Murder Chief as Model Husband', *Daily Express*, 3 October, 1918.
48   Ibid.
49   Ibid.
50   Peters in conversation with Arthur Ransome, 8 February 1919, Arthur Ransome, *Journal of a Month in Russia*, unpublished manuscript, Brotherton Library, University of Leeds.
51   Peters, interview in *Izvestia*, 29th October 1918.
52   Peace Treaty between Latvia and the Russian Soviet Federative Socialist Republic (RSFSR), sometimes referred to as *The Treaty of Riga*, 11th August, 1920.
53   Чекисты [Chekisti, Chekists] (Moscow 1987), p. 117.
54   Peters, 'The work I carried out in Petrograd'. Report to the Central Committee of the RKP (b), 15th July 1919.
55   Ibid.
56   John Pollack, 'Peters the Terrorist — Seizing Officer's Wives', *Daily Mail*, London, 28th June 1919.
57   Peters, 'The work I carried out in Petrograd'. op. cit.
58   Angelica Balabanoff, *My Life as a Rebel* (First published 1938; London 1973), pp. 223-35; and Alexander Berkman, *The Bolshevik Myth*, (First published 1925; London 1989), pp. 241-2. In fact, "Count" Pirro turns out to have been one Alberts Pirro (born 9th January, 1893); a professional swindler, fraudster and international confidence trickster from Latvia, who served multiple prison terms in Latvia during the 1920s and 1930s. In his memoirs, *Ar zobinu, uguni un sarkano karogu. (Mana melnā grāmata),* (With Sword, Fire and Red Flag (My Black Book.)), Pirro claims to have worked in Russia for the Commissariat for Foreign Affairs (1918-1921), as a secretary for the Foreign Commissar Georgy Chicherin; to have been employed in Butyrka prison in Moscow, registering foreign

prisoners; and to have travelled widely in Bukhara, Persia, Afghanistan, Siberia, China, France, Switzerland, Germany and the Baltic states. Whatever the truth behind these tales, Pirro was clearly employed by the Cheka in some capacity during this period. Information from Artis Zvirgzdiņš, email to the author 9th March 2018.

59   Martin Gilbert, *Winston S. Churchill, Vol. IV, Stricken World* (London, 1975), p. 351.

60   Lenin, 'Speech at the Fourth Conference of Gubernia Extraordinary Commissions', 6th February, 1920, *Collected Works*, Vol. 42, pp. 166-74.

61   *Izvestia*, 27th January 1920.

62   Lenin, Telegram to I. T. Smilga and G. K Orjonikidze, 3rd March, 1920, *Collected Works*, Vol. 44, p. 351

63   M. N. Roy, *Memoirs* (Bombay and London, 1964), p. 420.

64   Ibid. p. 473.

65   Ibid. p. 299.

66   Bryant, *Mirrors of Moscow*, (First published, New York, 1923. Westport, 1973), pp. 61-3.

67   M. N. Roy, *Memoirs*, op. cit., pp. 421-5.

68   Unpublished letter from Jēkabs Peterss to Lenin, CPSU Central Committee Archive, IML, 5/I/1274.

69   Lenin, *Complete Collected Works* (Russian edition), Vol. 54, p. 196.

70   Valentīns Šteinbergs, 'Delo "Miss Mei"' (The Case of Miss May), *Rodina* (Moscow) 10, 1992; & 'Svecha na vetru' *Zemlia* (Riga) 5th January-2nd February 1993.

71   S. J. Taylor, *Stalin's Apologist* (New York & Oxford, 1990), p. 125.

72   Interview with Horace "Harry" Young, London, 8th September 1986.

73   Aleksandr Zirnis, Diary entry 10th September 1918.

74   Andrew Cook, *Ace of Spies — the True Story of Sidney Reilly* (revised edition, London 2004).

75   Harry Ferguson, *Operation Kronstadt* (New York 2009), p. 292.

76   Gordon Brook-Shepherd, *Iron Maze — The Western Secret Services and the Bolsheviks*, (London, 1998), p. 330

77   J. Peters, 'private file', No. 897xp. [KGB]

78   OGPU Diploma No. 7521, awarded 'to Chekist fighter comrade Peters, J. Kh.', 18th December 1927 (copy in author's possession). J. Peters, 'private file', No. 897xp.

79   'Mutiny of Two Moscow Battalions', *Daily Express*, 21st November 1930.

80   'Revolt in Russia — Artillery Rushed to Moscow — Executioner Leads Soviet Forces — Stalin Rumour' — *Daily Express*, 22nd November 1930

81   'Mystery of Russian Revolt — Stain's Secret Plans for a Dash from Moscow', *Daily Express*, 24th November 1930.

82   Yakov Peters, 'On the Results of the Plenary Session of the Central Committee and the Moscow Committee RKP', 1st January 1931.

83   Valentīns Šteinbergs, 'Delo "Miss Mei"', op. cit.

84   Ibid.

85   Ibid.

86   *Represijas prêt Latvieshiem PSRS 1937-1938* (Repressions against Latvians in the USSR 1937-1938), Latvijas Valsts Arhivs, Riga 2009.

87   The popularly used abbreviation of the Moscow Soviet of People's Deputies, the city administration of Moscow, 1918-1941.

88   Donald Rumbelow, *The Houndsditch Murders and the Siege of Sidney Street* (updated edition, London 2009), p. 203.

89   V. M. Lurie & V. Ya. Kochik, *GRU – Dela I Lyudi* (GRU: The Deeds and the People), St. Petersburg & Moscow 2002), pp. 178-9.

90   Ibid.

91   Boris Volodarsky, *Soviet Intelligence Services in the Spanish Civil War, 1936-1939*, unpublished PhD thesis (LSE, London June 2010), p. 172.

92   V. M. Lurie & V. Ya. Kochik, *GRU – Dela I Lyudi*, op. cit., pp. 178-9.

93   Julian Semjonov, who used Salniņš as the prototype for his espionage hero, Maxim Isajev, in a series of novels and films says that he got the idea for the novel *Password is not*

225

Necessary from reading a phrase in a telegramme sent to Moscow in 1922: 'our man, who has been active in Vladivostok, has now been transferred abroad to continue his work in emigration'. Just like in Semjonov's novel, the spy in Vladivostok worked under cover at a White Guardist newspaper.

94 V. M. Lurie & V. Ya. Kochik, *GRU – Dela I Lyudi*, op. cit., pp. 178-9.

95 Ibid.

96 Ivan Vinarov, *Kämpfer der lautlosen Front*, (Fighters on the Secret Front), Militarverlag der DDR, Berlin, 1976 (First published in Bulgarian, Sofia 1969), pp. 88-95.

97 Ibid.

98 V. M. Lurie & V. Ya. Kochik, *GRU – Dela I Lyudi*, op. cit.., p. 363, and Boris Volodarsky, *Soviet Intelligence Services in the Spanish Civil War, 1936-1939*, op. cit., p. 74.

99 Mao obviously liked this phrase. He used it again, in an amended form [Every Communist must grasp the truth, "Political power grows out of the barrel of a gun"], in 'Problems of War and Strategy', 6th November 1938, Mao Tse-Tung, *Selected Works*, Vol. II (Peking, 1965), p. 224.

100 Boris Volodarsky, *Soviet Intelligence Services in the Spanish Civil War, 1936-1939*, op. cit., p. 172.

101 Ivan Vinarov, *Kämpfer der lautlosen*, op. cit, pp. 128-36.

102 Ibid. p. 136.

103 Ibid. p. 133.

104 A. I. Kolpakidi & D. P. Prokhorov, *Vneshnaya razvedka Rossii*. (The Foreign Intelligence Service of Russia) Saint Petersburg & Moscow, 2001, vol. 1, pp. 182-3.

105 V. M. Lurie & V. Ya. Kochik, *GRU – Dela I Lyudi*, op. cit., pp. 178-9.

106 Boris Volodarsky, *Soviet Intelligence Services in the Spanish Civil War, 1936-1939*, op. cit., p. 157.

107 Ibid. pp. 74-5.

108 Boris Volodarsky, *Stalin's Agent — The life and death of Alexander Orlov* (Oxford, 2015), p. 75.

109 V. M. Lurie & V. Ya. Kochik, *GRU – Dela I Lyudi*, op. cit., pp. 178-9.

110 Ibid.

111 Ibid.

112 Ibid.

113 Ibid.

114 Ibid.

115 Ivan Vinarov, *Kämpfer der lautlosen Front*, op. cit., pp. 204-5.

116 Boris Volodarsky, *Soviet Intelligence Services in the Spanish Civil War, 1936-1939*, op. cit., pp. 65-6.

117 *Начальник разведки* (The Head of Intelligence), Russian, 90 min, documentary film, directed by Romualds Pipars, Moscow, 1989.

118 Interview with Boris Borisov, Riga 28th June 1989.

13

1912 to 2012
The Man who was Away

But here the little boy spoke up — said he, 'We thought you knew;
He's done six months in Goulburn gaol — he's got six more to do.'
Thus in one comprehensive flash he made it clear as day,
The mystery of Peter's life — the man who was away.

Banjo Paterson[1]

The last official sighting of Jānis Žāklis was in Germany in 1912. His unexplained disappearance, and the unpublicised decision of the London police not to pursue him, helped create the legend of Peter the Painter. But what happened to the man behind the myth, and to the family he left behind in Latvia?

My introduction to the Žāklis family came in Riga in May 2004 when I met Ausma Žākle-Kalējs, a distant cousin of the elusive fugitive and mother of the well known composer and organist Aivars Kalējs.[2] Ausma was born in Courland in 1923. Her parents, Kārlis Žāklis (1897-1972) and Lidija Šēnberga (1899-1990), met in Petrograd as refugees during the First World War. Afterwards they returned to Latvia and ran a small farm called Kvieši in the parish of Kursīši, near Saldus. Seven families lived in the farmhouse in which Ausma grew up. During the Second World War the house was turned into a military headquarters by the German army, but the family continued to work the land until the Red Army arrived and confiscated everything. In January 1945 Ausma married Otto Kalējs (1920-1978). When the Russians arrived Otto was arrested but managed to escape and walked to Riga, where he found work at the VEF factory and sent for Ausma. Ausma found work in a knitting shop, and then trained as a teacher, before becoming a secretary for the Council of Ministers of the new Latvian Soviet Socialist Republic. She typed the manuscripts of Vilis Lācis, the novelist turned politician who headed the Soviet government in Latvia until 1959. Otto studied art and began a new career as a sculptor.[3] His statue of Lenin stood in Jelgava from 1974 to 1990.

Together with Ausma and two Latvian friends, my wife Irene and I set off in search of more clues to the fate of the Žāklis family in Courland. Relatives from Ausma's branch of the extended Žāklis clan were still very much part of the Courland landscape, on farms dotted around the parish of Jaunlutriņi outside Saldus. Ausma's cousins at Plaudoni farm showed us the family burial plot at nearby Kalnakunči, and pointed out the final resting place of a Jānis Žāklis who died in 1940. His gravestone said that he had been head forester. But this namesake was not the Jānis Žāklis who was Peter the Painter.[4] The family of the Žāklis we were interested in lived at Svitē, but the cousins at Plaudoni had never met them. Their parents had told them that the family didn't go there because the mother of the man we were looking for was unpleasant, they didn't like her.[5]

In those days, three families had lived at Svitē. In the Soviet times it was turned into a *Kolkhoz* (collective farm) and stables.

Our next stop was Rednieki, the ancestral home of the Žāklis clan. The farm's owner now is Juris Žāklis, born in 1968, the grandson of Miķelis Žāklis; a direct cousin of Peter the Painter.[6] Meeting Juris was like shaking hands with Peter the Painter himself. The two men share an uncanny resemblance (see image 69), as though the iconic image of the Latvian anarchist wanted in London had suddenly come to life. Juris Žāklis took us the short distance down the narrow dusty lanes to Svitē, the birthplace of Peter the Painter. Nestling among the trees on a low hill overlooking rolling fields, the farmhouse was instantly recognisable as the building depicted in the photographs left behind by Peter the Painter at 59 Grove Street in London. The only occupants now appeared to be a collection of alcoholics, who were mystified at the sudden appearance of so many visitors. We took our photographs and left.

Aivars Kalējs was due to give an organ recital at Lutrini parish church, and we had arranged to meet him there. Before the service began, the parish priest made an announcement from the pulpit: if there were any members of the congregation who knew anything about the families Žāklis, Angers, Sakne or Tālbergs, would they please stay behind after the service; there were people here from London who would like to talk to them. Afterwards, a man came forward with the address in Saldus of Malvīne Sakne. Malvīne was not at home when we arrived at the address. A neighbour said the old lady had been ill and directed us to the flat of her daughter, where she was being looked after. Finally we were there, talking to ninety-five-year-old Malvīne Sakne in the Saldus flat of her daughter, Ira Gruntmane.

Malvīne was born in 1910, the same year that Peter the Painter appeared in London. It was Malvīne who owned Svitē; the alcoholics we had met were squatters, whom she allowed to live there rent-free. Malvīne married Jānis Sakne, the son of Herman and Anna Sakne, Peter the Painter's older sister. Ira Gruntmane was the grand-niece of *our* Jānis Žāklis. Five years after meeting Ira in Saldus, I talked to her son (the present owner of Svitē), Ugis Gruntmanis, in London and showed him the photographs of Svitē belonging to Peter the Painter. Ugis immediately picked out a photo of two small children, and identified them as the children of Anna Sakne. 'The oldest is my grandpa Jānis, he died when I was six-years-old'.[7] Talking to Malvīne was difficult because of her age and ill-health. She had forgotten so many things, had trouble hearing and was virtually blind. Malvīne was born at Iernesti, the neighbouring farm to Redneiki, and had owned the property until 1949, when she was evicted by the Russians. Her daughter Ira reminded her of a family story about the Uncle Jānis who had disappeared abroad. Malvīne thought he had gone to America at the end of the 1920s. She couldn't remember. Malvīne cried as we left, touched by the interest of 'the young ones'.[8]

Before we went, Ira Gruntmane told us that the granddaughter of Kārlis Žāklis, Peter the Painter's older brother, still lived in Saldus, on the other side of town. She was away at present, but would put us in touch as soon as she was able to speak to her. When we met Ira again it was in Riga a few days later. She brought with her a legal document in Russian; the deed of sale for Svitē, when

Margrieta Žākle passed the ownership of the farm to her son-in-law Herman Sakne in 1913. The timing of the transaction was to prove significant. But first we were going back to Saldus, to meet the granddaughter of Kārlis Žāklis.

Līvija Rēfelde was born in 1930 and had worked for the post office. Her mother, Maria Žākle (1903-1979) was the daughter of Peter the Painter's big brother, Kārlis, the man who had been spared execution in 1906 by the strange intervention of Baron Keyserling. Līvija and her husband talked to us in their small wood timbered house on the edge of Saldus. Līvija knew nothing about her great grandparents, Peter the Painter's mother and father. But she said that her grandfather Kārlis doted on her. He liked to drink and whenever he got drunk he would try to catch hold of her and kiss her. Kārlis's son, another Jānis Žāklis, served in the army of the Latvian Republic before the first Soviet occupation in the summer of 1940. Afterwards he was arrested and sent to Siberia, where he died. The first Soviet occupation ended in 1941, when the German army occupied Latvia. From the spring of 1943, Latvian men were conscripted into the "volunteer" Latvian Legion, technically a formation of the Waffen SS, to circumvent the international law prohibiting foreign nationals serving in the German army. Approximately 115,000 Latvians served in the German forces before the war ended. Almost one third of them lost their lives on the battlefield. Līvija's brother, Fricis Žāklis, was one of those conscripted. When he came home after the war Fricis studied at Riga Academy of Art. Līvija proudly displayed some of his paintings of animals and scenes from nature.

I asked Līvija about Peter the Painter's four sisters, her great aunts. I already knew about the eldest sister, Anna Sakne. Of the other three, Līvija said that the youngest, Milda Ciba, had two sons, Arnolds and Kārlis, who lived in Baldone and owned a mill there. Milda died on 5th February, 1972. Katerina (Kate) married a man called Melbārdis. She had died not so very long ago. Her son Madgers was conscripted by the Germans during the war and deported by the Russians afterwards. He too died in Siberia. Charlotte Marija married a teacher called Gertners. After the war their son, Kārlis Gertners, disappeared into the forest and joined the *Mežabrāļi* (Forest Brothers), the Latvian resistance movement that fought until 1957 against the second Soviet occupation of Latvia. Kārlis Gertners died fighting, but his daughter Ruta Zaksa was still living in Saldus.[9] I met Ruta in 2012, when she came to the launch of the Latvian edition of this book in Riga.

While Līvija talked, I was struck by just how much the fate of the family that Jānis Žāklis left behind was a microcosm of the history of Latvia. My reverie was broken by Līvija telling me what she knew about her grandfather's missing brother; the story her grandfather Kārlis had told her mother; about the siege in the countryside, when Jānis Žāklis was rescued by the girl he married. And that he left Latvia with his wife in 1906, and that the family never heard directly from him again. Only years later someone outside the family told grandfather Kārlis that his brother had a ribbon making factory in America.[10]

From Saldus we went to Sabile, in search of Ābeļ, the 58 hectare farm at Pedvāle where Jānis Žāklis lived with his parents, under police observation, before the outbreak of the 1905 revolution. Driving into Pedvāle we saw an old lady in a headscarf sitting at the side of the road, and stopped to ask directions.

The lady was Milda Eglīte, born in 1919. Incredibly, she knew all about Ābeļ. Her parents had lived there after the Žāklis family gave up the farm in 1914, just before the outbreak of the First World War. When the war started there were terrible battles and Milda's parents had to go to Russia as refugees until 1917, when they returned to Latvia. Following Milda's directions we were soon at Ābeļ. The farm had been renovated and only the ruins of the old buildings survived. The owner of the new house, Skaistkalni (Beautiful Hills), said that Ābeļ had been built in 1892, and in later years it was known as Vecabelu (Old apple trees). The farm supported chickens, cows, and apple orchards. The original owner of the farm, Baron Briņķ of Matkule, lost Ābeļ and the surrounding land in a game of cards with his friend Baron Firk sometime around 1912/1913. All that remains of Abel today is a pile of stones and the ruin of the original cellar. The present farmhouse was built on the site of the servants' quarters at Ābeļ; so the Žāklis family were wealthy enough to employ domestic staff. The original buildings came down after WW2; the open field was turned into a great apple orchard, and there was also a tea house. As we got ready to leave, the owner showed us a secret hiding place in the house, by the stairs, which had once been used to hide local *Mežabrāļi*; another sign that the spirit of resistance embodied in Jānis Žāklis had deep roots in this part of Latvia.

All we had learned from the family was that Jānis Žāklis had gone to America, and that years later they had been told that he owned a ribbon-making factory somewhere. Žāklis did go to America. But despite Malvīne Sakne's vague notion that it was sometime in the 1920s, the evidence points to it being at the end of 1906. The family members we met in Courland were unaware that Žāklis returned to Europe in 1908, and were dumbfounded to learn about his involvement in the Houndsditch affair. None of the relatives we spoke to knew of anyone in the family who had any direct contact with Jānis Žāklis after he left Latvia. With the exception of his benevolent Uncle Juris, the army officer who sent Žāklis money to finance his studies in Europe, the family claim never to have heard from him again, despite otherwise being a tightly knit clan. More likely, those in the know took the secret with them to the grave. But the fact that Margrieta Žākle, a widow since 1908, chose 1913 to sell Svitē may indicate that she knew something others didn't. Because, by strange coincidence, 1913 is also the year in which Jānis Žāklis appears to have started life anew on the other side of the world. Perhaps the sale of the family farm provided the financial means to do so.

In August 2003 I interviewed the Latvian historian Andris Puļķis (1944-2003), a member of the editorial team that produced the updated edition of the *Memorial Books to the Fallen Fighters* of 1905. Puļķis was adamant that in 1913 Jānis Žāklis emmigrated to Australia. He told me that Žāklis had a lot of money from expropriations in Europe, and that he stayed in Australia and became a 'successful businessman'.[11] Puļķis had not suddenly invented this information for my benefit. Another Latvian historian, Dr Liga Lapa, recalls being told many years ago that Žāklis had gone to Australia: 'An account about the setting off to Australia of … Jānis Žāklis (whose *nom de guerre* was Mērnieks), was narrated orally to me by members of the editorial committee of the *Book of remembrance* who were veterans of the revolutionary movement. However, I have failed to find any documentary confirmation of their account.'[12]

When I met him in Riga, Puļķis was aged fifty-eight but looked older due to terminal illness. He needed constant medication, was unable to leave his flat, and found it difficult to talk or remember the details of his research. In the 1970s he had become fascinated with the Latvian anarchists and wanted to include articles and archive material on them in the re-issued memorial books. But this didn't sit well with his bosses at the Institute, or the guardians of history at the KGB. He was threatened that if he persisted in trying to publish such material he would loose his job and be forced to move to a smaller flat, and perhaps some unfortunate accident might befall him. Among the archive material in his possession were original reports from the Riga gendarmerie and Interpol about Jānis Žāklis. It was this material, he says, that indicated that Žāklis emigrated to Australia and stayed there. But under pressure from his superiors, who threatened dire consequences if he attempted to publish, Pulkis became so depressed and despondent at the prospect of never being able to use the material that finally he destroyed it. His reference to Interpol as the source of the information is incongruous. Interpol was created only in 1923. If the report of Žāklis being in Australia was dated 1913 it must have originated from some Russian, European, or Australian police source. An enquiry to Interpol from Australia in the 1920s could only have been made as part of the vetting process for an application for naturalisation. So far, despite extensive archival research in England, Latvia and Australia, no such information has been discovered.

Puļķis believed that Jānis Žāklis funded his move to Australia, and his new career as a businessman, with money accrued from expropriations in Europe. But a more likely source of finance, given the dating of his emigration to 1913, is the sale of the Žāklis family farm. Margrieta Žākle used the money from the sale to pay off the debts of all her children. The only sibling not named in the legal document as benefiting from the sale is the absent Jānis.[13] It seems probable that he got his share on the quiet, and used that money, rather than the proceeds of robberies, to build a new life under a new name.

If Jānis Žāklis was still hoping for a new insurrection in Latvia, then the arrest of Juris Laiviņš in Valka at the beginning of May 1913 must have come as a heavy blow after the disastrous events in London. By then, the twenty-nine-year-old Žāklis had been a committed revolutionary for twelve years. He had tasted prison, proved himself a tough urban guerrilla commander in 1905, and experienced Latvia's violent rural uprising and the savage repression which followed. Afterwards he survived to become the most important figure in the burgeoning Latvian anarchist movement, and for six years to reorganise and coordinate the armed resistance to Russian state terror in the Baltic. The strain of clandestine life in America and Europe must have been considerable. The collapse of his grandiose plan to turn London into the organisational hub of a resurgent Latvian anarchist movement left him not just a wanted man, but the most notorious anarchist in the world. The prospect of a new uprising in Latvia was remote. All of Žāklis's closest friends and comrades were burned-out, dead or in prison. Juris Laiviņš was the last. His arrest must have forced Žāklis to take stock of his few remaining options, and to rethink the direction of his life. Until then he had lead a charmed existence. It must have been obvious to him that his good luck, which had kept him from sharing the fate of his comrades, must one day run out. Jānis Žāklis quietly stepped off the inexorable path to martyrdom and embraced life.

Jānis Žāklis could have been planning to go to Australia all along. He arrived in London in 1910 to be with Fricis Svars, from whom he seemed inseparable. Before the Siege of Sidney Street, Svars wrote that he was planning to travel to 'that long dreamed about land Australia', with his wife and 'three other men'.[14] Jānis Žāklis may have been one of them. There were already Latvian anarchists in Australia at this period who maintained links with their comrades in Europe. In October 1913 the Latvian anarchist journal *Melnais Karogs*, published in Paris, acknowledged receipt of a £1 donation from Australia;[15] and in March 1914 the same journal listed donations from ten supporters in Sidney, including eight members of the Latvian Association of Sydney (Sidnejas latviešu pulciņš).[16] The man soliciting this money was Charles Limbits (Kārlis Limbītis), a Latvian who arrived in Sydney aboard the *Indrapura* on 26th March 1905 and on the same ship in 1912.[17] According to the minutes of a meeting of the Sydney Latvians on 4th January, 1914, 'comrade Limbits requested permission to read some letters. The letters were read. The first letter describes relationships between socialists and anarchists and further requests comrade Limbits to collect material support for imprisoned anarchists. The meeting considers this to be a private matter and the Association will not enter into debate about it, indicating that comrade Limbits, or his authorised representative, can act in this matter according to conscience.'[18]

That Limbits was in communication with *Melnais Karogs* in Paris would have made him an obvious person to contact, should Žāklis have needed assistance when he arrived in Australia. The Australian police were certainly on the lookout for him. Records show that between 1911 and 1917, the police in Australia contacted the City of London police in three separate cases, where they suspected they had Peter the Painter in custody. On each occasion the reply of the London police, who deemed the hunt for Peter the Painter to be a pointless exercise, was always the same: there was no evidence to justify an extradition request, and no further action was required.

The first case concerned August Maren, a former member of the LSDSP from Kuldīga, who had been imprisoned in Latvia until 1908. Maren had arrived in Australia from London, where he had been on the periphery of the same social circles in which the *Liesma* anarchists moved. For a time he had even lived in the boarding house run by Teodor and Lonny Jansons, where three days after his departure for Australia the police arrested Alfrēds Dzirkalis. But Maren had no involvement in the activities of *Liesma*. His arrest in Australia, in August 1911, resulted from a romantic dispute over a girl, Sarah Ligum, between Maren and two Latvian friends, Ernest and Adolph Dreger. The feud culminated in the arrest of Ernest Dreger for illegal possession of a shotgun. The disgruntled Dreger brothers sought retribution by telling the police that Maren had boasted to them of being connected to the Houndsditch gang. The Australian police kept Maren in custody for two months, while they sought further information from London with which to build a more substantial case. But with no evidence and mounting adverse publicity in the Australian press, the case against Maren was finally dropped and he was released. Maren later enlisted in the Australian army, as Peter Johnson, and served for three years in France during WWI. He was killed in a traffic accident in Sydney, in March 1929.

The second case where the Australian authorities requested help from London appeared much more compelling. Max Selling, a twenty-nine-year-old "Russian", was arrested on 9th August 1913; and sentenced to 14 years at Sydney Quarter Sessions, on 3rd September 1913, for attempting to forge a £5 bank note. The New South Wales police reported: 'When the Detectives entered Selling's room he made an attempt to get possession of a fully loaded automatic pistol which was close at hand. Selling is a Russian and only arrived in Australia from London about five months prior to his arrest. He can speak four different languages and is a determined, cunning, intellectual man.'[19] Believing their prisoner to be Peter the Painter, the police in Sydney sent Selling's photograph and fingerprints to London. The London police showed the photograph to Mr and Mrs Katz, the landlords at 59 Grove Street, but they were adamant that the picture was not of their former lodger, Peter Piatkov. The City Police identified the fingerprints of Selling as those of a criminal known to them as Johan Kaikon. Both Selling and Kaikon were aliases. Files in the National Archives of Australia reveal he was known by at least six such aliases, but that his real name was that of a Latvian, Kārlis Emīls Krastiņš.[20] But despite being Latvian and born in 1883, the same year as Jānis Žāklis, he was not the wanted man.

The third case, in 1917, involved Paul Hubert, a chef at the café Francotelli in Melbourne. According to the Melbourne police, Hubert was 'a well educated man and speaks several languages. He is an excellent hand at throwing a knife or using a revolver and has frequently given exhibitions of his skill and ability in this direction… He poses as a Frenchman but doubts exist as to his real nationality, although it is generally believed that he is a Russian and a political refugee. All his associates are foreigners, and he arrived in Sydney, Australia, about 6 years ago. This man was connected with a shooting sensation in which two Russian dancers, named Alexander and Sophia Yakoleff met their deaths … on the 13th August 1915. He was then a chef at the Union Hotel, Sydney, and was known by the name of Paul Jerome Hubert de' Beaudin.'[21]

Once again, a photograph of the arrested man was shown to people who knew Peter Piatkov in London, including Mr and Mrs Katz at Grove Street. All of them agreed that it was not a picture of Peter the Painter. In fact the photograph of Hubert most resembled the American adventurer and showman Buffalo Bill.

The final, bizarre account of Peter the Painter in Australia was published in 1934, in the autobiography of former Detective Sergeant Benjamin Leeson. After recovering from the wound he received at Sidney Street, Leeson was invalided out of the police force and in 1911 embarked on a voyage to Australia to recover his health. That much is fact. But the fantastical and paranoid story he constructed of what ensued is absolute science fiction.

In Leeson's account the man behind the violent events in London was none other than Joseph Stalin. Stalin controlled a secret international red brotherhood of anarchists that extended to Australia. When his ship first docked in Albany, Western Australia, Leeson says he was approached on the quayside by 'two foreign-looking individuals'[22] who asked him whether anyone named Leeson had come ashore. Leeson hastily returned to the ship, but the dastardly foreigners followed the ship to Melbourne, where they accosted him again. After shaking off these sinister figures Leeson moves on to Sydney, where he decides to go on an excursion to the Blue Mountains, just outside the city. But who should he meet while buying his ticket at the central railway station but Peter the Painter, whom he claims to recognise immediately because he had often seen him in the saloon bar of the King's Head pub in the East End of London. This claim is ridiculous. Jānis Žāklis did not drink and was not known to socialise in pubs. Leeson had never had an opportunity to see him in London, he was unknown to the police before the Houndsditch shootings and disappeared immediately afterwards, and the only published photographs him were those used on the police wanted poster.

Once aboard the train Leeson is joined in his compartment by Peter the Painter: 'We were alone. I guessed that he would be armed, and sundry straying of his hand to his hip-pocket, as if to assure himself of the readiness of his gun to his hand, confirmed my guess. Neither of us gave any sign of recognition, merely passing the time of day and sundry other remarks of little importance. 'Do you come from England?' asked the Painter. 'Yes,' said I, and a silence fell. It was an awkward situation. There was I, alone with an armed desperado who knew who I was, and who knew that I knew who he was... It was a tense moment, he wondering when I was going to show my hand, I asking myself how soon I should be looking down the barrel of a revolver. But nothing happened. My destination was a place named Wentworth Falls, and though I would have liked to extract a little information from Peter as to his movements after Sidney Street, I was not exactly sorry when the train lumbered into the station. Perfunctory farewells on either side, and I stepped out on to the platform, leaving Peter to travel — who knows where?'[23]

It was Ausma Kalējs who alerted me to the existence of an Australian branch of the Žāklis family. Her cousin Laimonis Vinegers emigrated there with his wife, Velta, in 1949. Their daughter, Ināra Baiba, was born in Australia in 1951 and grew up to become a biochemist. She married another Latvian-Australian, psychologist Aldis Putniņš, and they had three children. When I contacted Aldis in November 2003, he was already familiar with the Peter the Painter story, but unaware of the family connection. In 1994 Laimonis wrote down his family memories, in which he mentioned that he knew of relatives who lived at Klavine (the home of Peter the Painter's brother, Kārlis), but that he had never met them.[24] On another occasion, Laimonis remarked to Aldis that 'he thought a distant relative of his might have come to Australia (but he was unsure).'[25]

Laimonis Vinegers (1918-1996) was the third son of Kate Vinegere (née Žākle), the daughter of the Jānis Žāklis buried at Kalnakunchi. In 1939 he graduated from the Latvian State Technical College and entered the Latvian State University, but in 1940 he was called up for national service just before Soviet troops occupied Latvia and found himself absorbed into the Red Army. When the German invasion of 1941 forced the Russians to retreat, Laimonis was in Pskov on the Russian border, where he was able to use his job as a motorbike dispatch rider to escape back to Latvia. In danger of being arrested by the Russians as a deserter and by the Germans as a spy, he ditched his uniform and motorbike and lived rough while travelling on foot across Latvia. Later he became involved in distributing leaflets for one of the Latvian resistance groups and was arrested by the Gestapo. But because of his youth and his background as a mechanical engineering student, he was offered work as a mechanic in the Luftwaffe as an alternative to harsher treatment. So Laimonis joined the Luftwaffe and even flew on some bombing sorties as a navigator or bombardier. Eventually he ended up in Germany and at the end of the war was placed in a prisoner-of-war camp in Belgium.[26] Laimonis' mother, Kate Vinegere, was a communist and remained in Soviet Latvia. She died in 1972 and is buried in the Rainis Cemetary in Riga, alongside her other two sons, Valdis and Gunārs, both killed fighting the Germans in 1945 as soldiers of the Red Army. The fate of the three brothers, fighting in the uniforms of rival occupation forces, afflicted so many Latvian families in the 1940s as to be emblematic of Latvia.

The family's story of post war emigration came full circle in the summer of 2011, when I met the two Australian grandsons of Laimonis Vinegers in Riga. Tālis Putniņš and his younger brother, Krišjānis, had been brought up in Australia as fluent Latvian speakers. Both had taken the decision to emigrate back to Latvia. Tālis worked as a lecturer at the Stockholm School of Economics in Riga, and had recently acted as an economics consultant to the Latvian government. Krišjānis was the proprietor of a thriving music venue in Old Riga, Folkklubs ALA. Tālis had invested a great deal of time and effort into investigating the Žāklis family tree. I accompanied him and his brother on another trip to Rednieki, for a family reunion with Juris Žāklis. And I met Tālis' wife, Vēsma Upeniece, another Australian-Latvian. Unbelievably, the name of Vēsma's maternal grandfather was Griģis Svars. Curious about a possible family connection with the Fricis Svars killed in the Siege of Sidney Street, Vēsma once asked her grandmother, Marianna Svars (née Seskis), if she knew anything about him. The usually mild-mannered old lady suddenly became agitated and burst out, 'I know nothing about Fricis Svars, and I never want to hear that name again!'[27] Her aggressive reply, so out of character, suggested that there must indeed have been a family connection. When I talked to Vēsma in Riga we could only speculate about why her grandmother, who emigrated to Australia after the Second World War, should have been so upset at the mention of Fricis Svars. But the surname Svars is so uncommon in Latvia that there must have been a family connection.[28] Now, over a hundred years after Sidney Street, it seemed that a relative of Fricis Svars was married to a relative of Jānis Žāklis.

If Jānis Žāklis arrived in Australia in 1913, he would not have been eligible for naturalisation until after the First World War. From 1916 to 1920 he would have been obliged to register with the police as an alien. Afterwards, he could naturalise as a citizen of the Commonwealth of Australia, and become (technically) a British subject. All of these things would be documented in Australian government archives. His involvement in business would have eased the process of naturalisation, but also offers a clue to finding him. Many Latvians were only labourers or sailors at the time of their naturalisation. The key to documenting his life in Australia is discovering the name he adopted.

Somewhere in the files of the National Archives of Australia there will be a photograph which will provide that name. Finding 'the one who was away' remains a long and arduous process. With no documented proof yet, I could only trust my instinct that Andris Puļķis was right, and that Jānis Žāklis lived out his life in Australia. The investigation was still on-going when the Latvian edition of this book was published in 2012.[29]

Confirmation of Puļķis's theory came unexpectedly in 2015, when I was contacted by a Latvian journalist in Riga asking some rather innocuous questions about Peter the Painter for a magazine article she was writing. When it appeared the article was a rather lurid re-hash of my book. But it ended with a triumphant flourish, claiming to have discovered something that I had missed: that ten years before in 2005, when Latvia was celebrating the centenary of the 1905 revolution, a young Australian claiming to be the great-great-grandson of Jānis Žāklis had walked into the Latvian War Museum (LKM) in Riga looking for information about his relative. In support of his claim the young man produced a photograph taken from the family album in Australia. It was identical to one in the museum's collection depicting Jānis Žāklis in 1906, a photograph unpublished until my book came out seven years later.[30] At first I was sceptical, not least because the source of the information was Dainis Poziņš, Head of Medieval and Modern History at the museum, whom I had known since 2003, but for some inexplicable reason he had never thought the incident worth mentioning to me. I flew to Riga to ask Dainis for his version of the meeting.

Seated in his office in Riga, Dainis said that an Australian aged somewhere in his mid-twenties had arrived at the museum looking for information about Jānis Žāklis. The young man had been inspired to come to Latvia (his first visit to the country) after watching a documentary on television in Australia, *The Houndsditch Murders* (LWT 2003), in which I first identified Peter the Painter as Jānis Žāklis and mentioned that the photographs of Žāklis which I used for comparison with those of Peter the Painter had come from the Latvian War Museum. The Australian had arrived in Riga hoping to find members of his Latvian family, but speaking no Latvian and with no clue of where to look he had drawn a blank. Dainis told me he was amazed at the striking resemblance between the young man and pictures of Žāklis. And his showing Dainis the 1906 photograph of Žāklis 'from the family album' in Australia seemed pretty convincing. Dainis said he spoke to the Australian for about thirty minutes and gave him a few photocopied pages of information to take away with him. At the time Dainis hadn't attributed much significance to the visit; his recollection of the conversation was vague and he had forgotten all about it until his memory was jogged by the Latvian journalist ten years later. Now he appeared understandably embarrassed that I was making such a fuss. Worse still, Dainis confessed that his notes of the meeting, including the name and address of his Australian visitor, were subsequently lost during a computer data transfer that went wrong. He thought that the Australian was from Sydney and that the family had always lived there under their own name, which he supposed was Žākle (spelt how, he wasn't sure). When I pressed him for details of the conversation Dainis said that the Australian told him that no one in the family knew much about their relative's life prior to arriving in Australia, except that he had had a lot of adventures in

Latvia, but it was 'taboo' to speak about the subject. The family in Australia was started by Jānis Žāklis in 'the 1920s'. They knew of no contact with Latvia or Latvians, and the old man had only ever wanted to have a normal life and to keep away from trouble.[31]

In Sydney, Tālis Putniņš trawled through the records held by the New South Wales State Library looking for any variant on the name Žākle or Žāklis: telephone directories, the electoral role, historical records from 1900 onwards (including the 1930 NSW census); records of births, deaths and marriages; military records; NSW unassisted immigrant passenger lists 1826-1922 and incoming passenger lists in Australia more generally. Finally he searched naturalisation records held by the Australian National Archives. Nothing useful was found. Given the lack of records in any of these sources for variants on Žākle/Žāklis in NSW or more broadly Australia, it is difficult to imagine that is the name the family went by in Australia.[32] But taken together with the testimony of Andris Puļķis, who first told me that Jānis Žāklis had gone to Australia and had stayed there, and whom Dainis Poziņš agrees (even though Puļķis destroyed the proof) is an absolutely credible source, the 2005 visit of the Australian great-great-grandson is confirmation that Jānis Žāklis did emigrate to Australia, that he started a family there in the 1920s, and that there are living relatives still in Australia today. Peter the Painter emigrated to Australia intending to start a new life and not be found, and that is exactly what he succeeded in doing. The mystery continues only because the name used by his family in Australia is still unknown; but I know they are there. Finding that name holds the key to uncovering the missing details of Peter the Painter's life and death.

If the world's most wanted anarchist settled down in Australia, reinvented himself as a respectable businessman and made the best of the rest of his life, no one should blame him. What at first may appear as an anti-climax to an epic story of class war and revolution may also serve as a reminder that this story is about real people, not mindless lemmings. And that survival can demand as much bravery as the willingness to die for a noble cause.

Notes

1   Banjo Paterson, *The Man Who Was Away* (1894). Andrew "Banjo" Paterson (1864-1941), Australian journalist and bush poet, best remembered for his ballad *Waltzing Matilda*.

2   Tragically, Ausma Kalējs was knocked down and killed by a car while crossing the road in Riga in October 2004.

3   Interview with Ausma Kalējs, Riga 29th May 2004.

4   It wasn't until July 2018 that Ira Gruntmane (granddaughter of Anna Žākle-Sakne) took me to the grave of Peter the Painter's father, Jānis Žāklis (1851-1908) at the Žākle family cemetery at Čakšu kapi, Jaunlutriņu pagasts, outside Saldus.

5   Interview with Maruta Sproge, 'Plaudoni', Jaunlutrini 30th May 2004.

6   Juris Žāklis is married to Marite Skare (born 1971); they have two daughters, Agnese and Gundega.

7   Interview with Ugis Gruntmanis, London 19th December 2009. Dr. Ugis Gruntmanis MD practiced diabetes, metabolism and endocrinology, and internal medicine in Dallas, Texas until 2018.

8   Malvine Sakne died the following year, in 2005.

9   Interview with Līvija Rēfelde , Saldus 5th June 2004.

10 Ibid.

11 Interview with Andris Pulkis, Riga 28th August 2003.

12 Liga Lapa, 'The 1905 revolution and Latvian immigration to Australia', *Early Latvian Settlers In Australia*, edited by Aldis Putniņš (Sterling Star, South Yara, Australia, 2010), p. 194.

13 From the official land document deed (copy from Ira Gruntmane to the author, Riga, 5th June 2004): On 9th December 1913, Margarieta Žākle (née Talberga) sold Svitte No. 51, Lutrini, with all land and buildings to Hermanis Sakne for 8,300 roubles. Hermanis Sakne paid a down-payment of 1,020 roubles; the balance was provided by a bank mortgage of 7,300 roubles, spread over 50 years 6 months, at 4.5% interest. Out of the sale of the farm, the bank paid off the debts of Karlis Žāklis, Katrina and Milda Žākle and Anna Sakne. The debts of Maria Gertner were settled in a separate act in April 1913. Transfer of property rights were completed on 11th March 1914.

14 Fricis Svars, letter to his father, 1st January 1911. New English translation by Irene Ruff, 2010.

15 *Melnais Karogs* No. 17, Paris October 1913.

16 *Melnais Karogs* No. 19, Paris March 1914. The published names of the donors in Sidney were given as Andersons, Kleinsmith, C. Limberts, Bandinieks, W. Ausing, Gunelis, Osolinish, B. Weiz, F. Bremer and Melchis.

17 National Archives of Australia (NAA): SP11/5 Limbit, Charles, gives the date of his arrival as 1905; SP11/2 Latvian/Limbit, C, gives the date as 1912.

18 Aldis Putniņš, *Veclatviešu organizācijas Austrālijā 1913-1948* (Australia, 1987), p. 14.

19 NAA: A1/1914/497, Report by Superintendent T. Lynch, Police Department Detective Branch, 19th September 1913.

20 NAA: C123/1408, Karl Emil KRASTIN (alias Max Selling), Security Service, New South Wales dossier, 1939-1945. Item 1366854 (Sydney); MT269/1, Vic/Russia/SELLING, Max, 1917-1918, item 6555914 (Melbourne); A1/1914/497, Max Selling, 1913-1914, item 28030.

21 Files of the City of London Police, 'Houndsditch Murders', Box 1.21/No.96, Letter from Superintendent Shaw, Criminal Investigation Branch, Melbourne, 7th September 1917, London Metropolitan Archives.

22 Benjamin Leeson, *Lost London* (London 1934), p. 219.

23 Ibid.

24 Laimonis Vinegers, *Ciltsraksti — otrais uzmetums* (Adelaide, 1994).

25 Email from Aldis Putniņš, 18th November 2003.

26 Email from Aldis Putniņš, 24th November 2003.

27 Email from Tālis Putniņš, 5th February 2009.

28 Conversation with Vēsma Putniņš (née Upeniece), Riga 21st July 2011.

29 Filips Rufs, *Pa stāvu liesmu debesīs: Nenotveramā latviešu anarhista Pētera Māldera laiks un dzīve*, translated by Lauris Gundars (Dienas Grāmata, Riga 2012).

30 Evija Puķe-Jansone, *Anarhijas dēls* (Anarchy's son), *Legendas* August 2015 (98).

31 Interview with Dainis Poziņš, Riga, 2nd August 2015.

32 Email from Tālis Putniņš, 6th September 2015.

Index

241

Ralph Anstis, WARREN JAMES AND THE DEAN FOREST RIOTS, *The Disturbances of 1831*
£14.00 • 242pp *paperback* • 191x235mm • ISBN 978-0-9564827-7-8

John E. Archer, 'BY A FLASH AND A SCARE', *Arson, Animal Maiming, and Poaching in East Anglia 1815-1870*
£17.00 • 206pp *paperback* • 191x235mm • ISBN 978-0-9564827-1-6

Victor Bailey, CHARLES BOOTH'S POLICEMEN, *Crime, Police and Community in Jack-the-Ripper's London*
£17.00 • 162pp *paperback* • *2 colour and 8 b/w images* • 140x216mm • ISBN 978-0-9564827-6-1

Victor Bailey, ORDER AND DISORDER IN MODERN BRITAIN, *Essays on Riot, Crime, Policing and Punishment*
£15.00 • 214pp *paperback* • *5 b/w images* • 191x235mm • ISBN 978-0-9570005-5-1

Roger Ball, Dave Beckwith, Steve Hunt, Mike Richardson, STRIKERS, HOBBLERS, CONCHIES & REDS, *A Radical History of Bristol, 1880-1939*
£18.50 • 366pp *paperback* • *101 b/w images* • 156x234mm • ISBN 978-0-9929466-0-9

John Belchem, 'ORATOR' HUNT, *Henry Hunt and English Working Class Radicalism*
£17.50 • 248pp *paperback* • 191x235mm • ISBN 978-0-9564827-8-5

Alastair Bonnett & Keith Armstrong (eds.), THOMAS SPENCE: THE POOR MAN'S REVOLUTIONARY
£15.00 • 214pp *paperback* • 156x234mm • ISBN 978-0-9570005-9-9

Bob Bushaway, BY RITE, *Custom, Ceremony and Community in England 1700-1880*
£16.00 • 206pp *paperback* • 191x235mm • ISBN 978-0-9564827-6-1

Malcolm Chase, THE PEOPLE'S FARM, *English Radical Agrarianism 1775-1840*
£12.00 • 212pp *paperback* • 152x229mm • ISBN 978-0-9564827-5-4

Malcolm Chase, EARLY TRADE UNIONISM, Fraternity, *Skill and the Politics of Labour*
£17.00 • 248pp *paperback* • 191x235mm • ISBN 978-0-9570005-2-0

Nigel Costley, WEST COUNTRY REBELS
£20.00 • 220pp *full colour illustrated paperback* • 216x216mm • ISBN 978-0-9570005-4-4

James Epstein, THE LION OF FREEDOM, *Feargus O'Connor and the Chartist Movement, 1832-1842*
£17.00 • 296pp *paperback* • 156x234mm • ISBN 978-0-9929466-1-6

James Epstein, RADICAL EXPRESSION, *Political Language, Ritual, and Symbol in England, 1790-1850*
£15.00 • 220pp *paperback* • 156x234mm • ISBN 978-0-9929466-2-3

Chris Fusher, CUSTOM, WORK & MARKET CAPITALISM, *The Forest of Dean Colliers, 1788-1888*
£14.00 • 198pp *paperback* • 156x234mm • ISBN 978-0-9929466-7-8

Ariel Hessayon (ed.), THE REFINER'S FIRE, *The Collected Works of TheaurauJohn Tany*
£25.00 • 552pp *paperback* • 156x234mm • ISBN 978-0-9570005-7-5

Catherine Howe, HALIFAX 1842, *A Year of Crisis*
£14.50 • 202pp *paperback* • 156x234mm • ISBN 978-0-9570005-8-2

Also from
BREVIARY STUFF PUBLICATIONS

Barry Reay, THE LAST RISING OF THE AGRICULTURAL LABOURERS,
Rural Life and Protest in Nineteenth-Century England
£15.00 • 192pp *paperback* • 191x235mm • ISBN 978-0-9564827-2-3

Buchanan Sharp, IN CONTEMPT OF ALL AUTHORITY, *Rural Artisans and Riot in the West of England, 1586-1660*
£15.00 • 204pp *paperback* • 191x235mm • ISBN 978-0-9564827-0-9

Dorothy Thompson, THE CHARTISTS, *Popular Politics in the Industrial Revolution*
£17.00 • 280pp *paperback* • 191x235mm • ISBN 978-0-9570005-3-7

E. P. Thompson, WHIGS AND HUNTERS, *The Origin of the Black Act*
£16.00 • 278pp *paperback* • 156x234mm • ISBN 978-0-9570005-2-0
£30.00 • 278pp *hardback* • 156x234mm • ISBN 978-0-9929466-6-1

David Walsh, MAKING ANGELS IN MARBLE, *The Conservatives, the Early Industrial Working Class and Attempts at Political Incorporation*
£15.00 • 268pp *paperback* • 191x235mm • ISBN 978-0-9570005-0-6

David Walsh, THE SONS OF BELIAL, *Protest and Community Change in the North-West, 1740-1770*
£16.00 • 272pp *paperback* • 156x234mm • ISBN 978-0-9929466-9-2

Roger Wells, INSURRECTION, *The British Experience 1795-1803*
£22.00 • 372pp *paperback* • 191x235mm • ISBN 978-0-9564827-3-0

Roger Wells, WRETCHED FACES, *Famine in Wartime England 1793-1801*
£23.00 • 412pp *paperback* • 191x235mm • ISBN 978-0-9564827-4-7

David Worrall, RADICAL CULTURE, *Discourse, Resistance and Surveillance, 1790-1820*
£15.00 • 186pp *paperback* • 156x234mm • ISBN 978-0-9929466-4-7

Lightning Source UK Ltd.
Milton Keynes UK
UKHW011501041120
372791UK00004B/540

9 780992 946654